Cracking the

SAT*

Physics
Subject Test

2009–2010 Edition

Cracking the

SAT*

Physics
Subject Test

2009–2010 Edition

Steven A. Leduc

PrincetonReview.com

Random House, Inc. New York

The Independent Education Consultants Association recognizes The Princeton Review as a valuable resource for high school and college students applying to college and graduate school.

The Princeton Review, Inc.
2315 Broadway
New York, NY 10024
E-mail: editorialsupport@review.com

*SAT is a registered trademark of the College Board.

ISBN 978-0-375-42911-8
ISSN 1521-9453

Editor: Selena Coppock
Production Editor: Meave Shelton
Production Coordinator: Kim Howie

Printed in the United States of America.

10 9 8 7 6 5 4 3 2 1

2009–2010 Edition

John Katzman, Chairman, Founder
Michael J. Perik, President, CEO
Stephen Richards, COO, CFO
John Marshall, President, Test Preparation Services
Rob Franek, VP Test Prep Books, Publisher

Editorial
Seamus Mullarkey, Editorial Director
Laura Braswell, Senior Editor
Rebecca Lessem, Senior Editor
Selena Coppock, Editor
Heather Brady, Editor

Production Services
Scott Harris, Executive Director, Production Services
Kim Howie, Production Coordinator

Production Editorial
Meave Shelton, Production Editor
Emmeline Parker, Production Editor

Research & Development
Ed Carroll, Agent for National Content Directors
Liz Rutzel, Project Editor

Random House Publishing Group
Tom Russell, Publisher
Nicole Benhabib, Publishing Manager
Ellen L. Reed, Production Manager
Alison Stoltzfus, Associate Managing Editor
Elham Shabahat, Publishing Assistant

Acknowledgments

My thanks and appreciation to John Katzman, Steve Quattrociocchi, Jeff Rubenstein, Kris Gamache, Dan Edmonds, and Suellen Glasser, for making me feel at home; to Rachel Warren, Kate O'Neill, Melissa Kavonic, and Jeff Soloway for their support and fantastic editing, and to the production team for their beautiful work. Thanks to Paul Kanarek for his friendship, counsel, and encouragement.

Special thanks to Chris Pentzell for his work on the latest revision of this book.

A special thanks to Adam Robinson, who conceived of and perfected the Joe Bloggs approach to standardized tests and many of the other successful techniques used by The Princeton Review.

Dedication

This work is dedicated to the memory of my great aunt, Norma Perron Lamb Piette.

Contents

Introduction

The SAT Subject Tests are a series of one-hour exams developed and administered by the Educational Testing Service (ETS) and the College Board. Unlike the SAT, the SAT Subject Tests are designed to measure specific knowledge in specific areas. There are many different tests in many different subject areas, such as biology, history, French, and math. They are scored separately on a scale from 200 to 800.

How Are SAT Subject Tests Used by College Admissions?

Since the tests are given in specific areas, colleges use them as another piece of admissions information and, often, to decide whether an applicant can be exempted from college course requirements. For example, a certain score may excuse you from a basic science class or a foreign language requirement.

Should I Take the SAT Subject Tests? How Many? When?

About one third of the colleges that require SAT scores also require that you take two or three SAT Subject Test(s). Your first order of business is to start reading those college catalogs. College guidebooks, admissions offices, and guidance counselors should have this information as well.

As to which tests you should take, the answer is simple. Take the SAT Subject Tests

- on which you will do well

- that the colleges to which you are applying may require you to take.

Some colleges have specific requirements, while others do not. Again, start asking questions before you start taking tests. Once you find out which tests are required, if any, part of your decision making is done. The next step is to find out which of the tests will highlight your particular strengths. Choosing your tests means having to evaluate your own strengths and skills. Possibilities range from English literature, U.S. and world history, biology, chemistry, and physics to a variety of foreign languages.

As for when, take the tests as close as possible to the corresponding coursework you may be doing. If you plan to take the SAT Physics Subject Test, for example, and you are currently taking physics in high school, don't postpone the test until next year.

When Are the SAT Subject Tests Offered?

In general, you can take from one to three Subject Tests per test date in October, November, December, January, March, May, and June at test sites across the country. Not all subjects are offered at each administration, so check the dates carefully.

How Do I Register for the Tests?

To register by mail, pick up a registration form and student bulletin at your guidance counselor's office. You can also register at the College Board website at www.collegeboard.com. This site also contains useful information, such as the test dates and fees. If you have questions, you can talk to a representative at the College Board by calling 1-866-756-7346 from within the U.S. or 212-713-7789 from outside the U.S.

You may have your scores sent to you, to your school, and to four colleges of your choice. Additional reports will be sent to additional colleges for additional money. The scores take about six weeks to arrive. You may also check your scores on the web 8–14 days after taking the test.

What's a Good Score?

That's hard to say, exactly. A good score is one that fits in the range of scores for which the college of your choice usually accepts. However, if your score falls below the normal score range for Podunk University, that doesn't mean you won't go to Podunk University. Schools are usually fairly flexible in what they are willing to look at as a "good" score for a particular student.

Along with your score, you will also receive a percentile rank. That number tells you how you fit in with the other test takers. In other words, a percentile rank of 60 means that 40 percent of the test takers scored above you and 60 percent scored below you.

What's on the SAT Physics Subject Test?

The SAT Physics Subject Test contains 75 multiple-choice questions, and the time limit is 1 hour. The topics covered (which are listed below) are those most likely to be studied in a standard college-prep level high school physics course. The following list includes the major topics covered on the SAT Physics Subject Test, along with the corresponding chapters in this book and an approximate percentage of the questions on each.

Approximate Percentage of Major Topic Questions

Mechanics (Chapters 2–8)   36–42%
Kinematics, Dynamics, Energy and Momentum,
Circular Motion and Rotation, Vibrations and SHM, Gravity

Thermal Physics (Chapter 9)   6–11%
Temperature and Heat, Kinetic Theory, Thermodynamics

Electricity and Magnetism (Chapters 10–14)   18–24%
Electric Fields, Forces, Potentials, Magnetic Fields and Forces,
Electric Circuits, Electromagnetic Induction

Waves and Optics (Chapters 15–16)   15–19%
General Wave Properties, Doppler Effect, Reflection and
Refraction, Interference, Diffraction, Polarization, Ray Optics

Modern Physics (Chapter 17)   6–11%
Quantum Phenomena, Atoms, Nuclear Physics, Relativity,

Miscellaneous Topics   6–11%
History, Overlapping Questions, Graph Analysis, Measurement,
Math Skills, Astrophysics, Superconductivity, Chaos Theory

Since you have only about 45 seconds (on average) to answer each question, you won't be surprised to find that the math on the SAT Physics Subject Test is pretty straightforward; any mathematical calculations that do come up require no more than basic arithmetic, algebra, and trigonometry. The numbers will be simple, because you are not allowed to use a calculator on the test, and no formula sheet is given (or can be brought). You also cannot bring scratch paper; all scratch work must be done directly in the test booklet.

How Is the Test Scored and How Well Do I Need to Do?

On this test, each of the 75 questions is followed by 5 possible responses (A through E), and your job, of course, is to choose the best answer. Your *raw score* is equal to the number of questions you got right minus a fraction $\left(\dfrac{1}{4}\right)$ of the number of questions you answered wrong, rounded to the nearest whole number.

If you leave a question blank, it isn't counted as either right or wrong. For example, let's say that of the 75 questions, you got 42 right, 26 wrong, and you left 7 blank.

They figure out your raw score as follows:

$$42 - \frac{1}{4}(26) = 35.5 \;\longrightarrow\; \text{round to} \to \text{raw score} = 36$$

Then they convert this raw score to a *scaled score*. The SAT Subject Test scores are reported on a 200 to 800 scale (in multiples of 10). So your raw score of 36 may be converted to a scaled score of, say, 650. This is the score that's reported to you.

How would this score of 650 measure up? The averages vary slightly from administration to administration, but the average score on the November 1995 SAT Physics Subject Test was 653, the average score on the May 2000 test was 635, and the average score for 2007 college-bound seniors was 647, so a score of 650 would be considered at or above average. Notice that you can get more than a third of the questions wrong and still get an average score! Naturally, different colleges have different admission criteria. Some may report the average scores of their entering freshmen, so talk with your school counselor and check with the admissions offices of the colleges in which you're interested to see if they release their SAT averages.

Some Test-Taking Tips

When approaching the practice tests or the actual SAT Physics Subject Test, there are some helpful strategies you can use to help maximize your score.

Know the Directions to Part A Now

There are two parts to the SAT Physics Subject Test: Part A and Part B. Part A, which accounts for the first 12 or 13 questions, consists of four groups of 2 to 4 questions each. The questions within any one group all relate to a single situation, and the five possible answer choices are actually given before the questions. The most important thing to remember is that in Part A, an answer choice may be used once, more than once, or not at all in each group. For example, if the first group of questions in Part A are questions 1 to 4, then the answer to question 1 might be B, question 2 could be D, question 3 could be A, and question 4 could be D again. Note that in this group choice, D was the correct answer twice and choices C and E were not used at all. The questions on Part A of the test actually look like the following:

Questions 1-3 refer to the following quantities:

    (A) Wavelength
    (B) Frequency
    (C) Period
    (D) Wave speed
    (E) Amplitude

1. Which quantity is a fixed constant for all electromagnetic waves in a vacuum?

2. For a standing wave on a string that is fixed at both ends, which quantity is inversely proportional to the wave speed?

3. What is the distance between adjacent crests on a traveling wave?

(The answers to these questions are D, C, and A, in case you're curious.) Be prepared for this first section of the SAT Physics Subject Test, and don't waste valuable time by rereading the directions to Part A on the day of the test. Know the directions by heart.

Part B consists of the remaining questions. While some of the questions may be in groups of 2 or 3, all the questions in Part B are of the usual "question followed by 5 answer choices" variety, and each has a unique correct answer. The following is an example of a Part B question:

14. A block of mass m slides with constant speed down a ramp whose incline angle is θ. If F_1 is the magnitude of the gravitational force acting parallel to the ramp and F_2 is the magnitude of the normal force acting on the block, what is the value of F_1/F_2?

(A) $m \tan \theta$
(B) $m \cot \theta$
(C) 1
(D) $\cot \theta$
(E) $\tan \theta$

The answer to this problem is E.

Know That You Can Skip Questions Entirely

You might think that to get a great score, you need to answer nearly every question correctly. But don't stress out—this isn't the case at all. It's perfectly acceptable to skip some questions entirely, and, in fact, if you do this you'll have more time to answer questions that are easier for you—ones you have a better chance of getting right.

Perhaps some statistics will show you that it's okay to skip questions. The average score on the SAT Physics Subject Test is about 650 (on the familiar 200 to 800 scale). Scoring above 700 would put you in the top third of all test takers. You could skip about 30—that's right, 30—questions and still get a 700. If your goal is a 750, which would place you in the top fifth of all test takers, you could skip about 20 questions. And you could skip about 10 questions and still earn the top score of 800. Takes some of the pressure off, doesn't it?

Of course, to get those scores while skipping all of those questions, you would need to answer all the others correctly. It's probably more than likely that you'd get a few wrong. So let's look at a more realistic sample-test scenario. There are 75 questions on the SAT Physics Subject Test. You get 1 point for each question you answer correctly, 0 points for any question you skip (and thus leave blank), and $\frac{1}{4}$ point is subtracted for each question you answer incorrectly. So, let's say you skip 13 questions entirely, answer 50 questions correctly, and answer 12 incorrectly. Your raw score would be $50 - \left(\frac{1}{4}\right)(12) = 47$, which would convert to a scaled score of about 700 to 720. If you had skipped more questions, 17 instead of 13, and still answered 50 correctly (but 8 incorrectly), your raw score would be even higher:

$$50 - \left(\frac{1}{4}\right)(8) = 48,$$ which would be converted to a scaled score of about 720 or higher.

So the strategy is clear: If you get to a question that you know nothing about—one on which you can't eliminate even a single answer choice, don't let it fluster you—just skip it.

Process of Elimination Is Your Best Friend

On the SAT Physics Subject Test, like so many other multiple-choice tests, the Process of Elimination (POE for short) is your most valuable test-taking strategy. One of the advantages to taking a multiple-choice test is that the correct answer to every question is right there on the page! Often it's easier to identify (and eliminate!) wrong answer choices than it is to figure out the correct one. So after reading a question, the first thing you should do is read the answer choices. If you know a choice can't be right, cross it out. And remember: If even **part** of an answer choice is wrong, it's **all** wrong.

Also, it's important to notice that if two (or more) choices are equivalent—that is, if two or more choices would be valid together—then you can automatically eliminate **all** of them. After all, each question has just one correct answer; it can't have two (or more). As an example, look at Question 21 on page 8. By Newton's Second Law, $F_{net} = m\mathbf{a}$, choices B and C are equivalent because if $\mathbf{a}$ were zero, then the F_{net} would also be zero (and vice versa); that is, if B were correct, then C would *also* have to be correct. Since the question can't have two correct answers, eliminate both B and C.

Use POE as much as you can because even if a question is difficult and you are able to eliminate one or more choices, it is generally to your advantage not to skip the question, but instead to guess among the remaining choices and move on.

Never Spend Too Much Time on Any One Question

The questions on the SAT Physics Subject Test are not organized by level of difficulty, and every question on the test—whether it's easy, medium, or difficult—is worth the same amount: one point. You don't get extra credit for correctly answering a difficult question. If you see a question that seems tough, try to eliminate some choices. If you can't, just skip it. Never waste time agonizing over a tough question when there are easier questions you *can* answer.

Bubble in Your Answers in Groups

Going back and forth from the test book to your answer sheet after every single question can eat up lots of time. A better strategy is to bubble in your answers in groups. As you finish a question, write the answer as a big capital letter directly underneath the question number. After you've finished a page or two, transfer your answers to the answer sheet. Of course, make sure you bubble in your answer sheet correctly; as you get to each question number, say it (to yourself), along with the letter you've written down below the question number, and transfer that to the answer sheet. If you've skipped a question, be sure to leave that one blank on the answer sheet. It's important to keep your eye on the time because after time is called, you will not be allowed to bubble in anything on your answer sheet. So when you're getting to the end of the test (say, the last 5 to 10 minutes), it's a good idea to bubble in your answers one at a time, just to be sure you get them all in before time is called.

Make Two Passes Through the Test

The point of the two-pass system is to make sure you answer all the questions you find easy first before spending time on questions you find more difficult. Read through the questions in the order in which they're presented in the test book. If you can answer one relatively quickly, do so, and write the answer as a big capital letter directly below the question number. If it's a question that you think you could answer, but it looks like it might take a little while, circle the question number, and move on. If it's a question that you decide should be skipped entirely, put a big "X" through the question itself and then place a dash directly underneath the question number. As you move through the test, periodically check your watch to see how you're doing on time (remember, the time limit is one hour). Continue like this—deciding whether each question is answerable now, later, or never—until you reach question number 75 (which is always the last question). You have now completed your first pass through the test.

Next, go back to the beginning and make your second pass. Find the questions you circled and try them again. If your second attempt at these questions is bogging you down, just pick one of the answer choices that you didn't eliminate, write the letter below the question number, and move on. Continue like this, either bubbling in your answers in groups, or one at a time if time is growing short, and complete your second pass. Finally, if you have any time remaining, consider starting a third pass.

Question 21

This is what a question you can answer on the first pass should look like. Use POE and write your answer under the question number.

21. A ball is thrown straight upward and falls
D back to the ground 3 seconds later. At the moment the ball reaches its highest point

(A) its potential energy is minimized
(B) its acceleration is zero
(C) the net force on the ball is zero
(D) its velocity is changing
(E) the force of gravity on the ball is greater than when it was first thrown

22. Which one of the following expressions gives the kinetic energy of a proton of mass m that travels at speed of $(4/5)x$, where c is the speed of light?

(A) $\frac{1}{2}m(0.8c)^2$

(B) $(\frac{1}{0.8}-1)mc^2$

(C) $\frac{1}{0.8}mc^2$

(D) $(\frac{1}{0.6}-1)mc^2$

(E) $\frac{1}{0.6}mc^2$

Question 22
Skip questions if you cannot eliminate any answers. Cross out questions you choose to skip so you don't waste time during your second pass.

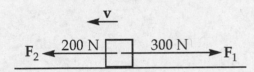

23. C

The figure above shows the two unbalanced forces acting on a block. If the velocity of the block is to the left, then
(A) the work done by F_1 is positive
(B) the work done by F_2 is negative
(C) the momentum of the block is decreasing
(D) the net force is in the same direction as the velocity
(E) the kinetic energy of the block is increasing

Question 23
Circle questions you want to return to during your second pass. This allows you to come back to time-consuming questions if you have time at the end of the test.

How Should I Prepare for the Test?

Most students take the SAT Physics Subject Test after they've taken a year-long college-prep course in physics at their high schools. The test is offered in May and June, so you can take it near the end of the school year while the material is still fresh. It's offered again in the fall (October, November, and December) and in January and March, so you have the option to take it at these times as well.

Naturally, it's important to be familiar with the topics—to understand the basics of the theory, to know the definitions of the fundamental quantities, and to recognize and be able to use the equations. Then, you should get some practice applying what you've learned to answering questions like the ones you'll see on the test.

This book contains hundreds of practice questions that review all of the content areas covered on the test. A few sections are preceded by an asterisk (*) to indicate that they contain higher-level discussions; feel free to skip these sections until you've mastered the basic ones. Each chapter (except the first) is followed by sample multiple-choice questions. One of the most important aspects of this book is that *answers and explanations are provided for every example and question*. You'll learn as much—if not more—from actively reading the explanations as you will from reading the text and examples.

In addition, two full-length practice tests are provided. These are designed to simulate a real SAT Physics Subject Test and will give you additional practice for the real thing. Again, a complete solution is provided for every question in both of these sample tests. The difficulty level of the examples and questions in this book is at or slightly above SAT Subject Test level, so if you have the time and motivation to attack these questions and learn from the solutions, you should feel confident that you will do your very best on the actual test.

Practice test questions are also available directly from the College Board on its website, www.collegeboard.com. The College Board also publishes a book entitled *The Official Study Guide for All SAT Subject Tests*. You can purchase this book at your local bookstore, through an online bookstore, or through the College Board's website.

You can also go to the website to get information about the SAT Physics Subject Test, including test descriptions, test dates, and test centers, and you can register for the SAT Subject Tests online.

I wish you all the best as you study for the SAT Physics Subject Test. Good luck!

—*Steve Leduc*

For more information visit **www.PrincetonReview.com**.

Chapter 1
Math Review

The few questions on the SAT Physics Subject Test that require you to know mathematics are straight forward and actually need little math beyond some algebra and maybe a little trig. In this chapter we are going to help you brush up on some knowledge you probably don't use every day, such as trig and the properties of vectors and how they are used. The material in this chapter is pretty clear-cut, so you should know this stuff backward and forward for the test.

SCIENTIFIC NOTATION

It's usually much easier to write very large or very small numbers in scientific notation. For example, the speed of light through empty space is approximately 300,000,000 meters per second. In scientific notation, this number would be written as 3×10^8. Here's another example: In standard units, Newton's universal gravitational constant is about 0.0000000000667; in scientific notation, this number would be written as 6.67×10^{-11}. In general, we say that a number is in **scientific notation** when it's written in the form $a \times 10^n$, where $1 \leq a < 10$ and n is an integer. As the two examples above show, when a very large number is written in scientific notation, the value of n is a large positive integer, and when a very small number is written in scientific notation, n is a large negative integer. To multiply or divide two numbers written in scientific notation, just remember that $10^m \times 10^n = 10^{m+n}$ and $10^m/10^n = 10^{m-n}$. So, for example, $(3 \times 10^8)(2.5 \times 10^{-12}) = 7.5 \times 10^{-4}$ and $(8 \times 10^9)/(2 \times 10^{-5}) = 4 \times 10^{14}$.

BASIC TRIG REVIEW

If you're given a right triangle, there are certain special functions, called **trig functions**, of the angles in the triangle that depend on the lengths of the sides. We'll concentrate on three of these functions; the **sine**, **cosine**, and **tangent** (abbreviated sin, cos, and tan, respectively). Take a look at the following right triangle, *ABC*. The right angle is at *C*, and the lengths of the sides are labeled *a*, *b*, and *c*.

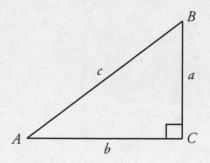

Triangles and Beans?
Pythagoras was actually a cult leader around 500 B.C. Some rules of his number-worshipping group included prohibitions against eating beans and wearing wool.

First, we'll mention one of the most important facts about any right triangle. The **Pythagorean theorem** tells us that the square of the *hypotenuse* (which is the name of the side opposite the right angle, always the longest side) is equal to the sum of the squares of the other two sides (called the *legs*):

$$a^2 + b^2 = c^2$$

Now for the trig functions. Let's consider angle A in the right triangle pictured above. The sine, cosine, and tangent of this angle are defined like this:

$$\sin A = \frac{\text{opposite}}{\text{hypotenuse}} = \frac{a}{c}, \qquad \cos A = \frac{\text{adjacent}}{\text{hypotenuse}} = \frac{b}{c}, \qquad \tan A = \frac{\text{opposite}}{\text{adjacent}} = \frac{a}{b}$$

By *opposite* we mean the length of the side that's opposite the angle, and by *adjacent* we mean the length of the side that's adjacent to the angle. The same definitions, in words, can be used for angle B as follows:

$$\sin B = \frac{\text{opposite}}{\text{hypotenuse}} = \frac{b}{c}, \qquad \cos B = \frac{\text{adjacent}}{\text{hypotenuse}} = \frac{a}{c}, \qquad \tan B = \frac{\text{opposite}}{\text{adjacent}} = \frac{b}{a}$$

Notice that $\sin A = \cos B$ and $\cos A = \sin B$.

SOHCAHTOA

Here's a word you should remember on test day so you can keep clear on the definitions of $\sin \theta$, $\cos \theta$, and $\tan \theta$: **SOHCAHTOA**. This isn't some magic word to chant over your test booklet; it simply helps you remember that

Sine = Opposite side over Hypotenuse $(S = \frac{O}{H})$

Cosine = Adjacent side over Hypotenuse $(C = \frac{A}{H})$

Tangent = Opposite over Adjacent side $(T = \frac{O}{A})$

The definitions

$$\sin \theta = \frac{\text{opposite}}{\text{hypotenuse}}, \qquad \cos \theta = \frac{\text{adjacent}}{\text{hypotenuse}}, \qquad \tan \theta = \frac{\text{opposite}}{\text{adjacent}}$$

can be used for any acute angle θ (theta) in a right triangle.

The values of the sine, cosine, and tangent of the acute angles in a 3-4-5 right triangle are listed in the specific example that follows:

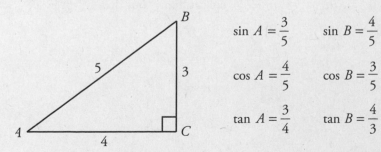

$\sin A = \frac{3}{5} \qquad \sin B = \frac{4}{5}$

$\cos A = \frac{4}{5} \qquad \cos B = \frac{3}{5}$

$\tan A = \frac{3}{4} \qquad \tan B = \frac{4}{3}$

We can also figure out the values of the sine, cosine, and tangent of the acute angles in a couple of special (and common) right triangles: the 30°-60° and the 45°-45° right triangles:

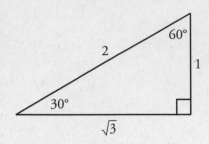

$$\sin 30° = \cos 60° = \frac{1}{2} = 0.50$$

$$\cos 30° = \sin 60° = \frac{\sqrt{3}}{2} \approx 0.87$$

$$\tan 30° = \frac{1}{\sqrt{3}} \approx 0.58, \quad \tan 60° = \sqrt{3} \approx 1.73$$

Triangle Mnemonics

A 30°-60°-90° triangle has 3 different angles with sides in proportions $1 - \sqrt{3} - 2$. A 45°- 45°-90° triangle has 3 distinct angles with sides in proportions $1\text{-}1\text{-}\sqrt{2}$. The number of distinct angles is what goes under the root sign.

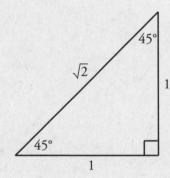

$$\sin 45° = \cos 45° = \frac{1}{\sqrt{2}} \approx 0.71$$

$$\tan 45° = 1$$

If we know the values of these functions for other acute angles, we can use them to figure out the missing sides of a right triangle. This is one of the most common uses of trig for the physics in this book. For example, consider the triangle below, with hypotenuse 5 and containing an acute angle, θ, of measure 30°:

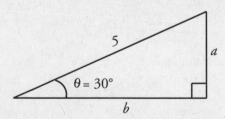

Sin 30° is 0.5, so because $\sin\theta = a/5$, we can figure out that

$$a = 5\sin\theta = 5\sin 30° \approx 5(0.5) = 2.5$$

We can use the Pythagorean theorem to figure out b, the length of the other side. Or, if we are told that cos 30° is about 0.87, then since $\cos\theta = b/5$, we'd find that

$$b = 5 \cos\theta = 5 \cos30° \approx 5(0.87) = 4.4$$

This gives us

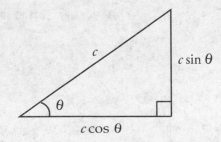

These values can be checked by the Pythagorean theorem, since

$$2.5^2 + 4.4^2 \approx 5^2.$$

This example illustrates this important, general fact: If the hypotenuse of a right triangle is c, then the length of the side opposite one of the acute angles, θ, is $c \sin\theta$, and the length of the side adjacent to this angle is $c \cos\theta$ as follows:

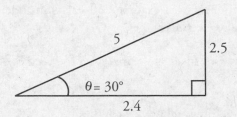

VECTORS

Definition

Distance

Distance is a scalar quantity. It refers to the amount of ground an object has covered.

A **vector** is a quantity that involves both magnitude and direction and obeys the **commutative law for addition**, which we'll explain in a moment. A quantity that does not involve direction is a **scalar**. For example, *55 miles per hour* is a scalar quantity, while *55 miles per hour, to the north* is a vector quantity. Speed and distance are scalar quantities. Other examples of scalars include: mass, work, energy, power, temperature, and electric charge.

The scalars of distance and speed are paired with the vectors of displacement and velocity, respectively.

Vectors can be denoted in several ways, including:

$$\mathbf{A}, A, \vec{A}$$

In textbooks, you'll usually see one of the first two, but when it's handwritten, you'll see one of the last two. In this book we will show all vector quantities in bold. For example, *A* would be the scalar quantity, and **A** the vector quantity.

Graphically, a vector is represented as an arrow whose length represents the magnitude and whose direction represents, well, the direction.

A /   **A** = 9 m/s northeast

B ←   **B** = 4 m/s west

Displacement

Displacement is a vector quantity. It refers to how far out of place an object is from its original position.

Displacement (which is net distance [magnitude] traveled plus direction) is the prototypical example of a vector:

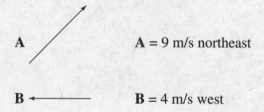

$$\underbrace{\mathbf{A}}_{\text{displacement}} = \underbrace{\text{4 miles}}_{\text{magnitude}}\ \underbrace{\text{to the north}}_{\text{direction}}$$

When we say that vectors obey the commutative law for addition, we mean that if we have two vectors of the same type, for example, another displacement,

$$\mathbf{B} = \underbrace{3 \text{ miles}}_{\text{magnitude}} \underbrace{\text{to the east}}_{\text{direction}}$$

then **A** + **B** must equal **B** + **A**. The vector sum **A** + **B** means the vector **A** followed by **B**, while the vector sum **B** + **A** means the vector **B** followed by **A**. That these two sums are indeed identical is shown in the following figure:

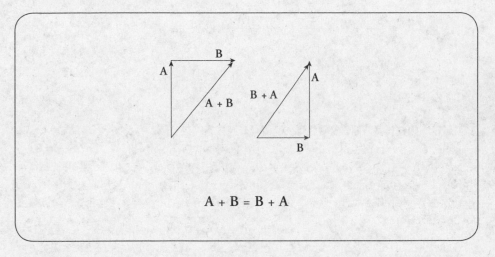

$$\mathbf{A} + \mathbf{B} = \mathbf{B} + \mathbf{A}$$

Two vectors are equal if they have the same magnitude and the same direction.

Vector Addition (Geometric)

The figure above illustrates how vectors are added to each other geometrically. Place the tail (the initial point) of one vector at the tip of the other vector, then connect the exposed tail to the exposed tip. The vector formed is the sum of the first two. This is called the "tip-to-tail" method of vector addition.

1. Add the following two vectors.

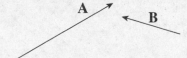

Here's How to Crack It

Place the tail of **B** at the tip of **A** and connect them:

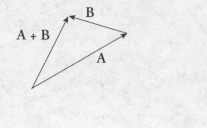

Scalar Multiplication of Vectors

A vector can be multiplied by a scalar (that is, by a number), which results in a vector. If the original vector is **A** and the scalar is 4, then the scalar multiple 4**A**. Simply has a magnitude that is four times greater than the original vector. The vector –4**A** would also be four times greater than **A**, but would point in the opposite direction.

$$\text{magnitude of } k\mathbf{A} = |k| \times (\text{magnitude of } \mathbf{A})$$

$$\text{direction of } k\mathbf{A} = \begin{cases} \text{the same as } \mathbf{A} \text{ if } k \text{ is positive} \\ \text{the opposite of } \mathbf{A} \text{ if } k \text{ is negative} \end{cases}$$

2. Sketch the scalar multiples 2**A**, $\frac{1}{2}$**A**, –**A**, and –3**A** of the vector **A**.

Here's How to Crack It

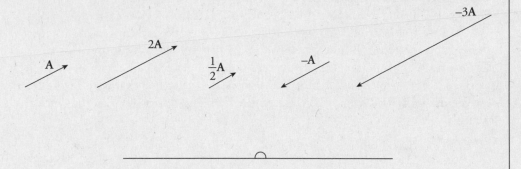

Vector Subtraction (Geometric)

To subtract one vector from another, for example, to get **A** – **B**, simply form the vector –**B**, which is the scalar multiple (–1)**B**, and add it to **A**.

$$\mathbf{A} - \mathbf{B} = \mathbf{A} + (-\mathbf{B})$$

3. For the two vectors **A** and **B**, find the vector **A** – **B**.

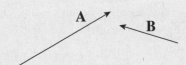

Here's How to Crack It

Flip **B** around—thereby forming –**B**—and add that vector to **A**.

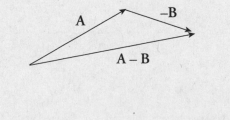

Components of Vectors

So as you can see, a vector can be defined as the sum of two (or more) vectors. The vectors that are added together to make up a vector are called its **components**. The vectors **B** and **C**, below, are called the **vector components** of **A**. Two-dimensional vectors, that is, vectors that lie flat in a plane, can be written as the sum of a horizontal vector and a vertical vector. For example, in the following diagram, the vector **A** is equal to the horizontal vector **B** plus the vertical vector **C**.

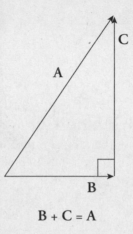

$$B + C = A$$

Since we are working with two dimensions, it is usually easiest to choose component vectors that lie along the x and y axes of the rectangular coordinate system, also known as the Cartesian coordinate system. The three arrows of the known vector and its component vectors create a right triangle. Setting up the components of the vectors in this way makes it much easier to add and subtract vectors and it allows you to use the Pythagorean theorem instead of some tricky trig.

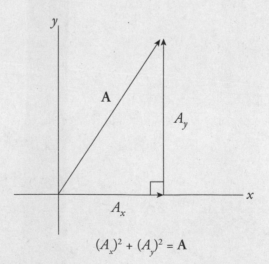

$$(A_x)^2 + (A_y)^2 = A$$

In the figure above, vector **A**, which is in the Cartesian plane is made up of the components A_x along the x axis and A_y along the y axis. A_x and A_y are called the **scalar components** of **A**.

A vector can be expressed in terms of its components using the **unit vectors i** and **j**.

i is a vector of magnitude one that points in the positive x direction, and **j** is a vector of magnitude one that points in the positive y direction.

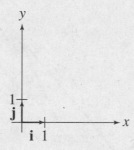

If the components of **A** are A_x and A_y, then $\mathbf{A} = A_x\mathbf{i} + A_y\mathbf{j}$.

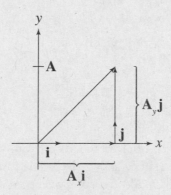

Vector Operations Using Components

Using perpendicular components makes the vector operations of addition, subtraction, and scalar multiplication pretty straightforward.

Vector Addition

Vectors **A** and **B** below are added together to form vector **C**.

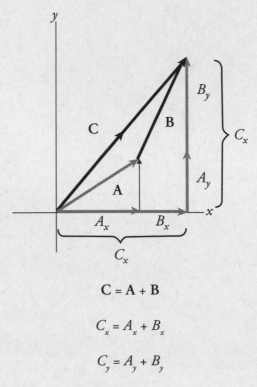

$$\mathbf{C} = \mathbf{A} + \mathbf{B}$$

$$C_x = A_x + B_x$$

$$C_y = A_y + B_y$$

To add two or more vectors, resolve each vector into its horizontal and vertical components. Add the components along the x-axis to form the x component of the resultant vector, and then add the components along the y-axis to form the y component of the resultant vector. You can use the values for C_x and C_y along with the Pythagorean theorem to determine the magnitude and direction of the resultant vector.

Vector Subtraction

To subtract vector B from vector A, use the same procedure. Resolve each vector into perpendicular components and subtract them in the indicated order.

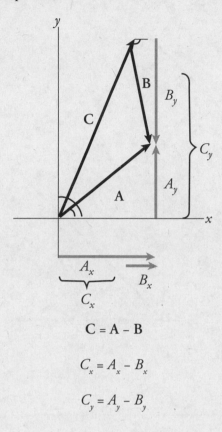

$$\mathbf{C} = \mathbf{A} - \mathbf{B}$$

$$C_x = A_x - B_x$$

$$C_y = A_y - B_y$$

Scalar Multiplication

Scalar multiplication just means that you increase the scale of the vector. (Or decrease it, if you multiply by a fraction.) Multiply each component by a given number.

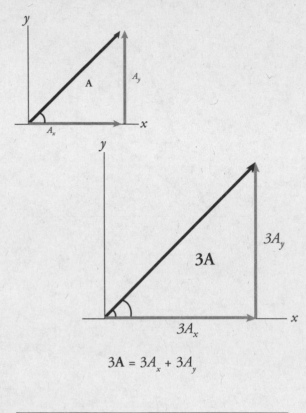

$$3\mathbf{A} = 3A_x + 3A_y$$

4. If the components of **A** are $A_x = 2$ and $A_y = -3$, and the components of **B** are $B_x = -4$ and $B_y = 2$, compute the components of each of the following vectors.

   a.   **A** + **B**
   b.   **A** − **B**
   c.   2**A**
   d.   **A** + 3**B**

Here's How to Crack It

a. Using unit vector notation, $\mathbf{A} = 2\mathbf{i} - 3\mathbf{j}$ and $\mathbf{B} = -4\mathbf{i} + 2\mathbf{j}$. Adding components, we see that $\mathbf{A} + \mathbf{B} = (2 + [-4])\mathbf{i} + ([-3] + 2)\mathbf{j} = -2\mathbf{i} - \mathbf{j}$. Therefore, the x component of the sum is -2 and the y component is -1.

b. $\mathbf{A} - \mathbf{B} = (2\mathbf{i} - 3\mathbf{j}) - (-4\mathbf{i} + 2\mathbf{j}) = (2 - [-4])\mathbf{i} + (-3 - 2)\mathbf{j} = 6\mathbf{i} - 5\mathbf{j}$. The x component is 6 and the y component is −5.

c. $2\mathbf{A} = 2(2\mathbf{i} - 3\mathbf{j}) = 4\mathbf{i} - 6\mathbf{j}$. 4 and − 6 are the x and y components, respectively.

d. $\mathbf{A} + 3\mathbf{B} = (2\mathbf{i} - 3\mathbf{j}) + 3(-4\mathbf{i} + 2\mathbf{j})$
   $= (2+3\,[-4])\mathbf{i} + (-3 + 3\,[2])\mathbf{j}$
   $= -10\mathbf{i} + 3\mathbf{j}$.
   −10 and 3 are the x and y components, respectively.

Magnitude of a Vector

Magnitude is a scalar number indicating the length of a vector. Use the Pythagorean theorem! You can use components C_x and C_y to find the magnitude of the new vector **C**.

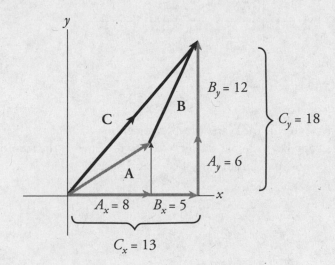

In this example, $C_x = 13$, $C_y = 18$, and vector **C** is the hypotenuse of the two.

$$a^2 + b^2 = c^2$$

$$13^2 + 18^2 = C^2$$

$$493 = C^2$$

Magnitude of C $\approx$ 22.2

Magnitude of a Vector Using SOHCAHTOA

You can use SOHCAHTOA to find A_x and A_y values. If **A** makes the angle θ with the x= axis, then its x- and y-components are $A\cos\theta$ and $A\sin\theta$, respectively (where A is the magnitude of **A**).

$$\mathbf{A} = \underbrace{A\cos\theta}_{A_x} + \underbrace{A\sin\theta}_{A_y}$$

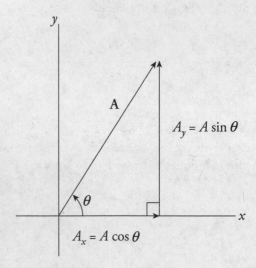

In general, any vector in the plane can be written in terms of two perpendicular component vectors. For example, vector $\mathbf{W}$ (shown below) is the sum of two component vectors whose magnitudes are $W\cos\theta$ and $W\sin\theta$:

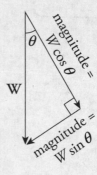

Keywords

scientific notation
trig functions
sine
cosine
tangent
Pythagorean theorem
SOHCAHTOA
vector
commutative law for addition
scalar
displacement
components
vector components
scalar components
unit vectors

Summary

o   Use SOHCAHTOA to remember the definitions of $\sin\theta$, $\cos\theta$, and $\tan\theta$.

o $\sin\theta = \dfrac{opposite}{hypotenuse}$

o $\cos\theta = \dfrac{adjacent}{hypotenuse}$

o $\tan\theta = \dfrac{opposite}{adjacent}$

o   A vector is a quantity that has a direction as well as a magnitude.

o   Add vectors by connecting vector arrows tip to tail and connecting the exposed tail to the exposed tip. The vector formed is the sum of the other vectors.

o   Because $\mathbf{A} - \mathbf{B} = \mathbf{A} + (-\mathbf{B})$, you can subtract a vector by multiplying it by –1 (flipping the point of the arrow to the opposite end) and adding the resultant vector to the other.

o   You can also add or subtract vectors by adding or subtracting their components.

o   Multiplying a vector by a positive scalar creates a vector in the same direction. Multiplying a vector by a negative scalar creates a vector in the opposite direction.

o   To find the magnitude (length) of a vector, you cannot simply add the lengths of the other two vectors. Resolve the vectors into horizontal and vertical components and use the Pythagorean theorem.

Chapter 2
Kinematics

Kinematics in many ways is the heart and soul of physics and, not surprisingly, a big deal on the SAT Physics Test. Kinematics is specifically the study of an object's motion in terms of its **displacement** (position in space), **velocity** (how fast an object is changing position), and **acceleration** (how fast an object is changing its velocity). In this chapter, we will explicitly define these terms and investigate how they relate to one another. Additionally we will go beyond one-dimensional motion and delve into in two-dimensional motion, that is, the world of projectile motion.

DISPLACEMENT

Displacement refers to an object's **change in position**. It's the vector that points from the object's initial position to its final position, regardless of the path actually taken. Since displacement means change in position, it is symbolized as **Δs**, where Δ denotes change in and **s** means spatial location.

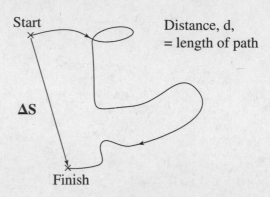

Displacement: A Strange Trip

The insect on the table below crawls 1 meter north, 2 meters east, 1 meter south, and finally 2 meters west.

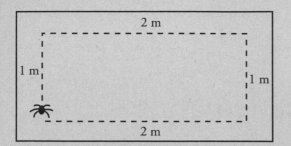

Even though the insect has crawled a total distance of 6 meters, its displacement is 0 meters. During the course of the bug's motion, it covered 6 meters of ground (distance = 6 m). Yet, when it is finished, it has not gone anywhere at all—there is no displacement for its motion (displacement = 0 m). Displacement is a vector quantity, and must incorporate **net** direction. The 1 meter north is canceled by the 1 meter south, and the 2 meters east is canceled by the 2 meters west.

If we know that the displacement is horizontal, then it can be called Δx; if the displacement is vertical, then it's Δy. The magnitude of this vector is the net distance traveled, not necessarily the actual distance traveled, d. Sometimes the word displacement refers to only this scalar quantity. Since a distance is being measured, the SI unit for displacement is the meter: [Δs] = m.

---

1. A rock is thrown straight upward from the edge of a 30 m cliff, rising 10 m then falling all the way down to the base of the cliff. Find the rock's displacement.

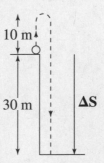

Here's How to Crack It

Displacement refers only to the object's initial position and final position, not the details of its journey. Since the rock started on the edge of the cliff and ended up on the ground 30 m below, its displacement is 30 m downward.

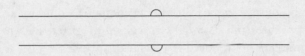

2. In a track-and-field event, an athlete runs exactly once around an oval track, a total distance of 500 m. Find the runner's displacement for the race.

Here's How to Crack It

If the runner returns to the same position from which she left, then her displacement is zero.

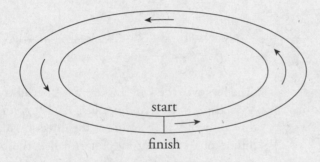

The *total* distance covered is 500 m, but the net distance—the displacement—is 0.

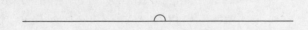

SPEED AND VELOCITY

When we're in a moving car, the speedometer tells us how fast we're going; it gives us our speed. But what does it mean to have a speed of, say, 10 m/s? It means that we're covering a distance of 10 meters every second. What if the car changes its speed as it drives (say, it stops at a traffic light)? We can look at a quantity that gives us information about the entire trip. By definition, **average speed** is the ratio of the total distance traveled to the time required to cover that distance.

Distance vs. Displacement
Note that distance is not the magnitude of the displacement unless the object has moved in a straight line.

$$\text{average speed} = \frac{\text{total distance}}{\text{time}}$$

The car's speedometer doesn't care in what direction the car is moving. You could be driving north, south, east, or west, the speedometer would make no distinction: *55 miles per hour, north* and *55 miles per hour, east* register the same on the speedometer as 55 miles per hour. Speed is a scalar quantity.

However, we also need to include *direction* in our descriptions of motion. We just learned about displacement, which takes both distance (net distance) and direction travelled into account. The vector that embodies both speed and direction is called **velocity**, symbolized **v**, and the definition of **average velocity** is:

$$\text{average velocity} = \frac{\text{displacement}}{\text{time}}$$

$$\bar{\mathbf{v}} = \frac{\Delta \mathbf{s}}{\Delta t}$$

The Skinny on Velocity

Since velocity is defined as the change in position per second, we can say the following (for motion along the x or y axis):

If **v** is positive, then the displacement is positive: The object is traveling in a positive direction.

If **v** is negative, then the displacement is negative: The object is traveling in a negative direction.

If **v** = 0, then the displacement is zero: The object is motionless.

(The bar over the **v** means *average*.) Because $\Delta \mathbf{s}$ is a vector, $\bar{\mathbf{v}}$ is also a vector, and because Δt is a *positive* scalar, the direction of **v** is the same as the direction of Δs. The magnitude of the velocity vector is called the object's **speed** and is expressed in units of meters per second (m/s).

Notice the distinction between speed and velocity. In everyday language, they're often used interchangeably. However, in physics, *speed* and *velocity* are technical terms with different definitions.

Speed has no direction and is always taken as a positive.

Velocity is speed and direction.

The magnitude of the average velocity is *not* called the average speed. Average speed is the *total* distance traveled divided by the elapsed time. Average velocity is the *net* distance traveled divided by the elapsed time.

3. Assume that the runner in sample question 3 completes the race in 1 minute and 20 seconds. Find her average speed and the magnitude of her average velocity.

Here's How to Crack It

Average speed is total distance divided by elapsed time. Since the length of the track is 500 m, the runner's average speed was (500 m)/(80 s) = 6.3 m/s. However, since her displacement was zero, her average velocity was zero also: $\mathbf{v} = \Delta s/\Delta t = $ (0 m)/(80 s) = 0 m/s.

4. Is it possible to move with constant speed but not constant velocity? Is it possible to move with constant velocity but not constant speed?

Here's How to Crack It

The answer to the first question is yes. For example, if you set your car's cruise control at 55 miles per hour but turn the steering wheel to follow a curved section of road, then the direction of your velocity changes (which means your velocity is not constant), even though your speed doesn't change.

The answer to the second question is *no*. Velocity means speed *and* direction; if the velocity is constant, then that means both speed and direction are constant. If speed were to change, then the velocity vector's magnitude would change (by definition), which immediately implies that the vector changes.

The Skinny on Acceleration

Since acceleration is defined as the change in velocity per second, we can say the following (for motion along the x or y axis):

If a is positive, then the change in velocity is positive: The object's velocity is increasing (becoming less negative).

If a is negative, then the change in velocity is negative: The object's velocity is decreasing (becoming less positive).

If a = 0, then the change in velocity is zero: The object's velocity is constant (not changing).

ACCELERATION

When you step on the gas pedal in your car, the car's speed increases; step on the brake and the car's speed decreases. Turn the wheel, and the car's direction of motion changes. In all of these cases, the velocity changes. To describe this change in velocity, we need a new term: **acceleration**. In the same way that velocity measures the rate of change of an object's position, acceleration measures the rate of change of an object's velocity. An object's **average acceleration** is defined as follows:

$$\text{average acceleration} = \frac{\text{change in velocity}}{\text{time}}$$

$$\overline{\mathbf{a}} = \frac{\Delta \mathbf{v}}{\Delta t}$$

The units of acceleration are meters per second, per second: $[a]$ = m/s^2. Because $\Delta \mathbf{v}$ is a vector, $\overline{\mathbf{a}}$ is also a vector; and because Δt is a *positive* scalar, the direction of $\overline{\mathbf{a}}$ is the same as the direction of $\Delta \mathbf{v}$.

Furthermore, if an object's original direction of motion is positive, then an increase in speed corresponds to a positive acceleration, while a decrease in speed corresponds to a negative acceleration (deceleration).

Notice that an object can accelerate even if its speed doesn't change. (Again, don't let the everyday usage of the word *accelerate* confuse you!) This is because acceleration depends on $\Delta \mathbf{v}$, and the velocity vector $\mathbf{v}$ changes if (1) speed changes, (2) direction changes, or (3) both speed and direction change. For instance, a car traveling around a circular racetrack is constantly accelerating even if the car's *speed* is constant because the direction of the car's velocity vector is constantly changing.

5. A car is traveling in a straight line along a highway at a constant speed of 80 miles per hour for 10 seconds. Find its acceleration.

Here's How to Crack It
Since the car is traveling at a constant velocity, its acceleration is zero. If there's no change in velocity, then there's no acceleration.

6. A car is traveling in a straight line along a highway at a speed of 20 m/s. The driver steps on the gas pedal and, 3 seconds later, the car's speed is 32 m/s. Find its average acceleration.

Here's How to Crack It

Assuming that the direction of the velocity doesn't change, it's simply a matter of dividing the change in velocity, 32 m/s – 20 m/s = 12 m/s, by the time interval during which the change occurred: $\bar{a} = \Delta v / \Delta t = (12 \text{ m/s}) / (3 \text{ s}) = 4 \text{ m/s}^2$.

7. Spotting a police car ahead, the driver of the car in the previous example slows from 32 m/s to 20 m/s in 2 sec. Find the car's average acceleration.

Here's How to Crack It

Dividing the change in velocity, 20 m/s – 32 m/s = –12 m/s, by the time interval during which the change occurred, 2 s, gives us $\bar{a} = \Delta v / \Delta t = (-12 \text{ m/s}) / (2 \text{ s}) = -6$ m/s^2. The negative sign means that the direction of the acceleration is opposite the direction of the velocity: The car is slowing down.

If an object has negative velocity, then a positive acceleration means it is slowing down and a negative acceleration means it is speeding up. This can be confusing. Just remember that if velocity and acceleration point in the same direction, the object is speeding up and if they point in opposite directions, it is slowing down.

speeding up

slowing down

Positive Acceleration vs. Speeding Up
Remember that positive acceleration doesn't necessarily mean the object is speeding up.

Negative Acceleration vs. Slowing Down
Remember that negative acceleration doesn't necessarily mean the object is slowing down.

Note: If velocity and acceleration are perpendicular, the object is turning.

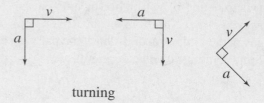

turning

We will discuss this further in Chapter 3.

UNIFORMLY ACCELERATED MOTION AND THE BIG FIVE

The simplest type of motion to analyze is motion in which the acceleration is *constant* (possibly equal to zero). Although true uniform acceleration rarely occurs in the real world, many common motions exhibit approximately constant acceleration and, in these cases, the kinematics of uniformly accelerated motion provide a pretty good description of what's happening. Notice that if the acceleration is constant, then taking an average yields nothing new, so $\bar{\mathbf{a}} = \mathbf{a}$.

Another thing that makes our discussion easier is that we'll only consider motion that takes place along a straight line. In these cases, there are only two possible directions of motion—one is positive, and the opposite direction is negative. Most of the quantities we've been dealing with—displacement, velocity, and acceleration—are vectors, which means that they include both a magnitude and a direction. With straight-line motion, we can show direction simply by attaching a plus or minus sign to the magnitude of the quantity, therefore we will drop the standard vector notation.

Fundamental Quantities: A Quick Review

The fundamental quantities are displacement (Δs), velocity (v), and acceleration (a). Acceleration is a change in velocity, from an initial velocity (v_i or v_0) to a final velocity (v_f or simply v—with no subscript). And, finally, the motion takes place during some elapsed time interval, Δt. Therefore, we have five kinematics quantities: Δs, v_0, v, a, and Δt. Since time usually begins at zero, we will replace Δt with t.

These five quantities are related by a group of five equations that we call the *Big Five*. They work in cases where acceleration is uniform, which are the cases we're considering.

		Variable that's missing
Big Five #1:	$\Delta s = \overline{v}t$ or $\frac{1}{2}(v_0 + v)t$	a
Big Five #2:	$v = v_0 + at$	Δs
Big Five #3:	$\Delta s = v_0 t + \frac{1}{2}at^2$	v
Big Five #4:	$\Delta s = vt - \frac{1}{2}at^2$	v_0
Big Five #5:	$v^2 = v_0^2 + 2a\Delta s$	t

In Big Five #1, the average velocity is simply the average of the initial velocity and the final velocity: $\overline{v} = \frac{1}{2}(v_0 + v)$. This is true because the acceleration is constant.

Each of the Big Five equations is missing one of the five kinematic quantities. The way you decide which equation to use when solving a problem is to determine which of the kinematic quantities is missing from the problem—that is, which quantity is neither given nor asked for—and then use the equation that doesn't contain that variable. For example, if the problem never mentions the final velocity—v is neither given nor asked for—you should use the equation that's missing v: Big Five #3.

The first part of Big Five #1 and Big Five #2 are simply the definitions of $\mathbf{v}$ and $\overline{\mathbf{a}}$ written in forms that don't involve fractions. The other Big Five equations can be derived from these two definitions and the equation $\overline{v} = \frac{1}{2}(v_0 + v)$, using a little algebra.

---

8. An object with an initial velocity of 4 m/s moves along a straight axis under constant acceleration. Three seconds later, its velocity is 14 m/s. How far did it travel during this time?

Here's How to Crack It
We're given v_0, t, and v, and we're asked for Δs. So a is missing; it isn't given and it isn't asked for, so we use Big Five #1.

$$\Delta s = \overline{v}t = \frac{1}{2}\left(v_0 + v\right)t = \frac{1}{2}\ (4\ \text{m/s} + 14\ \text{m/s})(3\ \text{s}) = 27\ \text{m}$$

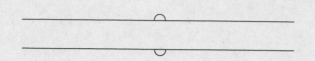

9. A car that's initially traveling at 10 m/s accelerates uniformly for 4 seconds at a rate of 2 m/s² in a straight line. How far does the car travel during this time?

Here's How to Crack It

We're given v_0, t, and a, and we're asked for s. So v is missing; it isn't given and it isn't asked for, so we use Big Five #3.

$$\Delta s = v_0 \Delta t + \frac{1}{2} at^2 = \left(10\ \text{m/s}\right)\left(4\,\text{s}\right) + \frac{1}{2}(2\ \text{m/s}^2\ )(4\ \text{s})^2 = 56\ \text{m}$$

10. A rock is dropped off a cliff that's 80 m high. If it strikes the ground with an impact velocity of 40 m/s, what acceleration did it experience during its descent?

Here's How to Crack It

If something is dropped, then that means it has no initial velocity: v_0, = 0. So, we're given v_0, Δs, and v, and we're asked for a. Since t is missing, we use Big Five #5.

Those Pesky Signs
Make sure you are clear which direction is positive. If an object ends more in the negative direction than it started, Δs is negative.

$$v^2 = v_0^2 + 2a\Delta s \Rightarrow v^2 = 2a\Delta s \quad \left(\text{since } v_0 = 0\right)$$

$$a = \frac{v^2}{2\Delta s} = \frac{\left(40\ \text{m/s}\right)^2}{2\left(80\ \text{m}\right)} = 10\ \text{m/s}^2$$

Notice that since a has the same sign as Δs, the acceleration vector points in the same direction as the displacement vector. This makes sense, because the object moves downward and the acceleration it experiences is due to gravity, which also points downward.

KINEMATICS WITH GRAPHS

So far, we've dealt with kinematics problems algebraically, but for this test, you should also be able to handle kinematics questions in which information is given graphically. The two most popular graphs in kinematics are position-versus-time graphs and velocity-versus-time graphs.

Position vs. Time

For example, think of an object that's moving along an axis in such a way that its position x as a function of time t is given by the following position-versus-time graph:

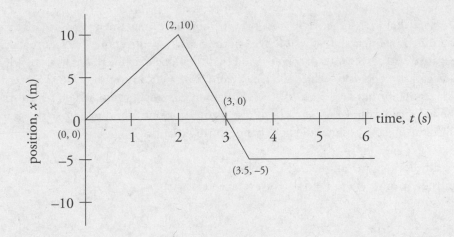

What does this graph tell us? It says that at time $t = 0$, the object was at $x = 0$. Then, in the next two seconds, its position changed from $x = 0$ to $x = 10$ m.

Then, at time $t = 2$ s, it reversed direction and headed back toward its starting point, reaching $x = 0$ at time $t = 3$ s, and continued, reaching position $x = -5$ m at time $t = 3.5$ s. Then the object remained at this position, $x = -5$ m, at least through time $t = 6$ s.

We can also determine the object's average velocity (and average speed) during particular time intervals. For example, its average velocity from time $t = 0$ to time $t = 2$ s is equal to the distance it traveled, $10 - 0 = 10$ m, divided by the elapsed time, 2 s.

$$\bar{v} = \frac{\Delta x}{\Delta t} = \frac{(10-0) \text{ m}}{(2-0) \text{ s}} = 5 \text{ m/s}$$

Notice that the ratio that gives us the average velocity, $\Delta x/\Delta t$, is also the slope of the x versus t graph. For a straight line, the slope is constant. Thus, average velocity and velocity are equal. Therefore:

> The slope of a position-versus-time graph gives the velocity.

What was the velocity from time $t = 2$ s to time $t = 3.5$ s? Well, the slope of the line segment joining the point $(t, x) = (2 \text{ s}, 10 \text{ m})$ to the point $(t, x) = (3.5 \text{ s}, -5 \text{ m})$ is

$$v = \frac{\Delta x}{\Delta t} = \frac{(-5-10) \text{ m}}{(3.5-2) \text{ s}} = -10 \text{ m/s}$$

The fact that $\mathbf{v}$ is negative tells us that the object's displacement was negative during this time interval; that is, it moved in the negative x direction. The fact that $\mathbf{v}$ is negative also agrees with the observation that the slope of a line that falls to the right is negative. What is the object's velocity from time $t = 3.5$ s to time $t = 6$ s? Since the line segment from $t = 3.5$ s to $t = 6$ s is horizontal, its slope is zero, which tells us that the velocity is also zero, but we can also figure this out from looking at the graph, since the object's position did not change during that time.

Finally, let's figure out the average velocity and average speed for the object's entire journey (from $t = 0$ to $t = 6$ s). The average velocity is

$$\bar{v} = \frac{\Delta x}{\Delta t} = \frac{(-5-0) \text{ m}}{(6-0) \text{ s}} = -0.83 \text{ m/s}$$

Slope
The slope of a line that goes up to the right is positive, the slope of a line that goes down to the right is negative, and the slope of a flat (horizontal) line is zero.

This is the slope of the imagined line segment that joins the point $(t, x) = (0 \text{ s}, 0 \text{ m})$ to the point $(t, x) = (6 \text{ s}, -5 \text{ m})$. The average speed is the total distance traveled by the object divided by the change in time. In this case, notice that the object traveled 10 m in the first 2 s, then 15 m (backward) in the next 1.5 s; it covered no distance from $t = 3.5$ s to $t = 6$ s. Therefore, the total distance traveled by the object is $d = 10 + 15 = 25$ m, which took 6 s, so

$$\text{average speed} = \frac{d}{\Delta t} = \frac{25 \text{ m}}{6 \text{ s}} = 4.2 \text{ m/s}$$

Note that the average velocity (or average speed) for the whole journey is not the same as taking the average of the velocities (or speeds) of the individual parts of the journey.

Also, remember that if any portion of a Position vs. Time graph is "curvy," this indicates that the object is accelerating.

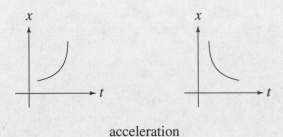

acceleration

Velocity vs. Time

Let's next consider an object moving along a straight axis in such a way that its velocity-versus-time graph looks like this:

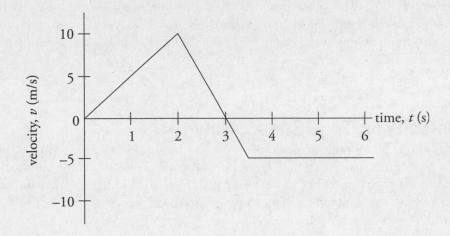

What does this graph tell us? It says that at time $t = 0$, the object's velocity was $v = 0$. Over the first two seconds, its velocity increased steadily to 10 m/s. At time $t = 2$ s, the velocity began to decrease, eventually becoming $v = 0$, at time $t = 3$ s. The velocity then became negative after $t = 3$ s, reaching $v = -5$ m/s at time $t = 3.5$ s. From $t = 3.5$ s on, the velocity remained a steady -5 m/s.

What can we ask about this motion? First, the fact that the velocity changed from $t = 0$ to $t = 2$ s tells us that the object accelerated. The acceleration during this time was

$$a = \frac{\Delta v}{\Delta t} = \frac{(10-0) \text{ m/s}}{(2-0) \text{ s}} = 5 \text{ m/s}^2$$

Now notice that the ratio that defines the acceleration, $\Delta v / \Delta t$, also defines the slope of the v versus t graph. Therefore

> The slope of a velocity-versus-time graph gives the acceleration.

What was the acceleration from time $t = 2$ s to time $t = 3.5$ s? The slope of the line segment joining the point $(t, v) = (2 \text{ s}, 10 \text{ m/s})$ to the point $(t, v) = (3.5 \text{ s}, -5 \text{ m/s})$ is

$$a = \frac{\Delta v}{\Delta t} = \frac{(-5-10) \text{ m/s}}{(3.5-2) \text{ s}} = -10 \text{ m/s}^2$$

The fact that a is negative tells us that the object's velocity change was negative during this time—that is, the object accelerated in the negative direction. In fact, after time $t = 3$ s, the velocity became more negative, telling us that the direction of motion was negative at increasing speed. What is the object's acceleration from time $t = 3.5$ s to time $t = 6$ s? Since the line segment from $t = 3.5$ s to $t = 6$ s is horizontal, its slope is zero, which tells us that the acceleration is zero, but you can also see this from looking at the graph; the object's velocity did not change during this time interval.

Velocity vs. Time Graphs; How Far?

We can ask another question when we see a velocity-versus-time graph: How *far* did the object travel during a particular time interval? For example, let's figure out the displacement of the object from time $t = 4$ s to time $t = 6$ s. During this time interval, the velocity was a constant -5 m/s, so the displacement was $\Delta x = v\Delta t = (-5 \text{ m/s})(2\text{s}) = -10$ m.

We've actually determined the area between the graph and the horizontal axis—after all, the area of a rectangle is *base × height* and, for the shaded rectangle shown on the next page, the *base* is Δt and the *height* is v. So, *base × height* equals $\Delta t × v$, which is displacement.

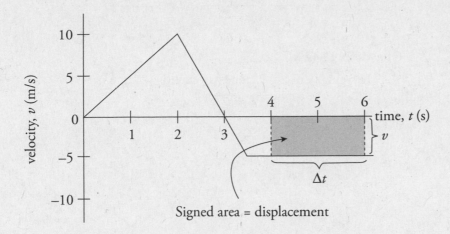

Signed area = displacement

We call this the *signed area* because regions below the horizontal axis are negative quantities (since the object's velocity is negative, its displacement is negative). Therefore, by counting areas above the horizontal axis as positive and areas below the horizontal axis as negative, we can make the following claim:

> Given a velocity-versus-time graph, the area between the graph and the *t*-axis is equal to the object's displacement.

What is the object's displacement from time $t = 0$ to $t = 3$ s? Using the fact that displacement is the area bounded by the velocity graph, we figure out the area of the triangle shown below.

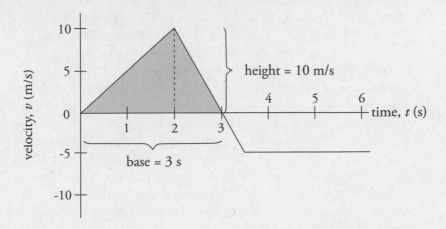

height = 10 m/s

base = 3 s

Displacement vs. Distance

If we wish to find the distance travelled using a velocity vs. time graph, then all areas are considered to be positive.

Since the area of a triangle is $\frac{1}{2} \times$ base $\times$ height, we find that $\Delta x = \frac{1}{2}$ (3 s)(10 m/s) = 15 m.

Questions 11-12

The velocity of an object as a function of time is given by the following graph:

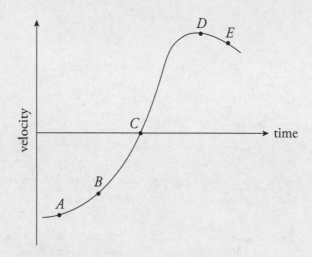

11. At which point (A, B, C, D, or E) is the magnitude of the acceleration the greatest?

12. How would you answer this same question if the graph shown were a position-versus-time graph?

Here's How to Crack It

11.   The acceleration is equal to the slope of the velocity-versus-time graph. Although this graph is not composed of straight lines, the concept of slope still applies; at each point, the slope of the curve is the slope of the tangent line to the curve. The slope is essentially zero at points *A* and *D* (where the curve is flat), small and positive at *B*, and small and negative at *E*. The slope at point *C* is large and positive, so this is where the object's acceleration is the greatest.

12.   If the graph shown were a position-versus-time graph, then the slope would be equal to the velocity. The slope of the given graph starts at zero (around point *A*), slowly increases to a small positive value at *B*, continues to slowly increase to a large positive value at *C*, and then, at around point *D*, quickly decreases to zero. Of the points designated on the graph, point *D* is the location of the greatest slope change, which means that this is the point of the greatest velocity change. Therefore, this is the point at which the magnitude of the acceleration is greatest.

FREE FALL

The simplest real-life example of motion under almost constant acceleration is the motion of objects in the earth's gravitational field, near the surface of the earth and ignoring any effects due to the air (mainly air resistance). With these effects ignored, an object can fall *freely*, that is, it can fall experiencing only acceleration due to gravity. Near the surface of the earth, the gravitational acceleration has a constant magnitude of about 9.8 m/s^2 (or, for our purposes, about 10 m/s^2); this quantity is denoted g (for *g*ravitational acceleration). And, of course, the gravitational acceleration vector, **g**, points *downward*.

Since the acceleration is constant, we can use the Big Five with a replaced by $+g$ or $-g$. To decide which of these two values to use for a, make a decision at the beginning of your calculations whether to call "down" the positive direction or the negative direction. If you call "down" the positive direction, then $a = +g$. If you call "down" the negative direction, then $a = -g$. Just to make things easier, you should always refer to the direction of the object's displacement as positive.

In each of the following examples, we'll ignore effects due to air resistance.

---

13. A rock is dropped from an 80-meter cliff. How long does it take to reach the ground?

Here's How to Crack It

Since the rock's displacement is down, we call down the positive direction, so $a = +g$. We're given v_0, s, and a, and asked for t. So v is missing; it isn't given and it isn't asked for, and we use Big Five #3.

$$\Delta s = v_0 t + \frac{1}{2}at^2 \Rightarrow \Delta s = \frac{1}{2}at^2 \text{ (since } v_0 = 0)$$

$$t = \sqrt{\frac{2\Delta s}{a}}$$

$$\sqrt{\frac{2\Delta s}{+g}} = \sqrt{\frac{2(+80 \text{ m})}{+10 \text{ m/s}^2}} = 4.0 \text{ s}$$

---

14. One second after being thrown straight down, an object is falling with a speed of 20 m/s. How fast will it be falling 2 seconds later?

Here's How to Crack It

Call down the positive direction, so $a = +g$ and $v_0 = +20$ m/s. We're given v_0, a, and t, and asked for v. Since s is missing, we use Big Five #2.

$$\Delta v = at$$
$$v - v_0 = at$$
$$v = v_0 + at = (+20 \text{ m/s}) + (+10 \text{ m/s}^2)(2 \text{ s}) = 40 \text{ m/s}$$

15. If an object is thrown straight upward with an initial speed of 8 m/s and takes 3 seconds to strike the ground, from what height was the object thrown?

Here's How to Crack It

The figure below shows that the displacement is down, so we call down the positive direction. Therefore, $a = +g$ and $v_0 = -8$ m/s (because up is the negative direction). We're given a, v_0, and t, and we need to find Δs. Since v is missing, we use Big Five #3.

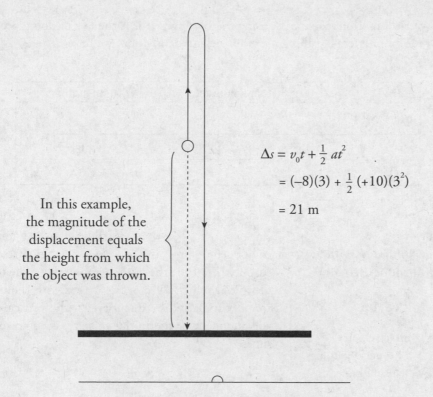

$$\Delta s = v_0 t + \frac{1}{2} a t^2$$
$$= (-8)(3) + \frac{1}{2} (+10)(3^2)$$
$$= 21 \text{ m}$$

In this example, the magnitude of the displacement equals the height from which the object was thrown.

PROJECTILE MOTION

In general, an object that moves near the surface of the earth will not follow a straight-line path; think of a baseball hit by a bat, a golf ball struck by a club, or a tennis ball hit from the baseline. If we launch an object at an angle other than straight upward, and consider only the effect of acceleration due to gravity, then the object will travel along a parabolic trajectory.

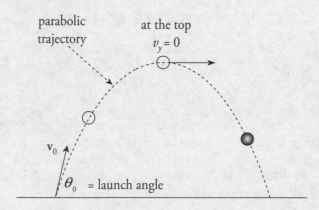

parabolic trajectory

at the top
$v_y = 0$

$\mathbf{v}_0$

θ_0 = launch angle

The force of gravity causes an object to fall but does not affect the objects horizontal motion. To simplify the analysis of parabolic motion, we analyze the horizontal and vertical motions separately, using the Big Five. This is the key to doing projectile motion problems. Calling *down* the negative direction, we have

	Horizontal motion:	**Vertical motion:**
position	$\Delta x = v_{0x}t$	$\Delta y = v_{0y}t + \frac{1}{2}(-g)t^2$
velocity	$v_x = v_{0x}$ (constant)	$v_y = v_{0y} + (-g)t$
acceleration	$a_x = 0$	$a_y = -g$

The Skinny on Projectile Motion
The perpendicular components of motion (horizontal and vertical) are independent of each other. Work them out separately.

Horizontal
A projectile launched with horizontal velocity (v_{0x}) maintains that velocity. There are no accelerations in the horizontal force, so the *x*-velocity is constant.

Vertical
The only vertical acceleration is 10 m/s^2 downward, so the v_y consistently decreases by this amount. At the top of the object's trajectory, $v_y = 0$.

The angle of launch determines the relationship of v_{0y} and v_{0x}.

If $\theta > 45°$, then $v_{0y} > v_{0x}$.

If $\theta < 45°$, then $v_{0y} < v_{0x}$.

The quantity v_{0x}, which is the horizontal (or *x*) component of the initial velocity, is equal to $v_0 \cos\theta_0$, where θ_0 is the **launch angle**, the angle that the initial velocity vector, **v**$_0$, makes with the horizontal. Similarly, the quantity v_{0y}, the vertical (or *y*) component of the initial velocity, is equal to $v_0 \sin\theta_0$.

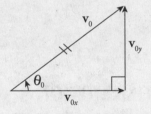

Free Fall vs. Horizontal Projection
The time it takes an object dropped from rest to fall a certain distance is the same as if it were projected horizontally with any speed.

16. An object is thrown horizontally with an initial speed of 10 m/s. How far will it drop in 4 seconds?

Here's How to Crack It
The first step is to decide whether this is a horizontal question or a vertical question, since you must consider these motions separately. The question "How far will it drop?" is a vertical question, so we'll use the set of equations listed above under vertical motion. Next, how far... ? implies that we will use the first of the vertical-motion equations, the one that gives vertical displacement, Δy.

Since the object is thrown horizontally, there is no vertical component to its initial velocity vector $\mathbf{v}_0$; that is, $v_{0y} = 0$. So

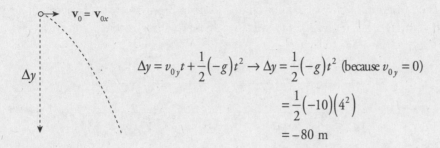

$$\Delta y = v_{0y}t + \frac{1}{2}(-g)t^2 \rightarrow \Delta y = \frac{1}{2}(-g)t^2 \text{ (because } v_{0y} = 0\text{)}$$

$$= \frac{1}{2}(-10)(4^2)$$

$$= -80 \text{ m}$$

The fact that Δy is negative means that the displacement is *down*. Also, notice that the information given about v_{0x} is irrelevant to the question.

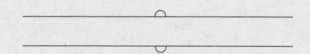

17. From a height of 100 m, a ball is thrown horizontally with an initial speed of 15 m/s. How far does it travel horizontally in the first 2 seconds?

Here's How to Crack It

The question "How far does it travel horizontally...?" immediately tells us that we should use the first of the horizontal-motion equations listed on the previous page.

$$\Delta x = v_{0x}t = (15 \text{ m/s})(2 \text{ s}) = 30 \text{ m}$$

The information that the initial vertical position is 100 m above the ground is irrelevant (except for the fact that it's high enough that the ball won't strike the ground before the 2 seconds have elapsed).

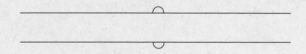

18. A projectile is traveling in a parabolic path for a total of 6 seconds. How does its horizontal velocity 1 s after launch compare to its horizontal velocity 4 s after launch?

Here's How to Crack It

The only acceleration experienced by the projectile is due to gravity, which is purely vertical, so there's no horizontal acceleration. If there's no horizontal acceleration, then the horizontal velocity cannot change during flight, and the projectile's horizontal velocity 1 s after it's launched is the same as its horizontal velocity 3 s later.

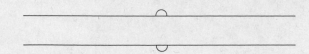

19. An object is projected upward with a 30° launch angle and an initial speed of 60 m/s. How many seconds will it be in the air? How far will it travel horizontally?

Here's How to Crack It

The total time the object spends in the air is equal to twice the time required to reach the top of the trajectory (because the parabola is symmetrical). So, as we did in the previous example, we can find the time required to reach the top by setting v_y equal to 0, and then double that amount of time:

$$v_y \overset{\text{set}}{=} 0 \;\Rightarrow\; v_{0y} + \left(-g\right)t = 0$$

$$t = \frac{v_{0y}}{g} = \frac{v_0 \sin\theta_0}{g} = \frac{\left(60 \text{ m/s}\right)\sin 30°}{10 \text{ m/s}} = 3 \text{ s}$$

Therefore, the *total* flight time (that is, up and down) is $T = 2t = 2 \times (3 \text{ s}) = 6 \text{ s}$.

Now, using the first horizontal-motion equation, we can calculate the horizontal displacement after 6 seconds.

$$\Delta x = v_{0x}T = \left(v_0 \cos\theta_0\right)T = \left[\left(60 \text{ m/s}\right)\cos 30°\right]\left(6 \text{ s}\right) = 310 \text{ m}$$

By the way, the full horizontal displacement of a projectile is called the projectile's **range**.

Chapter 2 Review Questions

Answers are on page 388.

1. An object that's moving with constant speed travels once around a circular path. Which of the following is/are true concerning this motion?

   I. The displacement is zero.
   II. The average speed is zero.
   III. The acceleration is zero.

   (A) I only
   (B) I and II only
   (C) I and III only
   (D) III only
   (E) II and III only

2. At time $t = t_1$, an object's velocity is given by the vector $\mathbf{v}_1$ shown below.

   A short time later, at $t = t_2$, the object's velocity is the vector $\mathbf{v}_2$.

   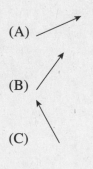

   If v_1 and v_2 have the same magnitude, which one of the following vectors best illustrates the object's average acceleration between $t = t_1$ and $t = t_2$?

   (A)

   (B)

   (C)

   (D)

   (E)

3. Which of the following is/are true?

   I. If an object's acceleration is constant, then it must move in a straight line.
   II. If an object's acceleration is zero, then its speed must remain constant.
   III. If an object's speed remains constant, then its acceleration must be zero.

   (A) I and II only
   (B) I and III only
   (C) II only
   (D) III only
   (E) II and III only

4. A baseball is thrown straight upward. What is the ball's acceleration at its highest point?

   (A) 0
   (B) $\frac{1}{2}g$, downward
   (C) g, downward
   (D) $\frac{1}{2}g$, upward
   (E) g, upward

5. How long would it take a car, starting from rest and accelerating uniformly in a straight line at 5 m/s², to cover a distance of 200 m?

   (A) 9.0 s
   (B) 10.5 s
   (C) 12.0 s
   (D) 15.5 s
   (E) 20.0 s

6. A rock is dropped off a cliff and strikes the ground with an impact velocity of 30 m/s. How high was the cliff?

   (A) 15 m
   (B) 20 m
   (C) 30 m
   (D) 45 m
   (E) 60 m

7. A stone is thrown horizontally with an initial speed of 10 m/s from a bridge. If air resistance could be ignored, how long would it take the stone to strike the water 80 m below the bridge?

(A) 1 s
(B) 2 s
(C) 4 s
(D) 6 s
(E) 8 s

8. A soccer ball, at rest on the ground, is kicked with an initial velocity of 10 m/s at a launch angle of 30°. Calculate its total flight time, assuming that air resistance is negligible.

(A) 0.5 s
(B) 1 s
(C) 1.7 s
(D) 2 s
(E) 4 s

9. A stone is thrown horizontally with an initial speed of 30 m/s from a bridge. Find the stone's total speed when it enters the water 4 seconds later. (Ignore air resistance.)

(A) 30 m/s
(B) 40 m/s
(C) 50 m/s
(D) 60 m/s
(E) 70 m/s

10. Which one of the following statements is true concerning the motion of an ideal projectile launched at an angle of 45° to the horizontal?

(A) The acceleration vector points opposite to the velocity vector on the way up and in the same direction as the velocity vector on the way down.
(B) The speed at the top of the trajectory is zero.
(C) The object's total speed remains constant during the entire flight.
(D) The horizontal speed decreases on the way up and increases on the way down.
(E) The vertical speed decreases on the way up and increases on the way down.

Keywords

kinematics
displacement
velocity
average speed
average velocity
speed
acceleration
average acceleration
uniform acceleration
launch angle
range
free fall

Summary

- Displacement is the vector that connects an object's initial position with its final position. It is the net distance traveled.

- Distance is the length of the particular path chosen (a scalar).

- Speed is a scalar quantity that has no direction and is always taken as a positive.

- Velocity is a vector that embodies speed and direction and measures the rate of change of an object's position.

- Acceleration measures the rate of change of an object's velocity.

- For cases in which acceleration is uniform, use the Big Five equations to find the missing variable that represents acceleration, displacement, initial velocity, final velocity, or elapsed time. Memorize the chart on page 37.

- The two most popular graphs in kinematics are the position-versus-time graph and the velocity-versus-time graph. The slope of a position-versus-time graph gives the velocity, while the slope of a velocity-versus-time graph gives the acceleration.

- On a velocity-versus-time graph, the area between the graph and the t-axis is equal to the object's displacement.

- Gravitational acceleration has a constant magnitude of about $9.8 m/s^2$. Use $10 m/s^2$ when you estimate.

- Since gravitational acceleration is constant, it can be replaced by either $+g$ or $-g$ with a + sign if down is the positive direction and a − sign if down is the negative direction. Always take the direction of an object's displacement as positive.

- Projectile motion is the parabolic formation caused by the pull of gravity on an object moving near the surface of the earth.

Chapter 3
Newton's Laws

In the previous chapter we studied the vocabulary and equations that describe motion. Now we will learn *why* things move the way they do; this is the subject of **dynamics.**

An interaction between two bodies, a push or a pull, is called a **force**. You see examples of forces every day. If you lift a book, you exert an upward force (created by your muscles) on it. If you pull on a rope that's attached to a crate, you create a **tension** in the rope that pulls the crate. When a skydiver is falling through the air, the earth is exerting a downward pull called **gravitational force,** and the air exerts an upward force called **air resistance**. When you stand on the floor, the floor provides an upward, supporting force called the **normal force**. If you slide a book across a table, the table exerts a **frictional force** against the book, so the book slows down and then stops. Static cling provides a directly observable example of the **electrostatic force**.

Sir Isaac Newton published a book in 1687 called *The Mathematical Principles of Natural Philosophy*—referred to nowadays as simply *The Principia*—that began the modern study of physics as a scientific discipline. To score well on force questions on the SAT Physics Subject Test, you will need to know about three of the laws that Newton stated in *The Principia*. These laws form the basis of dynamics and are known as **Newton's laws of motion.**

THE FIRST LAW

> Newton's first law says that an object will continue in its state of motion unless compelled to change by a force impressed upon it.

If the object is at rest, then it will stay at rest, and if it is moving, then it will continue to move at a constant speed in a straight line.

Basically, no force means no change in velocity. This property of objects—their natural resistance to changes in their state of motion—is called **inertia**. In fact, the first law is often referred to as the **law of inertia**.

The Skinny on the First Law

Mass is a measure of inertia; the more mass an object has the more the object resists changing its velocity. For example, if you hit a bowling ball with a bat, there's not much change in the ball's velocity. But if you hit a baseball with a bat with the same force, there's a bigger change in velocity. Since a bowling ball has more mass, it has more inertia.

THE SECOND LAW

Newton's second law predicts what will happen when a force *does* act on an object: The object's velocity will change and it will accelerate. More precisely, it says that its acceleration, **a**, will be directly proportional to the magnitude of the total—or *net*—force (F_{net}) and inversely proportional to the object's mass, *m*.

> $$F_{net} = m\mathbf{a}$$
>
> This is the most important equation in mechanics!

The Skinny on the Second Law

This law defines force. The second law relates the acceleration an object of a certain mass experiences when a force is applied to it. The larger the force on the object, the larger its acceleration. It's like the difference between pulling a wagon filled with heavy packages alone and having a friend help you pull. The wagon pulled by your joint force has a greater acceleration.

F_{net} is the sum of all the forces acting on an object. Beware, there can be forces acting on an object without causing a net acceleration. This happens when the forces cancel each other out—that is $F_{net} = 0$ N.

The mass of an object is directly related to its weight: The heavier an object is, the more mass it has. Two identical boxes, one empty and one full, have different masses. The box that's full has the greater mass, because it contains more stuff; more stuff means more mass. Mass is measured in **kilograms (kg)**. (Note: An object whose mass is 1 kg weighs about 2.2 pounds.) It takes twice as much force to produce the same acceleration of a 2 kg object than of a 1 kg object. **Mass** measures an object's inertia—its resistance to acceleration.

Forces are represented by vectors; they have magnitude and direction. If several different forces act on an object simultaneously, then the net force, F_{net}, is the vector sum of all these forces. (The phrase *resultant force* is also used to mean *net force*.)

Since $F_{net} = ma$, and m is a *positive* scalar, the direction of **a** always matches the direction of F_{net}. Finally, since $F = ma$, the units for F equal the units of m times the units of a.

$$[F] = [m][a]$$
$$= kg{\cdot}m/s^2$$

A force of 1 $kg{\cdot}m/s^2$ is renamed 1 **newton** (abbreviated N). A medium-size apple weighs about 1 N.

Force vs. Motion
Remember that an object does not have to move in the direction of the net force, in the same way that an object doesn't have to move in the direction of acceleration.

The relationship between the direction of net force and velocity is the same as the relationship between acceleration and velocity. Forward forces speed up objects, backward forces slow down objects, and forces perpendicular to the velocity are responsible for turning.

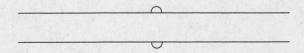

speeding up   slowing down   turning

1. What net force is required to maintain a 5,000 kg object moving at a constant velocity of magnitude 7,500 m/s?

Here's How to Crack It
The first law says that any object will continue in its state of motion unless a force acts on it. Therefore, no net force is required to maintain a 5,000 kg object moving at a constant velocity of magnitude 7,500 m/s. Here's another way to look at it: Constant velocity means $a = 0$, so the equation $F_{net} = ma$ immediately gives $F_{net} = 0$.

2. How much force is required to cause an object of mass 2kg to have an acceleration of 4 m/s^2?

Here's How to Crack It
According to the second law, $\mathbf{F}_{net} = m\mathbf{a} = (2 \text{ kg})(4 \text{ m/s}^2) = 8$ N.

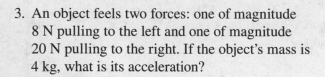

3. An object feels two forces: one of magnitude 8 N pulling to the left and one of magnitude 20 N pulling to the right. If the object's mass is 4 kg, what is its acceleration?

Here's How to Crack It
Forces are represented by vectors and can be added and subtracted. Therefore, an 8 N force to the left added to a 20 N force to the right yields a net force of 20 − 8 = 12 N to the right. Then Newton's second law gives $\mathbf{a} = \mathbf{F}_{net}/m = (12 \text{ N to the right})/(4 \text{ kg}) = 3 \text{ m/s}^2$ to the right.

THE THIRD LAW

Newton's third law is commonly remembered as, to every action, there is an equal, but opposite, reaction.

The Skinny on the Third Law
Two objects must interact for a force to exist. When both objects interact, each body experiences a force due to the other interacting body. If A and B are the two interacting masses, let F_1 be the force acting on A due to B; F_2 is the force acting on B due to A. F_1 and F_2 are the same magnitude but have opposite directions. $\mathbf{F}_1 = -\mathbf{F}_2$.

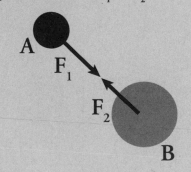

More precisely, if object 1 exerts a force on object 2, then object 2 exerts a force back on object 1, equal in strength but in the opposite direction. These two forces, $\mathbf{F}_{1\text{-on-}2}$ and $\mathbf{F}_{2\text{-on-}1}$, are called an **action/reaction pair.**

4. A woman riding a bicycle collides head-on with a parked school bus. Which object feels greater force?

Here's How to Crack It

Newton's third law states that the force exerted by the bus on the woman/bike will be equal in magnitude to the force that the woman/bike exerts on the bus. What is different is the effect of the force. Since $\mathbf{F}_{net} = m\mathbf{a}$, the bus (with larger mass) will experience a smaller acceleration than the woman on the bike.

WEIGHT

For this test, remember that although they are used interchangeably in everyday life, mass and weight are not the same thing; there is a clear distinction between them in physics. The **weight** of an object is the gravitational force exerted on it by Earth (or by whatever planet on which it happens to be). Mass, in contrast, is an intrinsic property of an object that measures its inertia: An object's mass does not change with location. If you put a baseball in a rocket and send it to the moon, its *weight* on the moon would be less than its weight on Earth (because the moon's gravitational pull is weaker than Earth's due to its much smaller mass), but its mass would be the same.

Since weight is a force, we can use $\mathbf{F}_{net} = m\mathbf{a}$ to compute it. What acceleration would gravitational force impose on an object? The gravitational acceleration, of course! Therefore, setting $\mathbf{a} = g$, the equation $\mathbf{F}_{net} = m\mathbf{a}$ becomes

$$\mathbf{F}_w = m\mathbf{g}$$

This is the equation for the weight of an object of mass m (weight is often symbolized just by $\mathbf{w}$, rather than $\mathbf{F}_w$). Notice that mass and weight are proportional but not identical. Furthermore, mass is measured in kilograms, while weight is measured in newtons.

5. What is the mass of an object that weighs 500 N?

Here's How to Crack It

Since weight is m multiplied by g, mass is F_w (weight) divided by g. Therefore, $m = F_w/g = (500 \text{ N})/(10 \text{ m/s}^2) = 50$ kg.

---

6. A person weighs 200 pounds. Given that a pound is a unit of weight equal to 4.45 N, what is this person's mass?

Here's How to Crack It

This person's weight in newtons is $(200 \text{ lb})(4.45 \text{ N/lb}) = 890$ N, so his mass is $m = F_w/g = (890 \text{ N})/(10 \text{ m/s}^2) = 89$ kg

---

7. A book whose mass is 2 kg rests on a table. Find the magnitude of the force exerted by the table on the book.

Here's How to Crack It

The book experiences two forces: The downward pull of the earth's gravity and the upward, supporting force exerted by the table. Since the book is at rest on the table, its acceleration is zero, so the net force on the book must be zero. Therefore, the magnitude of the support force must be equal to the magnitude of the book's weight, which is $F_w = mg = (2 \text{ kg})(10 \text{ m/s}^2) = 20$ N.

---

8. A can of paint with a mass of 6 kg hangs from a rope. If the can is to be pulled up to a rooftop with an acceleration of 1 m/s², what must be the tension in the rope?

Here's How to Crack It

First draw a picture. Represent the object of interest (the can of paint) as a heavy dot, and draw the forces that act on the object as arrows connected to the dot. This is called a **free-body (or force) diagram**.

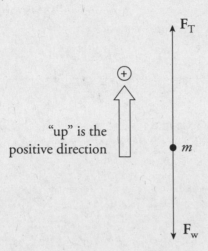

We have the tension force in the rope, F_T (also symbolized merely by T), which is upward, and the weight, F_w, which is downward. Calling *up* the positive direction, the net force is $F_T - F_w$. The second law, $F_{net} = ma$, becomes $F_T - F_w = ma$, so

$$F_T = F_w + ma = mg + ma = m(g + a) = 6(10 + 1) = 66 \text{ N}$$

9. A can of paint with a mass of 6 kg hangs from a rope. If the can is to be pulled up to a rooftop with a constant velocity of 1 m/s, what must be the tension in the rope?

Here's How to Crack It

The phrase "constant velocity" automatically means $a = 0$ and, therefore, $F_{net} = 0$. In the diagram above, F_T would need to have the same magnitude as F_w in order for the can to be moving at a constant velocity. Thus, in this case, $F_T = F_w = mg = (6)(10) = 60$ N.

THE NORMAL FORCE

Normal Force Notation
The normal force is denoted by $\mathbf{F_N}$, or simply by $\mathbf{N}$. (If you use the latter notation, be careful not to confuse it with N, the abbreviation for the newton.)

When an object is in contact with a surface, the surface exerts a contact force on the object. The component of the contact force that's *perpendicular* to the surface is called the **normal force** on the object. (In physics, the word *normal* means *perpendicular*.) The normal force is what prevents objects from falling through tabletops or you from falling through the floor.

10. A book whose mass is 2 kg rests on a table. Find the magnitude of the normal force exerted by the table on the book.

Normal vs. Weight
The normal is not always equal to mg. It is whatever needs to be in a given problem to make sure the object does not break through the surface. Use $\mathbf{F_{net}} = m\mathbf{a}$ to calculate it.

Here's How to Crack It

The book experiences two forces: The downward pull of Earth's gravity and the upward, supporting force exerted by the table. Since the book is at rest on the table, its acceleration is zero, so the net force on the book must equal zero. Therefore, the magnitude of the support force must equal the magnitude of the book's weight, which is $F_w = mg = (2)(10) = 20$ N. This means the normal force must be 20 N as well: $F_N = 20$ N. (Notice that this is a repeat of sample question 6, except that now we have a name for the "upward, supporting force exerted by the table." It's called the normal force.)

Also note that weight and the normal force are not an action-reaction pair, even though they are equal. The forces in an action-reaction pair work on different objects (e.g. the Earth pulls the book and the book pulls the Earth). The normal force and the book's weight act on the same object.

FRICTION

When an object is in contact with a surface, the surface exerts a contact force on the object. The component of the contact force that's parallel to the surface is called the **friction force** on the object. Friction, like the normal force, arises from electrical interactions between atoms that make up the object and those that make up the surface.

We'll look at two main categories of friction: (1) **static friction** and (2) **kinetic (sliding) friction**. If you attempt to push a heavy crate across a floor, at first you meet with resistance, but then you push hard enough to get the crate moving. The force that acted on the crate to cancel out your initial pushes was static friction, and the force that acts on the crate as it slides across the floor is kinetic friction. Static friction occurs when there is no relative motion between the object and the surface (no sliding); kinetic friction occurs when there is relative motion (when there's sliding).

The strength of the friction force depends, in general, on two things: the nature of the surfaces and the strength of the normal force. The nature of the surfaces is represented by the **coefficient of friction**, denoted by μ (*mu*). The greater this number is, the stronger the friction force will be. For example, the coefficient of friction between rubber-soled shoes and a wooden floor is 0.7, but between rubber-soled shoes and ice, it's only 0.1. Also, since kinetic friction is generally weaker than static friction (it's easier to keep an object sliding once it's sliding than it is to start the object sliding in the first place), there are two coefficients of friction: one for static friction (μ_s) and one for kinetic friction (μ_k). For a given pair of surfaces, it's virtually always true that $\mu_k < \mu_s$. The magnitude of these two types of friction forces are given by the following equations:

$$\mathbf{F}_{\text{static friction, max}} = \mu_s\, \mathbf{F}_N$$
$$\mathbf{F}_{\text{kinetic friction}} = \mu_k\, \mathbf{F}_N$$

Notice that the equation for the magnitude of the static friction force is for the *maximum* value. This is because static friction can vary, counteracting weaker forces that are less than the minimum force required to move an object. For example, suppose an object feels a normal force of $F_N = 100$ N, and the coefficient of static friction between it and the surface it's on is 0.5. Then, the *maximum* force that static friction can exert is $(0.5)(100 \text{ N}) = 50$ N. However, if you push on the object with a force of, say, 20 N, then the static friction force will be 20 N (in the opposite direction), *not* 50 N: The object won't move. The net force on a stationary object must be zero. Static friction can take on all values, up to a certain maximum, and you must overcome the maximum static friction force to get the object to slide.

The direction of $\mathbf{F}_{\text{kinetic friction}} = \mathbf{F}_{f\,(\text{kinetic})}$ is opposite to that of motion (sliding), and the direction of $\mathbf{F}_{\text{static friction}} = \mathbf{F}_{f\,(\text{static})}$ is opposite to that of the intended motion.

Kinetic vs. Static

For a person walking, the friction between the person's shoes and the floor is static (no sliding) and is directed forward (in the direction the person is walking). The person pushes on the floor in the backward direction. Static friction prevents it from moving backward, and so therefore must be forward.

Questions 11-12

A crate of mass 20 kg is sliding across a wooden floor. The coefficient of kinetic friction between the crate and the floor is 0.3.

11. Determine the magnitude of the friction force acting on the crate.

12. If the crate is being pulled by a force of 90 N (parallel to the floor), find the acceleration of the crate.

Here's How to Crack It
First draw a free-body diagram.

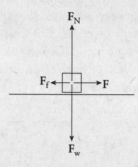

11. The normal force on the object balances the object's weight, so $F_N = mg = (20 \text{ kg})(10 \text{ m/s}^2) = 200$ N. Therefore, $F_{f \text{(kinetic)}} = \mu_k F_N = (0.3)(200\text{N}) = 60$ N.

12. The net horizontal force that acts on the crate is $F - F_f = 90 \text{ N} - 60 \text{ N} = 30$ N, so the acceleration of the crate is $a = F_{net}/m = (30 \text{ N})/(20 \text{ kg}) = 1.5 \text{ m/s}^2$.

13. A crate of mass 100 kg rests on the floor. The coefficient of static friction is 0.4. If a force of 250 N (parallel to the floor) is applied to the crate, what's the magnitude of the force of static friction on the crate?

Here's How to Crack It
The normal force on the object balances its weight, so $F_N = mg = (100 \text{ kg})(10 \text{ m/s}^2) = 1,000$ N. Therefore, $F_{\text{static friction, max}} = F_{f \text{(static), max}} = \mu_s F_N = (0.4)(1,000 \text{ N}) = 400$ N. This is the maximum force that static friction can exert, but in this case it isn't the actual value of the static friction force. Since the applied force on the crate is only 250 N, which is less than the $F_{f \text{(static)}}$, max, the force of static friction will be less also: $F_{f \text{(static)}} = 250$ N, and the crate will not slide.

PULLEYS

Pulleys are devices that change the direction of the tension force in the cords that slide over them. For the purposes of this text and the SAT Physics Subject Test, we'll consider each pulley to be frictionless and massless, which means their masses are so much smaller than the objects attached to the ends of them, that they can be ignored.

In the case of two single masses m_1 and m_2 that are attached to a pulley and cord, the downward forces are due to the weight (mass and gravity exerted on it) of the masses. The upward forces are due to the tension (**T**) in the cord.

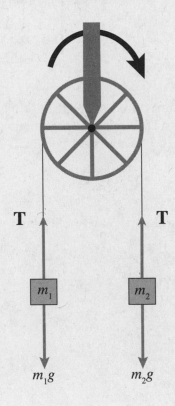

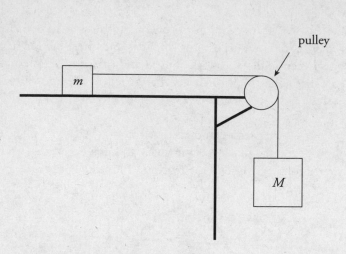

pulley

14. In the diagram above, assume that the tabletop
is frictionless. Determine the acceleration of the
blocks once they're released from rest.

Here's How to Crack It
There are two blocks, so we need to draw two free-body diagrams.

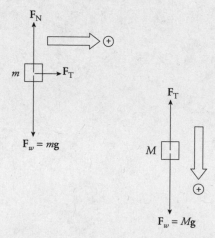

To get the acceleration of each one, we use Newton's second law, $\mathbf{F}_{net} = m\mathbf{a}$.

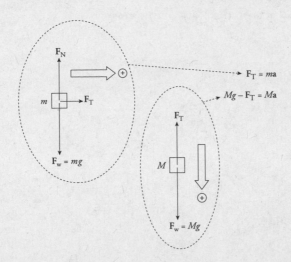

Notice that there are two unknowns, $\mathbf{F}_T$ and $\mathbf{a}$, but we can eliminate $\mathbf{F}_T$ by adding the two equations, and then we can solve for $\mathbf{a}$.

A quicker way of solving for the acceleration is to treat the entire system (blocks plus spring) as one object. Since we are only concerned with forces acting on the object, we can ignore tension. The string is part of the object. Then we need only consider forces acting in the direction of motion (Mg) and forces opposite the direction of motion (none). Our mass in Newton's second law becomes $M+m$, so $\mathbf{F}_{net} = m\mathbf{a}$ becomes $Mg =(M+m)\,\mathbf{a}$, giving us the same answer for acceleration.

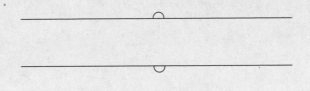

$$\left. \begin{array}{l} \mathbf{F}_T = m\mathbf{a} \\ Mg - \mathbf{F}_T = M\mathbf{a} \end{array} \right\}$$
Add the equations to eliminate $\mathbf{F}_T$.

$$Mg = m\mathbf{a} + M\mathbf{a}$$
$$= \mathbf{a}\,(m + M)$$

$$\frac{Mg}{m + M} = \mathbf{a}$$

15. Using the diagram from the previous example, assume that $m = 2$ kg, $M = 10$ kg, and the coefficient of kinetic friction between the small block and the tabletop is 0.5. What is the acceleration of the blocks?

Here's How to Crack It

Once again, draw a free-body diagram for each object. Notice that the only difference between these diagrams and the ones in the previous example is the inclusion of friction, F_f, that acts on the block on the table.

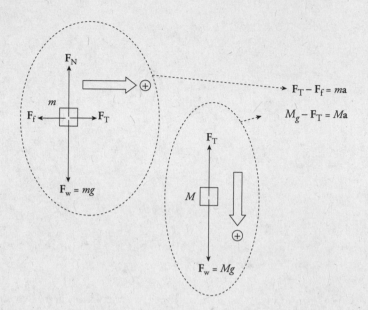

As before, we have two equations that contain two unknowns (a and F_T).

$$F_T - F_f = m\mathbf{a} \quad (1)$$
$$Mg - F_T = M\mathbf{a} \quad (2)$$

We add the equations (thereby eliminating F_T) and solve for $\mathbf{a}$. Notice that, by definition, $F_f = \mu F_N$ and from the free-body diagram for m, we see that $F_N = mg$, so $F_f = \mu mg$:

$$Mg - F_f = m\mathbf{a} + M\mathbf{a}$$
$$Mg - \mu mg = \mathbf{a}(m + M)$$

$$\frac{M - \mu m}{m + M} g = \mathbf{a}$$

Or, using our shorter method:

$$Mg - M_k mg = (M + m)\,\mathbf{a}$$

forward   backward   Total mass
force   force

Substituting in the numerical values given for m, M, and μ, we find that $\mathbf{a} = \dfrac{3}{4}g$ (or 7.5 m/s²).

16. In the previous example, calculate the magnitude of the tension in the cord.

Here's How to Crack It

Since the value of **a** has been determined, we can use either of the two original equations to calculate $\mathbf{F}_T$. Using equation (2), $Mg - \mathbf{F}_T = M\mathbf{a}$ (because it's simpler), we find

$$\mathbf{F}_T = Mg - M\mathbf{a} = Mg - M \cdot \frac{3}{4}g = \frac{1}{4}Mg = \frac{1}{4}(10)(10) = 25\,\text{N}$$

As you can see, we would have found the same answer if we'd used equation (1):

$$\mathbf{F}_T - \mathbf{F}_f = m\mathbf{a} \implies \mathbf{F}_T = \mathbf{F}_f + m\mathbf{a} = \mu mg + m\mathbf{a} = \mu mg + m \cdot \frac{3}{4}g = mg\left(\mu + \frac{3}{4}\right)$$

$$= (2)10(0.5 + 0.75)$$
$$= 25\,\text{N}$$

INCLINED PLANES

An **inclined plane** is basically a ramp. If an object of mass, m, is on the ramp, then the force of gravity on the object, $\mathbf{F}_w = m\mathbf{g}$, has two components: one that's parallel to the ramp ($mg\sin\theta$) and one that's normal to the ramp ($mg\cos\theta$), where θ is the incline angle. The force driving the block down the inclined plane is the component of the block's weight that's parallel to the ramp: $mg\sin\theta$.

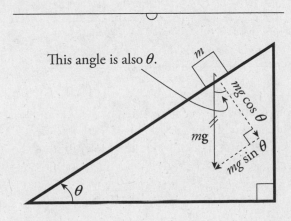

This angle is also θ.

17. A block slides down a frictionless, inclined plane that makes a 30° angle with the horizontal. Find the acceleration of this block.

Here's How to Crack It

Let m be the mass of the block, so the force that pulls the block down the incline is $mg \sin\theta$, and the block's acceleration down the plane is

$$a = \frac{F}{m} = \frac{mg \sin \theta}{m} = g \sin \theta = g \sin 30° = \frac{1}{2} g = 5 \text{ m/s}^2$$

You can use the 30-60-90 ratio $(x : x\sqrt{3} : 2x)$ to determine sin 30°.

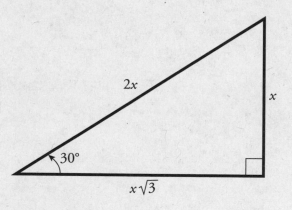

Sine is opposite over hypotenuse, $\frac{x}{2x} = \frac{1}{2}$.

So, $g \sin 30° = \frac{1}{2}g = 5\text{m/s}^2$. (Always use 10m/s² for gravity.)

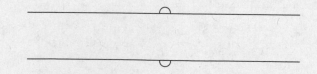

18. A block slides down an inclined plane that makes an angle θ with the horizontal. If the coefficient of kinetic friction is μ, find the acceleration of the block.

Here's How to Crack It

First draw a free-body diagram. Notice that in the diagram shown below, the weight of the block, $F_w = m\mathbf{g}$, has been written in terms of its scalar components: $F_w \sin \theta$ parallel to the ramp, and $F_w \cos \theta$ normal to the ramp.

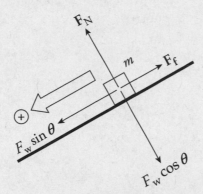

The force of friction, F_f, that acts up the ramp (opposite to the direction in which the block slides) has magnitude $F_f = \mu F_N$. But the diagram shows that $F_N = F_w \cos\theta$, so $F_f = \theta(mg \cos\theta)$. Therefore, the net force down the ramp is

$$F_w \sin\theta - F_f = mg \sin\theta - \mu mg \cos\theta = mg(\sin\theta - \mu\cos\theta).$$

Then, setting F_{net} equal to ma, we solve for a:

$$a = \frac{F_{net}}{m} = \frac{mg\left(\sin\theta - \mu\cos\theta\right)}{m}$$
$$= g\left(\sin\theta - \mu\cos\theta\right)$$

UNIFORM CIRCULAR MOTION

In Chapter 2, we considered two types of motion: straight-line motion and parabolic motion. We will now look at motion that follows a circular path, such as a rock on the end of a string, a horse on a merry-go-round, and (to a good approximation) the moon around Earth and Earth around the sun.

Let's simplify matters and consider the object's speed around its path to be constant. This is called **uniform circular motion**. You should remember that in these situations, although the speed may be constant, the velocity is not because the direction of the velocity is always changing. Since the velocity is changing, there must be acceleration. This acceleration doesn't change the speed of the object; it changes only the direction of the velocity to keep the object on its circular path. Also, to produce an acceleration, there must be a force; otherwise, the object would move off in a straight line (Newton's first law).

The figure on the left below shows an object moving along a circular trajectory, along with its velocity vectors at two nearby points. The vector $\mathbf{v}_1$ is the object's velocity at time $t = t_1$, and $\mathbf{v}_2$ is the object's velocity vector a short time later (at time $t = t_2$). The velocity vector is always tangential to the object's path (whatever the shape of the trajectory). Notice that since we are assuming constant speed, the lengths of $\mathbf{v}_1$ and $\mathbf{v}_2$ (their magnitudes) are the same.

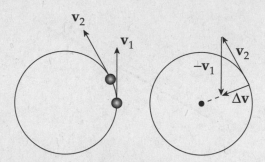

Since $\Delta \mathbf{v} = \mathbf{v}_2 - \mathbf{v}_1$ points toward the center of the circle (see the figure on the right), so does the acceleration, since $\mathbf{a} = \Delta \mathbf{v}/\Delta t$. And because the acceleration vector points toward the center of the circle, it's called **centripetal acceleration**, or $\mathbf{a}_c$. The centripetal acceleration is what turns the velocity vector to keep the object traveling in a circle.

The magnitude of the centripetal acceleration depends on the object's speed, v, and the radius, r, of the circular path according to the following equation:

$$a_c = \frac{v^2}{r}$$

19. An object of mass 5 kg moves at a constant speed of 6 m/s in a circular path of radius 2 m. Find the magnitude of the object's acceleration and the net force responsible for its motion.

Here's How to Crack It

By definition, an object moving at constant speed in a circular path is undergoing uniform circular motion. Therefore, it experiences a centripetal acceleration of magnitude v^2/r, which is always directed toward the center of the circle.

$$a_c = \frac{v^2}{r} = \frac{\left(6 \text{ m/s}\right)^2}{2 \text{ m}} = 18 \text{ m/s}^2$$

Newton's second law, coupled with the equation for centripetal acceleration, gives:

$$F_c = ma_c = m\frac{v^2}{r}$$

This equation gives the magnitude of the force. As for its direction, remember that because $F = ma$, the directions of **F** and **a** are always the same. Since centripetal acceleration points toward the center of the circular path, so does the force that produces it. Therefore, it's called **centripetal force**. The centripetal force acting on this object has a magnitude of $F_c = ma_c = (5 \text{ kg})(18 \text{ m/s}^2) = 90 \text{ N}$.

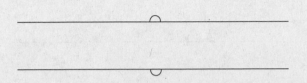

20. A 10 kg mass is attached to a string that has a breaking strength of 1,500 N. If the mass is whirled in a horizontal circle of radius 90 cm, what is the maximum speed it can have? (Neglect the effects of gravity.)

Here's How to Crack It

The first thing to do in problems like this is to identify what force(s) provide the centripetal force. In this example, the tension in the string provides the centripetal force:

$$\mathbf{F_T} \text{ provides } \mathbf{F_c} \Rightarrow F_T = \frac{mv^2}{r} \Rightarrow v = \sqrt{\frac{rF_T}{m}} \Rightarrow v_{max} = \sqrt{\frac{rF_{T,\,max}}{m}}$$

$$= \sqrt{\frac{(0.90 \text{ m})(1500 \text{ N})}{10 \text{ kg}}}$$

$$= 12 \text{ m/s}$$

21. A roller-coaster car enters the circular-loop part of the ride. At the very top of the circle (where the people in the car are upside down), the speed of the car is v and the acceleration points straight down. If the radius of the loop is r and the total mass of the car (plus passengers) is m, find the magnitude of the normal force exerted by the track on the car at this point.

What is the Centripetal Force?

The centripetal force is not a new force that makes things move in circles. Rather, real forces (eg. gravity, friction, tension, the normal) provide the centripetal force necessary to maintain circular motion.

Centripetal vs. Centrifugal

Centripetal force is the force necessary to maintain circular motion, directed toward the center. The so-called "centrifugal force" is what an object feels as it moves in a circle (an outward "force"). This is not actually a force, but the effect of the object's inertia (its resistance to acceleration).

Here's How to Crack It

There are two forces acting on the car at its highest point: the normal force exerted by the track and the gravitational force, both of which point downward.

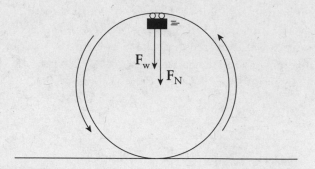

The combination of these two forces, $\mathbf{F}_N + \mathbf{F}_w$, provides the centripetal force, so

$$F_N + F_w = \frac{mv^2}{r} \Rightarrow F_N = \frac{mv^2}{r} - F_w$$

22. In the previous example, if the net force on the car at its highest point is straight down, why doesn't the car fall straight down?

Here's How to Crack It

Remember that force tells an object how to accelerate. If the car had zero velocity at this point, then it would fall straight down, but the car has a nonzero velocity (to the left) at this point. The fact that the acceleration is downward means that, at the next moment v will point down and to the left at a slight angle, ensuring that the car remains on a circular path, in contact with the track.

23. In the previous examples, what is the minimum speed necessary to keep the roller coaster on the track at all times?

Here's How to Crack It

The position where the roller coaster is most in danger of leaving the track is at the top.

$$F_N + F_w = \frac{mv^2}{r}$$

The slower the object moves, the smaller F_N gets (F_w is a constant). Therefore, the minimum speed occurs when $F_N = 0$. (The rollercoaster loses contact with the track, but only for a moment.)

$$F_w = \frac{mv^2}{r}$$

$$mg = \frac{mv^2}{r}$$

$$V = \sqrt{gr}$$

If the centripetal force acting on an object were suddenly removed, Newton's first law says that the object would move in a straight line with constant velocity (until another force acts on it). This means that the object would move in the direction it was moving when the force was removed (i.e., tangent to the circle).

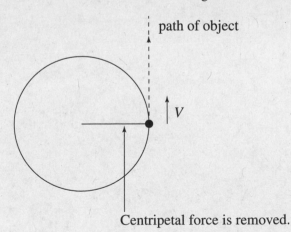

path of object

V

Centripetal force is removed.

Chapter 3 Review Questions

Answers are on page 390.

1. A person standing on a horizontal floor feels two forces: the downward pull of gravity and the upward supporting force from the floor. These two forces

   (A) have equal magnitudes and form an action/reaction pair
   (B) have equal magnitudes but do not form an action/reaction pair
   (C) have unequal magnitudes and form an action/reaction pair
   (D) have unequal magnitudes and do not form an action/reaction pair
   (E) None of the above

2. A person who weighs 800 N steps onto a scale that is on the floor of an elevator car. If the elevator accelerates upward at a rate of 5 m/s², what will the scale read?

   (A)   400 N
   (B)   800 N
   (C) 1000 N
   (D) 1200 N
   (E) 1600 N

3. A frictionless inclined plane of length 20 m has a maximum vertical height of 5 m. If an object of mass 2 kg is placed on the plane, which of the following best approximates the net force it feels?

   (A)   5 N
   (B) 10 N
   (C) 15 N
   (D) 20 N
   (E) 30 N

4. A 20 N block is being pushed across a horizontal table by an 18 N force. If the coefficient of kinetic friction between the block and the table is 0.4, find the acceleration of the block.

   (A) 0.5 m/s²
   (B) 1 m/s²
   (C) 5 m/s²
   (D) 7.5 m/s²
   (E) 9 m/s²

5. The coefficient of static friction between a box and a ramp is 0.5. The ramp's incline angle is 30°. If the box is placed at rest on the ramp, the box will

   (A) accelerate down the ramp
   (B) accelerate briefly down the ramp but then slow down and stop
   (C) move with constant velocity down the ramp
   (D) not move
   (E) Cannot be determined from the information given

6.

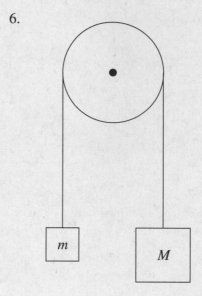

Assuming a frictionless, massless pulley, determine the acceleration of the blocks once they are released from rest.

(A) $\dfrac{m}{M+m}g$

(B) $\dfrac{M}{M+m}g$

(C) $\dfrac{M}{m}g$

(D) $\dfrac{M+m}{M-m}g$

(E) $\dfrac{M-m}{M+m}g$

7. If all of the forces acting on an object balance so that the net force is zero, then

(A) the object must be at rest
(B) the object's speed will decrease
(C) the object will follow a parabolic trajectory
(D) the object's direction of motion can change, but cannot its speed
(E) None of the above

8. A block of mass m is at rest on a frictionless, horizontal table placed in a laboratory on the surface of the earth. An identical block is at rest on a frictionless, horizontal table placed on the surface of the moon. Let $\mathbf{F}$ be the net force necessary to give the earth-bound block an acceleration of $\mathbf{a}$ across the table. Given that g_{moon} is one sixth of g_{earth}, the force necessary to give the moon-bound block the same acceleration $\mathbf{a}$ across the table is

(A) $\dfrac{\mathbf{F}}{12}$

(B) $\dfrac{\mathbf{F}}{6}$

(C) $\dfrac{\mathbf{F}}{3}$

(D) $\mathbf{F}$

(E) $6\mathbf{F}$

9. A crate of mass 100 kg is at rest on a horizontal floor. The coefficient of static friction between the crate and the floor is 0.4, and the coefficient of kinetic friction is 0.3. A force $\mathbf{F}$ of magnitude 344 N is then applied to the crate, parallel to the floor. Which of the following is true?

(A) The crate will accelerate across the floor at 0.5 m/s².
(B) The static friction force, which is the reaction force to $\mathbf{F}$ as guaranteed by Newton's third law, will also have a magnitude of 344 N.
(C) The crate will slide across the floor at a constant speed of 0.5 m/s.
(D) The crate will not move.
(E) None of the above

10. Two crates are stacked on top of each other on a horizontal floor; crate #1 is on the bottom, and crate #2 is on the top. Both crates have the same mass. Compared with the strength of the force $\mathbf{F}_1$ necessary to push only crate #1 at a constant speed across the floor, the strength of the force $\mathbf{F}_2$ necessary to push the stack at the same constant speed across the floor is greater than F_1 because

(A) the force of the floor on crate #1 is greater
(B) the coefficient of kinetic friction between crate #1 and the floor is greater
(C) the force of kinetic friction, but not the normal force, on crate #1 is greater
(D) the coefficient of static friction between crate #1 and the floor is greater
(E) the weight of crate #1 is greater

11. An object moves at constant speed in a circular path. Which of the following statements is/are true?

   I. The velocity is constant.
   II. The acceleration is constant.
   III. The net force on the object is zero since its speed is constant.

(A) II only
(B) I and III only
(C) II and III only
(D) I and II only
(E) None of the above

Keywords

dynamics
force
tension
gravitational force
air resistance
normal force
frictional force
electrostatic force
Newton's laws of motion
inertia
law of inertia
kilograms (kg)
mass
newton
action/reaction pair
weight
free body (force) diagram
normal force
friction force
static friction
kinetic (sliding) friction
coefficient of friction
pulley
inclined plane
uniform circular motion
centripetal acceleration
centripetal force

Summary

o   Newton's first law: An object at rest stays at rest. No force means no change in velocity.

o   Newton's second law: Acceleration (**a**) is directly proportional to the net applied force ($\mathbf{F}_{net}$) and inversely proportional to the object's mass (m) $\mathbf{F}_{net} = m\mathbf{a}$.

o   Newton's third law: For every action (or force) there is an equal and opposite reaction (force). The forces are equal in magnitude, opposite in direction, and act on different bodies.

o   The weight of an object is the gravitational pull exerted on it by the planet on which the object exists. Mass, conversely, does not change with location; it is a measure of an object's inertia.

o   The normal force is the component of the contact force that's perpendicular to the surface when an object is in contact with the surface.

o   Friction is the component of the contact force that is parallel to the surface when an object is in contact with the surface.

o   Kinetic (sliding) friction occurs when there is relative motion (the object is actually sliding across the floor).

o   Pulleys change the direction of the tension force in the cords that slide over them.

o   An inclined plane is a ramp. When an object is on the inclined plane, then the force of gravity $\mathbf{F}_w = m\mathbf{g}$ has two components: one parallel to the ramp ($mg \sin \theta$) and one that's normal (perpendicular) to the ramp ($mg \cos \theta$), where θ is the inclined plane.

o   Uniform circular motion considers an object's circular path at a constant speed. The velocity is not constant because the direction is always changing. Because velocity changes, acceleration changes as well.

o   In uniform circular motion, velocity is directed tangent to the circle and acceleration is directed toward the center.

Chapter 4
Work, Energy, and Power

It's difficult to give a precise definition of energy. Loosely speaking, energy is a quantity which gives an object or system the ability to accomplish something (what we will define as **work**). There are different forms of energy because there are different kinds of forces. There's kinetic energy (the energy due to motion), gravitational energy (a meteor crashing into the earth), elastic energy (a stretched rubber band), thermal energy (an oven), radiant energy (sunlight), electrical energy (a lamp plugged into a wall socket), nuclear energy (nuclear power plants), and mass energy (the heart of Einstein's equation $E = mc^2$).

Energy can come into a system or leave it via various interactions that produce changes. For the SAT Physics Subject Test, you should think of **force** as the agent of change, **energy** as the measure of change, and **work** as the way of transferring energy from one system to another. And one of the most important laws in physics—the **law of conservation of energy**, also known as the **first law of thermodynamics**—says that the total amount of energy in a given process will stay constant—that is, it will be **conserved**. For example, electrical energy can be converted into light and heat (this is how a light bulb works), but the amount of electrical energy coming in to the lightbulb equals the total amount of light and heat given off. Energy cannot be created or destroyed; it can only be transferred (from one system to another) or transformed (from one form to another).

WORK

When you lift a book from the floor, you exert a force on it over a distance, and when you push a crate across a floor, you also exert a force on it over a distance. The application of force over a distance and the resulting change in energy of the system give rise to the concept of **work**. When you hold a book in your hand, you exert a force (normal force) on the book, but since the book is at rest, the force does not act through a distance, so you do no work on the book. Although you did work on the book as you lifted it from the floor, once it's at rest in your hand, you are no longer doing work on it.

Definition. If a constant force $\mathbf{F}$ acts over a distance d, and $\mathbf{F}$ is parallel to $\mathbf{d}$, then the work done by $\mathbf{F}$ is the product of force and distance.

$$W = \mathrm{F}d$$

Notice that, although work depends on two vectors ($\mathbf{F}$ and $\mathbf{d}$ where $\mathbf{d}$ points in the direction of motion), work itself is *not* a vector. Work is a scalar quantity.

---

1. You slowly lift a book of mass 2 kg at constant velocity a distance of 3 m. How much work did you do on the book?

Here's How to Crack It

In this case, the force you exert must balance the weight of the book (otherwise the velocity of the book wouldn't be constant), so $F = mg = (2 \text{ kg})(10 \text{ m/s}^2) = 20$ N. Since this force is straight upward and the displacement of the book is also straight upward, $\mathbf{F}$ and $\mathbf{d}$ are parallel, so the work done by your lifting force is $W = Fd = (20 \text{ N})(3 \text{ m}) = 60 \text{ N·m}$. The unit for work, the newton-meter (N·m) is renamed a **joule**, and abbreviated J. So the work done is 60 J.

The definition above takes care of cases in which $\mathbf{F}$ is parallel to the motion. If $\mathbf{F}$ is not parallel to the motion, then the definition needs to be generalized.

Definition. If a constant force **F** acts over a distance **d**, and θ is the angle between **F** and **d**, then the work done by **F** is the product of the component of force in the direction of the motion and the distance.

$$W = (\text{F } cos\theta)d$$

When the formula for work works

$W = Fd\ cos\theta$ only works when the Force does not change as the object moves.

2. A 15 kg crate is moved along a horizontal floor by a warehouse worker who's pulling on it with a rope that makes a 60° angle with the horizontal. The tension in the rope is 200 N and the crate slides a distance of 10 m. How much work is done on the crate by the worker?

Here's How to Crack It

The figure below shows that $\mathbf{F}_T$ and **d** are not parallel. It's only the component of the force acting along the direction of motion, $\mathbf{F}_T \cos\theta$, that does any work.

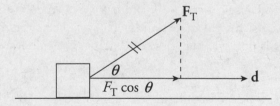

Therefore

$$W = (F_T \cos \theta)d = (200 \text{ N} \cdot \cos 60°)(10 \text{ m}) = 1{,}000 \text{ J}$$

3. In question 2, assume that the coefficient of kinetic friction between the crate and the floor is 0.4.

    (a) How much work is done by the normal force?

    (b) How much work is done by the friction force?

Here's How to Crack It

    (a) Clearly, the normal force is not parallel to the motion, so we use the general definition of work. Since the angle between $\mathbf{F}_N$ and $\mathbf{d}$ is 90° (by the definition of *normal*) and cos 90° = 0, the normal force does zero work.

    (b) The friction force, $\mathbf{F}_f$, is also not parallel to the motion; it's *antiparallel*. That is, the angle between $\mathbf{F}_f$ and $\mathbf{d}$ is 180°. Since cos 180° = –1, and the strength of the normal force is $F_N = F_f = mg =$ (15 kg)(10 m/s²) = 150 N, the work done by the friction force is

$$W = -\mathbf{F}_f d = -\mu_k F_N d = -(0.4)(150 \text{ N})(10 \text{ m}) = -600 \text{ J}$$

The two previous examples show that work—which, as we said, is a scalar quantity—may be positive, negative, or zero. If the angle between $\mathbf{F}$ and $\mathbf{d}$ (θ) is less than 90°, then the work is positive (because $\cos\theta$ is positive in this case); if $\theta = 90°$, the work is zero (because cos 90° = 0); and if $\theta > 90°$, then the work is negative (because $\cos\theta$ is negative). In other words, if a force helps the motion, the work done by the force is positive, but if the force opposes the motion, then the work done by the force is negative.

For situations where θ is something other than 0°, 90°, or 180°, it is sometimes useful to break the force into components, $F_\perp$ and $F_\parallel$.

Work and Circular Motion
Remember that all centripetal forces do no work, since the force is directed toward the center and the motion is tangent to the circle.

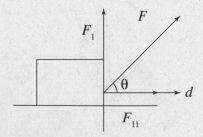

Where $F_\parallel$ is the component in the direction of motion (or opposite if it is negative) and $F_\perp$ is the component perpendicular to the direction of motion. We can now write this formula as $W = F_\parallel d$.

A box slides down an inclined plane (incline angle = 40°). The mass of the block, m, is 40 kg, the coefficient of kinetic friction between the box and the ramp, μ_k, is 0.3, and the length of the ramp, d, is 10 m. (Use: sin 40° ≈ 0.6 and cos 40° ≈ 0.8.)

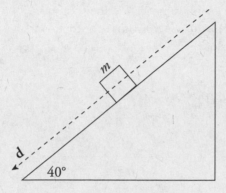

4. How much work is done by gravity?

5. How much work is done by the normal force?

6. How much work is done by friction?

7. What is the total work done?

Here's How to Crack It

4. Remember that the force that's directly responsible for pulling the box down the plane ($F_\parallel$) is the component of the gravitational force that's parallel to the ramp: $\mathbf{F}_w \sin \theta = mg \sin \theta$ (where θ is the incline angle). This component is parallel to the motion, so the work done by gravity is:

$$W_{\text{by gravity}} = (mg \sin\theta)d = (40 \text{ kg})(10 \text{ N/kg})(\sin 40°)(10 \text{ m}) = 2{,}400 \text{ J}$$

Notice that the work done by gravity is positive, as we would expect it to be, since gravity is helping the motion. Also, be careful with the angle θ. The general definition of work reads $W = (F \cos \theta)d$, where θ is the angle between $\mathbf{F}$ and $\mathbf{d}$. However, the angle between $\mathbf{F}_w$ and $\mathbf{d}$ is *not* 40° here, so the work done by gravity is not $(mg \cos 40°)d$. The angle θ used in the calculation above is the incline angle. This is why $W = F_\parallel d$ is a useful way of writing the formula.

5. Since the normal force is perpendicular to the motion, the work done by this force is zero.

6. The strength of the normal force is $F_w \cos \theta$ (where θ is the incline angle), so the strength of the friction force is $F_f = \mu_k F_N = \mu_k F_w \cos \theta = \mu_k mg \cos \theta$. Since F_f is antiparallel to d, the cosine of the angle between these vectors (180°) is −1, so the work done by friction is

$$W_{\text{by friction}} = -F_f d = -(\mu_k mg \cos \theta)(d) = \\ -(0.3)(40 \text{ kg})(10 \text{ N/kg})(\cos 40°)(10 \text{ m}) = -960 \text{ J}$$

Notice that the work done by friction is negative, as we expect it to be, since friction is opposing the motion.

7. Since work is a scalar, we can find the total work done simply by adding the values of the work done by each of the forces acting on the box:

$$W_{\text{total}} = \Sigma W = W_{\text{by gravity}} + W_{\text{by normal force}} + W_{\text{by friction}} = \\ 2{,}400 + 0 + (-960) = 1{,}440 \text{ J}$$

WORK DONE BY A VARIABLE FORCE

If a force remains constant over the distance through which it acts, then the work done by the force is just the product of force and distance. However, if the force doesn't remain constant, then the work done by the force isn't just a simple product. Focusing only on displacements that are along a straight line (say the x axis), let F be a force whose component in the x direction varies with position according to the equation $F = F(x)$. If we have a graph of F *versus* x, then the work done by F as it acts from $x = x_1$ to $x = x_2$ is equal to the area bounded by the graph of F, the x axis, and the vertical lines $x = x_1$ and $x = x_2$.

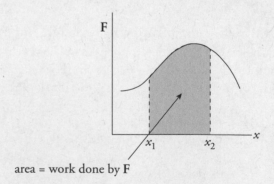

area = work done by F

8. The force exerted by a spring when it's displaced by x from its natural length is given by the equation $\mathbf{F}(x) = -kx$, where k is a positive constant. What is the work done by a spring as it pushes out from $x = -x_2$ to $x = -x_1$ (where $x_2 > x_1$) ?

Here's How to Crack It
We sketch the graph of $\mathbf{F}(x) = -kx$ and calculate the area under the graph from $x = -x_2$ to $x = -x_1$.

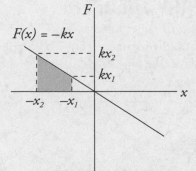

Here, the region is a trapezoid with area $A = \dfrac{1}{2}(\text{base}_1 + \text{base}_2) \times \text{height}$, so

$$W = A = \frac{1}{2}(kx_2 + kx_1)(x_2 - x_1)$$

$$= \frac{1}{2}k(x_2 + x_1)(x_2 - x_1)$$

$$= \frac{1}{2}k\left(x_2^2 - x_1^2\right).$$

KINETIC ENERGY

Consider an object at rest ($v_0 = 0$), and imagine that a steady force is exerted on it, causing it to accelerate. Let's be more specific; let's say that the object's mass is m, and let F be the force acting on the object, pushing it in a straight line. The object's acceleration is $\mathbf{a} = \mathbf{F}/m$, so after the object has traveled a distance Δs under the action of this force, its final speed, v, is given by Big Five #5:

$$v^2 = v_0^2 + 2a\Delta s = 2a\Delta s = 2\frac{\mathbf{F}}{m}\Delta s \quad \Rightarrow \quad \mathbf{F}\Delta s = \frac{1}{2}mv^2$$

But the quantity $\mathbf{F}\Delta s$ is the work done by the force, so $W = \dfrac{1}{2}mv^2$. The work done on the object has transferred energy to it, in the amount $\dfrac{1}{2}mv^2$.

The energy an object possesses by virtue of its motion is therefore defined as $\frac{1}{2}mv^2$ and is called **kinetic energy**.

$$K = \frac{1}{2}mv^2$$

THE WORK–ENERGY THEOREM

Kinetic energy is expressed in joules just like work, since in the case at which we just looked, $W = K$. In fact, the total work done on an object—or the work done by the net force—is equal to the object's change in kinetic energy; this is known as the **work–energy theorem**.

$$W_{\text{total}} = \Delta K$$

Kinetic energy, like work, is a scalar quantity.

9. What is the kinetic energy of a baseball (mass = 0.15 kg) moving with a speed of 20 m/s?

Here's How to Crack It
From the definition,

$$K = \frac{1}{2}mv^2 = \frac{1}{2}\left(0.15 \text{ kg}\right)\left(20 \text{ m/s}\right)^2 = 30 \text{ J}$$

10. How much work would it take to stop an object that has 30 J of kinetic energy?

Here's How to Crack It

To stop an object means to change its kinetic energy to zero. So, if the initial kinetic energy is 30 J, then the change in kinetic energy has to be 0 − 30 = −30 J. By the work–energy theorem, $W_{total} = \Delta K$, the total amount of work that would be required is −30 J.

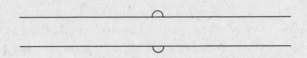

11. An object initially has 10 J of kinetic energy. Two forces act on it, one performing 40 J of work and the other (friction) performing −20 J. What is the final kinetic energy of this object?

Here's How to Crack It

The total work done is (40 J) + (−20 J) = 20 J. So, by the work–energy theorem, $W_{total} = \Delta K$, we have 20 J = ΔK. Since $\Delta K = K_f - K_i$, we find that $K_f = K_i + \Delta K = 10$ J + 20 J = 30 J.

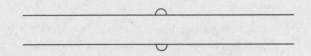

12. A pool cue striking a stationary billiard ball (mass = 0.25 kg) gives the ball a speed of 2 m/s. If the force of the cue on the ball was 25 N, over what distance did this force act?

Here's How to Crack It

The kinetic energy of the ball as it leaves the cue is

$$K = \frac{1}{2}mv^2 = \frac{1}{2}(0.25 \text{ kg})(2 \text{ m/s})^2 = 0.5 \text{ J}$$

The work W done by the cue gave the ball this kinetic energy, so

$$W = \Delta K \Rightarrow W = K_f \Rightarrow Fd = K \Rightarrow d = \frac{K}{F} = \frac{0.5 \text{ J}}{25 \text{ N}} = 0.02 \text{ m} = 2 \text{ cm}$$

Note that this could have been solved by using $F_{net} = ma$ to find the acceleration, and then using Big 5 #5 to find the displacement.

Kinematics vs. Work–Kinetic Energy
For objects moving in a straight line with a constant force, you can use the work–kinetic energy theorem or Big 5 #5 and $F_{net} = ma$ for problems where time is not involved.

POTENTIAL ENERGY

Kinetic energy is the energy an object has by virtue of its motion, but potential energy is independent of motion and arises from the object's position. For example, a ball at the edge of a tabletop has energy that could be transformed into kinetic energy if it falls off. An arrow in an archer's pulled-back bow has energy that could be transformed into kinetic energy if the archer releases the arrow. Both of these examples illustrate the concept of **potential energy** (symbolized as U or PE), the energy an object or a system has by virtue of its position. In each case, work was done on the object to put it in the given position (the ball was lifted to the tabletop, the arrow was pulled back), and since work is the means of transferring energy, these things have *stored energy that can be retrieved*, as kinetic energy. When an object falls, gravity does positive work, thereby giving the object kinetic energy. We can think of this situation differently by imagining that the kinetic energy came from a "storehouse" of energy. This energy is called potential energy.

Because there are different types of forces, there are different types of potential energy. The ball at the edge of the tabletop provides an example of **gravitational potential energy**, U_{grav}, which is the energy stored by virtue of an object's position in a gravitational field. This energy would be converted to kinetic energy as gravity pulled the ball down to the floor. For now, let's concentrate on gravitational potential energy.

Assume the ball has a mass m of 2 kg, and that the tabletop is h = 1.5 m above the floor. How much work did gravity do as the ball was lifted from the floor to the table? The strength of the gravitational force on the ball is $\mathbf{F}_w$ = mg = (2 kg)(10 N/kg) = 20 N. The force $\mathbf{F}_w$ points downward, and the ball's motion was upward, so the work done by gravity during the ball's ascent was

$$W_{by\ gravity} = -\mathbf{F}_w h = -mgh = -(20\ \text{N})(1.5\ \text{m}) = -30\ \text{J}$$

Someone performed +30 J of work to raise the ball from the floor to the tabletop. That energy is now stored, and if someone gave the ball a push to send it over the edge, by the time the ball reached the floor it would acquire a kinetic energy of 30 J. So we'd say that the change in the ball's gravitational potential energy in moving from the floor to the table was +30 J. That is

$$\Delta U_{grav} = -W_{by\ gravity}$$

Notice that potential energy, like work (and kinetic energy), is expressed in joules.

In general, if an object of mass m is raised a height h (which is small enough that g stays essentially constant over this altitude change), then the increase in the object's gravitational potential energy is

$$\Delta U_{grav} = mgh$$

An important fact that makes the above equation possible is that the work done by gravity as the object is raised does not depend on the path taken by the object. The ball could be lifted straight upward or on some curvy path—it would make no difference. Gravity is said to be a **conservative** force because of this property.

If we decide on a reference level to call $h = 0$, then we can say that the gravitational potential energy of an object of mass m at a height h is $U_{grav} = mgh$. To use this last equation, it's essential that we choose a reference level for height. For example, consider a passenger in an airplane reading a book. If the book is 1 m above the floor of the plane then, to the passenger, the gravitational potential energy of the book is mgh, where $h = 1$ m. However, to someone on the ground looking up, the floor of the plane may be, say, 9,000 m above the ground. So, to this person, the gravitational potential energy of the book is mgH, where $H = 9,001$ m. What both would agree on, though, is that the difference in potential energy between the floor of the plane and the position of the book is $mg \times (1$ m$)$, since the airplane passenger would calculate the difference as $mg \times (1$ m $- 0$ m$)$, while the person on the ground would calculate it as $mg \times (9,001$ m $- 9,000$ m$)$.

13. A stuntwoman (mass = 60 kg) scales a 20-meter-tall rock face. What is her gravitational potential energy (relative to the ground)?

Here's How to Crack It
Calling the ground $h = 0$, we find

$$U_{grav} = mgh = (60 \text{ kg})(10 \text{ N/kg})(20 \text{ m}) = 12,000 \text{ J}$$

CONSERVATION OF MECHANICAL ENERGY

We have seen energy in its two basic forms: kinetic energy (K) and potential energy (U). The sum of an object's kinetic and potential energies is called its **mechanical energy**, E.

$$E = K + U$$

(Notice that because U is relative, so is E.) Assuming that no nonconservative forces (friction, for example) act on an object or a system as it undergoes some change, mechanical energy is conserved. That is, the initial mechanical energy, E_i, is equal to the final mechanical energy, E_f, or

$$K_i + U_i = K_f + U_f$$

This is the simplest form of the law of conservation of total energy, which we mentioned at the beginning of this section.

---

14. A ball of mass 2 kg is gently pushed off the edge of a tabletop that is 1.8 m above the floor. Find the speed of the ball as it strikes the floor.

Here's How to Crack It

Ignoring the friction due to the air, we can apply conservation of mechanical energy. Calling the floor our $h = 0$ reference level, we write

$$K_i + U_i = K_f + U_f$$
$$0 + mgh = \frac{1}{2}mv^2 + 0$$
$$v = \sqrt{2gh}$$
$$= \sqrt{2(10 \text{ m/s}^2)(1.8 \text{ m})}$$
$$= 6 \text{ m/s}$$

Simplify
The formula $v = \sqrt{2gh}$ is useful and worth remembering for the test.

Notice that the ball's potential energy decreased, while its kinetic energy increased. This is the basic idea behind conservation of mechanical energy: One form of energy decreases while the other increases. (Also, notice that although the question gives you the mass of the ball, it wasn't necessary since the mass m cancelled out of the equation.)

---

15. A box is projected up a long ramp (incline angle with the horizontal = 30°) with an initial speed of 8 m/s. If the surface of the ramp is very smooth (essentially frictionless), how high up the ramp will the box go? What distance along the ramp will it slide?

Here's How to Crack It

Because friction is negligible, we can apply conservation of mechanical energy. Calling the bottom of the ramp our $h = 0$ reference level, we write

$$K_i + U_i = K_f + U_f$$

$$\frac{1}{2}mv_0^2 + 0 = 0 + mgh$$

$$h = \frac{\frac{1}{2}v_0^2}{g}$$

$$= \frac{\frac{1}{2}(8 \text{ m/s})^2}{10 \text{ m/s}^2}$$

$$= 3.2 \text{ m}$$

Since the incline angle is $\theta = 30°$, the distance, d, it slides up the ramp is found in the following way.

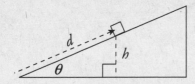

$$h = d \sin\theta$$

$$d = \frac{h}{\sin\theta} = \frac{3.2 \text{ m}}{\sin 30°} = 6.4 \text{ m}$$

16. Wile E. Coyote (mass = 40 kg) falls off a 50-meter-high cliff. On the way down, the force of air resistance has an average strength of 40 N. Find the speed with which he crashes into the ground.

Simplify
When a nonconservative force does work, an alternate equation is $W_{TOTAL} = \Delta K$, where the work done by gravity replaces the change in potential energy.

Here's How to Crack It

The force of air resistance opposes the downward motion, so it does negative work on the coyote as he falls: $W_r = -F_r h$. Calling the ground $h = 0$, we find that

$$K_i + U_i + W_r = K_f + U_f$$

$$0 + mgh + \left(-F_r h\right) = \frac{1}{2} mv^2 + 0$$

$$v = \sqrt{2h\left(g - F_r / m\right)} = \sqrt{2(50)(10 - 40/40)} = 30 \text{ m/s}$$

POWER

Simply put, **power** is the rate at which work is done (or energy is transferred, which is the same thing). Suppose you and I each do 1,000 J of work, but I do the work in 2 minutes while you do it in 1 minute. We both did the same amount of work, but you were quicker; you were more powerful. Here's the definition of power.

$$\text{Power} = \frac{\text{Work}}{\text{time}} \qquad \text{— in symbols} \rightarrow \qquad P = \frac{W}{t}$$

The unit of power is the joule per second (J/s), which is renamed the **watt** and symbolized W (not to be confused with the symbol for work, W). One watt is 1 joule per second: 1 W = 1 J/s.

---

17. A mover pushes a large crate (mass $m = 75$ kg) from the inside of the truck to the back end (a distance of 6 m), exerting a steady push of 300 N. If he moves the crate this distance in 20 s, what is his power output during this time?

Here's How to Crack It

The work done on the crate by the mover is $W = \mathbf{F}d = (300 \text{ N})(6 \text{ m}) = 1,800$ J. If this much work is done in 20 s, then the power delivered is $P = W/t = (1,800 \text{ J})/(20 \text{ s}) = 90$ W. Note that $P = W/t = \mathbf{F}d/t = \mathbf{F}v$; the formula $P = \mathbf{F}v$ is often useful.

Chapter 4 Review Questions

Answers are on page 393.

1. A force **F** of strength 20 N acts on an object of mass 3 kg as it moves a distance of 4 m. If **F** is perpendicular to the 4 m displacement, the work it does is equal to

   (A)   0 J
   (B)   60 J
   (C)   80 J
   (D)   600 J
   (E) 2,400 J

2. Under the influence of a force, an object of mass 4 kg accelerates from 3 m/s to 6 m/s in 8 s. How much work was done on the object during this time?

   (A) 27 J
   (B) 54 J
   (C) 72 J
   (D) 96 J
   (E) Cannot be determined from the information given

3. A box of mass m slides down a frictionless inclined plane of length L and vertical height h. What is the change in its gravitational potential energy?

   (A) $-mgL$
   (B) $-mgh$
   (C) $-mgL/h$
   (D) $-mgh/L$
   (E) $-mghL$

4. An object of mass m is traveling at constant speed v in a circular path of radius r. How much work is done by the centripetal force during one half of a revolution?

   (A) πmv^2
   (B) $2\pi mv^2$
   (C) 0
   (D) $\pi mv^2 r$
   (E) $2\pi mv^2 r$

5. While a person lifts a book of mass 2 kg from the floor to a tabletop, 1.5 m above the floor, how much work does the gravitational force do on the book?

   (A) −30 J
   (B) −15 J
   (C)   0 J
   (D)   15 J
   (E)   30 J

6. A block of mass 3 kg slides down a frictionless inclined plane of length 6 m and height 4 m. If the block is released from rest at the top of the incline, what is its speed at the bottom?

   (A)   5 m/s
   (B)   6 m/s
   (C)   8 m/s
   (D)   9 m/s
   (E) 10 m/s

7. A block of mass 3 kg slides down an inclined plane of length 6 m and height 4 m. If the force of friction on the block is a constant 16 N as it slides from rest at the top of the incline, what is its speed at the bottom?

   (A) 2 m/s
   (B) 3 m/s
   (C) 4 m/s
   (D) 5 m/s
   (E) 6 m/s

8. As a rock of mass 4 kg drops from the edge of a 40-meter-high cliff, it experiences air resistance, whose average strength during the descent is 20 N. At what speed will the rock hit the ground?

   (A)   8 m/s
   (B) 10 m/s
   (C) 12 m/s
   (D) 16 m/s
   (E) 20 m/s

9. An astronaut drops a rock from the top of a crater on the moon. When the rock is halfway down to the bottom of the crater, its speed is what fraction of its final impact speed?

(A) $\dfrac{1}{4\sqrt{2}}$

(B) 1/4

(C) $\dfrac{1}{2\sqrt{2}}$

(D) 1/2

(E) $\dfrac{1}{\sqrt{2}}$

10. A force of 200 N is required to keep an object sliding at a constant speed of 2 m/s across a rough floor. How much power is being expended to maintain this motion?

(A) 50 W
(B) 100 W
(C) 200 W
(D) 400 W
(E) Cannot be determined from the information given

Keywords

force
energy
work
law of conservation of energy
first law of thermodymamics
conserved
total work
kinetic energy
work–energy theorem
potential energy
gravitational potential energy
conservative
mechanical energy
power
joule
watt

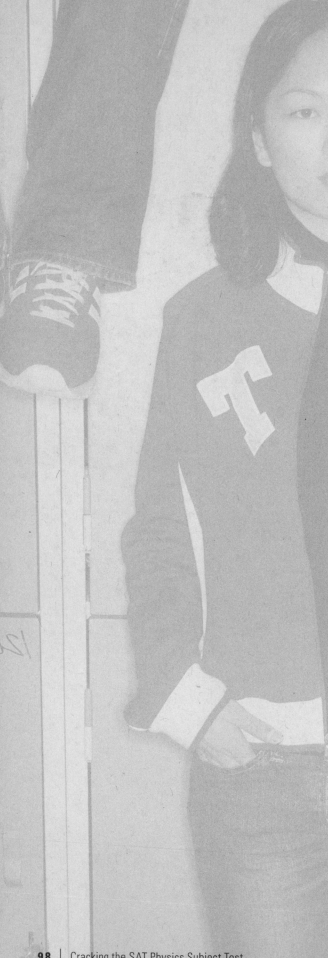

Summary

- Work done by a constant force is the product of force and distance and the resulting change of energy $W = Fd \cos \theta$.

- Forward forces do positive work, backward forces do negative work, perpendicular forces do no work.

- Work done by a variable force is measured by graphing **F** versus the horizontal, and then finding the area bounded by the graph of *F*, the *x*-axis, and vertical lines indicating the beginning and end of the period of force.

- Kinetic energy refers to the energy an object possesses by virtue of its motion and equals $\frac{1}{2}mv^2$.

- The work–energy theorem states that the total work done on an object is equal to the object's change in kinetic energy.

- Potential energy is the energy an object has by virtue of its position. Work done on an object to put it in a given position is stored in the object that can be retrieved.

- Conservation of mechanical energy is the sum of an object's kinetic and potential energies. Nonconservative forces, such as friction, are disregarded, so the initial mechanical energy is equal to the final mechanical energy.

- Power is the measure of work over time $P = \dfrac{W}{t}$. It is the rate at which work is done.

Chapter 5
Linear Momentum

When an object moves, it is necessary to account for both its mass and its velocity. Think for a minute about the difference in being hit with an inflatable beach ball traveling at 15 m/s (33 mi/h) or being hit by a motorcycle traveling at the same velocity. Ouch! Mass is definitely important. Velocity's "impact" (pun intended) is revealed by considering the difference between a baseball hit by an eight-year-old little leaguer and one hit by an adult Major League player. In this chapter, we will discuss linear momentum, impulse, what happens when objects collide, and the center of mass of a system of objects.

ANOTHER LOOK AT NEWTON'S SECOND LAW

When Newton first expressed his second law, he didn't write $F_{net} = m\mathbf{a}$. Instead, he expressed the law in terms of something we refer to nowadays as linear momentum.

> **Linear momentum** is the product of mass and velocity and is symbolized by **p**.
>
> $$\mathbf{p} = m\mathbf{v}$$
>
> Newton's second law can be written as
>
> $$\overline{\mathbf{F}} = \frac{\Delta \mathbf{p}}{\Delta t}$$

$\overline{\mathbf{F}} = \dfrac{\Delta \mathbf{p}}{\Delta t}$ is the same as $\overline{F} = m\overline{a}$, since $\Delta \mathbf{p}/\Delta t = \Delta(m\mathbf{v})/\Delta t = m(\Delta \mathbf{v}/\Delta t) = m\overline{a}$.

1. What is the linear momentum of a car of mass 1,000 kg that is moving at a speed of 20 m/s and of a truck of mass 5,000 kg moving at the same speed?

The Skinny on Momentum

Momentum is defined by the following equation: $\mathbf{p} = m\mathbf{v}$, where m is the mass of the object and $\mathbf{v}$ the velocity of the object. Momentum is measured in units of kg m/s and is a vector (so it has both magnitude and direction). The more momentum an object has the more you don't want to be hit by it.

Here's How to Crack It

The magnitude of the car's linear momentum is

$$p_{car} = m_{car}v = (1{,}000 \text{ kg})(20 \text{ m/s}) = 20{,}000 \text{ kg} \times \text{m/s}.$$

while the magnitude of the truck's linear momentum is

$$p_{truck} = m_{truck}v = (5{,}000 \text{ kg})(20 \text{ m/s}) = 100{,}000 \text{ kg} \times \text{m/s}.$$

Although the car and truck have the same speed, the truck has more momentum because it has more mass.

IMPULSE

The product of force and the time during which it acts is known as **impulse**, a term you should be familiar for this test.

Impulse is a vector quantity that's symbolized by **J**.

$$J = \bar{F}\Delta t$$

Newton's second law can be written in yet another form, in terms of impulse.

$$J = \Delta p$$

Sometimes this is referred to as the **impulse–momentum theorem**, but it's just another way of writing Newton's second law.

---

2. A football team's kicker punts the ball (mass = 0.42 kg) and gives it a launch speed of 30 m/s. Find the impulse delivered to the football by the kicker's foot and the average force exerted by the kicker on the ball, given that the impact time is 0.0020 s.

Here's How to Crack It

Impulse is equal to the change in linear momentum, so

$$J = \Delta p = p_f - p_i = p_f = mv = (0.42 \text{ kg})(30 \text{ m/s}) = 13 \text{ kg} \times \text{m/s}$$

Using the equation $\bar{F} = \dfrac{J}{\Delta t}$, we find that the average force exerted by the kicker is

$$\bar{F} = \frac{J}{\Delta t} = \frac{13 kg \times m/s}{2 \times 10^{-3} s} = 6,500 kg \times m/s^2 = 6,500 N.$$

That Hurts!
Since concrete is hard and has no cushion, this makes the impact time of any object striking concrete very short. Forces that exist over a short period of time are called impulsive forces. A large change in momentum divided by a short time interval makes for a painful landing on a concrete floor.

Questions 3-5

An 80 kg stuntman jumps out of a window that's 45 m above the ground.

3. How fast is he falling when he reaches ground level?

4. He lands on a large, air-filled target, coming to rest in 1.5 s. What average force does he feel while coming to rest?

5. What if he had instead landed on the ground (impact time = 10 ms)?

Here's How to Crack It

3. His gravitational potential energy turns into kinetic energy: $mgh = \frac{1}{2}mv^2$, so

$$v = \sqrt{2gh} = \sqrt{2(10)(45)} = 30 \text{ m/s}$$

(You could also have answered this question using Big Five #5.)

4. Using $\overline{\mathbf{F}} = \Delta \mathbf{p} / \Delta t$, we find that

$$\overline{\mathbf{F}} = \frac{\Delta \mathbf{p}}{\Delta t} = \frac{\mathbf{p}_f - \mathbf{p}_i}{\Delta t} = \frac{0 - m\mathbf{v}_i}{\Delta t} = \frac{-(80 \text{ kg})(30 \text{ m/s})}{1.5 \text{ s}} = -1{,}600 \text{ N} \Rightarrow \overline{F} = 1{,}600 \text{ N}$$

Time
Seconds are represented in questions as s. If you see a quantity that refers to time labeled with ms, it is using milliseconds. Because impact happens so quickly, a smaller quantity of time is necessary.

5. In this case

$$\overline{\mathbf{F}} = \frac{\Delta \mathbf{p}}{\Delta t} = \frac{\mathbf{p}_f - \mathbf{p}_i}{\Delta t} = \frac{0 - m\mathbf{v}_i}{\Delta t} = \frac{-(80 \text{ kg})(30 \text{ m/s})}{10 \times 10^{-3} \text{ s}} = 240{,}000 \text{ N} \Rightarrow \overline{F} = 240{,}000 \text{ N}$$

This force is equivalent to about 27 tons(!), more than enough force to break bones and cause fatal brain damage. Notice how crucial the impact time is: Increasing the slowing-down time reduces the acceleration and the force, ideally enough to prevent injury. This is the purpose of safety devices such as air bags in cars.

6. A small block is struck by a force F whose strength varies with time according to the following graph:

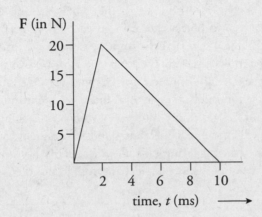

What is the impulse delivered to the block?

Here's How to Crack It

The impulse delivered to the block is equal to the area under the curve. The region is a triangle, so its area, $\frac{1}{2}$ base × height, can be calculated as follows:

$$J = \frac{1}{2}(10 \text{ ms})(20 \text{ N}) = 0.1 \text{ N} \times \text{s}$$

CONSERVATION OF LINEAR MOMENTUM

> The **law of conservation of linear momentum** states that in an isolated system, the total linear momentum will remain constant.

You may recall that Newton's third law says that when one object exerts a force on a second object, the second object exerts an equal but opposite force on the first. Since Newton's second law says that the impulse delivered to an object is equal to the resulting change in its linear momentum, $J = \Delta p$, the two interacting objects experience equal but opposite momentum changes (assuming that there are no external forces), which implies that the total linear momentum of the system will remain constant. In fact, given any number of interacting objects, each pair that comes in contact will undergo equal but opposite momentum changes, so the result described for two interacting objects will actually hold for any number of objects, given that the only forces they feel are from each other.

When is Momentum Conserved?

Remember that momentum is conserved in an isolated system. This means that if an object collides with a wall, the floor, or any permanently immovable object, momentum is NOT conserved.

7. An astronaut is floating in space near her shuttle when she realizes that the cord that's supposed to attach her to the ship has become disconnected. Her total mass (body + suit + equipment) is 91 kg. She reaches into her pocket, finds a 1 kg metal tool, and throws it out into space with a velocity of 6 m/s directly away from the ship. If the ship is 10 m away, how long will it take her to reach it?

Here's How to Crack It

Here, the astronaut + tool are the system. Because of conservation of linear momentum

$$m_{astronaut}\,\mathbf{v}_{astronaut} + m_{tool}\,\mathbf{v}_{tool} = 0$$

$$m_{astronaut}\,\mathbf{v}_{astronaut} = -m_{tool}\,\mathbf{v}_{tool}$$

$$\mathbf{v}_{astronaut} = -\frac{m_{tool}}{m_{astronaut}}\,\mathbf{v}_{tool}$$

$$= -\frac{1\text{ kg}}{90\text{ kg}}(-6\text{ m/s}) = +0.067\text{ m/s}$$

Using *distance = rate × time*, we find

$$t = \frac{d}{v} = \frac{10\text{ m}}{0.067\text{ m/s}} = 150\text{ s} = 2\frac{1}{2}\text{ min}$$

COLLISIONS

Conservation of linear momentum is routinely used to analyze **collisions**. Although the objects involved in a collision exert forces on each other during the impact, these forces are only *internal* (they occur within the system), and the system's total linear momentum is conserved.

Collisions are classified into two major categories: (1) **elastic** and (2) **inelastic**. A collision is said to be *elastic* if kinetic energy is conserved. Ordinary collisions are never truly elastic because there is always a change in energy due to energy transferred as heat, deformation of the objects, or the sound of the impact. However, if the objects do not deform very much (for example, two billiard balls or a hard glass marble bouncing off a steel plate), then the loss of initial kinetic energy is small enough to be ignored, and the collision can be treated as virtually elastic. *Inelastic* collisions, then, are ones in which the total kinetic energy is different after the collision. An extreme example of inelasticism is **completely** (or **perfectly** or **totally**) **inelastic**. In this case, the objects stick together after the collision and move as one afterward. In all cases of isolated collisions (elastic or not), conservation of linear momentum states that

> ## The Skinny on Collisions
> Elastic Collision: In an isolated system, momentum and kinetic energy are conserved.
>
> Inelastic Collision: Momentum is conserved and kinetic energy is **NOT** conserved.
>
> Perfectly or Totally Inelastic Collision: Momentum is conserved, kinetic energy is **NOT** conserved, and the objects stick together.

$$\text{total } \mathbf{p}_{\text{before collision}} = \text{total } \mathbf{p}_{\text{after collision}}$$

8. Two balls roll toward each other. The red ball has a mass of 0.5 kg and a speed of 4 m/s just before impact. The green ball has a mass of 0.3 kg and a speed of 2 m/s. After the head-on collision, the red ball continues forward with a speed of 2 m/s. Find the speed of the green ball after the collision. Was the collision elastic?

Here's How to Crack It

First remember that momentum is a vector quantity, so the direction of the velocity is crucial. Since the balls roll toward each other, one ball has a positive velocity while the other has a negative velocity. Let's call the red ball's velocity before the collision positive; then $v_{\text{red}} = +4$ m/s, and $v_{\text{green}} = -2$ m/s. Using a prime (′) to denote after the collision, conservation of linear momentum gives us the following:

$$\text{total } \mathbf{p}_{\text{before}} = \text{total } \mathbf{p}_{\text{after}}$$

$$m_{\text{red}}\mathbf{v}_{\text{red}} + m_{\text{green}}\mathbf{v}_{\text{green}} = m_{\text{red}}\mathbf{v}'_{\text{red}} + m_{\text{green}}\mathbf{v}'_{\text{green}}$$

$$(0.5)(+4) + (0.3)(-2) = (0.5)(+2) + (0.3)\mathbf{v}'_{\text{green}}$$

$$\mathbf{v}'_{\text{green}} = +1.3 \text{ m/s}$$

Notice that the green ball's velocity was reversed (from − to +) as a result of the collision; this typically happens when a lighter object collides with a heavier object. To see whether the collision was elastic, we need to compare the total kinetic energies before and after the collision. In this case, however, we don't need to do a complicated calculation, since both objects experienced a decrease in speed as a result of the collision. Kinetic energy was lost, so the collision was inelastic; this is usually the case with collisions between ordinary size objects. Most of the lost energy was transferred as heat; the two objects are both slightly warmer as a result of the collision.

9. Two balls roll toward each other. The red ball has a mass of 0.5 kg and a speed of 4 m/s just before impact. The green ball has a mass of 0.3 kg and a speed of 2 m/s. If the collision is perfectly inelastic, determine the velocity of the composite object after the collision.

Here's How to Crack It

If the collision is perfectly inelastic, then, by definition, the masses stick together after impact, moving with a velocity, $\mathbf{v}$. Applying conservation of linear momentum, we find

$$\text{total } \mathbf{p}_{\text{before}} = \text{total } \mathbf{p}_{\text{after}}$$

$$m_{\text{red}}\mathbf{v}_{\text{red}} + m_{\text{green}}\mathbf{v}_{\text{green}} = (m_{\text{red}} + m_{\text{green}})\mathbf{v}'$$

$$(0.5)(+4) + (0.3)(-2) = (0.5 + 0.3)\mathbf{v}'$$

$$\mathbf{v}' = +1.8 \text{ m/s}$$

Questions 10-11

A block of mass $M = 4$ kg is moving with velocity $V = 6$ m/s toward a target block of mass m = 2 kg, which is stationary ($v = 0$). The objects collide head-on, and immediately after the collision, the speed of block m is 4 times the speed of block M.

10. What is the speed of block M after the collision?

11. Is the collision elastic?

Here's How to Crack It

10.   If we let V' be the speed of block M immediately after the collision, then the speed of block m will be $4V'$. By applying conservation of linear momentum, we find that

$$\text{total } \mathbf{p}_{\text{before}} = \text{total } \mathbf{p}_{\text{after}}$$
$$MV = MV' + m(4V')$$
$$(4)(6) = (4)(V') + (2)(4V')$$
$$24 = 12V'$$
$$V' = 2 \text{ m/s}$$

Therefore, the speed of block M immediately after the collision is 2 m/s (and the speed of block m immediately after the collision is 8 m/s).

11.   A collision is elastic if the total kinetic energy is conserved. Since

$$K_{\text{before}} = \frac{1}{2}MV^2 + \frac{1}{2}mv^2 = \frac{1}{2}MV^2 = \frac{1}{2}(4 \text{ kg})(6 \text{ m/s})^2 = 72 \text{ J}$$

and

$$K_{\text{after}} = \frac{1}{2}MV'^2 + \frac{1}{2}mv'^2 = \frac{1}{2}(4 \text{ kg})(2 \text{ m/s})^2 + \frac{1}{2}(2 \text{ kg})(8 \text{ m/s})^2 = 72 \text{ J}$$

$K_{\text{before}} = K_{\text{after}}$, so the collision is elastic.

In the case of two dimensional collisions (e.g. two cars colliding at an intersection or two billiard balls colliding and moving off at angles), remember that there are two conservation of momentum equations.

$$\text{total } p_{\text{before, x}} = \text{total } p_{\text{before, x}}$$
$$\text{total } p_{\text{before, y}} = \text{total } p_{\text{after, y}}$$

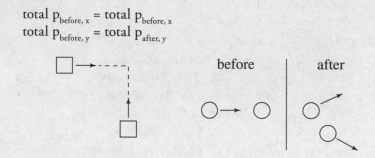

Examples of Two-Dimensional Collisions

CENTER OF MASS

The center of mass is the point where all of the mass of an object can be considered to be concentrated; it's the dot that represents the object of interest in a free-body diagram.

For a homogeneous body (that is, one for which the density is uniform throughout), the center of mass is where you intuitively expect it to be: at the geometric center. Thus, the center of mass of a uniform sphere or cube or box is at its geometric center.

If we have a collection of discrete particles, the center of mass of the system can be determined mathematically as follows. First, consider the case where the particles all lie on a straight line. Call this the x-axis. Select some point to be the origin ($x = 0$) and determine the positions of each particle on the axis. Multiply each position value by the mass of the particle at that location, and get the sum for all the particles. Divide this sum by the total mass, and the resulting x value is the center of mass:

$$x_{\text{cm}} = \frac{m_1 x_1 + m_2 x_2 + \cdots + m_n x_n}{m_1 + m_2 + \cdots + m_n}$$

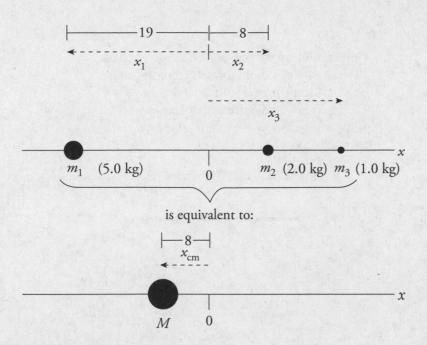

The system of particles behaves as if all its mass, $M = m_1 + m_2 + \ldots + m_n$, were concentrated at a single location, x_{cm}. The subscript cm in x_{cm} stands for center of mass.

In the example above, $x_{cm} = \dfrac{5(-19) + 2(8) + 1(15)}{5 + 2 + 1} = \dfrac{-95 + 16 + 15}{8} = \dfrac{-64}{8} = -8$. The system behaves as if an object with mass 8 were 8 units to the left of the origin.

If the system consists of objects that are not confined to the same straight line, use the equation above to find the x coordinate of their center of mass, and the corresponding equation

$$y_{cm} = \frac{m_1 y_1 + m_2 y_2 + \cdots + m_n y_n}{m_1 + m_2 + \cdots + m_n}$$

to find the y coordinate of their center of mass.

If the net external force on the system is zero, then the center of mass will not accelerate.

> **Another Instance of Newton's Second**
> From the equations for the center of mass, we see that
> $$\mathbf{F}_{net} = M\mathbf{a}_{cm}$$
> In other words, the net (external) force acting on the system causes the center of mass to accelerate according to Newton's second law.

12. Object *A*, of mass 5 kg, and object B, of mass 10 kg, hang from light threads from the ends of a uniform bar of length 18 and mass 15 kg. The masses *A* and *B* are at distances 6 and 12, respectively, below the bar. Find the center of mass of this system.

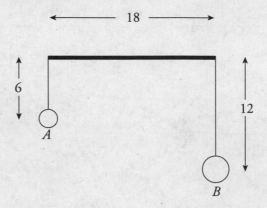

Here's How to Crack It

The center of mass of the bar alone is at its midpoint (because it is uniform), so we can treat the total mass of the bar as being concentrated at its midpoint. Constructing a coordinate system with this point as the origin, we now have three objects: one with mass 5 at $(-9, -6)$, one with mass 10 at $(9, -12)$, and one with mass 15 at $(0, 0)$.

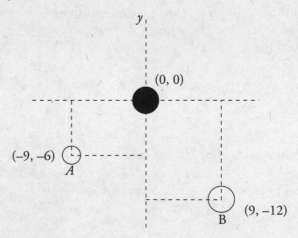

Choice of Origin
Remember, you can choose your origin anywhere, but a good strategy is to use the location mentioned in the problem. If it asks, "How far from the left is the center of mass?" choose the left as your origin.

We figure out the x and y coordinates of the center of mass separately.

$$x_{cm} = \frac{m_1 x_1 + m_2 x_2 + m_3 x_3}{m_1 + m_2 + m_3} = \frac{(5)(-9) + (10)(9) + (15)(0)}{5 + 10 + 15} = \frac{45}{30} = 1.5$$

$$y_{cm} = \frac{m_1y_1 + m_2y_2 + m_3y_3}{m_1 + m_2 + m_3} = \frac{(5)(-6) + (10)(-12) + (15)(0)}{5 + 10 + 15} = \frac{-150}{30} = -5$$

Therefore, the center of mass is at

$$(x_{cm}, y_{cm}) = (1.5, -5)$$

relative to the midpoint of the bar.

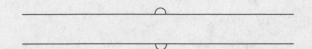

Questions 13-14

A man of mass 70 kg is standing at one end of a stationary, floating barge of mass 210 kg. He then walks to the other end of the barge, a distance of 90 meters. Ignore any frictional effects between the barge and the water.

13. How far will the barge move?

14. If the man walks at an average velocity of 8 m/s, what is the average velocity of the barge?

Here's How to Crack It

13. Since there are no external forces acting on the man + barge system, the center of mass of the system cannot accelerate. In particular, since the system is originally at rest, the center of mass cannot move. Letting $x = 0$ denote the midpoint of the barge (which is its own center of mass, assuming it is uniform), we can figure out the center of mass of the man + barge system:

$$x_{cm} = \frac{m_1x_1 + m_2x_2}{m_1 + m_2} = \frac{(70)(-45) + (210)(0)}{70 + 210} = \frac{-3,150}{280} = -11.25$$

So the center of mass is a distance of 11.25 meters from the midpoint of the barge, and since the man's mass is originally at the left end, the center of mass is a distance of 11.25 meters to the left of the barge's midpoint.

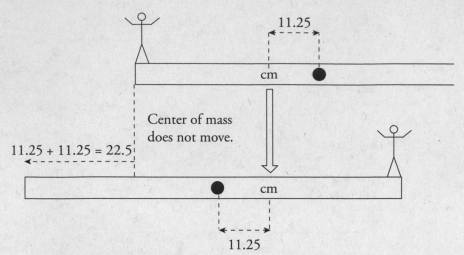

When the man reaches the other end of the barge, the center of mass will, by symmetry, be 11.25 meters to the *right* of the midpoint of the barge. But, since the position of the center of mass cannot move, this means the barge itself must have moved a distance of 11.25 + 11.25 = 22.5 meters to the left.

14. Let the time it takes the man to walk across the barge be denoted by t; then $t = \dfrac{90\,\text{m}}{8\ \text{m/s}}$. In this amount of time, the barge moves a distance of 22.5 meters in the *opposite* direction, so the velocity of the barge is

$$v_{\text{barge}} = \frac{-22.5\,\text{m}}{t} = \frac{-22.5\,\text{m}}{\dfrac{90\,\text{m}}{8\,\text{m/s}}} = -\frac{180\,\text{m}^2/\text{s}}{90} = -2\,\text{m/s}$$

Keywords

isolated system
linear momentum
impulse
impulse-momentum theorem
law of conservation of linear momentum
collisions
elastic
inelastic
perfectly (completely, totally) inelastic
center of mass

Chapter 5 Review Questions

Answers are on page 395.

1. An object of mass 2 kg has a linear momentum of magnitude 6 kg • m/s. What is this object's kinetic energy?

   (A) 3 J
   (B) 6 J
   (C) 9 J
   (D) 12 J
   (E) 18 J

2. A ball of mass 0.5 kg, initially at rest, acquires a speed of 4 m/s immediately after being kicked by a force of strength 20 N. For how long did this force act on the ball?

   (A) 0.01 s
   (B) 0.02 s
   (C) 0.1 s
   (D) 0.2 s
   (E) 1 s

3. A box with a mass of 2 kg accelerates in a straight line from 4 m/s to 8 m/s due to the application of a force whose duration is 0.5 s. Find the average strength of this force.

   (A) 2 N
   (B) 4 N
   (C) 8 N
   (D) 12 N
   (E) 16 N

4. A ball of mass m traveling horizontally with velocity **v** strikes a massive vertical wall and rebounds back along its original direction with no change in speed. What is the magnitude of the impulse delivered by the wall to the ball?

   (A) 0
   (B) $\frac{1}{2}mv$
   (C) mv
   (D) $2mv$
   (E) $4mv$

5. Two objects, one of mass 3 kg and moving with a speed of 2 m/s and the other of mass 5 kg and speed 2 m/s, move toward each other and collide head-on. If the collision is perfectly inelastic, find the speed of the objects after the collision.

   (A) 0.25 m/s
   (B) 0.5 m/s
   (C) 0.75 m/s
   (D) 1 m/s
   (E) 2 m/s

6. Object #1 moves toward object #2, whose mass is twice that of object #1 and which is initially at rest. After their impact, the objects lock together and move with what fraction of object #1's initial kinetic energy?

   (A) $\frac{1}{18}$

   (B) $\frac{1}{9}$

   (C) $\frac{1}{6}$

   (D) $\frac{1}{3}$

   (E) None of the above

7. Two objects move toward each other, collide, and separate. If there was no net external force acting on the objects, but some kinetic energy was lost, then

   (A) the collision was elastic and total linear momentum was conserved
   (B) the collision was elastic and total linear momentum was not conserved
   (C) the collision was not elastic and total linear momentum was conserved
   (D) the collision was not elastic and total linear momentum was not conserved
   (E) None of the above

8. Three thin, uniform rods each of length L are arranged in the shape of an inverted U.

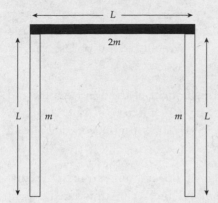

The two rods on the arms of the U each have mass m; the third rod has mass $2m$. How far below the midpoint of the horizontal rod is the center of mass of this assembly?

(A) $\dfrac{L}{8}$

(B) $\dfrac{L}{4}$

(C) $\dfrac{3L}{8}$

(D) $\dfrac{L}{2}$

(E) $\dfrac{3L}{4}$

9. A wooden block of mass M is moving at speed V in a straight line.

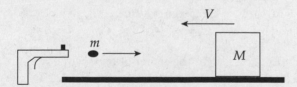

How fast would the bullet of mass m need to travel to stop the block (assuming that the bullet became embedded inside)?

(A) $mV/(m + M)$
(B) $MV/(m + M)$
(C) mV/M
(D) MV/m
(E) $(m + M)V/m$

10. Which of the following best describes a perfectly inelastic collision free of external forces?

(A) Total linear momentum is never conserved.
(B) Total linear momentum is sometimes conserved.
(C) Kinetic energy is never conserved.
(D) Kinetic energy is sometimes conserved.
(E) Kinetic energy is always conserved.

Summary

- Linear momentum is the product of mass and velocity, and is symbolized by **p**. Use the formula $\mathbf{p} = m\mathbf{v}$.

- Impulse is the product of the average force and the time during which it acts. This force occurs only briefly and equals the object's change in momentum.

- Conservation of linear momentum states that when two objects interact in an isolated system, the total linear momentum of the system will remain constant.

- Collisions of objects are classified as elastic or inelastic. Elastic collisions conserve kinetic energy. After an inelastic collision, the total kinetic energy is different from what it was before the collision.

- A perfectly inelastic collision is where the objects stick and move together.

- Center of mass is the point where all of the mass of an object can be considered to reside. For a homogeneous body, the center of mass is at the geometric center of the object. For a group of objects, establish an x/y coordinate system, multiply the position value of each object by its mass and get the sum for all the particles. Divide this sum by the total mass. The resulting value is the center of mass in terms of x- and y-coordinates. (Treat the x-value and y-value separately.)

- In an isolated system the center of mass will not accelerate.

Chapter 6
Rotational Motion

So far we've studied only translational motion—objects sliding, falling, or rising—but you'll also need to know about spinning objects for the SAT Physics Subject Test. We will now look at rotation, which completes our study of motion.

ROTATION AND TRANSLATION

All motion is some combination of **translation** and **rotation**, which are illustrated in the figures below. Consider any two points in the object under study, connected by a straight line. If this line always remains parallel to itself while the object moves, then the object is translating only. However, if this line does not always remain parallel to itself while the object moves, then the object is rotating.

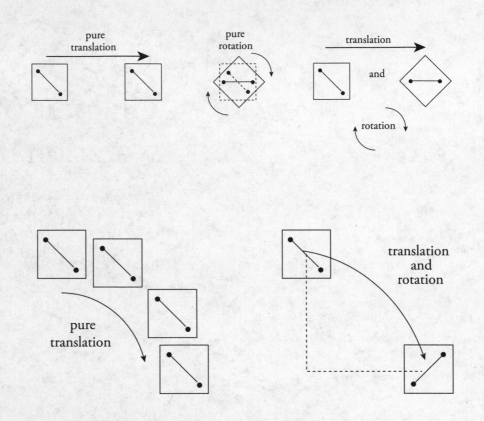

ROTATIONAL DYNAMICS

The dynamics of translational motion involve describing the acceleration of an object in terms of its mass (inertia) and the forces that act on it: $\mathbf{F}_{net} = m\mathbf{a}$. The dynamics of rotational motion involve describing the angular (rotational) acceleration of an object in terms of its **rotational inertia** and the **torques** that act on it.

TORQUE

Torque is the quantity that measures how effectively a force causes rotation. Consider a uniform rod that pivots around one of its ends. For simplicity, let's assume that the rod is at rest. What effect, if any, would each of the four forces in the figure below have on the potential rotation of the rod?

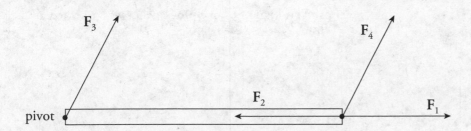

Our intuition tells us that F_1, F_2, and F_3 would *not* cause the rod to rotate, but F_4 would. What's different about F_4? It has torque.

The torque of a force can be defined as follows. Let r be the distance from the pivot (axis of rotation) to the point of application of the force **F**, and let θ be the angle between vectors **r** and **F**.

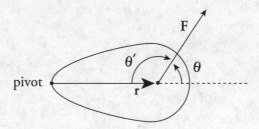

Then the magnitude of the torque of **F**, denoted by τ (*tau*), is defined as

$$\tau = r F \sin \theta.$$

In the previous figure, the angle between the vectors **r** and **F** is θ. Imagine sliding **r** over so that its initial point is the same as that of **F**.

The angle between two vectors is the angle between them when they start at the same point.

However, we can use the supplementary angle θ' in place of θ in the definition of torque. This is because torque depends on $\sin\theta$, and the sine of an angle and the sine of its supplement are always equal. Therefore, when figuring out torque, use whichever of these angles is most convenient.

Let's see if this mathematical definition of torque proves what we suspected about forces F_1, F_2, F_3, and F_4.

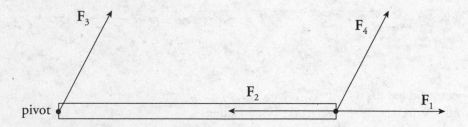

The angle between $\mathbf{r}$ and $\mathbf{F}_1$ is 0, and $\theta = 0$ tells us that $\sin\theta = 0$, so by the definition of torque, $\tau = 0$ as well. The angle between $\mathbf{r}$ and $\mathbf{F}_2$ is 180°, and $\theta = 180°$ gives us $\sin\theta = 0$, so $\tau = 0$. For $\mathbf{F}_3$, $\mathbf{r} = 0$ (because $\mathbf{F}_3$ acts *at* the pivot, so the distance from the pivot to the point of application of $\mathbf{F}_3$ is zero); since $\mathbf{r} = 0$, the torque is 0 as well. However, for $\mathbf{F}_4$, neither $\mathbf{r}$ nor $\sin\theta$ is zero, so $\mathbf{F}_4$ has a nonzero torque. Of the four forces shown in that figure, only $\mathbf{F}_4$ has torque and would produce rotational acceleration.

There's another way to determine the value of the torque. Of course, it gives the same result as the method given above, but this method is often easier to use. Look at the same object and force.

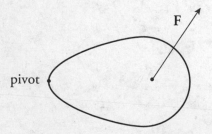

Instead of determining the distance from the pivot point to the point of application of the force, we will now determine the (perpendicular) distance from the pivot point to what's called the **line of action** of the force. This distance is the **lever arm** (or **moment arm**) of the force **F** relative to the pivot and is symbolized by l.

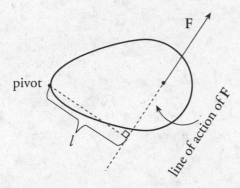

The torque of **F** is defined as the product

$$\tau = l\mathbf{F}$$

(Just as the lever arm is sometimes called the moment arm, the torque is also called the **moment** of the force.) The fact that these two definitions of torque, $\tau = \mathbf{r}F\sin\theta$ and $\tau = l\mathbf{F}$, are equivalent follows from the fact that $l = \mathbf{r}\sin\theta$.

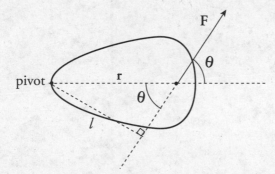

Since l is the component of **r** that's perpendicular to **F**, it is also symbolized by $\mathbf{r}_{\perp}$ ("r perp"). So the definition of torque can be written as $\tau = \mathbf{r}_{\perp}F$.

These two equivalent definitions of torque make it clear that only the component of **F** that's perpendicular to **r** produces torque. The component of **F** that's *parallel* to **r** does not produce torque. Notice that $\tau = \mathbf{r}F\sin\theta = \mathbf{r}F_{\perp}$, where $F_{\perp}$ ("F perp") is the component of **F** that's perpendicular to **r**.

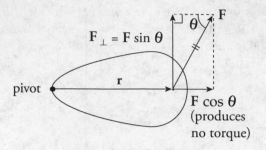

$$\mathbf{F}_\perp = \mathbf{F} \sin \theta$$

pivot

r

$\mathbf{F} \cos \theta$
(produces
no torque)

So the definition of torque can also be written as $\tau = r\mathbf{F}_\perp$.

1. A student pulls down with a force of 40 N on a
   rope that winds around a pulley of radius 5 cm.

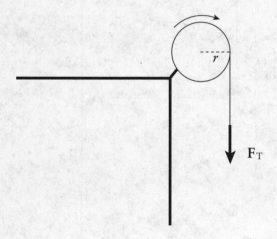

$\mathbf{F}_T$

What's the torque of this force?

Here's How to Crack It
Since the tension force, $\mathbf{F}_T$, is tangent to the pulley, it is perpendicular to the radius vector $\mathbf{r}$ at the point of contact.

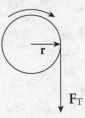

Therefore, the torque produced by this tension force is

$$\tau = \mathbf{r}\mathbf{F}_T = (0.05 \text{ m})(40 \text{ N}) = 2 \text{ N} \times \text{m}$$

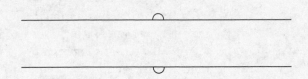

2. The cylinder below is free to rotate around its center. What is the net torque on the cylinder?

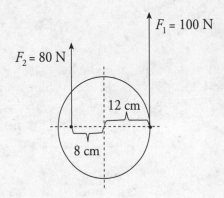

Here's How to Crack It

Each of the two forces produces a torque, but these torques oppose each other. The torque of $\mathbf{F}_1$ is counterclockwise, and the torque of $\mathbf{F}_2$ is clockwise.

The **net torque** is the sum of all the torques. Counting a counterclockwise torque as positive and a clockwise torque as negative, we have

$$\tau_1 = +\mathbf{r}_1\mathbf{F}_1 = +(0.12 \text{ m})(100 \text{ N}) = +12 \text{ N} \times \text{m}$$

and

$$\tau_2 = -r_2 F_2 = -(0.08 \text{ m})(80 \text{ N}) = -6.4 \text{ N} \times \text{m}$$

so

$$\tau_{net} = \Sigma \tau = \tau_1 + \tau_2 = (+12 \text{ N·m}) + (-6.4 \text{ N·m}) = +5.6 \text{ N} \times \text{m}$$

EQUILIBRIUM

An object is said to be in **translational equilibrium** if the sum of the forces acting on it is zero—that is, if $F_{net} = 0$. Similarly, an object is said to be in **rotational equilibrium** if the sum of the torques acting on it is zero—that is, if $\tau_{net} = 0$. The term *equilibrium* by itself means both translational and rotational equilibrium. An object in equilibrium may be in motion. $F_{net} = 0$ does not mean that the velocity is zero, it only means that the velocity is constant. Similarly, $\tau_{net} = 0$ does not mean that the angular velocity is zero; it only means that it's constant. If an object is at rest, then it is said to be in **static equilibrium**.

3. A block of mass M shown in the figure below hangs motionless. What's the tension in each of the ropes?

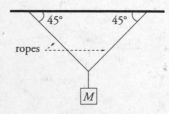

Here's How to Crack It

Let $\mathbf{T}_1$ be the tension in the left-hand rope and let $\mathbf{T}_2$ be the tension in the right-hand rope. We'll write each of these forces in terms of their horizontal and vertical components.

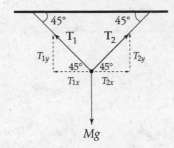

Look at the point where the two ropes meet. Since the system is in static equilibrium, the net force on this point must be zero. This means the horizontal forces must balance and the vertical forces must balance. Since the horizontal forces balance, this means $T_{1x} = T_{2x}$, so

$$T_1 \cos 45^\circ = T_2 \cos 45^\circ$$

which gives us $T_1 = T_2$. Since the tensions are the same, we can drop the subscripts and simply refer to the tension in each rope as T.

Now, to balance the vertical forces, we notice that the total upward is $T_{1y} + T_{2y} = T_y + T_y = 2T_y$ and the force downward is Mg, the weight of the block. Therefore,

$$2T_y = Mg$$
$$2T \sin 45^\circ = Mg$$
$$2T \times \frac{\sqrt{2}}{2} = Mg$$
$$T = \frac{Mg}{2}$$

This gives us the tension in each of the ropes noted in the figure.

---

4. The figure below shows a homogeneous bar of mass M and length L, with one end attached to a hinge on a wall and the other end supported by a string. What's the tension in the string?

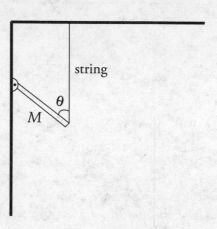

Here's How to Crack It

Let T be the tension in the string, let L be the length of the bar. The weight of the bar acts at the center of mass (halfway down the bar) so the force diagram looks like the following:

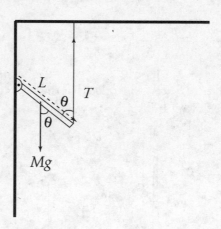

Look at the point where the bar is attached to the wall. Since the system is in static equilibrium, the net torque about this point must be zero. The weight of the bar produces a clockwise torque, of magnitude $(L/2)\, Mg \sin \theta$, and the tension in the string produces a counterclockwise torque, of magnitude $LT \sin \theta$. Since these torques balance, we have

$$LT \sin\theta = (L/2)Mg \sin\theta$$
$$T = \frac{1}{2}\, Mg$$

There is a force acting on the rod by the wall, but since that point is taken to be the pivot, its torque = 0. This "wall force" could, in theory, have both an x and a y component, depending on what is needed to make sure the rod doesn't move. Since there are no other x forces in this example, there will be no x component of the wall force.

ANGULAR MOMENTUM

So far we've developed rotational analogs for displacement, velocity, acceleration, and force. We will finish by developing a rotational analog for linear momentum; it's called **angular momentum**.

Consider a small point mass m at distance r from the axis of rotation, moving with velocity $\mathbf{v}$ and acted upon by a tangential force $\mathbf{F}$.

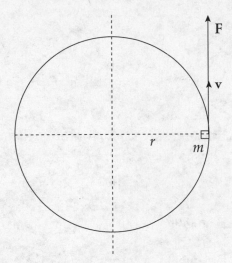

Then, by Newton's second law

$$\mathbf{F} = \frac{\Delta p}{\Delta t} = \frac{\Delta(mv)}{\Delta t}$$

If we multiply both sides of this equation by r and notice that $r\mathbf{F} = \tau$, we get

$$\tau = \frac{\Delta(rmv)}{\Delta t}$$

Therefore, to form the analog of the law $\mathbf{F} = \Delta p/\Delta t$ (force equals the rate-of-change of linear momentum), we say that torque equals the rate-of-change of angular momentum, and the angular momentum (denoted by L) of the point mass m is defined by the equation

$$L = rmv$$

If the point mass m does not move in a circular path, we can still define its angular momentum relative to any reference point.

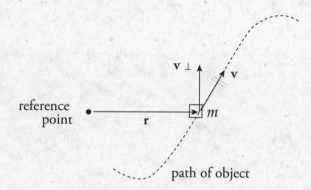

If $\mathbf{r}$ is the vector from the reference point to the mass, then the angular momentum is

$$L = rmv_\perp$$

where $v_\perp$ is the component of the velocity that's perpendicular to $\mathbf{r}$.

For a rotating object, the angular momentum equals the sum of the angular momentum of each individual particle. This can be written as $L = IW$, where I is the object's **movement of inertia** and W is the angular velocity (to be discussed later). I is basically a measure of how difficult it is to start an object rotating (analogous to mass in the translational world). I increases with mass and average radius from the axis of rotation.

CONSERVATION OF ANGULAR MOMENTUM

Newton's second law says that

$$F_{net} = \frac{\Delta p}{\Delta t}$$

so if $F_{net} = 0$, then **p** is constant. This is conservation of linear momentum.

The rotational analog of this is

$$\tau_{net} = \frac{\Delta L}{\Delta t}$$

So if $\tau_{net} = 0$, then L is constant. This is **conservation of angular momentum**. Basically, this law says that if the torques on a body balance so that the net torque is zero, then the body's angular momentum can't change.

The most common example of this phenomenon is when a figure skater spins. As the skater pulls her arms inward, she moves more of her mass closer to the rotation axis and decreases her rotational inertia, I. Since the external torque on her is negligible, her angular momentum must be conserved. Since $L = I\omega$, a decrease in I causes an increase in ω, and she spins faster.

ROTATIONAL KINEMATICS

If we mark several dots along a radius on a disk and call this radius the *reference line*, and the disk rotates around its center, we can use the movement of these dots to talk about angular displacement, angular velocity, and angular acceleration.

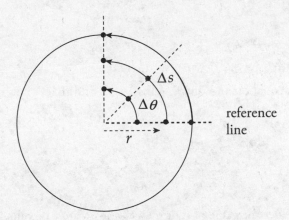

If the disk rotates as a rigid body, then all three dots shown have the same **angular displacement**, $\Delta\theta$. In fact, this is the definition of a **rigid body**: In a rigid body, all points along a radial line always have the same angular displacement.

Just as the time rate-of-change of displacement gives velocity, the time rate-of-change of angular displacement gives angular velocity, symbolized by ω (*omega*).

The definition of the **average angular velocity** is

$$\bar{\omega} = \frac{\Delta \theta}{\Delta t}$$

Finally, just as the time rate-of-change of velocity gives acceleration, the time rate-of-change of angular velocity gives angular acceleration, or α (*alpha*).

The definition of the **average angular acceleration** is

$$\bar{\alpha} = \frac{\Delta \omega}{\Delta t}$$

On the rotating disk illustrated on the previous page, we said that all points undergo the same angular displacement at any given time interval; this means that all points on the disk have the same angular velocity, ω, but not all points have the same linear velocity, *v*. This follows from the definition of **radian** measure. Expressed in radians, the angular displacement, $\Delta \theta$, is related to the arc length, Δs, by the equation

$$\Delta \theta = \frac{\Delta s}{r}$$

Rearranging this equation and dividing by Δt, we find that

$$\Delta s = r \Delta \theta \quad \Rightarrow \quad \frac{\Delta s}{\Delta t} = r \frac{\Delta \theta}{\Delta t} \quad \Rightarrow \quad \bar{v} = r \bar{\omega} \Rightarrow v = rw$$

Therefore, the greater the value of *r*, or $v = r\omega$ the greater the value of *v*. Points on the rotating body farther from the rotation axis move faster than those closer to the rotation axis.

From the equation $v = r\omega$, we can derive the relationship that connects angular acceleration and linear acceleration.

$$a = r\alpha$$

It's important to realize that the acceleration a in this equation is *not* centripetal acceleration, but rather tangential acceleration, which arises from a change in speed caused by an angular acceleration. By contrast, centripetal acceleration does not produce a change in speed. Often, tangential acceleration is written as a_t to distinguish it from centripetal acceleration (a_c).

---

5. A rotating, rigid body makes one complete revolution in 2 s. What is its average angular velocity?

Here's How to Crack It

One complete revolution is equal to an angular displacement of 2π radians, so the body's average angular velocity is

$$\bar{\omega} = \frac{\Delta\theta}{\Delta t} = \frac{2\pi \ \text{rad}}{2 \ \text{s}} = \pi \ \text{rad/s}$$

---

6. The angular velocity of a rotating disk increases from 2 rad/s to 5 rad/s in 0.5 s. What's the disk's average angular acceleration?

Here's How to Crack It
By definition

$$\overline{a} = \frac{\Delta\omega}{\Delta t} = \frac{(5-2)\ \text{rad/s}}{0.5\ \text{s}} = 6\ \text{rad/s}^2$$

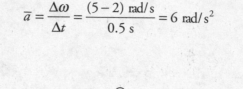

7. Derive an expression for centripetal acceleration in terms of angular speed.

Here's How to Crack It
For an object revolving with linear speed v at a distance r from the center of rotation, the centripetal acceleration is given by the equation $a_c = v^2/r$. Using the fundamental equation $v = r\omega$, we find that

$$a_c = \frac{v^2}{r} = \frac{(r\omega)^2}{r} = \omega^2 r$$

THE BIG FIVE FOR ROTATIONAL MOTION

The simplest type of rotational motion to analyze is motion in which the angular acceleration is *constant* (and may be equal to zero). Rotational motion around a *fixed* axis of rotation is another restriction that makes for an easy analysis. In this case, there are only two possible directions for motion. One direction, counterclockwise, is called *positive* (+), and the opposite direction, clockwise, is called *negative* (−).

Let's review the quantities we've seen so far. The fundamental quantities for rotational motion are angular displacement ($\Delta\theta$), angular velocity (ω), and angular acceleration (α). Because we're dealing with angular acceleration, we know about changes in angular velocity, from initial velocity (ω_i or ω_0) to final velocity (ω_f or simply ω—with no subscript). And, finally, the motion takes place during some elapsed time interval, Δt. Therefore, we have five kinematics quantities: $\Delta\theta$, ω_0, ω, α, and Δt.

These five quantities are related by a group of five equations that we call the Big Five. They work in cases in which the angular acceleration is uniform. These equations are identical to the Big Five we studied in Chapter 2, but in these cases, the translational variables (s, v, or a) are replaced by the corresponding rotational variables (θ, ω, or α, respectively).

		Variable that's missing
Big Five #1:	$\Delta\theta = \bar{\omega}\Delta t$	α
Big Five #2:	$\omega = \omega_0 + \alpha t$	$\Delta\theta$
Big Five #3:	$\Delta\theta = \omega_0 t + \frac{1}{2}\alpha t^2$	ω
Big Five #4:	$\Delta\theta = \omega t - \frac{1}{2}\alpha t^2$	ω_0
Big Five #5:	$\omega^2 = \omega_0^2 + 2\alpha\Delta\theta$	Δt

In Big Five #1, the average angular velocity is simply the average of the initial angular velocity and the final angular velocity, $\bar{\omega} = \frac{1}{2}(\omega_0 + \omega)$, because angular acceleration is constant.

Each of the Big Five equations is missing exactly one of the five kinematics quantities and, as with the other Big Five you learned, the way you decide which equation to use is to determine which of the kinematics quantities is missing from the problem, and use the equation that's also missing that quantity. For example, if the problem never mentions the final angular velocity—ω is neither given nor asked for—then the equation that will work is the one that's missing ω; that's Big Five #3.

Notice that Big Five #1 and #2 are simply the definitions of $\bar{\omega}$ and $\bar{\alpha}$ written in forms that don't involve fractions.

---

8. An object with an initial angular velocity of 1 rad/s rotates with constant angular acceleration. Three seconds later, its angular velocity is 5 rad/s. Calculate its angular displacement during this time interval.

Here's How to Crack It

We're given ω_0, t, and ω, and asked for $\Delta\theta$. So α is missing, and we use Big Five #1.

$$\Delta\theta = \overline{\omega}\Delta t = \frac{1}{2}(\omega_0 + \omega)\Delta t = \frac{1}{2}(1 \text{ rad/s} + 5 \text{ rad/s})(3 \text{ s}) = 9 \text{ rad}$$

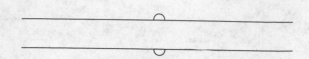

9. Starting with zero initial angular velocity, a sphere begins to spin with constant angular acceleration about an axis through its center, achieving an angular velocity of 10 rad/s when its angular displacement is 20 rad. What is the value of the sphere's angular acceleration?

Here's How to Crack It

We're given ω_0, $\Delta\theta$, and ω, and asked for α. Since t is missing, we use Big Five #5.

$$\omega^2 = \omega_0^2 + 2\alpha\Delta\theta \quad \Rightarrow \quad \omega^2 = 2\alpha\Delta\theta \text{ (since } \omega_0 = 0)$$

$$\alpha = \frac{\omega^2}{2\Delta\theta} = \frac{(10 \text{ rad/s})^2}{2(20 \text{ rad})} = 2.5 \text{ rad/s}^2$$

To summarize, here's a comparison of the fundamental quantities of translational and rotational motion and of the Big Five (assuming constant acceleration and a fixed axis of rotation).

	Translational	Rotational	Connection
displacement	Δs	$\Delta\theta$	$\Delta s = r\Delta\theta$
velocity	v	ω	$v = r\omega$
acceleration	a	α	$a = r\alpha$
Big Five #1	$\Delta s = \bar{v}t$	$\Delta\theta = \bar{\omega}\Delta t$	
Big Five #2	$v = v_0 + at$	$\omega = \omega_0 + \alpha t$	
Big Five #3	$\Delta s = v_0 t + \frac{1}{2}at^2$	$\Delta\theta = \omega_0 t + \frac{1}{2}\alpha t^2$	
Big Five #4	$\Delta s = vt - \frac{1}{2}at^2$	$\Delta\theta = \omega t - \frac{1}{2}\alpha t^2$	
Big Five #5	$v^2 = v_0^2 + 2a\Delta s$	$\omega^2 = \omega_0^2 + 2\alpha\Delta\theta$	

Chapter 6 Review Questions

Answers are on page 398.

1. An object of mass 0.5 kg, moving in a circular path of radius 0.25 m, experiences a centripetal acceleration of constant magnitude 9 m/s². What is the object's angular speed?

    (A) 2.3 rad/s
    (B) 4.5 rad/s
    (C) 6 rad/s
    (D) 12 rad/s
    (E) Cannot be determined from the information given

2. An object, originally at rest, begins spinning under uniform angular acceleration. In 10 s, it completes an angular displacement of 60 rad. What is the numerical value of the angular acceleration?

    (A) 0.3 rad/s²
    (B) 0.6 rad/s²
    (C) 1.2 rad/s²
    (D) 2.4 rad/s²
    (E) 3.6 rad/s²

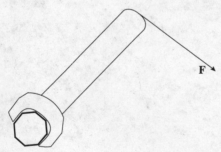

3. In an effort to tighten a bolt, a force **F** is applied as shown in the figure above. If the distance from the end of the wrench to the center of the bolt is 20 cm and **F** = 20 N, what is the magnitude of the torque produced by **F** ?

    (A) 0 N × m
    (B) 1 N × m
    (C) 2 N × m
    (D) 4 N × m
    (E) 10 N × m

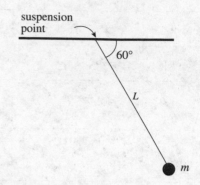

4. In the figure above, what is the torque about the pendulum's suspension point produced by the weight of the bob, given that the length of the pendulum, L, is 80 cm and $m = 0.50$ kg ?

    (A) 0.49 N × m
    (B) 0.98 N × m
    (C) 1.7 N × m
    (D) 2.0 N × m
    (E) 3.4 N × m

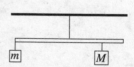

5. A uniform meter stick of mass 1 kg is hanging from a thread attached at the stick's midpoint. One block of mass $m = 3$ kg hangs from the left end of the stick, and another block, of unknown mass m, hangs below the 80 cm mark on the meter stick. If the stick remains at rest in the horizontal position shown above, what is m ?

    (A) 4 kg
    (B) 5 kg
    (C) 6 kg
    (D) 8 kg
    (E) 9 kg

Keywords

translation
rotation
rotational inertia (moment of inertia)
torque
line of action
lever arm (moment arm)
moment
net torque
translational equilibrium
rotational equilibrium
static equilibrium
angular momentum
conservation of angular momentum
angular displacement
rigid body
average angular velocity (or speed)
average angular acceleration
radian

Summary

- Rotational dynamics involves describing the acceleration of an object in terms of its mass (inertia) and the forces that act on it: $F_{net} = ma$.

- Torque is the quantity that measures how effectively a force causes rotation. The greater the distance from the axis of rotation (the pivot) where force is applied, the greater the torque will be.

- Equilibrium refers to the state of an object when the sum of the forces and torque acting on it is zero.

- Angular momentum is the rotational analog for linear momentum. It is the product of mass and velocity and the distance from the axis of rotation. It is symbolized by L. Use the formula $L = rmv_{\perp}$.

- Conservation of angular momentum states that if the torques on a body balance so that the net torque is zero, then the body's angular momentum cannot change.

- Rotational kinematics has symbols and concepts that are analogous to those of linear kinematics.

- When dealing with rotational kinematics, remember to use the Big Five to find the value of the missing variable.

Chapter 7
Laws of Gravitation

You will need to know about gravitation of planets and other objects for the SAT Physics Subject Test. This chapter will give you the equations you need for gravitation of the objects as well as their potential gravitational energy. We'll check in with the laws of our old friend Newton and learn about three laws devised by Johannes Kepler.

KEPLER'S LAWS

The SAT Physics Subject Test expects you to be familiar with three simple laws put forth by Johannes Kepler.

The Skinny on Kepler's Laws

First Law: The orbit of each planet is an ellipse and the sun is at one focus.

Second Law: An imaginary line from the sun to a moving planet sweeps out equal areas in equal intervals of time.

Third Law: The ratio of the square of a planet's period of revolution (the time for one complete orbit) to the cube of its average distance from the sun is a constant that is the same for all planets.

Kepler's First Law

Every planet moves in an elliptical orbit, with the sun at one **focus**. Just as a circle has a center—that special point inside the circle from which every point on the circle is the same distance—an ellipse has two **foci** (plural of focus): A pair of special points inside the ellipse such that the sum of the distance of every point on the ellipse to the two foci is always the same.

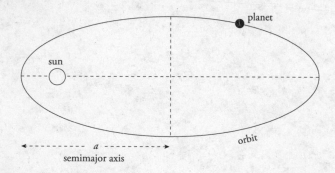

Kepler's Second Law

As a planet moves in its orbit, a line drawn from the sun to the planet sweeps out equal areas in equal time intervals.

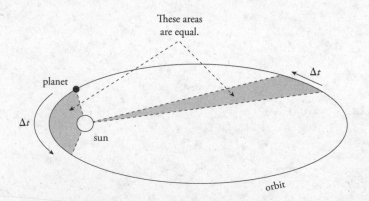

Therefore, the planet moves faster when it is nearer the sun than when it is farther away.

Kepler's Third Law

If T is the period (the time it takes the planet to make one orbit around the sun) and a is the length of the semimajor axis of a planet's orbit, then the ratio T^2/a^3 is the same for all the planets.

NEWTON'S LAW OF GRAVITATION

Newton eventually put forth another important theory about the Universe: Any two objects in the Universe exert an attractive force on each other—called the **gravitational force**—whose strength is proportional to the product of the objects' masses and inversely proportional to the square of the distance between them. If we let G be the **universal gravitational constant**, which is equal to 6.67×10^{-11} N • m²/kg², then the strength of the gravitational force is given by the equation

$$F = G\frac{m_1 m_2}{r^2}$$

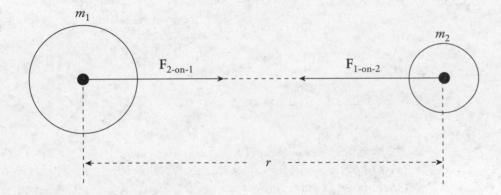

The forces $\mathbf{F}_{\text{1-on-2}}$ and $\mathbf{F}_{\text{2-on-1}}$ act along the line that joins the bodies and form an action/reaction pair.

THE GRAVITATIONAL ATTRACTION DUE TO AN EXTENDED BODY

Newton's law of gravitation is really a statement about the force between two point particles: objects that are very small in comparison with the distance between them. However, Newton also proved that a uniform sphere attracts another body as if all of the sphere's mass were concentrated at its center, so we can also apply Newton's law of gravitation to objects that are not small, relative to the distance between them.

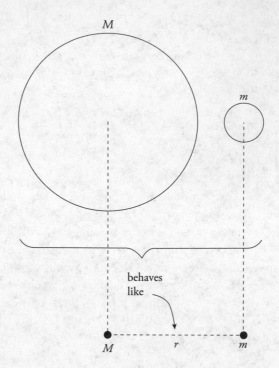

Therefore, r is the distance between the centers of mass of the two objects. For objects with uniform density, this is merely the distance from center to center.

The force of gravity is very small unless at least one of the objects is large, like a plant or moon. Let's try a problem that explores this.

1. The Sun has a mass of 2×10^{30} kg and Mars has a mass of 6×10^{23} kg. How does the acceleration of the Sun due to Mars compare to the acceleration of Mars due to the Sun?

Here's How to Crack It

The force on the Sun is $F = m_S a_S$, and the force on Mars is $F = m_M a_M$. Since F is the same in both of these equations—because F is their mutual gravitational attraction—we can write

$$m_S a_S = m_M a_M \quad \Rightarrow \quad \frac{a_S}{a_M} = \frac{m_M}{m_S} = \frac{6 \times 10^{23} \text{ kg}}{2 \times 10^{30} \text{ kg}} = 3 \times 10^{-7}$$

So, the acceleration of the Sun is much smaller than that of Mars; it's only 3×10^{-7} as much. Because of Mars's much smaller mass, it's affected more by the gravitational force, which is why Mars orbits the Sun and not the other way around.

2. An object on the surface of the earth weighs 90 N. If the object is moved to an altitude of 2R (R= the radius of the earth), what will be its new weight?

Here's How to Crack It

The weight of an object is the force of gravity acting on the object, which is equal to

$$\frac{GM_{earth}M_{object}}{r^2}$$

On the surface of Earth, $r = R$, so

$$W = \frac{GM_{earth}M_{object}}{R^2}$$

Altitude is measured from the surface of Earth. Since r is the distance to the center of Earth, $r = R + 2R = 3R$.

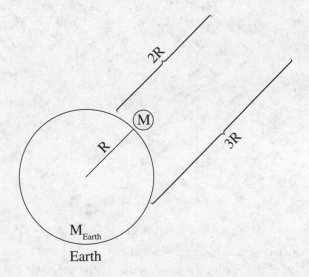

Therefore, the new $W = \frac{GM_{earth}M_{object}}{(3R)^2} = \frac{1}{9}W_{old}$

Since the old weight was 90 N, the new weight will be $\frac{1}{9} \times (90N) = 10N$.

G or g?

Remember that G is a universal constant equal to 6.67×10^{-11} Nxm^2 /kg^2. g depends upon what planet or moon an object is on. Near the surface, $mg = \frac{GMm}{R^2}$ where M and R are the mass and radius of the planet or moon. Cancelling m, we see that $g = \frac{GM}{R^2}$.

3. If M is the mass of Earth, then the mass of the Moon is about M/80 and the mass of the Sun is about 330,000M. If R is the distance between Earth and the Moon, then the distance between Earth and the Sun is about 400R. So, which exerts a greater gravitational force on the earth: the Moon or the Sun?

Here's How to Crack It

According to Newton's law of gravitation, the gravitational forces on Earth exerted by the Moon and by the Sun are:

$$F_{\text{by moon}} = G\frac{M \times \frac{1}{80}M}{R^2} \quad \text{and} \quad F_{\text{by sun}} = G\frac{M \times 330{,}000M}{(400R)^2}$$

Simplifying these expressions, we compare the values of

$$F_{\text{by moon}} = \frac{1}{80} \times G\frac{M^2}{R^2} \quad \text{and} \quad F_{\text{by sun}} = \frac{330{,}000}{160{,}000} \times G\frac{M^2}{R^2}$$

$$\approx 2 \times G\frac{M^2}{R^2}$$

We now see that the gravitational force exerted by the Sun is greater than that exerted by the Moon (by a factor of about $2/\frac{1}{80} = 160$).

4. An artificial satellite of mass m travels at a constant speed in a circular orbit of radius R around the earth (mass M). What is the speed of the satellite?

Here's How to Crack It

The centripetal force on the satellite is provided by Earth's gravitational pull. Therefore

$$\frac{mv^2}{R} = G\frac{Mm}{R^2}$$

Solving this equation for v yields

$$v = \sqrt{G\frac{M}{R}}$$

Notice that the satellite's speed doesn't depend on its mass; even if it were a baseball, if its orbit radius were R, then its orbit speed would still be $\sqrt{GM/R}$.

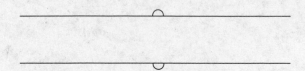

5. A communications satellite of mass m is orbiting the earth at constant speed in a circular orbit of radius R. If R is increased by a factor of 4, what happens to T, the satellite's orbit period (the time it takes to complete one orbit)?

Here's How to Crack It

From question 4, we know that

$$v = \sqrt{G\frac{M}{R}}$$

Now, since $v = 2\pi R/T$, we have

$$\frac{2\pi R}{T} = \sqrt{G\frac{M}{R}}$$

$$T = \frac{2\pi R}{\sqrt{G\dfrac{M}{R}}} = \frac{2\pi R\sqrt{R}}{\sqrt{GM}}$$

This tells us that T is proportional to $R\sqrt{R}$, so if R increases by a factor of 4, then T will increase by a factor of $4\sqrt{4} = 8$.

GRAVITATIONAL POTENTIAL ENERGY

Work and Gravity
By definition,
$U_{grav} = -W_{by\ grav}$

Remember that when we developed the equation $U = mgh$ for the gravitational potential energy of an object of mass m at height h above the surface of the earth, we took the surface of the earth to be our $U = 0$ reference level and assumed that the height, h, was small compared with the earth's radius. In that case, the variation in g was negligible, so g was thought of as a constant. The work done by gravity as an object was raised to height h was then simply $-F_{grav} \times \Delta s = -mgh$, so $U_{grav} = mgh$.

But now we'll take variations in g into account and develop a general equation for gravitational potential energy, one that isn't restricted to small altitude changes.

Consider an object of mass m at a distance r_1 from the center of the earth (or any spherical body) moving by some means to a position r_2.

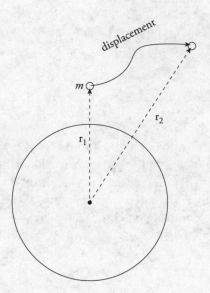

How much work did the gravitational force perform during this displacement? The answer is given by the equation.

$$W_{by\ grav} = GMm\left(\frac{1}{r_2} - \frac{1}{r_1}\right)$$

Therefore, since $\Delta U_{grav} = -W_{by\ grav}$, we get

$$U_2 - U_1 = -GMm\left(\frac{1}{r_2} - \frac{1}{r_1}\right)$$

Let's choose our $U = 0$ reference at infinity. That is, we decide to allow $U_2 \rightarrow 0$ as $r_2 \rightarrow \infty$. Then this equation becomes

$$U = -\frac{GMm}{r}$$

Notice that according to this equation (and our choice of $U = 0$ when $r = \infty$), the gravitational potential energy is always negative. This just means that energy has to be added to bring an object (mass m) bound to the gravitational field of M to a point very far from M, at which $U = 0$.

6. Find an expression for the minimum speed at which an object of mass m must be launched in order to escape Earth's gravitational field. (This is called **escape speed**.)

Here's How to Crack It

When launched, the object is at the surface of the earth ($r_0 = r_E$) and has an upward, initial velocity of magnitude v_0. To get it far away from the earth, we want to bring its gravitational potential energy to zero, but to find the minimum launch speed, we want the object's final speed to be zero by the time it gets to this distant location. So, by conservation of energy

$$K_0 + U_0 = K_f + U_f$$

$$\frac{1}{2}mv_i^2 + \frac{-GM_E m}{r_-} = 0 + 0$$

which gives

$$\frac{1}{2}mv_0^2 = \frac{GM_E m}{r_E} \quad \Rightarrow \quad v_0 = \sqrt{\frac{2GM_E}{r_E}}$$

7. A satellite of mass m is in a circular orbit of radius R around the earth (radius r_E, mass M). What is its total mechanical energy (where U_{grav} is considered zero as R approaches infinity)?

Here's How to Crack It

The mechanical energy, E, is the sum of the kinetic energy, K, and potential energy, U. You can calculate the kinetic energy, since you know that the centripetal force on the satellite is provided by the gravitational attraction of the earth.

$$\frac{mv^2}{R} = \frac{GMm}{R^2} \quad \Rightarrow \quad mv^2 = \frac{GMm}{R} \quad \Rightarrow \quad K = \frac{1}{2}mv^2 = \frac{GMm}{2R}$$

Therefore

$$E = K + U = \frac{GMm}{2R} + \frac{-GMm}{R} = -\frac{GMm}{2R}$$

Chapter 7 Review Questions

Answers are on page 400.

1. If the distance between two point particles is doubled, then the gravitational force between them

   (A) decreases by a factor of 4
   (B) decreases by a factor of 2
   (C) increases by a factor of 2
   (D) increases by a factor of 4
   (E) Cannot be determined without knowing the masses

2. At the surface of the earth, an object of mass m has weight w. If this object is transported to an altitude that's twice the radius of the earth, then, at the new location,

   (A) its mass is $\frac{m}{2}$ and its weight is $\frac{w}{2}$

   (B) its mass is m and its weight is $\frac{w}{2}$

   (C) its mass is $\frac{m}{2}$ and its weight is $\frac{w}{4}$

   (D) its mass is m and its weight is $\frac{w}{4}$

   (E) its mass is m and its weight is $\frac{w}{9}$

3. A moon of mass m orbits a planet of mass $100m$. Let the strength of the gravitational force exerted by the planet on the moon be denoted by F_1, and let the strength of the gravitational force exerted by the moon on the planet be F_2. Which of the following is true?

   (A) $F_1 = 100F_2$
   (B) $F_1 = 10F_2$
   (C) $F_1 = F_2$
   (D) $F_2 = 10F_1$
   (E) $F_2 = 100F_1$

4. The planet Pluto has 1/500 the mass and 1/15 the radius of Earth. What is the value of g on the surface of Pluto?

   (A) 0.3 m/s2
   (B) 1.6 m/s2
   (C) 2.4 m/s2
   (D) 4.5 m/s2
   (E) 7.1 m/s2

5. A satellite is currently orbiting Earth in a circular orbit of radius R; its kinetic energy is K_1. If the satellite is moved and enters a new circular orbit of radius $2R$, what will be its kinetic energy?

   (A) $\frac{K_1}{4}$

   (B) $\frac{K_1}{2}$

   (C) K_1

   (D) $2K_1$

   (E) $4K_1$

6. A moon of Jupiter has a nearly circular orbit of radius R and an orbit period of T. Which of the following expressions gives the mass of Jupiter?

   (A) $\frac{2\pi R}{T}$

   (B) $\frac{4\pi^2 R}{T}$

   (C) $\frac{2\pi R^3}{(GT^2)}$

   (D) $\frac{4\pi^2 R^2}{(GT^2)}$

   (E) $\frac{4\pi^2 R^3}{(GT^2)}$

7. The mean distance from Saturn to the sun is 9 times greater than the mean distance from Earth to the sun. How long is a Saturn year?

(A)   18 Earth years
(B)   27 Earth years
(C)   81 Earth years
(D) 243 Earth years
(E) 729 Earth years

8. The moon has mass M and radius R. A small object is dropped from a distance of $3R$ from the moon's center. The object's impact speed when it strikes the surface of the moon is equal to

$$\sqrt{kGM/R} \text{ for } k =$$

(A) $\dfrac{1}{3}$

(B) $\dfrac{2}{3}$

(C) $\dfrac{3}{4}$

(D) $\dfrac{4}{3}$

(E) $\dfrac{3}{2}$

9. Two satellites orbit the earth in circular orbits, each traveling at a constant speed. The radius of satellite A's orbit is R, and the radius of satellite B's orbit is $3R$. Both satellites have the same mass. How does F_A, the centripetal force on satellite A, compare with F_B, the centripetal force on satellite B ?

(A) $F_A = 9F_B$

(B) $F_A = 3F_B$

(C) $F_A = F_B$

(D) $F_B = 3F_A$

(E) $F_B = 9F_A$

Keywords

focus
foci
gravitational force
universal gravitational constant
escape speed
period
altitude

Summary

- Kepler's first law: Every planet moves in an elliptical orbit with the sun at one focus of both of them in an ellipse.

- Kepler's second law: A planet moves faster when it is closer to the sun than when it is further away.

- Kepler's third law: The ratio T^2/a^3 is the same for all the planets, where T is the time it takes the planet to make one orbit (the period) and a is the length of the semimajor axis of a planet's orbit.

- Newton's law of gravitation states that any two objects in the Universe exert on each other a gravitational force whose strength is proportional to the product of the object's masses and inversely proportional to the square of the distance between them.

- A uniform sphere attracts another body as if all of the sphere's mass were concentrated at its center.

- Gravitational potential energy comes into play when the height is large compared with the earth's radius. In this case, gravitation is a variable force.

- Altitude is measured from the earth's surface.

Chapter 8
Oscillations

In this chapter, we'll concentrate on a kind of periodic motion that's straightforward and that, fortunately, actually describes many real-life systems. This type of motion is called **simple harmonic motion**. Many of the examples of this that you'll see on the SAT Physics Subject Test involve a block that's oscillating on the end of a spring. Here we'll learn about this simple system, and we can apply our knowledge to many other oscillating systems.

SIMPLE HARMONIC MOTION (SHM): THE SPRING–BLOCK OSCILLATOR

When a spring is compressed or stretched from its natural length, a force is created. If the spring is displaced by x from its natural length, the force it exerts in response is given by the equation

$$\mathbf{F}_S = -kx$$

This is known as **Hooke's law.** The proportionality constant, k, is a positive number called the **spring** (or **force**) **constant** that indicates how stiff the spring is. The stiffer the spring, the greater the value of k. The minus sign in Hooke's law tells us that $\mathbf{F}_S$ and x always point in opposite directions. For example, referring to the figure below, when the spring is stretched (x is to the right), it then pulls back ($\mathbf{F}$ is to the left); when the spring is compressed (x is to the left), it then pushes outward ($\mathbf{F}$ is to the right). In all cases, the spring wants to return to its original length. As a result, the spring tries to restore the attached block to the **equilibrium position**, which is the position at which the net force on the block is zero. For this reason, we say that the spring provides a **restoring force**.

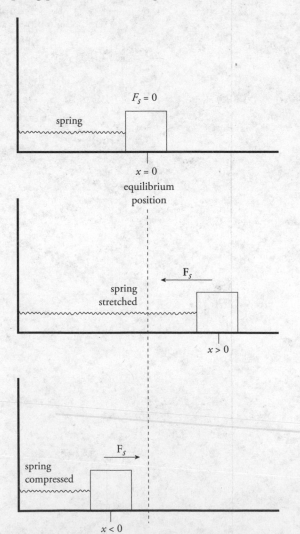

1. A 12 cm-long spring has a force constant (k) of 400 N/m. How much force is required to stretch the spring to a length of 14 cm ?

Here's How to Crack It

The displacement of the spring has a magnitude of $14 - 12 = 2$ cm $= 0.02$ m, so according to Hooke's Law, the spring exerts a force of magnitude $F = kx = (400$ N/m$)(0.02$ m$) = 8$ N. Therefore, we'd have to exert this much force to keep the spring in this stretched state.

Springs that obey Hooke's Law (called **ideal** or **linear springs**) provide an ideal mechanism for defining the most important kind of vibrational motion: simple harmonic motion.

Consider a spring with force constant k, attached to a vertical wall, with a block of mass m on a frictionless table attached to the other end.

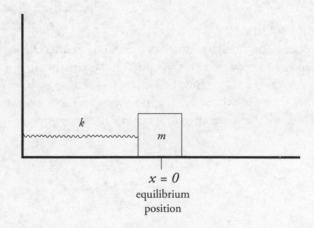

$x = 0$
equilibrium
position

Grab the block, pull it some distance from its original position, and release it. The spring will pull the block back toward equilibrium. Of course, because of its momentum, the block will pass through the equilibrium position and compress the spring. At some point, the block will stop, and the compressed spring will push the block back. In other words, the block will **oscillate**.

During the oscillation, the force on the block is zero when the block is at equilibrium (the point we designate as $x = 0$). This is because Hooke's law says that the strength of the spring's restoring force is given by the equation $F_S = kx$, so $F_S = 0$ at equilibrium. The acceleration of the block is also equal to zero at $x = 0$, since $F_S = 0$ at $x = 0$ and $a = F_S/m$. At the endpoints of the oscillation region, where the block's displacement, x, is largest, the restoring force and the magnitude of the acceleration are both at their maximum.

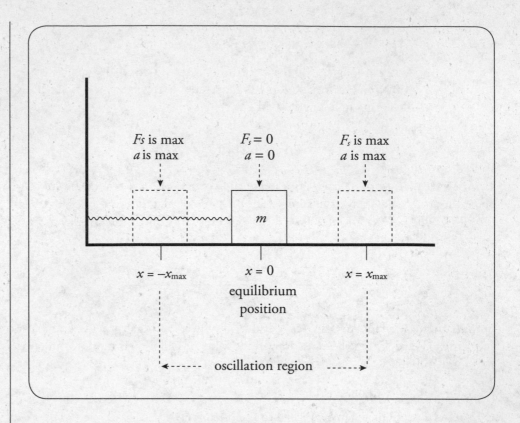

SHM in Terms of Energy

Another way to describe an oscillating block's motion is in terms of energy transfers. A stretched or compressed spring stores **elastic potential energy**, which is transformed into kinetic energy (and back again); this shuttling of energy between potential and kinetic causes the oscillations. For a spring with spring constant k, the elastic potential energy it possesses—relative to its equilibrium position—is given by the equation

$$U_S = \frac{1}{2}kx^2$$

Notice that the farther you stretch or compress a spring, the more work you have to do, and, as a result, the more potential energy is stored.

In terms of energy transfers, we can describe the block's oscillations as follows: When you initially pull out the block, you increase the elastic potential energy of the system. When you release the block, this potential energy turns into kinetic energy, and the block moves. As it passes through equilibrium, $U_S = 0$, so all the energy is kinetic. Then, as the block continues through equilibrium, it compresses the spring and the kinetic energy is transformed back into elastic potential energy.

By conservation of mechanical energy, the sum $K + U_s$ is a constant. Therefore, when the block reaches the endpoints of the oscillation region (that is, when $x = \pm x_{max}$), U_s is maximized, so K must be minimized; in fact, $K = 0$ at the endpoints. As the block is passing through equilibrium, $x = 0$, so $U_s = 0$ and K is maximized.

Please note, the figure on page 156 and the figure on this page are very important. Be sure you understand them and everything in this section before you take the test!

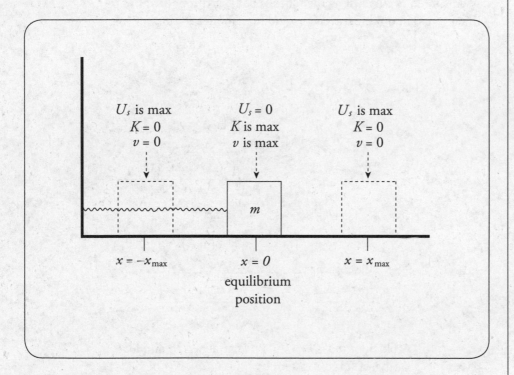

U_s is max $U_s = 0$ U_s is max
$K = 0$ K is max $K = 0$
$v = 0$ v is max $v = 0$

$x = -x_{max}$ $x = 0$ $x = x_{max}$

equilibrium
position

The maximum displacement from equilibrium is called the **amplitude** of oscillation, or A. So instead of writing $x = x_{max}$, we write $x = A$ (and $x = -x_{max}$ will be written as $x = -A$).

2. A block of mass $m = 0.2$ kg oscillates on a spring whose force constant k is 500 N/m. The amplitude of the oscillations is 4.0 cm. Calculate the maximum speed of the block.

Here's How to Crack It

First let's get an expression for the maximum elastic potential energy of the system, which occurs when $x = x_{max} = A$.

$$U_S = \frac{1}{2}kx^2 \implies U_{S, max} = \frac{1}{2}x_{max}^2 = \frac{1}{2}kA^2$$

When all this energy has been transformed into kinetic energy—which, as we discussed earlier, occurs just as the block is passing through equilibrium—the block will have maximum kinetic energy and maximum speed.

$$U_{S, max} \rightarrow K_{max} \implies \frac{1}{2}kA^2 = \frac{1}{2}mv_{max}^2$$

$$v_{max} = \sqrt{\frac{kA^2}{m}}$$

$$= \sqrt{\frac{(500 \text{ N/m})(0.04 \text{ m})^2}{0.2 \text{ kg}}}$$

$$= 2.0 \text{ m/s}$$

3. A block of mass $m = 2.0$ kg is attached to an ideal spring of force constant $k = 200$ N/m. The block is at rest at its equilibrium position. An impulsive force acts on the block, giving it an initial speed of 2.0 m/s. Find the amplitude of the resulting oscillations.

Here's How to Crack It

The block will come to rest when all of its initial kinetic energy has been transformed into the spring's potential energy. At this point, the block is at its maximum displacement from equilibrium, that is, it's at one of its amplitude positions, and

$$K_i + U_i = K_f + U_f$$

$$\frac{1}{2} m v_0^2 + 0 = 0 + \frac{1}{2} k A^2$$

$$A = \sqrt{\frac{m v_0^2}{k}}$$

$$= \sqrt{\frac{(2.0 \text{ kg})(2.0 \text{ m/s})^2}{200 \text{ N/m}}}$$

$$= 0.2 \text{ m.}$$

Because F_s varies as the object moves, the work done by or against the spring cannot be written as $Fd \cos\theta$. As with gravity, we must calculate work in terms of potential energy. If a block on a spring moves from x_1 to x_2, then

$$W_{spring} = -\Delta U_s = -(\frac{1}{2} k x_2^2 - \frac{1}{2} k x_1^2)$$

$$= \frac{1}{2} k (x_1^2 - x_2^2)$$

If an external force compresses or stretches the spring, then

$$W_{againstspring} = +\Delta U_s = \frac{1}{2} k (x_2^2 - x_1^2)$$

THE KINEMATICS OF SHM

Now that we've explored the dynamics of the block's oscillations in terms of force and energy, let's talk about motion—kinematics. As you watch the block oscillate, you should notice that it repeats each **cycle** of oscillation in the same amount of time. A cycle is a *round-trip*: for example, from position $x = A$ over to $x = -A$ and back again to $x = A$. The amount of time it takes to complete a cycle is called the **period** of the oscillations, or T. If T is short, the block is oscillating rapidly, and if T is long, the block is oscillating slowly.

Another way of describing the rate of the oscillations is to count the number of cycles that can be completed in a given time interval; the more completed cycles, the faster the oscillations. The number of cycles that can be completed per unit time is called the **frequency** of the oscillations, or f, and frequency is expressed in cycles per second. One cycle per second is one **hertz** (abbreviated **Hz**).

One of the most basic equations of oscillatory motion is

$$\text{period} = \frac{\#\ \text{seconds}}{\text{cycle}} \qquad \text{while} \qquad \text{frequency} = \frac{\#\ \text{cycles}}{\text{second}}$$

Therefore

$$T = \frac{1}{f} \qquad \text{and} \qquad f = \frac{1}{T}.$$

4. A block oscillating on the end of a spring moves from its position of maximum spring stretch to maximum spring compression in 0.25 s. Determine the period and frequency of this motion.

Here's How to Crack It

The period is defined as the time required for one full cycle. Moving from one end of the oscillation region to the other is only half a cycle. Therefore, if the block moves from its position of maximum spring stretch to maximum spring compression in 0.25 s, the time required for a full cycle is twice as much; $T = 0.5$ s. Because frequency is the reciprocal of period, the frequency of the oscillations is $f = 1/T = 1/(0.5\ \text{s}) = 2$ Hz.

5. A student observing an oscillating block counts 45 cycles of oscillation in one minute. Determine its frequency (in hertz) and period (in seconds).

Here's How to Crack It

The frequency of the oscillations, in hertz (which is the number of cycles per second), is

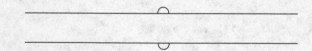

$$f = \frac{45\ \text{cycles}}{\text{min}} \times \frac{1\ \text{min}}{60\ \text{s}} = \frac{0.75\ \text{cycles}}{\text{s}} = 0.75\ \text{Hz}$$

Therefore

$$T = \frac{1}{f} = \frac{1}{0.75 \text{ Hz}} = 1.33 \text{ s}$$

One of the defining properties of the spring–block oscillator is that the frequency and period can be determined from the mass of the block and the force constant of the spring. The equations are as follows:

$$f = \frac{1}{2\pi}\sqrt{\frac{k}{m}} \qquad \text{and} \qquad T = 2\pi\sqrt{\frac{m}{k}}$$

Let's analyze these equations. Suppose we had a small mass on a very stiff spring; then we would expect that this strong spring would make the small mass oscillate rapidly, with high frequency and short period. Both of these predictions are proved true by the equations above because if m is small and k is large, then the ratio k/m is large (high frequency) and the ratio m/k is small (short period).

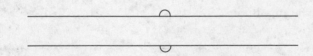

6. How would the period of the spring–block oscillator change if both the mass of the block and the spring constant were doubled?

Here's How to Crack It

The equation given above for the period shows that T depends on m/k. If both m and k are doubled, then the ratio m/k will be unchanged. Therefore, T will be unchanged too.

―――――――――――○―――――――――――

7. A block is attached to a spring and set into oscillatory motion, and its frequency is measured. If this block were removed and replaced by a second block with 1/4 the mass of the first block, how would the frequency of the oscillations compare to that of the first block?

Here's How to Crack It

Since the same spring is used, k remains the same. According to the equation given above, f is inversely proportional to the square root of the mass of the block: $f \propto 1/\sqrt{m}$. Therefore, if m decreases by a factor of 4, then f increases by a factor of $\sqrt{4} = 2$.

―――――――――――○―――――――――――

The equations we saw above for the frequency and period of the spring–block oscillator do not contain A, the amplitude of the motion.

> In simple harmonic motion, both the frequency and the period are independent of the amplitude.

The reason that the frequency and period of the spring–block oscillator are independent of amplitude is that F, the strength of the restoring force, is proportional to x, the displacement from equilibrium, as given by Hooke's law: $F_s = kx$.

―――――――――――○―――――――――――

8. A student performs an experiment with a spring–block simple harmonic oscillator. In the first trial, the amplitude of the oscillations is 3.0 cm, while in the second trial (using the same spring and block), the amplitude of the oscillations is 6.0 cm. Compare the values of the period, frequency, and maximum speed of the block between these two trials.

Here's How to Crack It

If the system exhibits simple harmonic motion, then the period and frequency are independent of amplitude. This is because the same spring and block were used in the two trials, so the period and frequency will have the same values in the second trial as they had in the first. But the maximum speed of the block will be greater in the second trial than in the first. Since the amplitude is greater in the second trial, the system possesses more total energy ($E = \frac{1}{2}kA^2$). So when the block is passing through equilibrium (its position of greatest speed), the second system has more energy to convert to kinetic, meaning that the block will have a greater speed. In fact, from question 2 we know that $v_{max} = A\sqrt{k/m}$, so since A is twice as great in the second trial than in the first, v_{max} will be twice as great in the second trial than in the first.

For undergoing simple harmonic motion, the position x can be expressed as a sine or cosine function in terms of t.

$$x = A\cos(2\pi ft + \varnothing) \ \text{ or } \ x = A\sin(2\pi ft + \varnothing)$$

$\varnothing$ is called the phase, and is determined by the initial conditions. For example, if $x=A$ at $t=0$, then choosing the cosine version of the equation would mean $\varnothing = 0$ =0. (Remember that $\cos 0 = 1$). $x = A\cos(2\pi ft)$.

---

9. For each of the following arrangements of two springs, determine the **effective spring constant**, k_{eff}. This is the force constant of a single spring that would produce the same force on the block as the pair of springs shown in each case.

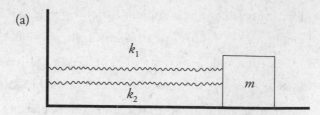

(a)

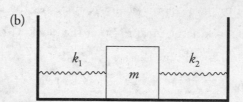

(b)

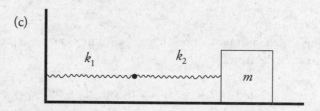

(c)

(d)   Determine k_{eff} in each of these cases if $k_1 = k_2 = k$.

Here's How to Crack It

(a)   Imagine that the block was displaced a distance x to the right of its equilibrium position. Then the force exerted by the first spring would be $F_1 = -k_1 x$ and the force exerted by the second spring would be $F_2 = -k_2 x$. The net force exerted by the springs would be

$$F_1 + F_2 = -k_1 x + -k_2 x = -(k_1 + k_2)x$$

Since $F_{eff} = -(k_1 + k_2)x$, we see that $k_{eff} = k_1 + k_2$.

(b)   Imagine that the block was displaced a distance x to the right of its equilibrium position. Then the force exerted by the first spring would be $F_1 = -k_1 x$ and the force exerted by the second spring would be $F_2 = -k_2 x$. The net force exerted by the springs would be

$$F_1 + F_2 = -k_1 x + -k_2 x = -(k_1 + k_2)x$$

As in part (a), we see that, since $F_{eff} = -(k_1 + k_2)x$, we get $k_{eff} = k_1 + k_2$.

(c)   Imagine that the block was displaced a distance x to the right of its equilibrium position. Let x_1 be the distance that the first spring is stretched, and let x_2 be the distance that the second spring is stretched. Then $x = x_1 + x_2$. But $x_1 = -F/k_1$ and $x_2 = -F/k_2$, so

$$\frac{-F}{k_1} + \frac{-F}{k_2} = x$$

$$-F\left(\frac{1}{k_1} + \frac{1}{k_2}\right) = x$$

$$F = -\left(\frac{1}{\dfrac{1}{k_1} + \dfrac{1}{k_2}}\right)x$$

$$F = -\frac{k_1 k_2}{k_1 + k_2}x$$

Therefore

$$k_{\text{eff}} = \frac{k_1 k_2}{k_1 + k_2}$$

(d)   If the two springs have the same force constant, that is, if $k_1 = k_2 = k$, then in the first two cases, the pairs of springs are equivalent to one spring that has twice their force constant: $k_{\text{eff}} = k_1 + k_2 = k + k = 2k$. In (c), the pair of springs is equivalent to a single spring with half their force constant.

$$k_{\text{eff}} = \frac{k_1 k_2}{k_1 + k_2} = \frac{kk}{k + k} = \frac{k^2}{2k} = \frac{k}{2}$$

THE SPRING–BLOCK OSCILLATOR: VERTICAL MOTION

So far we've looked at a block sliding back and forth on a horizontal table, but the block could also oscillate vertically. The only difference would be that gravity would cause the block to move downward, to an equilibrium position at which, in contrast with the horizontal SHM we've examined, the spring would *not* be at its natural length.

Consider a spring of negligible mass hanging from a stationary support. A block of mass m is attached to its end and allowed to come to rest, stretching the spring a distance d. At this point, the block is in equilibrium; the upward force of the

Vertical vs. Horizontal
Use what you know about horizontal motion of the spring–block oscillator. The only difference in vertical motion is that you must account for gravity.

spring is balanced by the downward force of gravity. Therefore

$$kd = mg \quad \Rightarrow \quad d = \frac{mg}{k}$$

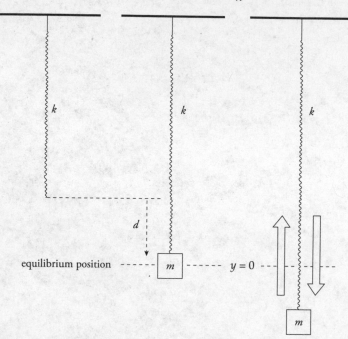

Next, imagine that the block is pulled down a distance A and released. The spring force increases (because the spring was stretched farther); it's stronger than the block's weight, and, as a result, the block accelerates upward. As the block's momentum carries it up, through the equilibrium position, the spring becomes less stretched than it was at equilibrium, so F_S is less than the block's weight. As a result, the block decelerates, stops, and accelerates downward again, and the up-and-down motion repeats.

When the block is at a distance y below its equilibrium position, the spring is stretched a total distance of $d + y$, so the upward spring force is equal to $k(d + y)$, while the downward force stays the same, mg.

The net force on the block is

$$F = k(d + y) - mg$$

but this equation becomes $F = ky$ because $kd = mg$ (as we saw above).

Since the resulting force on the block, $F = ky$, has the form of Hooke's law, we know that he vertical simple harmonic oscillations of the block have the same characteristics as do horizontal oscillations, with the equilibrium position, $y = 0$, not at the spring's natural length, but at the point where the hanging block is in equilibrium.

Questions 10-13

A block of mass $m = 1.5$ kg is attached to the end of a vertical spring of force constant $k = 300$ N/m. After the block comes to rest, it is pulled down a distance of 2.0 cm and released.

10. How far does the weight of the block cause the spring to stretch initially?

11. What are the minimum and maximum amounts of stretch of the spring during the oscillations of the block?

12. At what point(s) will the speed of the block be zero?

13. At what point(s) will the acceleration of the block be zero?

Here's How to Crack It

10. The weight of the block initially stretches the spring by a distance of

$$ d = \frac{mg}{k} = \frac{(1.5 \text{ kg})(10 \text{ N/kg})}{300 \text{ N/m}} = 0.05 \text{ m} = 5 \text{ cm} $$

11. Since the amplitude of the motion is 2.0 cm, the spring is stretched a maximum of 5 cm + 2.0 cm = 7 cm when the block is at the lowest position in its cycle, and a minimum of 5 cm − 2.0 cm = 3 cm when the block is at its highest position.

12. The block's speed is 0 at the two ends of its oscillation region, which are the points described in question 12.

13. The block's acceleration is 0 at its equilibrium position, which is the point described in question 11.

PENDULUMS

You may see a question about pendulums on the SAT Physics Subject Test, so we'll cover them in this chapter. A **simple pendulum** consists of a weight of mass *m* (called the *bob*) attached to a massless rod that swings, without friction, about the vertical equilibrium position. The restoring force is provided by gravity and as the figure below shows, the magnitude of the restoring force when the bob is at an angle θ to the vertical is given by the equation

$$F_{restoring} = mg \sin \theta$$

Although the displacement of the pendulum is measured by the angle that it makes with the vertical, instead of by its linear distance from the equilibrium position (as was the case for the spring–block oscillator), the simple pendulum has many of the same important features as the spring–block oscillator. For example

- displacement is zero at the equilibrium position.
- at the endpoints of the oscillation region (where $\theta = \pm \theta_{max}$), the restoring force and the tangential acceleration (a_t) have their greatest magnitudes, the speed of the pendulum is zero, and the potential energy is maximized.
- as the pendulum passes through the equilibrium position, its kinetic energy and speed are maximized.

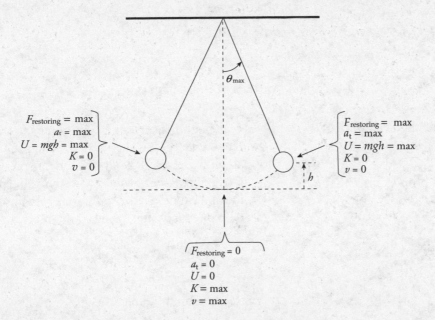

$F_{restoring} = max$
$a_t = max$
$U = mgh = max$
$K = 0$
$v = 0$

$F_{restoring} = max$
$a_t = max$
$U = mgh = max$
$K = 0$
$v = 0$

$F_{restoring} = 0$
$a_t = 0$
$U = 0$
$K = max$
$v = max$

Despite these similarities, there is one important difference. Simple harmonic motion results from a restoring force that has a strength that's proportional to the displacement. The magnitude of the restoring force on a pendulum is $mg \sin \theta$, which is *not* proportional to the displacement θ. Strictly speaking, the motion of a simple pendulum is not really simple harmonic. However, if θ is small, then $\sin \theta \approx \theta$ (measured in radians), so in this case, the magnitude of the restoring force is approximately $mg\theta$, which *is* proportional to θ. This means that if θ_{max} is small, the motion can be treated as simple harmonic.

If the restoring force is given by $mg\theta$, rather than $mg \sin \theta$, then the frequency and period of the oscillations depend only on the length of the pendulum and the value of the gravitational acceleration, according to the following equations.

$$f = \frac{1}{2\pi}\sqrt{\frac{g}{L}} \qquad \text{and} \qquad T = 2\pi\sqrt{\frac{L}{g}}$$

Notice that neither frequency nor period depends on the amplitude (the maximum angular displacement, θ_{max}); this is a characteristic feature of simple harmonic motion. Also notice that neither depends on the mass of the weight.

Chapter 8 Review Questions

Answers are on page 402.

1. Which of the following is/are characteristics of simple harmonic motion?

    I. The acceleration is constant.
    II. The restoring force is proportional to the displacement.
    III. The frequency is independent of the amplitude.

    (A) II only
    (B) I and II only
    (C) I and III only
    (D) II and III only
    (E) I, II, and III

2. A block attached to an ideal spring undergoes simple harmonic motion. The acceleration of the block has its maximum magnitude at the point where

    (A) the speed is the maximum
    (B) the potential energy is the minimum
    (C) the speed is the minimum
    (D) the restoring force is the minimum
    (E) the kinetic energy is the maximum

3. A block attached to an ideal spring undergoes simple harmonic motion about its equilibrium position ($x = 0$) with amplitude A. What fraction of the total energy is in the form of kinetic energy when the block is at position $x = \frac{1}{2}A$?

    (A) $\frac{1}{3}$

    (B) $\frac{3}{8}$

    (C) $\frac{1}{2}$

    (D) $\frac{2}{3}$

    (E) $\frac{3}{4}$

4. A student measures the maximum speed of a block undergoing simple harmonic oscillations of amplitude A on the end of an ideal spring. If the block is replaced by one with twice the mass but the amplitude of its oscillations remains the same, then the maximum speed of the block will

    (A) decrease by a factor of 4
    (B) decrease by a factor of 2
    (C) decrease by a factor of $\sqrt{2}$
    (D) remain the same
    (E) increase by a factor of 2

5. A spring–block simple harmonic oscillator is set up so that the oscillations are vertical. The period of the motion is T. If the spring and block are taken to the surface of the moon, where the gravitational acceleration is $\frac{1}{6}$ of its value here, then the vertical oscillations will have a period of

    (A) $\dfrac{T}{6}$

    (B) $\dfrac{T}{3}$

    (C) $\dfrac{T}{\sqrt{6}}$

    (D) T

    (E) $T\sqrt{6}$

6. A linear spring of force constant k is used in a physics lab experiment. A block of mass m is attached to the spring and the resulting frequency, f, of the simple harmonic oscillations is measured. Blocks of various masses are used in different trials, and in each case, the corresponding frequency is measured and recorded. If f^2 is plotted versus $1/m$, the graph will be a straight line with slope

   (A) $4\pi^2/k^2$
   (B) $4\pi^2/k$
   (C) $4\pi^2 k$
   (D) $k/(4\pi^2)$
   (E) $k^2/(4\pi^2)$

7. A block of mass $m = 4$ kg on a frictionless, horizontal table is attached to one end of a spring of force constant $k = 400$ N/m and undergoes simple harmonic oscillations about its equilibrium position ($x = 0$) with amplitude $A = 6$ cm. If the block is at $x = 6$ cm at time $t = 0$, then which of the following equations (with x in centimeters and t in seconds) gives the block's position as a function of time?

   (A) $x = 6 \sin(10t + \frac{1}{2}\pi)$
   (B) $x = 6 \sin(10\pi t)$
   (C) $x = 6 \sin(10\pi t - \frac{1}{2}\pi)$
   (D) $x = 6 \sin(10t)$
   (E) $x = 6 \sin(10t - \frac{1}{2}\pi)$

8. A student is performing a lab experiment on simple harmonic motion. She has two different springs (with force constants k_1 and k_2) and two different blocks (of masses m_1 and m_2). If $k_1 = 2k_2$ and $m_1 = 2m_2$, which of the following combinations would give the student the spring–block simple harmonic oscillator with the shortest period?

   (A) The spring with force constant k_1 and the block of mass m_1
   (B) The spring with force constant k_1 and the block of mass m_2
   (C) The spring with force constant k_2 and the block of mass m_1
   (D) The spring with force constant k_2 and the block of mass m_2
   (E) All the combinations above would give the same period.

9. A simple pendulum swings about the vertical equilibrium position with a maximum angular displacement of 5° and period T. If the same pendulum is given a maximum angular displacement of 10°, then which of the following best gives the period of the oscillations?

   (A) $\dfrac{T}{2}$

   (B) $\dfrac{T}{\sqrt{2}}$

   (C) T

   (D) $T\sqrt{2}$

   (E) $2T$

10. A simple pendulum of length L and mass m swings about the vertical equilibrium position ($\theta = 0$) with a maximum angular displacement of θ_{max}. What is the tension in the connecting rod when the pendulum's angular displacement is $\theta = \theta_{max}$?

    (A) $mg \sin\theta_{max}$
    (B) $mg \cos\theta_{max}$
    (C) $mgL \sin\theta_{max}$
    (D) $mgL \cos\theta_{max}$
    (E) $mgL(1 - \cos\theta_{max})$

Keywords

simple harmonies motion
Hooke's law
spring (or force) constant
equilibrium position
restoring force
ideal (or linear) springs
oscillate
elastic potential energy
amplitude
cycle
period
frequency
hertz (Hz)
effective spring constant
simple pendulum
phase

Summary

- When a spring is stretched or compressed horizontally, a force is created as the spring tries to return to its equilibrium position. The force it exerts in response is given by Hooke's law: $\mathbf{F}_s = -kx$.

- During oscillation, the force on the block when it is at equilibrium is zero, while the speed is at a maximum.

- At amplitude, when displacement from equilibrium is largest, the force and magnitude of acceleration are both at their maximum.

- The shutting off of energy between potential and kinetic causes oscillations.

- Each cycle of oscillation occurs in the same amount of time.
    1. The amount of time it takes to complete a cycle is called a period and is expressed in seconds per cycle.
    2. The number of cycles that can be completed in a unit of time is called the frequency of the oscillations and is expressed in cycles per second.

- The forces at play in the vertical motion of a spring are very similar to those in horizontal motion. The only difference is that, due to gravity, the vertical motion of a spring equilibrium is not at the spring's natural length.

- For an object moving with simple harmonic motion, the period and frequency are independent of the amplitude.

- Displacement of a simple pendulum is measured by the angle that it makes with the vertical. A pendulum's restoring force is provided by gravity and is proportional to the displacement.

- For small angles, a pendulum exhibits simple harmonic motion.

- The period and frequency of a pendulum do not depend on the mass.

Chapter 9
Thermal Physics

In this chapter we will discuss heat and temperature, concepts that seem familiar from our everyday experience. The SAT Physics Subject Test expects you to know things about heat and temperature that go beyond what you see around you every day. In physics, **heat** is defined as thermal energy that's transmitted from one body to another. While an object is capable of containing **thermal energy** (due to the random motion of its molecules), it doesn't *contain* heat; heat is energy that's *in transit*. **Temperature**, on the other hand, is a measure of the concentration of an object's internal thermal energy and is one of the basic SI units.

TEMPERATURE SCALES

In the United States, temperatures are still often expressed in **degrees Fahrenheit** (°F). On this scale, water freezes at 32°F and boils at 212°F. In other countries, temperature is expressed in **degrees Celsius** (°C); water freezes at 0°C and boils at 100°C. The size of a Fahrenheit degree is smaller than a Celsius degree, and the conversion between the two scales is given by the formula

$$T\,(°F) = \frac{9}{5}T\,(°C) + 32$$

The Celsius scale is sometimes used in scientific work, but it's giving way to the **absolute temperature scale**, in which temperatures are expressed in **kelvins** (K). On the kelvin scale, water freezes at 273.15 K and boils at 373.15 K. Notice that the degree sign is *not* used for absolute temperature. The kelvin scale assigns a value of 0 K to the lowest theoretically possible temperature and a value of 273.16 K to the **triple point of water** (the temperature at which the three phases of water—liquid water, ice, and vapor—coexist).

> A kelvin is equal in size to a Celsius degree, and the conversion between kelvins and degrees Celsius is:
>
> $$T\,(K) = T\,(°C) + 273.15$$
>
> For the SAT Physics Subject Test, you can ignore the .15 and use the simpler conversion equation $T = T_{°C} + 273$.

---

1. Room temperature is 68°F. What's this temperature in kelvins?

Here's How to Crack It

First convert this to Celsius. Since $T°_F = \frac{9}{5}T°_C + 32$, it's also true that $T°_C = \frac{5}{9}(T°_F - 32)$, so 68°F is equal to $\frac{5}{9}(68 - 32) = 20°C$. Converting this to kelvins, we add 273; room temperature is 293 K.

PHYSICAL CHANGES DUE TO HEAT TRANSFER

When a substance absorbs or gives off heat, one of the following two things can happen:

      (1)   the temperature of the substance can change

             or

      (2)   the substance can undergo a phase change.

There are three phases of matter: **solid**, **liquid**, and **vapor** (or **gas**). When a solid **melts** (or **liquefies**), it becomes a liquid; the reverse process occurs when a liquid **freezes** (or **solidifies**) to become a solid. A liquid can **evaporate** (to become vapor), and vapor can **condense** to become liquid. These are the most common phase changes, but others exist: A solid can **sublimate**, going directly to vapor form, and vapor can experience **deposition**, going directly to solid.

Since either the first or second change—but *not both*—takes place upon heat transfer, let's study these changes separately.

Calorimetry I: Heat Transfer and Temperature Change

The change in temperature that a substance experiences upon a transfer of heat depends on two things: the identity and the amount of the substance present. For example, we could transfer 200 J of heat to a gold nugget and a piece of wood of equal mass and, even though they were infused with the same amount of thermal energy, the temperature of the gold would rise much more than the temperature of the wood. Also, if this heat were transferred to two nuggets of gold of unequal mass, the temperature of the smaller nugget would rise more than that of the larger one.

> The equation that connects the amount of heat, Q, and the resulting temperature change, ΔT, is
>
> $$Q = mc\,\Delta T$$
>
> where m is the mass of the sample and c is an intrinsic property of the substance called its **specific heat**. Notice that positive Q is interpreted as heat coming *in* (ΔT is positive, so T increases), while negative Q corresponds to heat going *out* (ΔT is negative, so T decreases).

2. Gold has a specific heat of 130 J/kg·°C, and wood has a specific heat of 1,800 J/kg·°C. If a piece of gold and a piece of wood, each of mass 0.1 kg, both absorb 2,340 J of heat, by how much will their temperatures rise?

Celsius vs. Kelvin
Since temperature measured in Kelvins is equal to temperature measured in Celsius plus a constant, ΔT in Kelvins is the same as ΔT in Celsius.

Here's How to Crack It
We're given c, m, and Q, and we know that $\Delta T = Q/(mc)$.

$$\Delta T_{gold} = \frac{Q}{mc}_{gold} = \frac{2,340 \text{ J}}{(0.1 \text{ kg})(130 \text{ J/kg} \cdot \text{°C})} = 180 \text{ °C}$$

$$\Delta T_{wood} = \frac{Q}{mc}_{wood} = \frac{2,340 \text{ J}}{(0.1 \text{ kg})(1,800 \text{ J/kg} \cdot \text{°C})} = 13 \text{ °C}$$

Notice that the temperature of gold increased by 180°C, but the temperature of the wood increased by only 13°C.

3. A block of Teflon of mass 0.05 kg at a temperature of 430°C is placed in a beaker containing 0.5 kg of water (10 times the mass of the Teflon block) at room temperature, 20°C. After a while, the Teflon and water reach **thermal equilibrium** (they're at the same temperature). If the specific heat of water is 4 times the specific heat of Teflon, what's the common final temperature of the Teflon and the water?

Here's How to Crack It
Heat always flows from hot to cold. Therefore, when the hot block of Teflon is placed in the cool water, the Teflon loses heat and the water absorbs it. If we let T_f be the final temperature of both the Teflon and the water, then

$$Q_{lost \text{ by Teflon}} = m_{Teflon} c_{Teflon} (T_f - 430°\text{C})$$

and

$$Q_{gained \text{ by water}} = m_{water} c_{water} (T_f - 20°\text{C})$$

By conservation of energy (ignoring the heat transfer to the air or the beaker), the heat lost by the Teflon is equal to the heat absorbed by the water. Since $Q_{\text{lost by Teflon}}$ is heat going *out*, it's negative, and since $Q_{\text{gained by water}}$ is heat coming *in*, it's positive. To account for the signs, we have to write

$$Q_{\text{lost by Teflon}} = -Q_{\text{gained by water}}$$

so

$$m_{\text{Teflon}} c_{\text{Teflon}} \left(T_f - 430°C \right) = -m_{\text{water}} c_{\text{water}} \left(T_f - 20°C \right)$$

$$T_f - 430°C = -\frac{m_{\text{water}} c_{\text{water}}}{m_{\text{Teflon}} c_{\text{Teflon}}} \left(T_f - 20°C \right)$$

$$T_f - 430°C = -40 \left(T_f - 20°C \right)$$

$$41 T_f = 1230°C$$

$$T_f = 30°C$$

Notice how little the temperature of the water changed. Water has a very high specific heat and can absorb large amounts of thermal energy without undergoing much of a temperature change. We could have used this same experiment to determine the specific heat of Teflon. Drop a known mass of Teflon at a given temperature into the water and then measure the temperature of the water once thermal equilibrium is reached. Knowing this final temperature, we could solve for c_{Teflon}.

Calorimetry II: Heat Transfer and Phase Changes

Remember that when an object absorbs or loses heat, either its temperature will change or the phase of the object will start to change, *but not both*. For example, if we start heating an ice cube that's at 0°C, the heat causes the ice cube to melt, but the temperature *remains at 0°C throughout the melting process*. Only when the ice cube has completely melted will any additional heat cause the temperature to rise.

The equation that applies during the melting of the ice cube (or during any other phase transition) is the following:

$$Q = mL$$

where L is the **latent heat of transformation**.

This equation tells us how much heat must be transferred to cause a sample of mass m to completely undergo a phase change. In the case of a solid-to-liquid (or vice versa) phase change, L is called the latent **heat of fusion**. For a phase change between liquid and vapor, L is called the latent **heat of vaporization**.

4. The heat of fusion for water is 334 kJ/kg. How much thermal energy is required to completely melt a 100-gram ice cube?

Here's How to Crack It

The change in phase from solid to liquid requires the input of heat; in this case, $Q = mL = (0.1 \text{ kg})(334 \text{ kJ/kg}) = 33.4 \text{ kJ}$.

5. A beaker contains 0.1 kg of water, initially at room temperature (20°C). If the specific heat of water is 4.2 J/kg × °C and the latent heat of vaporization is 2,300 kJ/kg, how much thermal energy would the water need to absorb to turn completely to steam?

Here's How to Crack It

First we need to heat the water to the boiling point, 100°C; then we need to continue to add heat until all the liquid is vaporized. The amount of thermal energy required for the first step is

$$
\begin{aligned}
Q_1 &= m_{\text{water}} c_{\text{water}} \left(100°C - 20°C\right) \\
&= (0.1 \text{ kg})\left(4.2 \text{ kJ/kg·°C}\right)\left(80°C\right) \\
&= 33.6 \text{ kJ}
\end{aligned}
$$

and the amount of energy required for the second step is

$$
Q_2 = m_{\text{water}} L_{\text{vap}} = (0.1 \text{ kg})(2,300 \text{ kJ/Kg}) = 230 \text{ kJ}
$$

Therefore, the total amount of thermal energy required is

$$
Q_{\text{total}} = Q_1 + Q_2 = 33.6 \text{ kJ} + 230 \text{ kJ} = 264 \text{ kJ}
$$

HEAT TRANSFER AND THERMAL EXPANSION

When a substance undergoes a temperature change, it changes in size. Steel beams that form railroad tracks expand when they get warmer; a balloon filled with air shrinks when it's placed in a freezer. The change in size of a substance due to a temperature change depends on the amount of the temperature change and the identity of the substance.

Let's first talk about changes in length (of the steel beam, for example). When its temperature is T_0, its length is L_0. Then, if its temperature changes to T_f, the length changes to L_f, such that

$$L_f - L_0 = \alpha L_i (T_f - T_0)$$

where α is the **coefficient of linear expansion** of the material. This equation is usually used in the simpler form

$$\Delta L = \alpha L_0 \Delta T$$

Nearly all substances have a positive value of α, which means that they expand upon heating.

6. A steel beam used in the construction of a bridge has a length of 30.0 m when the temperature is 15°C. On a very hot day, when the temperature is 35°C, how long will the beam be? (The coefficient of linear expansion for structural steel is $+1.2 \times 10^{-5}$/°C.)

Here's How to Crack It

The change in length of the beam is

$$\Delta L = \alpha L_0 \Delta T = \frac{1.2 \times 10^{-5}}{°C} \left(30.0 \text{ m}\right)\left(35°C - 15°C\right) = 7.2 \times 10^{-3} \text{ m} = 7.2 \text{ mm}$$

As we've mentioned, substances also undergo volume changes when heat is lost or absorbed. The change in volume, ΔV, corresponding to a temperature change, ΔT, is given by the equation

$$\Delta V = \beta V_0 \Delta T$$

where V_0 is the sample's initial volume and β is the **coefficient of volume expansion** of the substance. Since we're now looking at the change in a three-dimensional quantity (volume) rather than a one-dimensional quantity (length), for most solids, $\beta \approx 3\alpha$. Nearly all substances have a positive value of β, which means they expand upon heating. An extremely important example of a substance with a *negative* value of β is liquid water between 0°C and 4°C. Unlike the vast majority of substances, liquid water *expands* as it nears its freezing point and solidifies (which is why ice has a lower density and floats in water).

7. The mercury in a household glass-tube thermometer has a volume of 500 mm³ (= 5.0 × 10⁻⁷ m³) at $T = 19°C$. The hollow column within which the mercury can rise or fall has a cross-sectional area of 0.1 mm² (= 1.0 × 10⁻⁷ m²). Ignoring the volume expansion of the glass, how much will the mercury rise in the thermometer when its temperature is 39°C ? (The coefficient of volume expansion of mercury is 1.8 × 10⁻⁴/°C.)

Here's How to Crack It

First let's figure out by how much the volume of the mercury increases.

$$\Delta V = \beta V_0 \Delta T = \frac{1.8 \times 10^{-4}}{°C}\left(5.0 \times 10^{-7}\ \text{m}^3\right)\left(39°C - 19°C\right) = 1.8 \times 10^{-9}\ \text{m}^3$$

Now, since *volume = cross-sectional area × height*, the change in height of the mercury column will be

$$\Delta h = \frac{\Delta V}{A} = \frac{1.8 \times 10^{-9}\ \text{m}^3}{1.0 \times 10^{-7}\ \text{m}^2} = 1.8 \times 10^{-2}\ \text{m} = 1.8\ \text{cm}$$

THE KINETIC THEORY OF GASES

Unlike the condensed phases of matter—solid and liquid—the atoms or molecules that make up a gas do not move around relatively fixed positions. Rather, the molecules of a gas move freely and rapidly, in a chaotic swarm.

A confined gas exerts a force on the walls of its container because the molecules are zipping around inside the container, striking the walls and rebounding. The magnitude of the force per unit area is called **pressure**, and is denoted by P.

$$P = \frac{F}{A}$$

The SI unit for pressure is the N/m^2, the **pascal** (abbreviated **Pa**). As we'll see, the faster the gas molecules are moving, the more pressure they exert. Be careful not to confuse pressure and force. Pressure is force divided by the area over which the force acts. For example, if you placed a box weighing 1,000 N on a tabletop whose area was 1 m^2, then the pressure would be 1,000 pascals. But if that same box were placed on a thin vertical column whose top had an area of only 1 cm^2 (or 10^{-4} m^2), then the pressure would be 10,000,000 pascals. In each case, the force was the same, but the areas over which the force acted were different, which is why the pressures were different.

We also need a way to talk about the typically vast numbers of molecules in a given sample of gas. One **mole** of atoms or molecules contains

$$N_A = 6.022 \times 10^{23}$$

of these elementary quantities. The number N_A is known as **Avogadro's constant**, and the mass of one mole of any substance is its atomic or molecular mass (these values are given in the Periodic Table of Elements). For example, the mass of a carbon-12 atom (the most abundant isotope of carbon) has a mass of exactly 12 atomic mass units, and a mole of these atoms has a mass of 12 grams. Oxygen has an atomic mass of 16 g, so a mole of carbon dioxide (CO_2), which is made up of one carbon atom and two oxygen atoms, has a mass of 12 g + 2(16 g) = 44 g.

THE IDEAL GAS LAW

Three physical properties—pressure (P), volume (V), and temperature (T)—are commonly used to describe a gas. Ideal gases exhibit certain properties: the volume of the gas molecules is negligible compared with that of the container that holds them, they experience no electrical forces, and undergo elastic collisions. These three variables are related by the equation

$$PV = nRT$$

where n is the number of moles of gas and R is a constant (8.31 J/mol·K) called the **universal gas constant**. This equation is known as the **ideal gas law.**

This equation tells us that for a fixed volume of gas, an increase in P gives a proportional increase in T. The pressure increases when the gas molecules strike the walls of their container with more force, which occurs if they move more rapidly.

Also, the equation

$$K_{avg} = \frac{3}{2} k_B T$$

tells us that the average translational kinetic energy of the gas molecules is directly proportional to the absolute temperature of the sample.

From this we can find root-mean-square (a kind of average) speed of the gas molecule.

$$v_{rms} = \sqrt{\frac{3k_B T}{m}}$$

Because $k_B = R/N_A$ and $mN_A = M$ (the mass of one mole of the molecules—the **molar mass**), the equation for v_{rms} is also often written as follows:

$$v_{rms} = \sqrt{\frac{3RT}{M}}$$

Notice that these last two equations can only determine v_{rms}. It's important to realize that the molecules in the container have a wide *range* of speeds; some are much slower and others are much faster than v_{rms}. The root-mean-square speed is important because it gives us a type of average speed that's easy to calculate from the temperature of the gas.

8. What happens to the rms speed of the molecules in a sample of helium gas if the temperature is increased from –73°C to 527°C ?

Here's How to Crack It

When we use the ideal gas law or the formulas for v_{rms}, we have to use absolute temperatures—that is, temperatures expressed in kelvins. The conversion between degrees Celsius and kelvins is $T_{°C} + 273 = T$, so –73°C = 200 K and 527°C = 800 K. Therefore, the absolute temperature of the gas is increased by a factor of 4 (from 200 K to 800 K). Since v_{rms} is proportional to $\sqrt{T}$, if T increases by a factor of 4, then v_{rms} increases by a factor of $\sqrt{4} = 2$.

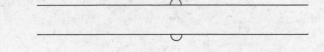

9. What happens to the pressure of a sample of helium gas if the temperature is increased from 200 K to 800 K, with no change in volume?

Here's How to Crack It

The ideal gas laws, $PV = nRT$, tells us that if V remains constant, then P is proportional to T. So, if T increases by a factor of 4, then so will P.

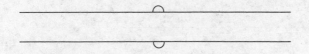

10. What happens to the pressure of a sample of helium gas if the volume is reduced from 6 liters to 3 liters, with no change in temperature?

Here's How to Crack It

The ideal gas law, $PV = nRT$, tell us that if T remains constant, then P is inversely proportional to V. So, if V decreases by a factor of 2, then P will increase by a factor of 2.

THE LAWS OF THERMODYNAMICS

We've learned about two ways in which energy can be transferred between a system and its environment. One is work, which takes place when a force acts over a distance. The other is heat, which takes place when energy is transferred due to a difference in temperature. The study of the energy transfers involving work and heat, and the resulting changes in internal energy, temperature, volume, and pressure is called **thermodynamics**.

The Zeroth Law of Thermodynamics

When two objects are brought into contact, heat will flow from the warmer object to the cooler one until they reach thermal equilibrium. This property of temperature is expressed by the **zeroth law of thermodynamics.**

> If objects 1 and 2 are each in thermal equilibrium with object 3, then objects 1 and 2 are in thermal equilibrium with each other.

The First Law of Thermodynamics

Simply put, the **first law of thermodynamics** is a statement of the conservation of energy that includes heat.

> Energy (in the form of heat) is neither created nor destroyed in any thermodynamic system.

The mathematical equation that corresponds to this law is

$$\Delta U = Q - W$$

Where ΔU is the change in internal energy of the system, Q is the heat added to the system, and W is the work done by the system. U depends on the state of the system.

Consider the following example. An insulated container filled with an ideal gas rests on a heat reservoir (something that can act as a heat source or a heat sink). The container is fitted with a snug, but frictionless, weighted piston that can be raised or lowered. The confined gas is the *system*, and the piston and heat reservoir are the *surroundings*.

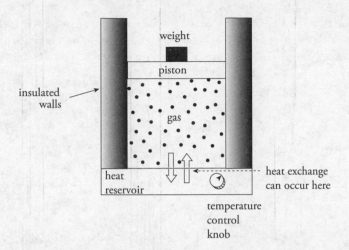

insulated walls

weight

piston

gas

heat reservoir

heat exchange can occur here

temperature control knob

The **state** of the gas is given once its pressure, volume, and temperature are known, and the equation that connects these state variables is the ideal gas law, $PV = nRT$. We'll imagine performing different experiments with the gas, such as heating it or allowing it to cool, increasing or decreasing the weight on the piston, and so on, and study the energy transfers (work and heat) and the changes in the state variables. If each process is carried out such that at each moment, the system and its surroundings are in thermal equilibrium, we can plot the pressure (P) versus the volume (V) on a diagram. By following the path of this **P–V diagram**, we can study how the system is affected as it moves from one state to another.

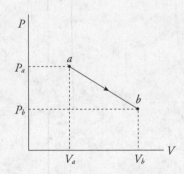

Work is done on or by the system when the piston is moved and the volume of the gas changes. For example, imagine that the gas pushes the piston upward, causing an increase in volume. The work done by the gas during its expansion is $W = F \Delta s$, but since $F = PA$, we have $W = PA \Delta s$, and because $A \Delta s = \Delta V$, we have

$$W = P \Delta V$$

This equation is also true if the piston is pushed down and the volume of the gas decreases. In this case, ΔV is negative, so W is negative. In general, then, W is positive when the system does work against its surroundings, and W is negative when the surroundings do work on the system.

The equation $W = P\Delta V$ assumes that the pressure P does not change during the process. If P *does* change, then the work is equal to the area under the curve in the P–V diagram; moving left to right gives a positive area (and positive work), while moving right to left gives a negative area (and negative work).

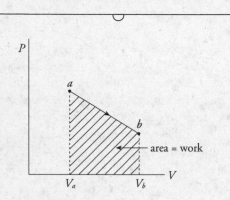

11. What's the value of W for the process ab following path 1 and for the same process following path 2, shown in the P–V diagram below?

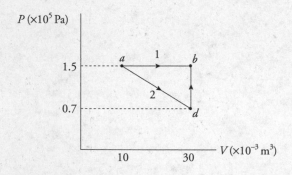

Here's How to Crack It
Path 1. Since, in path 1, P remains constant, the work done is just $P\Delta V$.

$$W = P\Delta V = (1.5 \times 10^5 \text{ Pa})[(30 \times 10^{-3} \text{ m}^3) - (10 \times 10^{-3} \text{ m}^3)] = 3{,}000 \text{ J}$$

Path 2. If the gas is brought from state *a* to state *b*, along path 2, then work is done only along the part from *a* to *d*. From *d* to *b*, the volume of the gas does not change, so no work can be performed. The area under the graph from *a* to *d* is

$$W = \frac{1}{2}h(b_1 + b_2) = \frac{1}{2}(\Delta V)(P_a + P_d)$$

$$= \frac{1}{2}(20 \times 10^{-3}\ \text{m}^3)[(1.5 \times 10^5\ \text{Pa}) + (0.7 \times 10^5\ \text{Pa})]$$

$$= 2{,}200\ \text{J}$$

As this example shows, the value of *W* depends not only on the initial and final states of the system, but also on the path between the two. In general, different paths give different values for *W*.

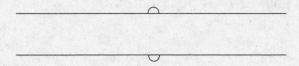

Questions 12-13

For the previous *P–V* diagram,

12. Find the work done by the system for the path *abda*.

13. Find the heat absorbed by the system along this same path.

Here's How to Crack It

12. From the previous problem, we learned that, for the process *ab*, W=3,000 J and for process *bd*, W=0. Since W=2,200 J for the process *ad*, then W for *da* would be -2,200 J (ΔV is negative.) Therefore, the total W=3,000 J - 2200 J = 800 J

13. Since *U* depends on the state of the system, for any closed path on a *P–V* diagram $\Delta U = 0$. Since $\Delta U = Q - W$, we have 0=Q - 800 J, therefore Q=800 J.

A process where the temperature remains constant is referred to as **isothermal**. If there is no heat exchanged between the system and its surroundings, the process is adiabatic.

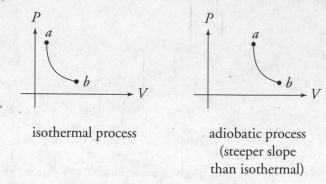

isothermal process

adiobatic process
(steeper slope
than isothermal)

The Second Law of Thermodynamics

Entropy

Consider a box containing two pure gases separated by a partition. What would happen if the partition were removed? The gases would mix, and the positions of the gas molecules would be random.

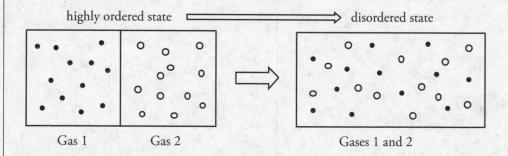

A closed system that shows a high degree of order tends to evolve in such a way that its degree of order decreases. In other words, *disorder* (or, as it's technically called, **entropy**) *increases*. If we started with the box on the right, containing the mixture of the gases, it would be virtually impossible that at any later time all the molecules of Gas 1 would happen to move to the left side of the box and, at the same time, the molecules of Gas 2 would spontaneously move to the right side of the box. If we were to watch a movie of this process, and saw the mixed-up molecules suddenly separate and move to opposite sides of the box, we'd assume that the film was running backward. In a way, the second law of thermodynamics defines the direction of time: Time flows in such a way that ordered systems become disordered. Disordered states do not spontaneously become ordered without any other change taking place. The following is the essence of one form of the **second law of thermodynamics**:

> The total amount of disorder—the total entropy—of a system plus its surroundings will never decrease.

Now, it is possible for the entropy of a system to decrease, but it'll always be at the expense of a greater increase in entropy in the surroundings. For example, when water freezes, its entropy decreases. The molecules making up an ice crystal have a more structured order than the random collection of water molecules in the liquid phase, so the entropy of the water decreases when it freezes. But when water freezes, it releases heat energy into its environment, which creates disorder in the surroundings. If we were to figure out the total change in entropy of the water *plus its surroundings*, we'd find that although the entropy of the water itself decreased, it was more than compensated by a greater amount of entropy *increase* in the surroundings. So, the *total* entropy of the system and its surroundings increased, in agreement with the second law of thermodynamics.

Efficiency of heat engines Converting work to heat is easy—rubbing your hands together shows that work can be converted to heat. What we'll look at now is the reverse process: How efficiently can heat be converted into work? A device that uses heat to produce useful work is called a **heat engine**. The internal-combustion engine in a car is an example. Certain types of engines take their working substance (a mixture of air and fuel in the case of a car engine) through a cyclic process, so that the cycle can be repeated. The basic components of any cyclic heat engine are simple: Energy in the form of heat comes into the engine from a high-temperature source, some of this energy is converted into useful work, the remainder is ejected as exhaust heat into a low-temperature sink, and the system returns to its original state to run through the cycle again.

Since we're looking at cyclic engines only, the system returns to its original state at the end of each cycle, so ΔU must be 0. Therefore, by the first law of thermodynamics, $Q_{net} = W$. So, the net heat absorbed by the system is equal to the work performed by the system. The heat that's absorbed from the high-temperature source is Q_H (H for *hot*), and the heat that is discharged into the low-temperature reservoir is Q_C (C for *cold*). Because heat coming *in* is positive and heat going *out* is negative, Q_H is positive and Q_C is negative, and the net heat absorbed is $Q_H + Q_C$. Instead of writing Q_{net} in this way, we usually write it as $Q_H - |Q_C|$, to show that Q_{net} is less than Q_H. The thermal efficiency, e, of the heat engine is equal to the ratio of what we get out to what we have to put in—that is, $e = Q_W/Q_H$. Since $W = Q_{net} = Q_H - |Q_C|$, we have

$$e = \frac{Q_H - |Q_C|}{Q_H} = 1 - \frac{|Q_C|}{Q_H}$$

Notice that unless $Q_C = 0$, the engine's efficiency is *always* less than 1. Here is another form of the second law of thermodynamics.

For any cyclic heat engine, some exhaust heat is always produced. Because $Q_C \neq 0$, no cyclic heat engine can operate at 100% efficiency; it is impossible to completely convert heat into useful work.

14. A heat engine draws 800 J of heat from its high-temperature source and discards 600 J of exhaust heat into its cold-temperature reservoir each cycle. How much work does this engine perform per cycle, and what is its thermal efficiency?

Here's How to Crack It

The work output per cycle is equal to the difference between the heat energy drawn in and the heat energy discarded.

$$W = Q_{\mathrm{H}} - \left|Q_{\mathrm{C}}\right| = 800 \text{ J} - 600 \text{ J} = 200 .$$

The efficiency of this engine is

$$e = \frac{W}{Q_{\mathrm{H}}} = \frac{200 \text{ J}}{800 \text{ J}} = 0.25 = 25\%$$

The Carnot Cycle

The most efficient heat engine follows what is known as the Carnot cycle: isothermal expansion, followed by adiabatic expansion, followed by isothermal compression, followed by adiabatic compression.

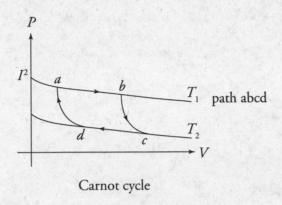

Carnot cycle

For the Carnot cycle, efficiency can be written as

$$e = \frac{T_H - T_C}{T_H} = 1 - \frac{T_C}{T_H}$$

where T_H and T_C are temperatures of the hot and cold reservoirs, respectively.

Chapter 9 Review Questions

Answers are on page 404.

1. How much heat is required to raise the temperature of a 0.04 kg stainless steel spoon from 20°C to 50°C if the specific heat of stainless steel is 0.50 kJ/kg × °C ?

   (A) 200 J
   (B) 400 J
   (C) 600 J
   (D) 800 J
   (E) 1,000 J

2. The melting point of copper is 1,080°C and its heat of fusion is 200 kJ/kg. If a copper coin at this temperature is completely melted by the absorption of 2,000 J of heat, what is the mass of the coin?

   (A) $\dfrac{1}{1,080 \text{ kg}}$

   (B) $\dfrac{1}{540 \text{ kg}}$

   (C) $\dfrac{1}{108 \text{ kg}}$

   (D) $\dfrac{1}{100 \text{ kg}}$

   (E) $\dfrac{1}{50 \text{ kg}}$

3. Water has the specific heat 4.186 kJ/kg·°C, a boiling point of 100°C, and a heat of vaporization of 2,260 kJ/kg. A sealed beaker contains 100 g of water that's initially at 20°C. If the water absorbs 100 kJ of heat, what will its final temperature be?

   (A) 100°C
   (B) 119°C
   (C) 143°C
   (D) 183°C
   (E) 239°C

4. On a cold winter day (5°C), the foundation block for a statue is filled with 2.0 m3 of concrete. By how much will the concrete's volume increase on a very warm summer day (35°C) if its coefficient of volume expansion is 4.0×10^{-5}/°C ?

   (A) 160 cm^3
   (B) 1,200 cm^3
   (C) 1,600 cm^3
   (D) 2,400 cm^3
   (E) 3,200 cm^3

5. An ideal gas is confined to a container whose volume is fixed. If the container holds n moles of gas, by what factor will the pressure increase if the absolute temperature is increased by a factor of 2 ?

   (A) $\dfrac{2}{(nR)}$

   (B) 2

   (C) $2nR$

   (D) $\dfrac{2}{n}$

   (E) $\dfrac{2}{R}$

6. Two large glass containers of equal volume each hold 1 mole of gas. Container 1 is filled with hydrogen gas (2 g/mol), and Container 2 holds helium (4 g/mol). If the pressure of the gas in Container 1 equals the pressure of the gas in Container 2, which of the following is true?

(A) The temperature of the gas in Container 1 is lower than the temperature of the gas in Container 2.
(B) The temperature of the gas in Container 1 is greater than the temperature of the gas in Container 2.
(C) The value of R for the gas in Container 1 is $\frac{1}{2}$ the value of R for the gas in Container 2.
(D) The rms speed of the gas molecules in Container 1 is lower than the rms speed of the gas molecules in Container 2.
(E) The rms speed of the gas molecules in Container 1 is greater than the rms speed of the gas molecules in Container 2.

7. Through a series of thermodynamic processes, the internal energy of a sample of confined gas is increased by 560 J. If the net amount of work done on the sample by its surroundings is 320 J, how much heat was transferred between the gas and its environment?

(A) 240 J absorbed
(B) 240 J dissipated
(C) 880 J absorbed
(D) 880 J dissipated
(E) None of the above

8. What's the total work performed on the gas as it's transformed from state a to state c, along the path indicated?

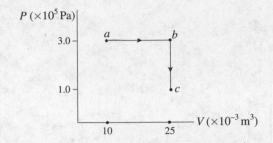

(A) 1,500 J
(B) 3,000 J
(C) 4,500 J
(D) 5,000 J
(E) 9,500 J

9. During each cycle, a heat engine absorbs 400 J of heat from its high-temperature source and discards 300 J of heat into its low-temperature sink. What is the efficiency of this engine?

(A) $\frac{1}{7}$

(B) $\frac{1}{4}$

(C) $\frac{3}{7}$

(D) $\frac{4}{7}$

(E) $\frac{3}{4}$

10. Of the following, which is the best description of the second law of thermodynamics?

(A) The total energy of the universe is a constant.
(B) The efficiency of a heat engine can never be greater than 50 percent.
(C) The amount of heat required to vaporize a liquid is greater than the amount of heat required to melt a solid of the same substance.
(D) The entropy of the universe is always increasing.
(E) As the altitude increases, the boiling point of water decreases.

Keywords

heat
thermal energy
temperature
degrees Fahrenheit
degrees Celsius
absolute temperature scale
kelvins (K)
triple point of water
solid
liquid
vapor
gas
melts
liquefies
freezes
solidifies
evaporate
condense
sublimate
deposition
specific heat
thermal equilibrium
latent heat of transformation
heat of fusion
heat of vaporization
coefficient of linear expansion
coefficient of volume expansion
pressure
pascal (Pa)
mole
Avogadro's constant
universal gas constant
ideal gas law
molar mass
thermodynamics
zeroth law of thermodynamics
first law of thermodynamics
state
P–V diagram
entropy
second law of thermodynamics
heat engine
adiabatic
isothermal
efficiency
Carnot cycle
internal energy

Summary

o Heat is thermal energy that is transferred from one body to another. Heat is energy that is in transit. Temperature is a measure of the concentration of an object's internal thermal energy.

o When a substance absorbs or gives off heat, either the temperature of the substance can change, or the substance can undergo a phase change, *but not both.*

o The change of a substance's temperature depends upon the specific heat of the substance and the amount of the substance present. Use the equation $Q = mc\,\Delta T$.

o The temperature of a substance remains constant during the substance's phase transition. Use the formula $Q = mL$.

o Heat transfer and thermal expansion are related in that when a substance undergoes a temperature change, it changes in size.

o Because the atoms or molecules that make up a gas move freely and rapidly in a chaotic swarm, a confined gas exerts a force in the walls of its container. To find this pressure, use the equation $P = \dfrac{F}{A}$.

o The ideal gas law, $PV = nRT$, covers ideal gases, which have the following properties:
   1. The volume of the gas molecules is negligible compared to that of the container which holds them.
   2. They experience no electrical forces.
   3. They undergo elastic collisions.

o The zeroth law of thermodynamics states that when two objects are brought into contact, heat flows from the warmer object to the cooler one.

o The first law of thermodynamics states that energy (in the form of heat) is neither created nor destroyed in any thermodynamic system.

o The second law of thermodynamics states that the total amount of disorder—the total entropy—of a system plus its surroundings will never decrease.

o A heat engine is a device that uses heat to produce useful work. To determine the efficiency of a heat engine, use the formula

$$e = \frac{Q_H - |Q_C|}{Q_H} = 1 - \frac{|Q_C|}{Q_H}.$$ Unless $Q_C = 0$, the

engine's efficiency is always less than 1.

o For a Carnot engine, $e = \dfrac{T_H - T_C}{T_H} = 1 - \dfrac{T_C}{T_H}$

o The change of internal energy is zero for a closed path on a P–V diagram.

Chapter 10
Electric Forces
and Fields

Perhaps not surprisingly, you do not need to know
a lot of chemistry for the SAT Physics Subject Test.
What you do need to know is that the basic components of atoms are protons, neutrons, and electrons. In
this chapter we will show you all that you will need to
know about these sub-atomic particles, Coulomb's law,
and the electrical field.

ELECTRIC CHARGE

Protons and neutrons form the nucleus of the atom (and are referred to collectively as *nucleons*), while the electrons keep their distance, swarming around the nucleus. Most of an atom consists of empty space. In fact, if a nucleus were the size of the period at the end of this sentence, then the electrons would be 5 meters away. So what holds atoms together? One of the most powerful forces in nature: the **electromagnetic force**. Protons and electrons have a quality called **electric charge** that gives them an attractive force. Electric charge comes in two varieties: positive and negative. A positive particle always attracts a negative particle, and particles of the same charge always repel each other. Protons are positively charged, and electrons are negatively charged. Neutrons are electrically neutral; they have no charge.

Charge It!
Protons: positive
Electrons: negative
Neutrons: neutral

Protons and electrons are intrinsically charged, but bulk matter is not. This is because the amount of charge on a proton exactly balances the charge on an electron. Since most atoms contain an equal number of protons and electrons, their overall electric charge is 0 because the negative charges cancel out the positive charges. Therefore, for matter to be **charged**, an atom must have unequal numbers of protons and electrons. This can be accomplished by either the removal or addition of electrons (that is, by the **ionization** of some of the object's atoms). If you remove electrons, then the object becomes positively charged, and if you add electrons, then it becomes negatively charged. Furthermore, charge is **conserved**. For example, if you rub a glass rod with a piece of silk, then the silk will acquire a negative charge and the glass will be left with an *equal* positive charge. *Net charge cannot be created or destroyed.* (*Charge* can be created or destroyed—it happens all the time—but *net* charge cannot.)

The magnitude of charge on an electron (and therefore on a proton) is denoted e. This stands for **elementary charge** because it's the basic unit of electric charge. The charge of an ionized atom must be a whole number times e because charge can be added or subtracted only in lumps of size e. For this reason we say that charge is **quantized**. To remind us of the quantized nature of electric charge, the charge of a particle (or object) is denoted by the letter q. In the SI system of units, charge is expressed in **coulombs** (abbreviated **C**). One coulomb is a tremendous amount of charge; the value of e is about 1.6×10^{-19} C.

COULOMB'S LAW

The electric force between two charged particles obeys the same mathematical law as the gravitational force between two masses—that is, it's an inverse-square law. The **electric force** between two particles with charges of q_1 and q_2, separated by a distance r, is given by the equation

$$F_E = k \frac{|q_1 q_2|}{r^2}$$

This is **Coulomb's law**.

The absolute value symbol is needed to give the magnitude of the force. Some books omit the absolute value symbol and state that a negative force indicates attraction while a positive force indicates repulsion. This, however, can lead to confusion. Remember that each charge feels this force, equal in magnitude and indirection (Newton's third law).

Since one of these forces points to the left and one points to the right, calling F_E negative is problematic. They both can't feel a negative force.

The value of the proportionality constant, k, depends on the material between the charged particles. In empty space (vacuum)—or air, for all practical purposes—it is called **Coulomb's constant** and has the value $k = 9 \times 10^9$ N $\times$ m^2/C^2.

Remember that the value of the universal gravitational constant, G, is 6.7×10^{-11} N $\times$ m^2/kg^2. The relative sizes of these fundamental constants show the relative strengths of the electric and gravitational forces. The value of k is orders of magnitude larger than G.

1. Consider two small spheres, one carrying a charge of +4.0 nC and the other a charge of −2.0 nC, separated by a distance of 2 cm. Find the electric force between them. ("n" is the abbreviation for "nano," which means 10^{-9}.)

Here's How to Crack It

The electric force between the spheres is given by Coulomb's law.

$$F_E = k \frac{|q_1 q_2|}{r^2} = \left(9 \times 10^9 \ \text{N} \times \text{m}^2 / \text{C}^2\right) \frac{\left(4.0 \times 10^{-9}\right)\left(2.0 \times 10^{-9} \ \text{C}\right)}{\left(2.0 \times 10^{-2} \text{m}\right)^2} = 1.8 \times 10^{-4} \ \text{N}$$

The force between the spheres is attractive and lies along the line that joins the charges, as we've illustrated below. The two forces shown form an action/reaction pair.

$$q_1 \oplus \xrightarrow{\quad \mathbf{F}_E \quad} \qquad \xleftarrow{\quad -\mathbf{F}_E \quad} \ominus q_2$$

Superposition

Consider three point charges: q_1, q_2, and q_3. The total electric force acting on, say, q_2 is simply the sum of $\mathbf{F}_{1\text{-on-2}}$ (the electric force on q_2 due to q_1, and $\mathbf{F}_{3\text{-on-2}}$ (the electric force on q_2 due to q_3).

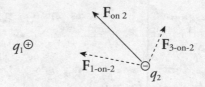

$$\mathbf{F}_{\text{on 2}} = \mathbf{F}_{1\text{-on-2}} + \mathbf{F}_{3\text{-on-2}}$$

The fact that electric forces can be added in this way is known as **superposition.**

2. Consider four equal, positive point charges that are situated at the vertices of a square. Find the net electric force on a negative point charge placed at the square's center.

Here's How to Crack It

Refer to the diagram below. The attractive forces due to the two charges on each diagonal cancel out $F_1 + F_3 = 0$, and $F_2 + F_4 = 0$ because the distances between the negative charge and the positive charges are all the same and the positive charges are all equivalent. Therefore, the net force on the center charge is zero.

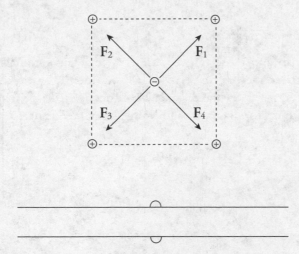

3. If the two positive charges on the bottom side of the square in the previous example were removed, what would be the net electric force on the negative charge? Write your answer in terms of the force that each positive charge exerts on the negative charge.

Here's How to Crack It

If we break down F_1 and F_2 into horizontal and vertical components, then the two horizontal components cancel each other out, and the two vertical components add.

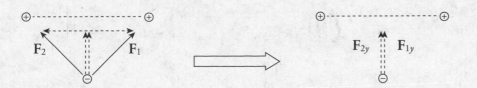

It is clear from the diagram on the left that $\mathbf{F}_{1y} = \mathbf{F}_1 \sin 45°$ and $\mathbf{F}_{2y} = \mathbf{F}_2 \sin 45°$. Also, the magnitude of $\mathbf{F}_1$ equals that of $\mathbf{F}_2$. So the net electric force on the negative charge is $\mathbf{F}_{1y} + \mathbf{F}_{2y} = 2\mathbf{F} \sin 45°$, where $\mathbf{F}$ is the strength of the force between the negative charge and each of the positive charges.

$$F_E = 2F \sin 45° = 2F \times \frac{\sqrt{2}}{2}$$
$$= F\sqrt{2}$$

The direction of the net force is straight upward, toward the center of the line that joins the two positive charges.

THE ELECTRIC FIELD

Objects on Earth (and those in orbit) experience a gravitational force directed toward the earth's center. For objects located outside the earth, this force varies inversely with the square of the distance and directly with the mass of the gravitational source. A vector diagram of the gravitational field surrounding the earth looks like the following:

We can think of the space surrounding the earth as permeated by a **gravitational field** that's created by the earth. Any mass that's placed in this field experiences a gravitational force due to this field.

The same process is used to describe the electric force. Rather than having two charges reach out across empty space to each other to produce a force, we can instead interpret the interaction in the following way: The presence of a charge creates an **electric field** in the space that surrounds it. Another charge placed in the field created by the first will experience a force due to the field.

Consider a point charge Q in a fixed position and assume that it's positive. Now imagine moving a tiny positive test charge q around to various locations near Q. At each location, measure the force that the test charge experiences, and call it $\mathbf{F}_{on\ q}$. Divide this force by the test charge q; the resulting vector is the **electric field vector**, $\mathbf{E}$, at that location.

$$\mathbf{E} = \frac{\mathbf{F}_{on\ q}}{q}$$

The reason for dividing by the test charge is simple. If we were to use a different test charge with, say, twice the charge of the first one, then each of the forces $\mathbf{F}$ we'd measure would be twice as much as before. But when we divided this new, stronger force by the new, greater test charge, the factors of 2 would cancel, leaving the same ratio as before. So this ratio tells us the intrinsic strength of the field due to the source charge, independent of whatever test charge we may use to measure it.

What would the electric field of a positive charge Q look like? Since the test charge used to measure the field is positive, every electric field vector would point radially away from the source charge. If the source charge is positive, the electric field vectors point away from it; if the source charge is negative, then the field vectors point toward it. Since the force decreases as we get farther away from the charge (as $1/r^2$), so does the electric field. This is why the electric field vectors farther from the source charge are shorter than those that are closer.

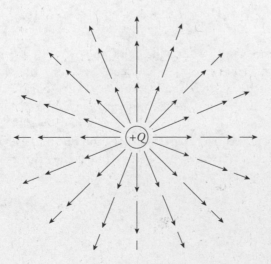

Since the force on the test charge q has a strength of kqQ/r^2, when we divide this by q, we get the expression for the strength of the electric field created by a point-charge source of magnitude Q.

$$E = k\frac{Q}{r^2}$$

To make it easier to sketch an electric field, we can draw lines through the vectors such that the electric field vector is tangent to the line everywhere it's drawn.

Now, your first thought might be that obliterating the individual field vectors deprives us of information, since the length of the field vectors told us how strong the field was. Well, although the individual field vectors are gone, the strength of the field can be figured out by looking at the density of the field lines. Where the field lines are denser, the field is stronger.

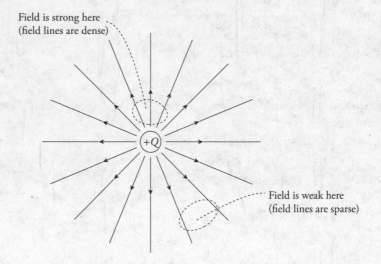

Electric field vectors can be added like any other vectors. If we had two source charges, their fields would overlap and effectively add; a third charge wandering by would feel the effect of the combined field. At each position in space, add the electric field vector due to one of the charges to the electric field vector due to the other charge: $\mathbf{E}_{total} = \mathbf{E}_1 + \mathbf{E}_2$. (This is superposition again.) In the diagram below, $\mathbf{E}_1$ is the electric field vector at a particular location due to the charge $+Q$, and $\mathbf{E}_2$ is the electric field vector at that same location due to the other charge, $-Q$. Adding these vectors gives the overall field vector $\mathbf{E}_{total}$ at that location.

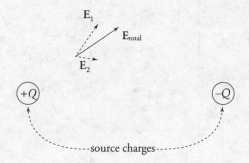

If this is done at enough locations, we can sketch the electric field lines.

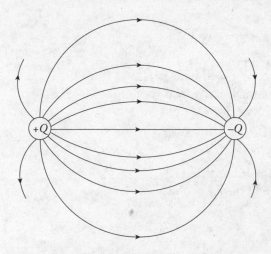

Notice that, as with electric field vectors, electric field lines always point away from positive source charges and toward negative ones. Two equal but opposite charges, like the ones shown in the diagram above, form a pair called an **electric dipole**.

If a positive charge $+q$ were placed in the electric field above, it would experience a force that is tangent to, and in the same direction as, the field line passing through $+q$'s location. After all, electric fields are sketched from the point of view of what a positive test charge would do. However, if a negative charge $-q$ were placed in the electric field, it would experience a force that is tangent to, but in the direction opposite from, the field line passing through $-q$'s location.

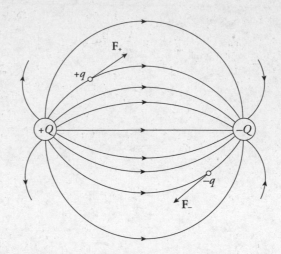

Finally, notice that electric field lines never cross.

---

4. A charge $q = +3.0$ nC is placed at a location at which the electric field strength is 400 N/C. Find the force felt by the charge q.

Here's How to Crack It

From the definition of the electric field, we have the following equation:

$$F_{on\ q} = q\mathbf{E}$$

Therefore, in this case, $F_{on\ q} = q\mathbf{E} = (3 \times 10^{-9}\ \text{C})(400\ \text{N/C}) = 1.2 \times 10^{-6}\ \text{N}.$

---

5. A dipole is formed by two point charges, each of magnitude 4.0 nC, separated by a distance of 6.0 cm. What is the strength of the electric field at the point midway between them?

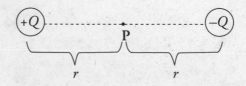

Here's How to Crack It

Let the two source charges be denoted $+Q$ and $-Q$. At Point P, the electric field vector due to $+Q$ would point directly away from $+Q$, and the electric field vector due to $-Q$ would point directly toward $-Q$. Therefore, these two vectors point in the same direction (from $+Q$ to $-Q$), so their magnitudes would add.

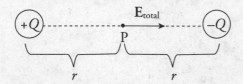

Using the equation for the electric field strength due to a single point charge, we find that

$$E_{total} = k\frac{Q}{r^2} + k\frac{Q}{r^2} = 2k\frac{Q}{r^2}$$

$$= 2(9 \times 10^9 \ N \times m^2 / C^2) \frac{4.0 \times 10^{-9} \ C}{[\frac{1}{2}(6.0 \times 10^{-2} \ m)]^2}$$

$$= 8.0 \times 10^4 \ N/C$$

6. If a charge $q = -5.0$ pC were placed at the midway point described in the previous example, describe the force it would feel. ("p" is the abbreviation for "pico-," which means 10^{-12}.)

Here's How to Crack It

Since the field E at this location is known, the force felt by q is easy to calculate.

$\mathbf{F}_{on \ q} = q\mathbf{E} = (-5.0 \times 10^{-12} \ C)(8.0 \times 10^4 \ N/C \text{ to the right}) = 4.0 \times 10^{-7} \ N \text{ to the } \textit{left}.$

7. What can you say about the electric force that a charge would feel if it were placed at a location at which the electric field was zero?

Here's How to Crack It
Remember that $F_{on\ q} = q\mathbf{E}$. So if $\mathbf{E} = 0$, then $F_{on\ q} = 0$. (Zero field means zero force.)

CONDUCTORS AND INSULATORS

Materials can be broadly classified based on their ability to permit the flow of charge. If electrons were placed on a metal sphere, they would quickly spread out and cover the outside of the sphere uniformly. These electrons would be free to flow through the metal and redistribute themselves, moving to get as far away from one another as they could. Materials that permit the flow of excess charge are called **conductors**; they conduct electricity. Metals are excellent conductors. Metals conduct electricity because the structure of a typical metal consists of a lattice of nuclei and electrons, with about one electron per atom not bound to its nucleus. Electrons are free to move about the lattice, creating a sort of sea of mobile electrons. This freedom allows excess charge to flow freely.

Insulators, however, closely guard their electrons, and even extra ones that might be added. Electrons are not free to roam throughout the atomic lattice. Examples of insulators are glass, wood, rubber, and plastic. If excess charge is placed on an insulator, it stays put.

Midway between conductors and insulators is a class of materials known as **semiconductors**. As the name indicates, they're less conducting than most metals, but more conducting than most insulators. Examples of semiconducting materials are silicon and germanium.

An extreme example of a conductor is the **superconductor**. This is a material that offers absolutely no resistance to the flow of charge; it is a *perfect* conductor of electric charge. Many metals and ceramics become superconducting when they are brought to extremely low temperatures.

8. A solid sphere of copper is given a negative charge. Discuss the electric field inside and outside the sphere.

Here's How to Crack It

The excess electrons that are deposited on the sphere move quickly to the outer surface (copper is a great conductor). Any excess charge on a conductor resides entirely on the outer surface.

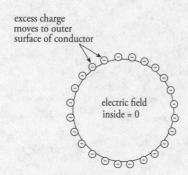

Once these excess electrons establish a uniform distribution on the outer surface of the sphere, there will be no net electric field within the sphere. Why not? Since there is no additional excess charge inside the conductor, there are no excess charges to serve as a source or sink of an electric field line cutting down into the sphere because field lines begin or end on excess charges.

> There can be no electric field within the body of a conductor.

In fact, you can shield yourself from electric fields simply by surrounding yourself with metal. Charges may move around on the outer surface of your cage, but within the cage, the electric field will be zero. Also, the electric field is always perpendicular to the surface, no matter what shape the surface may be.

You can see an example of this when you're listening to the car radio and you pass through a tunnel. In a tunnel, you're surrounded by metal, so the radio signals (which are electromagnetic waves composed of time-varying electric and magnetic fields) can't penetrate inside, and you won't get any reception.

9. If an electron with mass M_e makes a circular orbit of radius r around a proton with mass M_p, what is the speed v of the electron?

Here's How to Crack It

Since the gravitational attraction between the particles is negligible compared to the electrostatic attraction, we can say that $F_E = \dfrac{M_e v^2}{r}$ for the electron to move in a circular path. $F_E = \dfrac{k|q_1 q_2|}{r^2} = \dfrac{ke^2}{r^2}$ Therefore, $\dfrac{ke^2}{r^2} = \dfrac{M_e v^2}{r} \Rightarrow v = e\sqrt{\dfrac{k}{M_e r}}$

Chapter 10 Review Questions

Answers are on page 406.

1. If the distance between two positive point charges is tripled, then the strength of the electrostatic repulsion between them will decrease by a factor of

   (A) 3
   (B) 6
   (C) 8
   (D) 9
   (E) 12

2. Two 1 kg spheres each carry a charge of magnitude 1 C. How does F_E, the strength of the electric force between the spheres, compare with F_G, the strength of their gravitational attraction?

   (A) $F_E < F_G$
   (B) $F_E = F_G$
   (C) $F_E > F_G$
   (D) If the charges on the spheres are of the same sign, then $F_E > F_G$; but if the charges on the spheres are of opposite sign, then $F_E < F_G$.
   (E) Cannot be determined without knowing the distance between the spheres

3. The figure below shows three point charges, all positive. If the net electric force on the center charge is zero, what is the value of $\dfrac{y}{x}$?

   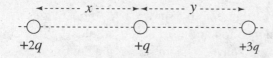

   $+2q$ $+q$ $+3q$

   (A) $\dfrac{4}{9}$

   (B) $\sqrt{\dfrac{2}{3}}$

   (C) $\sqrt{\dfrac{3}{2}}$

   (D) $\dfrac{3}{2}$

   (E) $\dfrac{9}{4}$

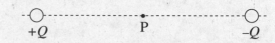

$+Q$ P $-Q$

4. The figure above shows two point charges, $+Q$ and $-Q$. If the negative charge were absent, the electric field at point P due to $+Q$ would have strength E. With $-Q$ in place, what is the strength of the total electric field at P, which lies at the midpoint of the line segment joining the charges?

   (A) 0

   (B) $\dfrac{E}{4}$

   (C) $\dfrac{E}{2}$

   (D) E

   (E) $2E$

5. A sphere of charge $+Q$ is fixed in position. A smaller sphere of charge $+q$ is placed near the larger sphere and released from rest. The small sphere will move away from the large sphere with

   (A) decreasing velocity and decreasing acceleration.
   (B) decreasing velocity and increasing acceleration.
   (C) decreasing velocity and constant acceleration.
   (D) increasing velocity and decreasing acceleration.
   (E) increasing velocity and increasing acceleration.

6. An object of charge $+q$ feels an electric force $\mathbf{F}_E$ when placed at a particular location in an electric field, $\mathbf{E}$. Therefore, if an object of charge $-2q$ were placed at the same location where the first charge was, it would feel an electric force of

(A) $\dfrac{-\mathbf{F}_E}{2}$

(B) $-2\mathbf{F}_E$

(C) $-2q\mathbf{F}_E$

(D) $\dfrac{-2\mathbf{F}_E}{q}$

(E) $\dfrac{-\mathbf{F}_E}{(2q)}$

7. A charge of $-3Q$ is transferred to a solid metal sphere of radius r. Where will this excess charge reside?

(A) $-Q$ at the center, and $-2Q$ on the outer surface

(B) $-2Q$ at the center, and $-Q$ on the outer surface

(C) $-3Q$ at the center

(D) $-3Q$ on the outer surface

(E) $-Q$ at the center, $-Q$ in a ring of radius $\frac{1}{2}r$, and $-Q$ on the outer surface

8. Which of the following statements is true?

(A) Electric field vectors point toward a positive source charge, and the resulting electric force on an electron would point in the same direction as the electric field vector.

(B) Electric field vectors point toward a positive source charge, and the resulting electric force on an electron would point in the opposite direction from the electric field vector.

(C) Electric field vectors point toward a negative source charge, and the resulting electric force on an electron would point in the same direction as the electric field vector.

(D) Electric field vectors point toward a negative source charge, and the resulting electric force on an electron would point in the opposite direction from the electric field vector.

(E) None of the above

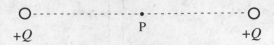

9. The figure above shows two point charges, $+Q$ and $+Q$. If the right-hand charge were absent, the electric field at Point P due to $+Q$ would have a strength of E. With the right-hand charge in place, what is the strength of the total electric field at P, which lies at the midpoint of the line segment joining the charges?

(A) 0

(B) $\dfrac{E}{4}$

(C) $\dfrac{E}{2}$

(D) $2E$

(E) $4E$

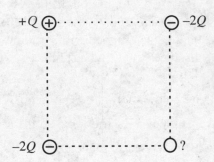

10. The figure above shows four point charges fixed in position at the corners of a square. What charge would have to be present at the bottom right location for the electric field at the center of the square to be zero?

(A) $+Q$
(B) $+Q\sqrt{2}$
(C) $+2Q$
(D) $+3Q$
(E) $+4Q$

Keywords

electromagnetic force
electric charge
charged
ionization
conserved
elementary charge
quantized
coulombs
electric force
Coulomb's law
Coulomb's constant
superposition
gravitational field
electric field
electric field vector
electric dipole
conductors
insulators
semiconductors
superconductor

Summary

o   Electric charge is a quality of protons and electrons that gives them an attractive force. Protons are positive, while electrons are negative. Neutrons have no electrical charge.

o   Use Coulomb's law ($F_E = k\dfrac{|q_1 q_2|}{r^2}$) to determine the magnitude electric force between two charged particles with charges of q_1 and q_2 separated by a distance of r^2.

o   Superposition refers to the fact that the total electric force acting on a charge can be determined by summing up the individual contributions to the force of each of the other charges. Electric force is a vector quantity.

o   The presence of a charge creates an electric field in the space that surrounds it. The electric field vectors farther from the source charge are shorter than those that are closer because the force decreases as we get further away from the charge.

o   The electric field points away from positive charges and toward negative charges.

o   Positive charge feel a force in the direction of the electric field and negative charges feel a force opposite to the electric field.

o   Conductors are materials, such as metals, that permit the flow of charge. Electrons are free to flow through metal and redistribute themselves.

o   Insulators are materials, such as wood, glass, rubber and plastic, which inhibit the flow of electrons. Electrons cannot travel through an insulator, so the charge stays put in the material in which it originated.

Chapter 11
Electric Potential and Capacitance

When an object moves in a gravitational field, it usually experiences a change in kinetic energy and in gravitational potential energy because there is work done on the object by gravity. Similarly, when a charge moves in an electric field, it generally experiences a change in kinetic energy and in electrical potential energy because of the work done on it by the electric field. In this chapter we will discuss electric potentials.

ELECTRICAL POTENTIAL ENERGY

As we said, when a charge moves in an electric field, unless its displacement is always perpendicular to the field, the electric force does work on the charge. If W_E is the work done by the electric force, then the change in the charge's **electrical potential energy** is defined by

$$\Delta U_E = -W_E$$

Notice that this is the same equation that defined the change in the gravitational potential energy of an object of mass m undergoing a displacement in a gravitational field ($\Delta U_G = -W_G$).

---

1. A positive charge $+q$ moves from position A to position B in a uniform electric field $\mathbf{E}$

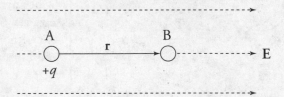

   What is its change in electrical potential energy?

Here's How to Crack It

Since the field is uniform, the electric force that the charge feels, $\mathbf{F}_E = q\mathbf{E}$, is constant. Since q is positive, $\mathbf{F}_E$ points in the same direction as $\mathbf{E}$, and, as the figure shows, they point in the same direction as the displacement, $\mathbf{r}$. This makes the work ($W = Fd$) done by the electric field equal to $W_E = F_E\mathbf{r} = qE\mathbf{r}$, so the change in the electrical potential energy is

$$\Delta U_E = -qE\mathbf{r}$$

Notice that the change in potential energy is negative, which means that potential energy has decreased; this always happens when the field does positive work. It's just like when you drop a rock to the ground: Gravity does positive work, and the rock loses gravitational potential energy.

---

2. Solve the previous problem, but consider the case of a negative charge, $-q$.

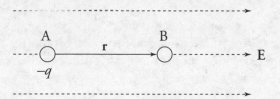

Here's How to Crack It

In this case, an outside agent must be pushing the charge to make it move because the electric force *naturally* pushes negative charges against field lines. Therefore, we expect that the work done by the electric field is negative. The electric force, $F_E = (-q)E$, points in the direction opposite to the displacement, so the work it does is $W_E = -F_E r = -qEr$, and the change in electrical potential energy is positive: $\Delta U_E = -W_E = -(-qEr) = qEr$. Since the change in potential energy is positive, the potential energy has increased; this always happens when the field does negative work. It's like when you lift a rock off the ground: Gravity does negative work, and the rock gains gravitational potential energy.

ELECTRIC POTENTIAL

Consider a point charge q_1 at a distance r_1 from a fixed charge q_2 moving by some means to a position r_2

How much work did the electric force perform during this displacement? The answer is given by the equation $W_E = -kq_1q_2(\dfrac{1}{r_2} - \dfrac{1}{r_1})$

Therefore, since $\Delta U_E = -W_E$ we get $U_2 - U_1 = kq_1q_2(\dfrac{1}{r_2} - \dfrac{1}{r_1})$

Let's choose our $U=U$ reference at infinity. Then this equation becomes $U_E = \dfrac{kq_1q_2}{r}$

Notice that if q_1 and q_2 have the same sign, U_E is positive. This means it took positive work by an external force to bring these charges together (since they repel each other). If q_1 and q_2 have opposite signs, U_E is negative. This means the electric force does positive work to bring these changes together (since they attract).

Let's look at another example:

Let W_E be the work done by the electric field on a charge q as it undergoes a displacement. If another charge that's twice as strong, say $2q$, were to undergo the same displacement, the electric force would be twice as great on this second charge, and the work done by the electric field would be twice as much, $2W_E$. Since the work would be twice as much in the second case, the change in electrical potential energy would be twice as great as well, but the ratio of the change in potential energy to the charge would be the same: $\dfrac{\Delta U_E}{q} = \dfrac{2\Delta U_E}{2q}$. This ratio says something about the *field* and the *displacement*, but not the charge that made the move. The change in **electric potential**, ΔV, is defined as this ratio.

$$\Delta V = \frac{\Delta U_E}{q}$$

Electric potential is electrical potential energy *per unit charge*; the units of electric potential are joules per coulomb. One joule per coulomb is called one **volt** (abbreviated V); so $\dfrac{1\text{J}}{\text{C}} = 1$ V.

Consider the electric field that's created by a point source charge Q. The electric potential at a distance r from Q is

$$V = k\frac{Q}{r}.$$

Notice that the potential depends on the source charge making the field and the distance from it.

3. Let $Q = 2 \times 10^{-9}$ C. What is the potential at a point P that is 2 cm from Q?

Here's How to Crack It

Relative to $V = 0$ at infinity, we have

$$V = k\frac{Q}{r} = \left(9 \times 10^9 \ \text{N} \times \text{m}^2/\text{C}^2\right)\frac{2 \times 10^{-9} \ \text{C}}{0.02 \ \text{m}} = 900 \ \text{V}.$$

Notice that, like potential energy, potential is a *scalar*. In the preceding example, we didn't have to specify the direction of the vector from the position of Q to the point P because it didn't matter. At *any* point on a sphere that's 2 cm from Q, the potential will be 900 V. These spheres around Q are called **equipotential surfaces**, and they're surfaces of constant potential. Their cross sections in any plane are circles and are, therefore, perpendicular to the electric field lines. The equipotentials are always perpendicular to the electric field lines.

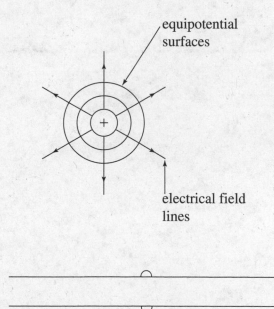

equipotential surfaces

electrical field lines

4. How much work is done by the electric field as a charge moves along an equipotential surface?

Here's How to Crack It
If the charge always remains on a single equipotential, then the potential, V, never changes. Therefore, $\Delta V = 0$, so $\Delta U_E = 0$. Since $W_E = -\Delta U_E$, the work done by the electric field is zero.

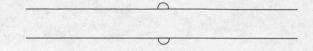

5. Two large, flat plates—one carrying a charge of $+Q$, the other $-Q$—are separated by a distance d. The electric field between the plates, **E**, is uniform. Determine the potential difference between the plates.

Here's How to Crack It
Imagine a positive charge q moving from the positive plate to the negative plate.

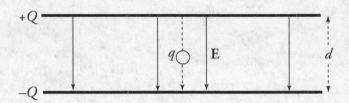

Since the work done by the electric field is

$$W_{E,+\rightarrow-} = F_E d = qEd$$

the potential difference between the plates is

$$V_- - V_+ = \frac{-W_{E,+\rightarrow-}}{q} = \frac{-qEd}{q} = -Ed$$

This tells us that the potential of the positive plate is greater than the potential of the negative plate, by the amount Ed.

CAPACITANCE

You may see a question on capacitors on the SAT Physics Subject Test, so let's discuss them now. Consider two conductors, separated by some distance, that carry equal but opposite charges, $+Q$ and $-Q$. This pair of conductors make up a system called a **capacitor**. Work must be done to create this separation of charge, and, as a result, potential energy is stored. Capacitors are basically storage devices for electrical potential energy.

The most common conductors are parallel metal plates or sheets, and these capacitors are called **parallel-plate capacitors**. We'll assume that the distance d between the plates is small compared to the dimensions of the plates, and in this case, the electric field between the plates is uniform.

The ratio of Q to the voltage, ΔV, for *any* capacitor, is called its **capacitance** (C).

$$C = \frac{Q}{\Delta V}$$

For a parallel-plate capacitor, we have

$$C = \frac{\varepsilon_0 A}{d}$$

Capacitance is a measure of the capacity for holding charge. The greater the capacitance, the more charge can be stored on the plates at a given potential difference. The capacitance of any capacitor depends only on the size, shape, and separation of the conductors. From the definition $C = Q/\Delta V$, the units of C are coulombs per volt. One coulomb per volt is renamed one **farad** (abbreviated F): 1 C/V = 1 F.

Questions 6-7

A 10-nanofarad parallel-plate capacitor holds a charge of magnitude 50 μC on each plate.

6. What is the potential difference between the plates?

7. If the plates are separated by a distance of 0.885 mm, what is the area of each plate?

6.   From the definition, $C = \dfrac{Q}{\Delta V}$, we find that

$$\Delta V = \frac{Q}{C} = \frac{50 \times 10^{-6}\ \text{C}}{10 \times 10^{-9}\ \text{F}} = 5{,}000\ \text{V}$$

7.   From the equation $C = \dfrac{\varepsilon_0 A}{d}$, we can calculate the area, A, of each plate.

$$A = \frac{Cd}{\varepsilon_0} = \frac{\left(10 \times 10^{-9}\ \text{F}\right)\left(0.885 \times 10^{-3}\ \text{m}\right)}{8.85 \times 10^{-12}\ \text{C}^2 / \text{N} \cdot \text{m}^2} = 1.0\ \text{m}^2$$

COMBINATIONS OF CAPACITORS

When a capacitor charges up, work must be done by an external force (for example a battery). This increases the potential energy stored by the capacitor. The potential Energy Stored is given by the formula

$$PE = \frac{1}{2}Q\Delta V = \frac{1}{2}CV^2 = \frac{1}{2}\frac{Q^2}{C}$$

Capacitors are often arranged in combination in electric circuits. Let's review two types of arrangements: the parallel combination and the series combination.

A collection of capacitors are said to be in **parallel** if they all share the same potential difference. The following diagram shows two capacitors wired in parallel.

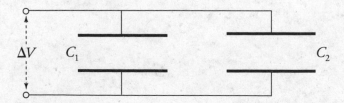

The top plates are connected by a wire and form a single equipotential; the same is true for the bottom plates. Therefore, the potential difference across one capacitor is the same as the potential difference across the other capacitor.

If we want to find the capacitance of a *single* capacitor that would perform the same function as this combination, and if the capacitances are C_1 and C_2, then the charge on the first capacitor is $Q_1 = C_1 \Delta V$ and the charge on the second capacitor is $Q_2 = C_2 \Delta V$. The total charge on the combination is $Q_1 + Q_2$, so the equivalent capacitance, C_p, must be

$$C_P = \frac{Q}{\Delta V} = \frac{Q_1 + Q_2}{\Delta V} = \frac{Q_1}{\Delta V} + \frac{Q_2}{\Delta V}$$

so

$$C_p = C_1 + C_2$$

which can be extended to more than 2 capacitors. So the **equivalent** capacitance of a collection of capacitors in parallel is found by adding the individual capacitances.

A collection of capacitors are said to be in **series** if they all share the same charge magnitude. The following diagram shows two capacitors wired in series.

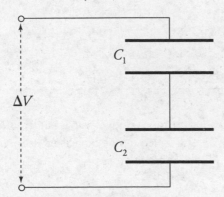

When a potential difference is applied, as shown, negative charge will be deposited on the bottom plate of the bottom capacitor; this will push an equal amount of negative charge away from the top plate of the bottom capacitor toward the bottom plate of the top capacitor. When the system has reached equilibrium, the charges on all the plates will have the same magnitude.

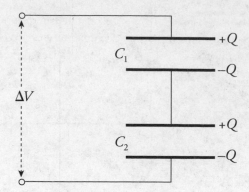

If the top and bottom capacitors have capacitances of C_1 and C_2, respectively, then the potential difference across the top capacitor is $\Delta V_1 = Q/C_1$, and the potential difference across the bottom capacitor is $\Delta V_2 = Q/C_2$. The total potential difference across the combination is $\Delta V_1 + \Delta V_2$, which equals ΔV. Therefore, the equivalent capacitance, C_S, must be

$$C_S = \frac{Q}{\Delta V} = \frac{Q}{\Delta V_1 + \Delta V_2} = \frac{Q}{\dfrac{Q}{C_1} + \dfrac{Q}{C_2}} = \frac{1}{\dfrac{1}{C_1} + \dfrac{1}{C_2}}$$

This can be written as

$$\frac{1}{C_S} = \frac{1}{C_1} + \frac{1}{C_2},$$

which can also be extended to more than 2 capacitators. As you can see, the *reciprocal* of the capacitance of a collection of capacitors in series is found by adding the reciprocals of the individual capacitances.

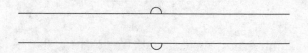

8. Given that $C_1 = 2$ μF, $C_2 = 4$ μF, and $C_3 = 6$ μF, calculate the equivalent capacitance for the following combination:

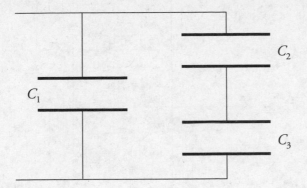

Here's How to Crack It

Notice that C_2 and C_3 are in series, and they are in parallel with C_1. That is, the capacitor equivalent to the series combination of C_2 and C_3 (which we'll call C_{2-3}) is in parallel with C_1. We can represent this as follows:

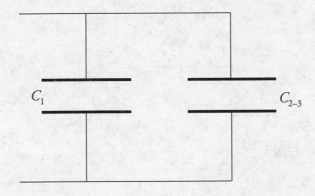

So the first step is to find C_{2-3}.

$$\frac{1}{C_{2-3}} = \frac{1}{C_2} + \frac{1}{C_3} \quad \Rightarrow \quad C_{2-3} = \frac{C_2 C_3}{C_2 + C_3}$$

Now this is in parallel with C_1, so the overall equivalent capacitance (C_{1-2-3}) is

$$C_{1-2-3} = C_1 + C_{2-3} = C_1 + \frac{C_2 C_3}{C_2 + C_3}$$

Substituting in the given numerical values, we get

$$C_{1-2-3} = (2 \ \mu\text{F}) + \frac{(4 \ \mu\text{F})(6 \ \mu\text{F})}{(4 \ \mu\text{F}) + (6 \ \mu\text{F})} = 4.4 \ \mu\text{F}$$

DIELECTRICS

One method of keeping the plates of a capacitor apart, which is necessary to maintain charge separation and store potential energy, is to insert an insulator (called a **dielectric**) between the plates.

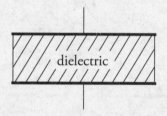

A dielectric always increases the capacitance of a capacitor.

Let's see why this is true. Imagine charging a capacitor to a potential difference of ΔV with charge $+Q$ on one plate and $-Q$ on the other. Now disconnect the capacitor from the charging source and insert a dielectric. What happens? Although the dielectric is not a conductor, the electric field that existed between the plates causes the molecules within the dielectric material to polarize; there is more electron density on the side of the molecule near the positive plate.

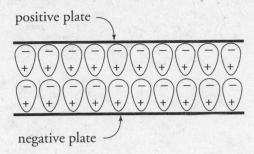

positive plate

negative plate

The effect of this is to form a layer of negative charge along the top surface of the dielectric and a layer of positive charge along the bottom surface; this separation of charge induces its own electric field $(\mathbf{E}_i)$, within the dielectric, which opposes the original electric field, $\mathbf{E}$, within the capacitor.

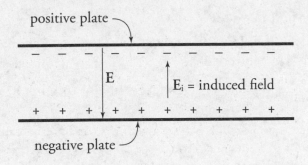

positive plate

$\mathbf{E}$ $\mathbf{E}_i$ = induced field

negative plate

So the overall electric field has been reduced from its previous value: $\mathbf{E}_{total} = \mathbf{E} + \mathbf{E}_i$, and $\mathbf{E}_{total} = \mathbf{E} - \mathbf{E}_i$. Let's say that the electric field has been reduced by a factor of κ (the Greek letter *kappa*) from its original value as follows

$$\mathbf{E}_{\text{with dielectric}} = \mathbf{E}_{\text{without dielectric}} - \mathbf{E}_i = \frac{\mathbf{E}}{\kappa}$$

Since $\Delta V = Ed$ for a parallel-plate capacitor, we see that ΔV must have decreased by a factor of κ. But $C = \dfrac{Q}{\Delta V}$, so if ΔV decreases by a factor of κ, then C increases by a factor of κ:

$$C_{\text{with dielectric}} = \kappa C_{\text{without dielectric}}$$
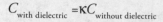

The value of κ, called the **dielectric constant**, varies from material to material, but it's always greater than 1.

———————————————○———————————————

9. A parallel-plate capacitor with air between its plates has a capacitance of $2 \times 10{-6}$ F. What will be the capacitance if the capacitor is fitted with a dielectric whose dielectric constant is 3 ?

Here's How to Crack It

The capacitance *with* a dielectric is equal to κ times the capacitance without, where κ is the dielectric constant. So

$$C_{\text{with dielectic}} = \kappa C_{\text{with dielectic}} = (3)(2 \times 10^{-6}\ \text{F}) = 6 \times 10^{-6}\ \text{F}.$$

Remember that a capacitor with a dielectric always has a greater capacitance than the same capacitor without a dielectric.

———————————————○———————————————

Chapter 11 Review Questions

Answers are on page 408.

1. Which of the following statements is/are true?

    I. If the electric field at a certain point is zero, then the electric potential at the same point is also zero.
    II. If the electric potential at a certain point is zero, then the electric field at the same point is also zero.
    III. The electric potential is inversely proportional to the strength of the electric field.

    (A) I only
    (B) II only
    (C) I and II only
    (D) I and III only
    (E) None are true

2. If the electric field does negative work on a negative charge as the charge undergoes a displacement from position A to position B within an electric field, then the electrical potential energy

    (A) is negative
    (B) is positive
    (C) increases
    (D) decreases
    (E) Cannot be determined from the information given

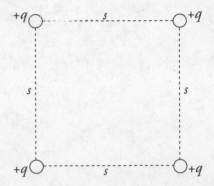

3. The work required to assemble the system shown above, bringing each charge in from an infinite distance, is equal to

    (A) $k\dfrac{4q^2}{s}$

    (B) $k\dfrac{(4+\sqrt{2})q^2}{s}$

    (C) $k\dfrac{6q^2}{s}$

    (D) $k\dfrac{(4+2\sqrt{2})q^2}{s}$

    (E) $k\dfrac{(8+2\sqrt{2})q^2}{s}$

4. Negative charges are accelerated by electric fields toward points

    (A) at lower electric potential
    (B) at higher electric potential
    (C) where the electric field is zero
    (D) where the electric field is weaker
    (E) where the electric field is stronger

5. A charge q experiences a displacement within an electric field from position A to position B. The change in the electrical potential energy is ΔU_E, and the work done by the electric field during this displacement is W_E. Then

(A) $V_B - V_A = \dfrac{W_E}{q}$

(B) $V_A - V_B = qW_E$

(C) $V_B - V_A = qW_E$

(D) $V_A - V_B = \dfrac{U_E}{q}$

(E) $V_B - V_A = \dfrac{U_E}{q}$

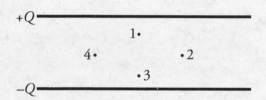

6. Which points in the uniform electric field (between the plates of the capacitor) shown above lie on the same equipotential?

(A) 1 and 2 only
(B) 1 and 3 only
(C) 2 and 4 only
(D) 3 and 4 only
(E) 1, 2, 3, and 4 all lie on the same equipotential, since the electric field is uniform.

7. The potential at point A in an electric field is 10V higher than at point B. If a negative charge, $q = -2$ C, is moved from point A to point B, then the potential energy of this charge will

(A) decrease by 20 J
(B) decrease by 5 J
(C) increase by 5 J
(D) increase by 20 J
(E) increase by 100 J

8. A parallel-plate capacitor is charged to a potential difference of ΔV; this results in a charge of $+Q$ on one plate and a charge of $-Q$ on the other. The capacitor is disconnected from the charging source, and a dielectric is then inserted. What happens to the potential difference and the stored electrical potential energy?

(A) The potential difference decreases, and the stored electrical potential energy decreases.
(B) The potential difference decreases, and the stored electrical potential energy increases.
(C) The potential difference increases, and the stored electrical potential energy decreases.
(D) The potential difference increases, and the stored electrical potential energy increases.
(E) The potential difference decreases, and the stored electrical potential energy remains unchanged.

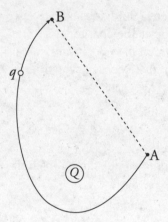

9. How much work would the electric field (created by the stationary charge Q) perform as a charge q is moved from point A to B along the curved path shown?
($V_A = 200$ V, $V_B = 100$ V, $q = -0.05$ C, length of line segment AB = 10 cm, length of curved path = 20 cm.)

(A) -10 J
(B) -5 J
(C) $+5$ J
(D) $+10$ J
(E) $+20$ J

Keywords

electrical potential energy
electric potential
volt
equipotential surfaces
capacitance
parallel-plate capacitors
farad
parallel
equivalent
series
dielectric
dielectric constant

Summary

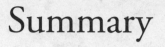

○ The change in the electrical potential energy of a charge is defined by $\Delta U_E = -W_E$. Essentially this is the same equation that defines a change in the gravitational potential energy.

○ Electric potential is electric potential energy per unit charge. The units of electric potential are joules per coulomb. The change in electric potential, ΔV, is defined as $\Delta V = \dfrac{\Delta U_E}{q}$.

○ Capacitance is a measure of the capacity for holding charge. The greater the capacitance, the more charge can be stored on the plates at a given potential difference.

○ Combinations of capacitors often seen in electric circuits. A collection of capacitors is parallel if the capacitors all share the same potential difference. A collection of capacitors is in a series if they all share the same charge magnitude.

○ Dielectrics are insulators that are placed between the plates of a capacitor so that the capacitor can maintain charge separation and store potential energy. A dielectric always increases the capacitance of a capacitor.

Chapter 12
Direct Current Circuits

In Chapter 10, we learned that an electrostatic field cannot be sustained within a conductor: The source charges move to the surface and the conductor forms a single equipotential. We will now look at conductors within which an electric field *can* be sustained because a power source maintains a potential difference across the conductor, allowing charges to continually move through it. This ordered motion of charge through a conductor is called **electric current**.

ELECTRIC CURRENT

Picture a piece of metal wire. Within the metal, electrons are zooming around at speeds of about a million m/s in random directions, colliding with other electrons and positive ions in the lattice. This is charge in motion, but it isn't a *net* movement of charge because the electrons move randomly. If there's no net motion of charge, there's no current. However, if we were to create a potential difference between the ends of the wire, meaning if we set up an electric field

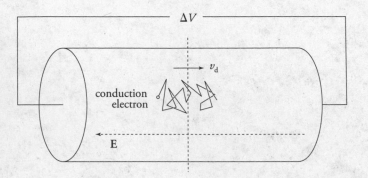

the electrons would experience an electric force, and they would start to drift through the wire. This is **current**. Although the electric field would travel through the wire at nearly the speed of light, the electrons themselves would still have to make their way through a crowd of atoms and other free electrons, so their **drift speed**, v_d, would be relatively slow: about a millimeter per second.

Current vs. Electron Flow
Remember that current is in the direction that positive charges would move (i.e. opposite the direction of electron flow).

To measure the current, we have to measure how much charge crosses a plane per unit time. If an amount of charge of magnitude ΔQ crosses an imaginary plane in a time interval Δt, then the current is:

$$I = \frac{\Delta Q}{\Delta t}$$

Because current is charge per unit time, it's expressed in coulombs per second. One coulomb per second is an **ampere** (abbreviated **A**), or amp. So 1 C/s = 1 A.

Although the charge carriers that constitute the current within a metal are electrons, the direction of the current is the direction that *positive* charge carriers would move. So, if the conduction electrons drift to the right, we'd say the current points toward the left.

RESISTANCE

Let's say we had a copper wire and a glass fiber that had the same length and cross-sectional area, and that we hooked up the ends of the metal wire to a source of potential difference and measured the resulting current. If we were to do the same thing with the glass fiber, the current would probably be too small to measure, but why? Well, the glass provided more resistance to the flow of charge. If the potential difference is ΔV and the current is I, then the **resistance** is

$$R = \frac{\Delta V}{I}$$

Notice that if the current is large, the resistance is low, and if the current is small, then resistance is high. The Δ in the equation above is often omitted, but you should always assume that in this context, $V = \Delta V$ = difference in electric potential, also called voltage.

Because resistance is voltage divided by current, it is expressed in volts per amp. One volt per amp is one **ohm** (Ω, *omega*). So, 1 V/A = 1 Ω.

---

1. If a voltage of 9 V is applied between the ends of the wire whose resistance is 0.2 Ω, what will be the resulting current?

Here's How to Crack It
From $I = V/R$, we get

$$I = \frac{V}{R} = \frac{9\,\text{V}}{0.2\,\Omega} = 45\,\text{A}.$$

Resistivity

The resistance of an object depends on two things: the material it's made of and its shape. For example, again think of the copper wire and glass fiber of the same length and area. They have the same shape, but their resistances are different because they're made of different materials. Glass has a much greater *intrinsic* resistance than copper does; it has a greater **resistivity**. For a wire of length L and cross-sectional area A made of a material with resistivity ρ, resistance is given by

$$R = \frac{\rho L}{A}$$

The resistivity of copper is around 10^{-8} $\Omega \bullet$ m, while the resistivity of glass is *much* greater, around 10^{12} $\Omega \bullet$ m.

ELECTRIC CIRCUITS

An electric current is maintained when the terminals of a voltage source (a battery, for example) are connected by a conducting pathway, in what's called a **circuit**. If the current always travels in the same direction through the pathway, it's called a **direct current**.

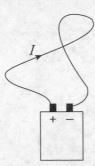

The job of the voltage source is to provide a potential difference called an **electromotive force**, or **emf**, which drives the flow of charge. The emf isn't really a force; it's the work done per unit charge, and it's measured in volts.

To try to imagine what's happening in a circuit in which a steady-state current is maintained, let's follow one of the charge carriers that's drifting through the pathway. (Remember, we're pretending that the charge carriers are positive, just like we imagine that test charges in an electric field are positive.) The charge is introduced by the positive terminal of the battery and enters the wire, where it's pushed by the electric field. It encounters resistance, bumping into the relatively stationary atoms that make up the metal's lattice and setting them into greater motion. So the electrical potential energy that the charge had when it left the battery is turning into heat. By the time the charge reaches the negative terminal, all of its original electrical potential energy is lost. To keep the current going, the voltage source must do positive work on the charge, forcing it to move from the negative terminal toward the positive terminal. The charge is now ready to make another journey around the circuit.

Energy and Power

When a carrier of positive charge q drops by an amount V in potential, it loses potential energy in the amount qV. If this happens in time t, then the rate at which this energy is transformed is equal to $(qV)/t = (q/t)V$. But q/t is equal to the current, I, so the rate at which electrical energy is transferred is given by the equation

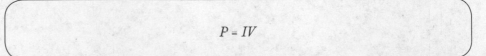

$$P = IV$$

This equation works for the power delivered by a battery to the circuit as well as for resistors. The power dissipated in a resistor, as electrical potential energy is turned into heat, is given by $P = IV$, but because of the relationship $V = IR$, we can express this in two other ways.

or

$$P = IV = I(IR) = I^2 R$$

$$P = IV = \frac{V}{R} \cdot V = \frac{V^2}{R}$$

Resistors become hot when current passes through them; the thermal energy generated is called **joule heat**.

Circuit Analysis

We will now develop a way of specifying the current, voltage, and power associated with each element in a circuit. Our circuits will contain three basic elements: batteries, resistors, and connecting wires. As we've seen, the resistance of an ordinary metal wire is negligible; resistance is provided by devices that control the current: **resistors**.

All the resistance of the system is concentrated in resistors, which are symbolized in a circuit diagram by this symbol

Batteries are denoted by the symbol

where the longer line represents the **positive** (higher potential) terminal, and the shorter line is the **negative** (lower potential) terminal.

Here's a simple circuit diagram.

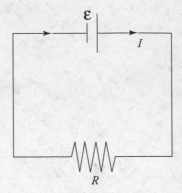

The emf (ε) of the battery is indicated, as is the resistance (R) of the resistor. It's easy to determine the current in this case because there's only one resistor. The equation $V = IR$, with V given by ε, gives us

$$I = \frac{\varepsilon}{R}$$

Combinations of Resistors

As you remember from chapter 11, two common ways of combining resistors within a circuit is to place them either in **series** (one after the other)

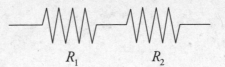

or in **parallel** (that is, side-by-side)

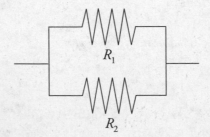

To simplify the circuit, our goal is to find the equivalent resistance of the resistors. Resistors are said to be in series if they all share the same current and if the total voltage drop across them is equal to the sum of the individual voltage drops.

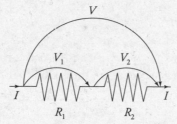

In this case, then, if V denotes the voltage drop across the combination, we have

$$R_{equiv} = \frac{V}{I} = \frac{V_1 + V_2}{I} = \frac{V_1}{I} + \frac{V_2}{I} = R_1 + R_2$$

This idea can be applied to any number of resistors in series (not just two).

$$R_S = R_1 + R_2 + \ldots$$

Resistors are said to be in parallel if they all share the same voltage drop, and the total current entering the combination is split among the resistors. Imagine that a current I enters the combination. It splits; some of the current, I_1, would go through R_1, and the remainder, I_2, would go through R_2.

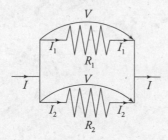

What's the same?
Remember, in a series circuit the current is the same through each resistor. In parallel, the voltage drop is the same.

So if V is the voltage drop across the combination, we have

$$I = I_1 + I_2 \quad \Rightarrow \quad \frac{V}{R_{\text{equiv}}} = \frac{V}{R_1} + \frac{V}{R_2} \quad \Rightarrow \quad \frac{1}{R_{\text{equiv}}} = \frac{1}{R_1} + \frac{1}{R_2}$$

This idea can be applied to any number of resistors in parallel (not just two). The reciprocal of the equivalent resistance for resistors in parallel is equal to the sum of the reciprocals of the individual resistances.

$$\frac{1}{R_P} = \frac{1}{R_1} + \frac{1}{R_i} + \ldots$$

Notice that the equation for the equivalent resistance for resistors in *series* is just like the equation for the equivalent capacitance for capacitors in *parallel* and vice versa. So be careful with series and parallel resistors versus capacitors—the formulas are the reverse of each other.

2. Calculate the equivalent resistance for the following circuit:

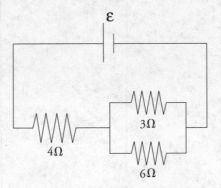

Here's How to Crack It
First find the equivalent resistance of the two parallel resistors.

$$\frac{1}{R_P} = \frac{1}{3\ \Omega} + \frac{1}{6\ \Omega} \quad \Rightarrow \quad \frac{1}{R_P} = \frac{1}{2\ \Omega} \quad \Rightarrow \quad R_P = 2\ \Omega$$

This resistance is in series with the 4 Ω resistor, so the overall equivalent resistance in the circuit is $R_{equiv} = 4\ \Omega + 2\ \Omega = 6\ \Omega$.

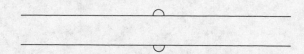

3. Determine the current through each resistor, the voltage drop across each resistor, and the power given off (dissipated) as heat in each resistor of the circuit below.

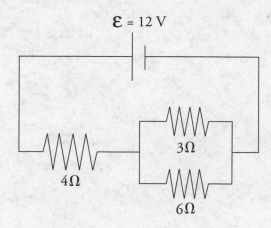

$\mathcal{E} = 12\ V$

4Ω

3Ω

6Ω

Here's How to Crack It

You might want to redraw the circuit each time we replace a combination of resistors by its equivalent resistance. From our work in the last question, we have

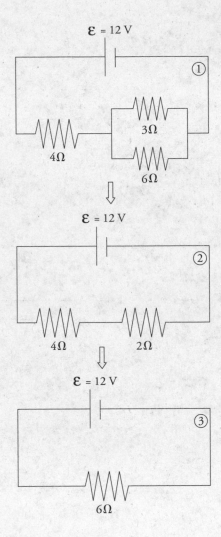

From diagram ③, which has just one resistor, we can figure out the current.

$$I = \frac{\varepsilon}{R_{equiv}} = \frac{12\text{ V}}{6\ \Omega} = 2\text{ A}$$

Now we can work our way back to the original circuit (diagram ①). In going from ③ to ②, we are going back to a series combination. Resistors in series share the same current, so we take the current, $I = 2$ A, back to diagram ②. The current through each resistor in diagram ② is 2 A.

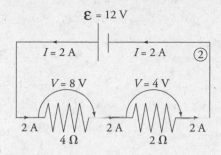

Since we know the current through each resistor, we can figure out the voltage drop across each resistor using the equation $V = IR$. The voltage drop across the 4 Ω resistor is (2 A)(4 Ω) = 8 V, and the voltage drop across the 2 Ω resistor is (2 A)(2 Ω) = 4 V. Notice that the total voltage drop across the two resistors is 8 V + 4 V = 12 V, which matches the emf of the battery.

Now for the last step: going from diagram ② back to diagram ①. Nothing needs to be done with the 4 Ω resistor; nothing about it changes in going from diagram ② to ①, but the 2 Ω resistor in diagram ② goes back to the parallel combination. Resistors in parallel share the same voltage drop. So we take the voltage drop, $V = 4$ V, back to diagram ①. The voltage drop across each of the two parallel resistors in diagram ① is 4 V.

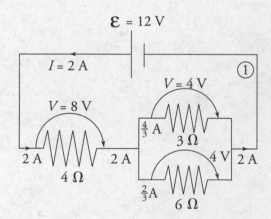

Since we know the voltage drop across each resistor, we can figure out the current through each resistor by using the equation $I = \dfrac{V}{R}$. The current through the 3 Ω resistor is $\dfrac{4\text{ V}}{3\ \Omega} = \dfrac{4}{3}$ A, and the current through the 6 Ω resistor is $\dfrac{4\text{ V}}{6\ \Omega} = \dfrac{2}{3}$ A. Notice that the current entering the parallel combination (2 A) equals the total current passing through the individual resistors ($\dfrac{4}{3}$ A $+ \dfrac{2}{3}$ A).

Finally, we will calculate the power dissipated as heat by each resistor. We can use any of the equivalent formulas: $P = IV$, $P = I^2R$, or $P = V^2/R$.

For the 4 Ω resistor: $P = IV = (2 \text{ A})(8 \text{ V}) = 16 \text{ W}$

For the 3 Ω resistor: $P = IV = (\frac{4}{3} \text{ A})(4 \text{ V}) = \frac{16}{3} \text{ W}$

For the 6 Ω resistor: $P = IV = (\frac{2}{3} \text{ A})(4 \text{ V}) = \frac{8}{3} \text{ W}$

So the resistors are dissipating a total of

$$16 \text{ W} + \frac{16}{3} \text{ W} + \frac{8}{3} \text{ W} = 24 \text{ W}.$$

If the resistors are dissipating a total of 24 J every second, then they must be provided with that much power. This is easy to check: $P = IV = (2 \text{ A})(12 \text{ V}) = 24 \text{ W}$.

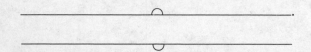

Questions 4-7

For the circuit below,

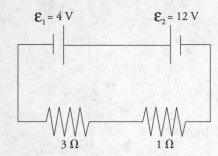

4. In which direction will current flow and why?

5. What's the overall emf?

6. What's the current in the circuit?

7. At what rate is energy consumed by, and provided to, this circuit?

Here's How to Crack It

4. The battery whose emf is ε_1 wants to send current clockwise, while the battery whose emf is ε_2 wants to send current counterclockwise. Since $\varepsilon_2 > \varepsilon_1$, the battery whose emf is ε_2 is the more powerful battery, so the current will flow counterclockwise.

5. Charges forced through ε_1 will lose, rather than gain, 4 V of potential, so the overall emf of this circuit is $\varepsilon_2 - \varepsilon_1 = 8$ V.

6. Since the total resistance is 3 Ω + 1 Ω = 4 Ω, the current will be
$$I = \frac{8\text{ V}}{4\ \Omega} = 2\text{A}.$$

7. Finally, energy will be dissipated in these resistors at a rate of $I^2 R_1 + I^2 R_2 = (2\text{ A})^2 (3\ \Omega) + (2\text{ A})^2 (1\ \Omega) = 16$ W. ε_2 will provide energy at a rate of $P_2 = IV_2 = (2\text{ A})(12\text{ V}) = 24$ W, while ε_1 will absorb at a rate of $P_1 = IV_1 = (2\text{ A})(4\text{ V}) = 8$ W. Once again, energy is conserved; the power delivered (24 W) equals the power taken (8 W + 16 W = 24 W).

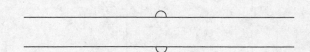

8. All real batteries contain internal resistance, r. Determine the current in the following circuit when the switch S is closed:

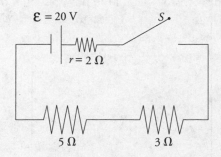

Here's How to Crack It

Before the switch is closed, there is no complete conducting pathway from the positive terminal of the battery to the negative terminal, so no current flows through the resistors. However, once the switch is closed, the resistance of the circuit is $2 \, \Omega + 3 \, \Omega + 5 \, \Omega = 10 \, \Omega$, so the current in the circuit is $I = \dfrac{20V}{10\Omega} = 2A$. Often the battery and its internal resistance are enclosed in a dotted line. See the following example.

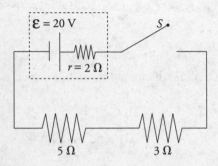

In this case, a distinction can be made between the emf of the battery and the actual voltage it provides once the current has begun. Since $I = 2$ A, the voltage drop across the internal resistance is $Ir = (2 \text{ A})(2 \, \Omega) = 4$ V, so the effective voltage provided by the battery to the rest of the circuit—called the **terminal voltage**—is lower than the ideal emf. It is $V = \varepsilon - Ir = 20 \text{ V} - 4 \text{ V} = 16$ V.

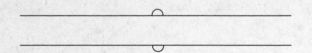

9. A student has three 30 Ω resistors and an ideal 90 V battery. (A battery is ideal if it has a negligible internal resistance.) Compare the current drawn from—and the power supplied by—the battery when the resistors are arranged in parallel versus in series.

Here's How to Crack It

Resistors in series always provide an equivalent resistance that's greater than any of the individual resistances, and resistors in parallel always provide an equivalent resistance that's smaller than their individual resistances. So, hooking up the resistors in parallel will create the smallest resistance and draw the greatest total current.

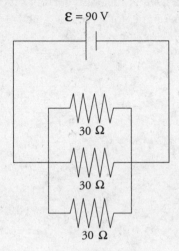

In this case, the equivalent resistance is

$$\frac{1}{R_P} = \frac{1}{30\ \Omega} + \frac{1}{30\ \Omega} + \frac{1}{30\ \Omega} \quad \Rightarrow \quad \frac{1}{R_P} = \frac{1}{10\ \Omega} \quad \Rightarrow \quad R_P = 10\ \Omega$$

and the total current is $I = \dfrac{\varepsilon}{R_P} = \dfrac{90\ \text{V}}{10\ \Omega} = 9\text{A}$. (You could verify that 3 A of current would flow in each of the three branches of the combination.) The power supplied by the battery will be $P = IV = (9\ \text{A})(90\ \text{V}) = 810\ \text{W}$.

If the resistors are in series, the equivalent resistance is $R_S = 30\ \Omega + 30\ \Omega + 30\ \Omega = 90\ \Omega$, and the current drawn is only $I = \dfrac{\varepsilon}{R_P} = \dfrac{90\ \text{V}}{90\ \Omega} = 1\text{A}$. The power supplied by the battery in this case is just $P = IV = (1\ \text{A})(90\ \text{V}) = 90\ \text{W}$.

10. A **voltmeter** is a device that's used to measure the voltage between two points in a circuit. An **ammeter** is used to measure current. Determine the readings on the voltmeter (denoted —Ⓥ—) and the ammeter (denoted —Ⓐ—) in the circuit below.

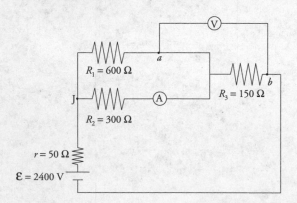

Here's How to Crack It

Assume that the ammeter is ideal; it has negligible resistance and doesn't alter the current that it's trying to measure. Similarly, assume that the voltmeter has an extremely high resistance, so it draws negligible current away from the circuit.

Our first goal is to find the equivalent resistance in the circuit. The 600 Ω and 300 Ω resistors are in parallel; they're equivalent to a single 200 Ω resistor. This is in series with the battery's internal resistance, r, and R_3. The overall equivalent resistance is therefore R_{equiv} = 50 Ω + 200 Ω + 150 Ω = 400 Ω, so the current supplied by the battery is $I = \dfrac{\varepsilon}{R_{equiv}} = \dfrac{2,400 \text{ V}}{400 \, \Omega}$ = 6 A. At the junction marked J, this current splits. Since R_1 is twice R_2, half as much current will flow through R_1 as through R_2; the current through R_1 is I_1 = 2 A, and the current through R_2 is I_2 = 4 A. The voltage drop across each of these resistors is $I_1 R_1 = I_2 R_2$ = 1,200 V (matching voltages verify the values of currents I_1 and I_2). Since the ammeter is in the branch that contains R_2, it will read I_2 = 4 A.

The voltmeter will read the voltage drop across R_3, which is $V_3 = IR_3$ = (6 A)(150 Ω) = 900 V. So the potential at point b is 900 V lower than at point a.

11. The diagram below shows a point *a* at potential $V = 20$ V connected by a combination of resistors to a point (denoted *G*) that is **grounded**. *The* ***ground*** *is considered to be at potential zero.* If the potential at point a is maintained at 20 V, what is the current through R_3 ?

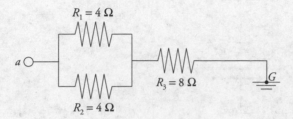

Here's How to Crack It

R_1 and R_2 are in parallel; their equivalent resistance is R_p, where

$$\frac{1}{R_P} = \frac{1}{4\,\Omega} + \frac{1}{4\,\Omega} \Rightarrow R_P = 2\,\Omega$$

R_P is in series with R_3, so the equivalent resistance is

$$R_{equiv} = R_P + R_3 = (2\,\Omega) + (8\,\Omega) = 10\,\Omega$$

and the current that flows through R_3 is

$$I_3 = \frac{V}{R_{equiv}} = \frac{20\text{ V}}{10\,\Omega} = 2\text{ A}$$

RESISTANCE–CAPACITANCE (RC) CIRCUITS

Capacitors are typically charged by batteries. Once the switch in the diagram on the left is closed, electrons are attracted to the positive terminal of the battery and leave the top plate of the capacitor. Electrons also accumulate on the bottom plate of the capacitor, and this continues until the voltage across the capacitor plates matches the emf of the battery. When this condition is reached, the current stops and the capacitor is fully charged.

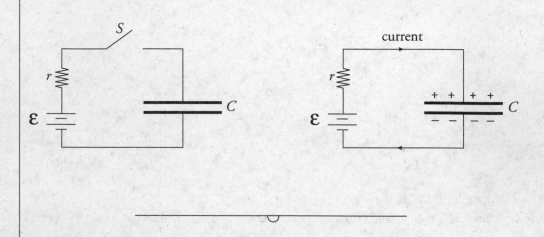

12. Find the charge stored and the voltage across each capacitor in the following circuit, given that $\varepsilon = 180$ V, $C_1 = 30\,\mu$F, $C_2 = 60\,\mu$F, and $C_3 = 90\,\mu$F.

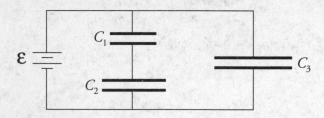

Here's How to Crack It

Once the charging currents stop, the voltage across C_3 is equal to the voltage across the battery, so $V_3 = 180$ V. This gives us $Q_3 = C_3V_3 = (90\,\mu\text{F})(180\text{ V}) = 16.2$ mC. Since C_1 and C_2 are in series, they must store identical amounts of charge, and, from the diagram, the sum of their voltages must equal the voltage of the battery. So if we let Q be the charge on each of these two capacitors, then $Q = C_1V_1 = C_2V_2$ and $V_1 + V_2 = 180$ V. The equation $C_1V_1 = C_2V_2$ becomes $(30\,\mu\text{F})V_1 = (60\,\mu\text{F})V_2$, so $V_1 = 2V_2$. Substituting this into $V_1 + V_2 = 180$ V gives us $V_1 = 120$ V and $V_2 = 60$ V.

The charge stored on each of these capacitors is

$$(30\,\mu\text{F})(120\text{ V}) = C_1 V_1 = C_2 V_2 = (60\,\mu\text{F})(60\text{ V}) = 3.6\text{ mC}$$

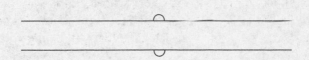

13. In the diagram below, $C_1 = 2$ mF and $C_2 = 4$mF. When Switch S is open, a battery (which is not shown) is connected between points a and b and charges capacitor C_1 so that $V_{ab} = 12$ V. The battery is then disconnected.

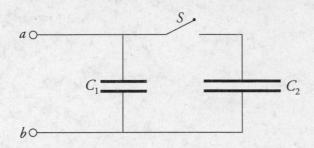

   After the switch is closed, what will be the common voltage across each of the parallel capacitors (once electrostatic conditions are reestablished)?

Here's How to Crack It

When C_1 is fully charged, the charge on (each of the plates of) C_1 has the magnitude $Q = C_1 V = (2\text{ mF})(12\text{ V}) = 24$ mC. After the switch is closed, this charge will be redistributed in such a way that the resulting voltages across the two capacitors, V', are equal. This happens because the capacitors are in parallel. So if Q'_1 is the new charge magnitude on C_1 and Q'_2 is the new charge magnitude on C_2, we have $Q'_1 + Q'_2 = Q$, so $C_1 V' + C_2 V' = Q$, which gives us

$$V' = \frac{Q}{C_1 + C_2} = \frac{24\text{ mC}}{2\text{ mF} + 4\text{ mF}} = 4\text{ V}$$

Chapter 12 Review Questions

Answers are on page 410.

1. A wire made of brass and a wire made of silver have the same length, but the diameter of the brass wire is 4 times the diameter of the silver wire. The resistivity of brass is 5 times greater than the resistivity of silver. If R_B denotes the resistance of the brass wire and R_S denotes the resistance of the silver wire, which of the following is true?

   (A) $R_B = \dfrac{5}{16} R_S$

   (B) $R_B = \dfrac{4}{5} R_S$

   (C) $R_B = \dfrac{5}{4} R_S$

   (D) $R_B = \dfrac{5}{2} R_S$

   (E) $R_B = \dfrac{16}{5} R_S$

2. For an ohmic conductor, doubling the voltage without changing the resistance will cause the current to

   (A) decrease by a factor of 4
   (B) decrease by a factor of 2
   (C) remain unchanged
   (D) increase by a factor of 2
   (E) increase by a factor of 4

3. If a 60-watt lightbulb operates at a voltage of 120 V, what is the resistance of the bulb?

   (A) $2\,\Omega$
   (B) $30\,\Omega$
   (C) $240\,\Omega$
   (D) $720\,\Omega$
   (E) $7,200\,\Omega$

4. A battery whose emf is 40 V has an internal resistance of $5\,\Omega$. If this battery is connected to a $15\,\Omega$ resistor R, what will be the voltage drop across R ?

   (A) 10 V
   (B) 30 V
   (C) 40 V
   (D) 50 V
   (E) 70 V

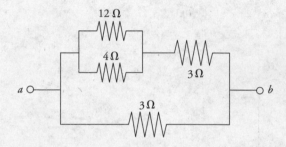

5. Determine the equivalent resistance between points a and b.

   (A) $0.167\,\Omega$
   (B) $0.25\,\Omega$
   (C) $0.333\,\Omega$
   (D) $1.5\,\Omega$
   (E) $2.0\,\Omega$

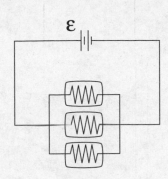

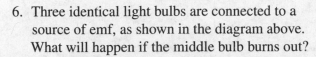

6. Three identical light bulbs are connected to a source of emf, as shown in the diagram above. What will happen if the middle bulb burns out?

(A) All the bulbs will go out.
(B) The light intensity of the other two bulbs will decrease (but they won't go out).
(C) The light intensity of the other two bulbs will increase.
(D) The light intensity of the other two bulbs will remain the same.
(E) More current will be drawn from the source of emf.

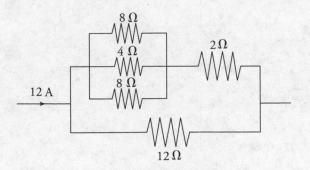

7. What is the voltage drop across the 12-ohm resistor in the portion of the circuit shown above?

(A)   24 V
(B)   36 V
(C)   48 V
(D)   72 V
(E)   144 V

8. What is the current through the 8-ohm resistor in the circuit shown above?

(A) 0.5 A
(B) 1.0 A
(C) 1.25 A
(D) 1.5 A
(E) 3.0 A

9. How much energy is dissipated as heat in 20 s by a $100\,\Omega$ resistor that carries a current of 0.5 A ?

(A)   50 J
(B)   100 J
(C)   250 J
(D)   500 J
(E)   1,000 J

10. Two resistors, A and B, are in series in a circuit that carries a nonzero current. If the resistance of Resistor A is 4 times greater than the resistance of Resistor B, which of the following correctly compares the currents through these resistors (I_A and I_B, respectively) and the voltage drops across them (V_A and V_B, respectively)?

(A) $I_A = I_B$ and $V_A = V_B$
(B) $I_A = I_B$ and $V_A = 4V_B$
(C) $I_A = I_B$ and $V_B = 4V_A$
(D) $I_A = 4I_B$ and $V_A = 4V_B$
(E) $I_B = 4I_A$ and $V_B = 4V_A$

Keywords

electric current
current
drift speed
ampere
resistance
ohm Ω
resistivity
circuit
direct current
electromotive force (emf)
joule heat
resistors
positive
negative
series
parallel
terminal voltage
internal resistance
voltmeter
ammeter
grounded
ground

Summary

o   Electric current is created when a potential dif-
    ference (an electric field) set up between the
    ends of a piece of wire cause the electrons in the
    wire to drift through the wire with a net move-
    ment of charge.

o   Resistance differs from material to material. A
    conductive material offers less resistance to the
    flow of electrons. Resistance is represented by
    the equation $R = \dfrac{\Delta V}{I}$. If the current is large,
    the resistance is low; if the current is small, re-
    sistance is high.

o   Electric circuits are paths along which electri-
    cal energy is released (as from a battery or other
    source of electrical energy). Electrical energy
    can only be released when the current has a
    complete conducting path available from one
    side of the potential difference to the other.

o   Power is the rate at which energy is released.
    Use the formula $P = IV$. This equation is rel-
    evant for the power delivered by the battery to a
    circuit as well as for resistors. Resistors dissipate
    energy as heat.

o   Circuit analysis is a way to specify the current,
    voltage, and power associated with each element
    in a circuit (batteries, resistors, and connecting
    wires).

o   Combinations of resistors occur in a series (one
    after the other) or in parallel (side-by-side).

o   Resistance–Capacitance (RC) circuits are sim-
    ple circuits for charging a capacitor. An RC
    circuit consists of a battery which holds the
    potential energy that will charge the capacitor,
    a switch that closes the circuit and allows the
    current to flow, as well as a resistor that will use
    the energy to produce heat.

Chapter 13
Magnetic Forces and Fields

In Chapter 10, we learned that electric charges are the source of electric fields and that other charges experience an electric force in those fields. The charges generating the field were assumed to be at rest. Electric charges *that move* are the source of **magnetic fields**, and other charges that move can experience a magnetic force in these fields. As you may recall, magnetic forces and fields make up a significant portion of the SAT Physics Subject Test; they are the focus of this chapter.

THE MAGNETIC FORCE ON A MOVING CHARGE

If a particle with charge q moves with velocity $\mathbf{v}$ through a magnetic field $\mathbf{B}$, it will experience a magnetic force, $\mathbf{F_B}$, with magnitude

$$F_B = |q|\, vB\sin\theta$$

where θ is the angle between $\mathbf{v}$ and $\mathbf{B}$. From this equation, we can see that if the charge is at rest, then $v = 0$ immediately gives us $F_B = 0$—magnetic forces only act on moving charges. Also, if $\mathbf{v}$ is parallel (or antiparallel) to $\mathbf{B}$, then $\mathbf{F_B} = 0$ since, in either of these cases, $\sin\theta = 0$. So only charges that cut across the magnetic field lines will experience a magnetic force. Furthermore, the magnetic force is maximized when $\mathbf{v}$ is perpendicular to $\mathbf{B}$, since if $\theta = 90°$, then $\sin\theta$ is equal to 1, its maximum value.

The direction of $\mathbf{F_B}$ is always perpendicular to both $\mathbf{v}$ and $\mathbf{B}$ and depends on the sign of the charge q (which is given by the right-hand rule).

Right-Hand Rule:

With your right hand (palm up), point your thumb in the direction of $\mathbf{V}$ and your fingers in the direction of $\mathbf{B}$. If q is positive, $\mathbf{F_B}$ points out of the palm. If q is negative, $\mathbf{F_B}$ points into the palm.

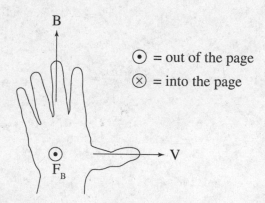

$\odot$ = out of the page

$\otimes$ = into the page

Notice that there are fundamental differences between the electric force and magnetic force on a charge. First, a magnetic force acts on a charge only if the charge is moving; the electric force acts on a charge whether it moves or not. Second, the direction of the magnetic force is always perpendicular to the magnetic field, while the electric force is always parallel (or antiparallel) to the electric field.

The SI unit for the magnetic field is the **tesla** (abbreviated **T**), which is one newton per ampere-meter. Another common unit for magnetic field strength is the **gauss** (abbreviated **G**); $1\ G = 10^{-4}\ T$.

1. A charge $+q = +6 \times 10–6$ C moves with speed $v = 4 \times 105$ m/s through a magnetic field of strength $B = 0.5$, T, as shown in the figure below. What is the magnetic force experienced by q ?

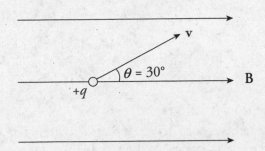

Here's How to Crack It
The magnitude of F_B is

$$F_B = qvB \sin\theta = (6 \times 10^{-6} \text{ C})(4 \times 10^5 \text{ m/s})(0.5 \text{ T}) \sin 30° = 0.6 \text{ N}.$$

The right-hand rule on the previous page was designed for situations in which the charged moves perpendicular to **B**. We can use it for our example if we point the thumb in the direction of **V** that is perpendicular to **B** (up). **B** points to the right and therefore **F**$_B$ is into the page.

2. A particle of mass m and charge $+q$ is projected with velocity v (in the plane of the page) into a uniform magnetic field **B** that points into the page. How will the particle move?

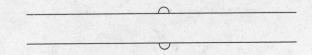

Here's How to Crack It

Since **v** is perpendicular to **B**, the particle will feel a magnetic force of strength qvB, which will be directed perpendicular to **v** (and to **B**) as shown.

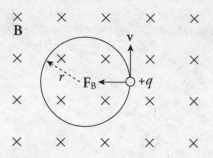

Since F_B is always perpendicular to **v**, the particle will undergo uniform circular motion; F_B will provide the centripetal force. Notice that, because F_B is always perpendicular to **v**, the magnitude of **v** will not change, just its direction.

The Skinny on Magnetic Fields

F_B is always perpendicular to both **V** and **B**.

Magnetic Forces cannot change the speed of an object, only its direction.

The Magnetic Field does no work on any charge.

The radius of the particle's circular path is found from the equation $F_B = F_C$.

$$q v B = \frac{m v^2}{r} \implies r = \frac{m v}{q B}$$

3. A particle of charge $-q$ is shot into a region that contains an electric field, **E**, crossed with a perpendicular magnetic field, **B**. If $E = 2 \times 10_4$ N/C and $B = 0.5$ T, what must be the speed of the particle if it is to cross this region without being deflected?

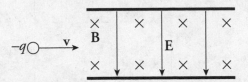

Here's How to Crack It

If the particle is to pass through undeflected, the electric force it feels has to be canceled by the magnetic force. In the diagram on the previous page, the electric force on the particle is directed upward and the magnetic force is directed downward. So F_E and F_B point in opposite directions, and for their magnitudes to balance, qE must equal qvB, so v must equal E/B, which in this case gives

$$v = \frac{E}{B} = \frac{2 \times 10^4 \text{ N/C}}{0.5 \text{ T}} = 4 \times 10^4 \text{ m/s}.$$

4. The figure below shows a uniform magnetic field, **B**, whose field lines point up in the plane of the page, and three particles, all with the same positive charge, q, and all moving with the same speed, **v**. Which particle—X, Y, or Z—will experience the greatest magnetic force?

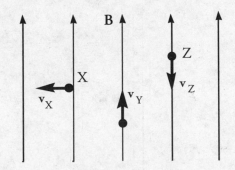

Here's How to Crack It

Since the velocity of particle Y is parallel to the direction of **B**, particle Y feels no magnetic force (the angle θ between $\mathbf{v}_Y$ and **B** is 0, and sin 0 = 0). Since the velocity of particle Z is antiparallel to the direction of **B**, particle Z also feels no magnetic force (the angle θ between $\mathbf{v}_Z$ and **B** is 180°, and sin 180° is also 0). However, the velocity of particle X is perpendicular to the direction of **B** (that is, θ = 90°), so the magnetic force on particle X is $qv\text{B}\sin\theta = qv\text{B}\sin 90° = qv\text{B}$. Therefore, particle X feels the greatest magnetic force.

THE MAGNETIC FORCE ON A CURRENT-CARRYING WIRE

Since magnetic fields affect moving charges, they should also affect current-carrying wires. After all, a wire that contains a current contains charges that move.

Let a wire of length ℓ be immersed in magnetic field **B**. If the wire carries a current I, then the magnitude of the magnetic force it feels is

$$\mathbf{F}_B = I\ell\text{B}\sin\theta$$

where θ is the angle between ℓ and **B**. Here, the direction of ℓ is the direction of the current, I. The direction of $\mathbf{F}_B$ is given by the right-hand rule as before, remembering that the direction of the current is the direction that positives would flow.

5. A U-shaped wire of mass m is lowered into a magnetic field **B** that points out of the plane of the page. What is the direction of the net magnetic force on the wire?

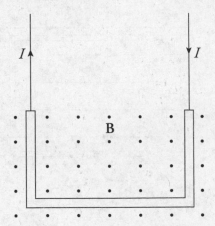

Here's How to Crack It

The total magnetic force on the wire is equal to the sum of the magnetic forces on each of the three sections of wire. The force on the first section (the right, vertical one), F_{B1}, is directed to the left and the force on the third piece (the left, vertical one), F_{B3}, is directed to the right. Since these pieces are the same length, these two oppositely directed forces have the same magnitude, $I\ell_1 B = I\ell_3 B$, and they cancel. So the net magnetic force on the wire is the magnetic force on the middle piece. Since I moves to the left and **B** is out of the page, F_{B2} is directed upward.

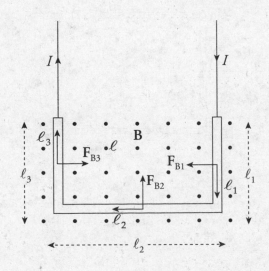

6. A rectangular loop of wire that carries a current I is placed in a uniform magnetic field, **B**, as shown in the diagram below. Describe the direction in which the loop will rotate.

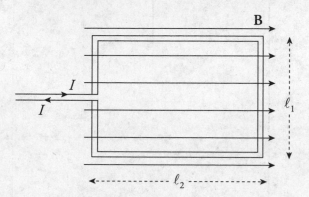

Here's How to Crack It

Ignoring the tiny gap in the vertical left-hand wire, we have two wires of length ℓ_1 and two of length ℓ_2. There is no magnetic force on either of the sides of the loop of length ℓ_2, because the current in the top side is parallel to **B** and the current in the bottom side is antiparallel to **B**. The magnetic force on the right-hand side points out of the plane of the page, while the magnetic force on the left-hand side points into the plane of the page.

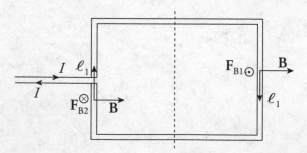

If the loop is free to rotate, then each of these two forces exerts a torque that tends to turn the loop in such a way that the right-hand side rises out of the plane of the page and the left-hand side rotates into the page.

MAGNETIC FIELDS CREATED BY CURRENT-CARRYING WIRES

As we said at the beginning of this chapter, the source of magnetic fields are electric charges that move; they may spin, circulate, move through space, or flow down a wire. For example, consider a long, straight wire that carries a current I. The current generates a magnetic field in the surrounding space that's proportional to I and inversely proportional to r, the distance from the wire.

$$B \propto \frac{I}{r}$$

The magnetic field "lines" are actually circles whose centers are on the wire. The direction of these circles is determined by a variation of the right-hand rule. Imagine grabbing the wire in your right hand with your thumb pointing in the direction of the current. Then the direction in which your fingers curl around the wire gives the direction of the magnetic field lines.

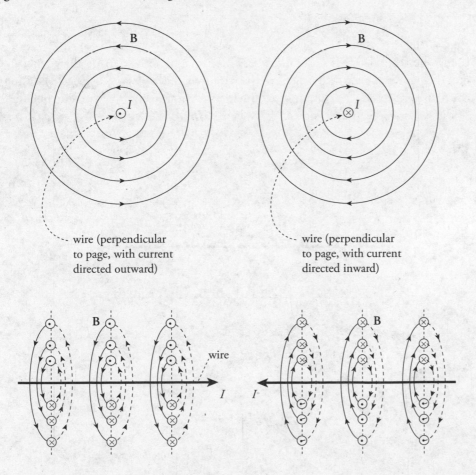

wire (perpendicular to page, with current directed outward)

wire (perpendicular to page, with current directed inward)

7. The diagram below shows a proton moving with velocity v_0, initially parallel to, and above, a long, straight wire. If the current in the wire is I as shown, what is the direction of the magnetic force on the proton?

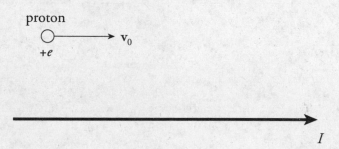

Here's How to Crack It

Using the second right-hand rule, we see the magnetic field B produced by the current points out of the page above the wire (where the proton is located). Using the first right-hand rule for a proton moving the right, feeling a magnetic field out of the page, we see that F_B points downward, toward the wire.

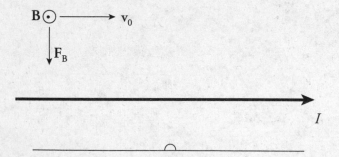

8. The diagram below shows a pair of long, straight, parallel wires, separated by a small distance, *r*. If equal currents are established in the wires, what is the magnetic field midway between the wires?

$$\text{Wire 1} \quad \text{Wire 2}$$

$$\odot \quad \cdot \quad \odot$$

$$I \quad \; P \quad \; I$$

Here's How to Crack It

Let $\mathbf{B}_1$ be the magnetic field due to Wire 1 and $\mathbf{B}_2$ be the magnetic field due to Wire 2. The total magnetic field at point P is just their vector sum, $\mathbf{B}_1 + \mathbf{B}_2$. Using the second right-hand rule, we know that $\mathbf{B}_1$ is directed counter-clockwise around Wire 1 and $\mathbf{B}_2$ is counter-clockwise around Wire 2. Therefore, at point P, $\mathbf{B}_1$ points upward and $\mathbf{B}_2$ points downward.

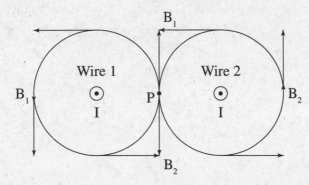

Since B is proportional to $\dfrac{I}{r}$ and I and r are the same for both wires, $\mathbf{B}_1$ and $\mathbf{B}_2$ cancel to zero.

Chapter 13 Review Questions

Answers are on page 412.

1. Which of the following is/are true concerning magnetic forces and fields?

   I. The magnetic field lines due to a current-carrying wire radiate away from the wire.
   II. The kinetic energy of a charged particle can be increased by a magnetic force.
   III. A charged particle can move through a magnetic field without feeling a magnetic force.

   (A) I only
   (B) II and III only
   (C) I and II only
   (D) III only
   (E) I and III only

2. The velocity of a particle of charge $+4.0 \times 10^{-9}$ C and mass 2×10^{-4} kg is perpendicular to a 0.1-tesla magnetic field. If the particle's speed is 3×10^4 m/s, what is the acceleration of this particle due to the magnetic force?

   (A) 0.0006 m/s^2
   (B) 0.006 m/s^2
   (C) 0.06 m/s^2
   (D) 0.6 m/s^2
   (E) None of the above

3. In the figure below, what is the direction of the magnetic force $\mathbf{F_B}$?

   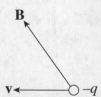

   (A) To the right
   (B) Downward, in the plane of the page
   (C) Upward, in the plane of the page
   (D) Out of the plane of the page
   (E) Into the plane of the page

4. In the figure below, what must be the direction of the particle's velocity, $\mathbf{v}$?

   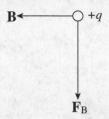

   (A) To the right
   (B) Downward, in the plane of the page
   (C) Upward, in the plane of the page
   (D) Out of the plane of the page
   (E) Into the plane of the page

5. Due to the magnetic force, a positively charged particle executes uniform circular motion within a uniform magnetic field, $\mathbf{B}$. If the charge is q and the radius of its path is r, which of the following expressions gives the magnitude of the particle's linear momentum?

   (A) qBr

   (B) $\dfrac{qB}{r}$

   (C) $\dfrac{q}{(Br)}$

   (D) $\dfrac{B}{(qr)}$

   (E) $\dfrac{r}{(qB)}$

6. A straight wire of length 2 m carries a 10-amp current. How much stronger is the magnetic field at a distance of 2 cm from the wire than it is at 4 cm from the wire?

   (A) 2
   (B) $2\sqrt{2}$
   (C) 4
   (D) $4\sqrt{2}$
   (E) 8

7. Due to the magnetic force, a positively charged particle undergoes uniform circular motion in a uniform magnetic field. Which of the following changes could cause the radius of the circular path to decrease?

   (A) Increase the mass of the particle
   (B) Increase the speed of the particle
   (C) Decrease the charge of the particle
   (D) Decrease the strength of the magnetic field
   (E) None of the above

8. In the figure below, what must be the direction of the magnetic field?

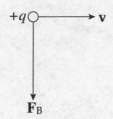

   (A) To the left, in the plane of the page
   (B) Upward, in the plane of the page
   (C) Downward, in the plane of the page
   (D) Out of the plane of the page
   (E) Into the plane of the page

9. A particle of charge –0.04 C is projected with speed 2×10^4 m/s into a uniform magnetic field, **B**, of strength 0.5 T. If the particle's velocity as it enters the field is perpendicular to **B**, what is the magnitude of the magnetic force on this particle?

   (A)   4 N
   (B)   8 N
   (C)   40 N
   (D)   80 N
   (E)   400 N

10. A charge of mass m and charge q is moving in a circle of radius r and speed v due to a uniform magnetic field **B**. If the speed is doubled to $2v$, what happens to the period, T?

   (A) T increases by a factor of 2
   (B) T increases by a factor of 4
   (C) T stays the same
   (D) T decreases by a factor of 2
   (E) T decreases by a factor of 4

Keywords

magnetic fields
tesla (T)
gauss (G)
magnetic force
right-hand rules

Summary

- When a particle with a charge (q) moves through a magnetic field (**B**), it experiences a magnetic force ($\mathbf{F_B}$). The direction of $\mathbf{F_B}$ perpendicular to both **V** and **B** and is given by the right-hand rule.

- Magnetic forces affect moving charges, and a current-carrying wire contains charges that move. The magnetic force that affects a wire that carries a current is represented by the equation $F_B = I\ell B \sin\theta$.

- Magnetic forces never change the speed of a charge, they only turn it.

- Magnetic forces do no work.

- Magnetic fields are created by current-carrying wires because of the motion of the electric charges that flow down a wire. The current (I) generates a magnetic field (B) in the surrounding space that is proportional to the current and inversely proportional to the distance from the wire (r). Use the equation $B \propto \dfrac{I}{r}$.

Chapter 14
Electromagnetic Induction

In Chapter 13, we learned that electric currents generate magnetic fields. We will now see how magnetism can generate electric currents.

MOTIONAL EMF

The figure below shows a conducting wire of length ℓ, moving with constant velocity **v** in the plane of the page through a uniform magnetic field **B** that's perpendicular to the page. The magnetic field exerts a force on the moving conduction electrons in the wire. Using the right-hand rule, the direction of the magnetic force, $\mathbf{F_B}$, on these electrons (which are negatively charged) is downward.

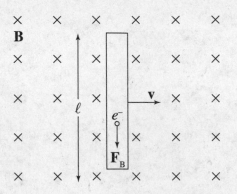

As a result, electrons will be pushed to the lower end of the wire, which will leave an excess of positive charge at its upper end. This separation of charge creates a uniform electric field, **E**, within the wire, pointing downward.

A charge q in the wire feels two forces: an electric force, $\mathbf{F_E} = q\mathbf{E}$, and a magnetic force of magnitude

$$F_B = q\mathbf{v}B$$

If q is negative, $\mathbf{F}_E$ is upward and $\mathbf{F}_B$ is downward; if q is positive, $\mathbf{F}_E$ is downward and $\mathbf{F}_B$ is upward. So, in both cases, the forces act in opposite directions. Once the magnitude of $\mathbf{F}_E$ equals the magnitude of $\mathbf{F}_B$, the charges in the wire are in electromagnetic equilibrium. This occurs when $qE = qvB$—that is, when $E = vB$.

The presence of the electric field creates a potential difference between the ends of the rod. Since negative charge accumulates at the lower end (which we'll call point a) and positive charge accumulates at the upper end (point b), point b is at a higher electric potential.

The potential difference V_{ba} is equal to $E\ell$ and, since $E = vB$, the potential difference can be written as $vB\ell$.

Now imagine that the rod is sliding along a pair of conducting rails connected at the left by a stationary bar. The sliding rod now completes a rectangular circuit, and the potential difference V_{ba} causes current to flow.

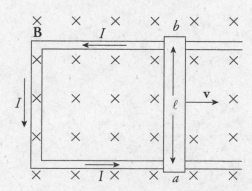

The motion of the sliding rod through the magnetic field creates an electromotive force, called **motional emf**:

$$\varepsilon = vB\ell$$

The existence of a current in the sliding rod causes the magnetic field to exert a force on it. Using the formula $F_B = I\ell B$ and the right-hand rule tells us that the direction of $\mathbf{F_B}$ on the rod is to the left. An external agent must provide this same amount of force to the right to maintain the rod's constant velocity and keep the current flowing. The power that the external agent must supply is $P = Fv = I\ell Bv$, and the electrical power delivered to the circuit is $P = IV_{ba} = I\varepsilon = IvB\ell$. Notice that these two expressions are identical. The energy provided by the external agent is transformed first into electrical energy and then into thermal energy as the conductors making up the circuit dissipate heat.

FARADAY'S LAW OF ELECTROMAGNETIC INDUCTION

Electromotive force can be created by the motion of a conductor through a magnetic field, but there's another way to create an emf from a magnetic field.

Magnetic Flux

The **magnetic flux**, Φ_B, through an area A is equal to the product of A and the magnetic field perpendicular to it: $\Phi_B = B\perp A = BA\cos\theta$. Magnetic flux measures the density of magnetic field lines that cross through an area. (Note that the direction of $\mathbf{A}$ is taken to be perpendicular to he plane of the loop.)

Questions 1-3

The figure shows two views of a circular loop of area 30 cm² placed within a uniform magnetic field, B (magnitude 0.2 T).

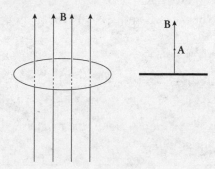

1. What's the magnetic flux through the loop?

2. What would be the magnetic flux through the loop if the loop were rotated 60°?

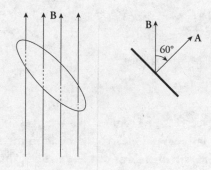

3. What would be the magnetic flux through the loop if the loop were rotated 90°?

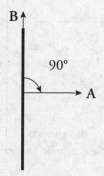

Here's How to Crack It

1. Since **B** is parallel to **A**, the magnetic flux is equal to BA.

$$\Phi_B = BA = (0.2 \text{ T}) \cdot 30 \text{ cm}^2 \cdot \left(\frac{1 \text{ m}}{100 \text{ cm}}\right)^2 = 6 \cdot 10^{-4} \text{ T} \times \text{m}^2$$

The SI unit for magnetic flux, the tesla·meter², is called a **weber** (abbreviated **Wb**). So $\Phi_B = 6 \times 10^{-4}$ Wb.

2. Since the angle between **B** and **A** is 60°, the magnetic flux through the loop is

$$\Phi_B = BA \cos 60° = (6 \times 10^{-4} \text{ Wb})(0.5) = 3 \times 10^{-4} \text{ Wb}$$

3. If the angle between **B** and **A** is 90°, the magnetic flux through the loop is zero, since cos 90° = 0.

Even though Φ_B is not a vector, we can think of it as having a direction, the direction A.

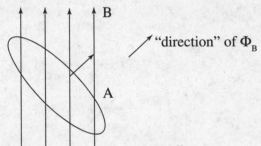

For the SAT Physics Subject Test, remember that changes in magnetic flux induce emf. According to **Faraday's law of electromagnetic induction**, the emf induced in a circuit is equal to the rate of change of the magnetic flux through the circuit. This can be written mathematically as

$$\varepsilon_{avg} = -\frac{\Delta\Phi_B}{\Delta t}$$

This induced emf can produce a current, which will then create its own magnetic field. The direction of the induced current is determined by the polarity of the induced emf and is given by **Lenz's law** (which also explains the minus sign in the equation above): The induced current will always flow in the direction that opposes the change in magnetic flux that produced it. If this were not so, then the magnetic flux created by the induced current would magnify the change that produced it, and energy would not be conserved.

Questions 4-5

The circular loop of Example 14.1 rotates at a constant angular speed through 60° in 0.5 s.

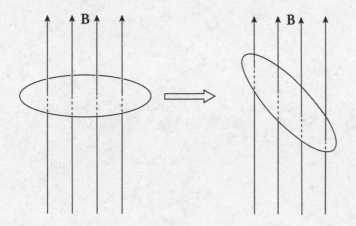

4. What's the induced emf in the loop?

5. In which direction will current be induced to flow?

Here's How to Crack It

4. As we found in Questions 1–3, the magnetic flux through the loop changes when the loop rotates. Using the values we determined earlier, Faraday's law gives

$$\varepsilon_{avg} = -\frac{\Delta\Phi_B}{\Delta t} = -\frac{\left(3\times10^{-4}\ \text{Wb}\right)-\left(6\times10^{-4}\ \text{Wb}\right)}{0.5\ \text{s}} = 6\times10^{-4}\ \text{V}$$

5. The original magnetic flux was 6×10^{-4} Wb upward, and was decreased to 3×10^{-4} Wb. So the change in magnetic flux is -3×10^{-4} Wb upward, or, equivalently, $\Delta\Phi_B = 3 \times 10^{-4}$ Wb, downward. To oppose this change, we would need to create some magnetic flux upward. The current would be induced in the counterclockwise direction (looking down on the loop) because the right-hand rule tells us that then the current would produce a magnetic field that would point up.

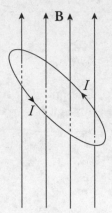

Current will flow only while the loop rotates, because emf is induced only when magnetic flux is changing. If the loop rotates 60° and then stops, the current will disappear.

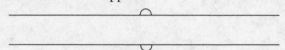

6. Consider the conducting rod that's moving with constant velocity v along a pair of parallel conducting rails (separated by a distance ℓ), within a uniform magnetic field, B.

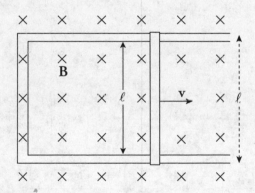

Find the induced emf and the direction of the induced current in the rectangular circuit.

Here's How to Crack It

The area of the rectangular loop is ℓx, where x is the distance from the left-hand bar to the moving rod.

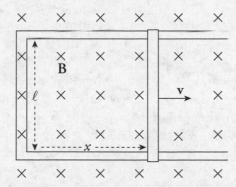

Because the area is changing, the magnetic flux through the loop is changing, which means that an emf will be induced in the loop. To calculate the induced emf, we first write $\Phi_B = BA = B\ell x$, then since $\Delta x / \Delta t = v$ (distance/time = speed), we get

$$\left|\mathcal{E}_{\text{avg}}\right| = \frac{\Delta\Phi_B}{\Delta t} = \frac{\Delta(B\ell x)}{\Delta t} = B\ell \frac{\Delta x}{\Delta t} = B\ell v$$

We can figure out the direction of the induced current from Lenz's law. As the rod slides to the right, the magnetic flux into the page increases. How do we oppose an increasing into-the-page flux? By producing out-of-the-page flux. For the induced current to generate a magnetic field that points out of the plane of the page, the current must be directed counterclockwise (according to the right-hand rule).

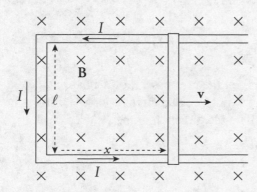

Notice that the magnitude of the induced emf and the direction of the current agree with the results we derived earlier, in the section on motional emf.

This example also shows how a violation of Lenz's law would lead directly to a violation of the law of conservation of energy. The current in the sliding rod is directed upward, as we saw from using Lenz's law, so the conduction electrons are drifting downward. The force on these drifting electrons—and thus the rod itself—is directed to the left, opposing the force that's pulling the rod to the right. If the current were directed downward, in violation of Lenz's law, then the magnetic force on the rod would be to the right, causing the rod to accelerate to the right with ever-increasing speed and kinetic energy, without the input of an equal amount of energy from the outside.

Questions 7-8

A permanent magnet creates a magnetic field in the surrounding space. The end of the magnet at which the field lines emerge is designated the north pole (N), and the other end is the south pole (S).

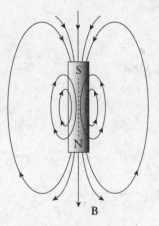

7. The figure on the next page shows a bar magnet moving down, through a circular loop of wire. What will be the direction of the induced current in the wire?

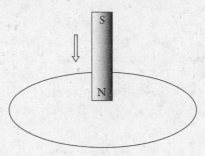

8. What will be the direction of the induced current in the wire if the magnet is moved as shown in the following diagram?

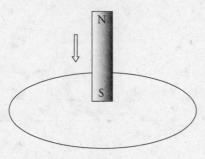

Here's How to Crack It

7. The magnetic flux down through the loop increases as the magnet is moved. By Lenz's law, the induced emf will generate a current that opposes this change. How do we oppose a change of *more flux downward*? By creating flux upward. So, according to the right-hand rule, the induced current must flow counterclockwise (because this current will generate an upward-pointing magnetic field).

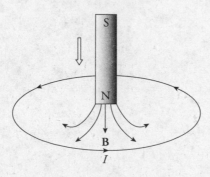

8. In this case, the magnetic flux through the loop is upward and, as the south pole moves closer to the loop, the magnetic field strength increases so the magnetic flux through the loop increases upward. How do we oppose a change of *more flux upward*? By creating flux downward. Therefore, in accordance with the right-hand rule, the induced current will flow clockwise (because this current will generate a downward-pointing magnetic field).

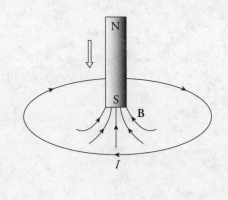

Chapter 14 Review Questions

Answers are on page 414.

1. A metal rod of length L is pulled upward with constant velocity v through a uniform magnetic field B that points out of the plane of the page.

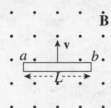

   What is the potential difference between points a and b?

   (A) 0

   (B) $\frac{1}{2}vBL$, with point a at the higher potential

   (C) $\frac{1}{2}vBL$, with point b at the higher potential

   (D) vBL, with point a at the higher potential

   (E) vBL, with point b at the higher potential

2. The circle and ellipse below have the same area.

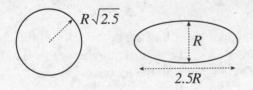

   If both loops are held so that their plane is perpendicular to a uniform magnetic field, B, how would Φ_C, the magnetic flux through the circular loop, compare to Φ_E, the magnetic flux through the elliptical loop?

   (A) $\Phi_C = 2.5\Phi_E$

   (B) $\Phi_C = \sqrt{2.5}\,\Phi_E$

   (C) $\Phi_C = \Phi_E$

   (D) $\Phi_E = \sqrt{2.5}\,\Phi_C$

   (E) $\Phi_E = 2.5\Phi_C$

3. The figure below shows a small circular loop of wire in the plane of a long, straight wire that carries a steady current I upward. If the loop is moved from distance x_2 to distance x_1 from the straight wire, what will be the direction of the induced current in the loop and the direction of the corresponding magnetic field it produces?

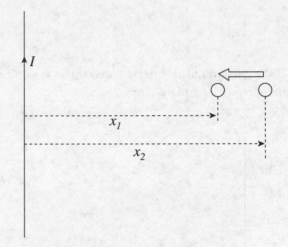

   (A) The induced current will be clockwise, and the magnetic field it produces will point out of the plane of the page.

   (B) The induced current will be clockwise, and the magnetic field it produces will point into the plane of the page.

   (C) The induced current will be counterclockwise, and the magnetic field it produces will point out of the plane of the page.

   (D) The induced current will be counterclockwise, and the magnetic field it produces will point into the plane of the page.

   (E) None of the above

4. A square loop of wire (side length = s) surrounds a long, straight wire such that the wire passes through the center of the square.

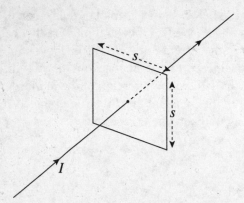

If the current in the wire is I, determine the current induced in the square loop.

(A) $\dfrac{2\mu_0 Is}{\pi\left(1+\sqrt{2}\right)}$

(B) $\dfrac{\mu_0 Is}{\pi\sqrt{2}}$

(C) $\dfrac{\mu_0 Is}{\pi}$

(D) $\dfrac{\mu_0 Is\sqrt{2}}{\pi}$

(E) 0

5. In the figure below, a permanent bar magnet is pulled upward with a constant velocity through a loop of wire.

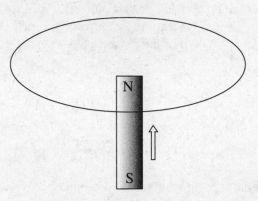

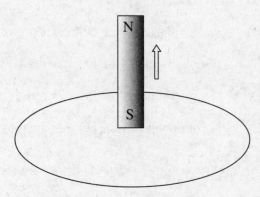

Which of the following best describes the direction(s) of the current induced in the loop (looking down on the loop from above)?

(A) Always clockwise
(B) Always counterclockwise
(C) First clockwise, then counterclockwise
(D) First counterclockwise, then clockwise
(E) No current will be induced in the loop.

Keywords

electromagnetic induction
motional emf
magnetic flux
weber (wb)
Faraday's law of electromagnetic induction
Lenz's law

Summary

○ Motional emf refers to the effects on a wire or other conductor that moves relative to a uniform magnetic field. The action pushes electrons to the lower end of the wire, and leaves an excess of positive charge at the upper end. This separation of charges creates a uniform electric field within the wire.

○ Faraday's law of electromagnetic induction states that the emf induced in a circuit is equal to the rate of change of the magnetic flux through the circuit. Use the equation $\varepsilon_{avg} = -\dfrac{\Delta\Phi_B}{\Delta t}$.

○ Magnetic flux measures the density of magnetic field lines that cross through an area. The magnetic flux (Φ_B) through an area A is equal to the product of A and the magnetic field perpendicular to it. Use the equation

$$\Phi_B = B_\perp A = BA \cos\theta.$$

○ Lenz's law states that the induced current will always flow in the direction that opposes the change in magnetic flux that produced it. If Lenz's law were not true, then the system would be in violation of the law of conservation of energy.

Chapter 15
Waves

Waves make up approximately 20 percent of the SAT Physics Subject Test. But what are they, exactly? Imagine holding the end of a long rope in your hand, with the other end attached to a wall. Move your hand up and down, and you'll create a wave that travels along the rope, from your hand to the wall. This is the basic idea of a **mechanical wave**: a disturbance transmitted by a medium from one point to another, without the medium itself being transported. In the case of water waves, wind or an earthquake can cause a disturbance in the ocean, and the resulting waves can travel thousands of miles. No water actually makes that journey; the water is only the medium that conducts the disturbance.

TRANSVERSE TRAVELING WAVES

Let's return to our long rope. Someone standing near the system would see peaks and valleys actually moving along the rope, in what's called a **traveling wave**.

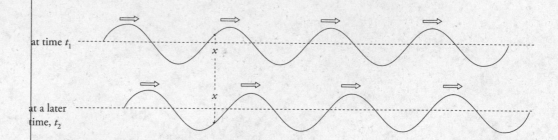

At any point (x) along the rope, the rope has a certain, and varying, vertical displacement. It's this variation in the vertical displacement that defines the shape of the wave. In the figure above, one particular location along the rope—marked x—is shown. Notice that, at time t_1, the vertical position y of the rope at x is slightly positive (it's above the horizontal). But at a later time, t_2, the vertical position of the rope at this same x is slightly negative (it's below the horizontal). It's clear that for a traveling wave, the displacement y of each point depends not only on x but also on t. An equation that gives y must therefore be a function of both position (x) and time (t). Because y depends on *two* independent variables, wave analysis can be difficult. But there's a way of looking at waves that simplifies things.

Instead of looking at a wave in which both variables (x and t) are changing, we'll allow *only one* of the variables to change. We'll use two points of view.

Point of View #1: x varies, t does not

Point of View #2: t varies, x does not

Point of View #1: x Varies, t Does Not

To keep t from varying, we must freeze time. How do we do this? By imagining a photograph of the wave. In fact, the figure above shows two snapshots: one taken at time t_1 and the second taken at a slightly later time, t_2. All the x's along the rope are visible (that is, x varies), but t does not. What features of the wave can we see in this point of view? Well, we can see the points at which the rope has its maximum vertical displacement *above* the horizontal; these points are called **crests**. The points at which the rope has its maximum vertical displacement *below* the horizontal are called **troughs**. These crests and troughs repeat themselves at regular intervals along the rope, and the distance between two adjacent crests (or two adjacent troughs) is the length of one wave, and is called the **wavelength** (λ, *lambda*). Also, the maximum displacement from the horizontal equilibrium position of the rope is known as the **amplitude** (A) of the wave. Be careful: A is just the distance from the "middle" to a crest, *not* from a trough to a crest.

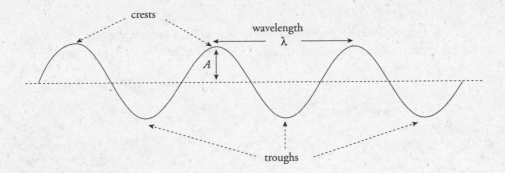

Point of View #2: *t* Varies, *x* Does Not

Now we will designate one position *x* along the rope to watch as time varies. One way to do this is to visualize two screens in front of the rope, with only a narrow gap between them. We can then observe how a single point on the rope varies as a wave travels behind the screen (the wave is traveling because we aren't freezing time here). This point on the rope moves up and down. Since the direction in which the rope oscillates (vertically) is perpendicular to the direction in which the wave **propagates** (or travels, horizontally), this wave is **transverse**. The time it takes for one complete vertical oscillation of a point on the rope is called the **period**, *T*, of the wave, and the number of cycles it completes in one second is called its **frequency**, *f*. The period and frequency are established by the source of the wave and $T = 1/f$.

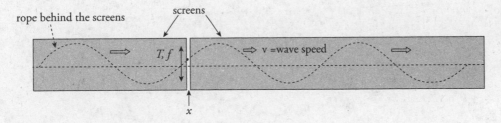

Four of the most important characteristics of any wave are its wavelength, amplitude, period, and frequency.

A fifth important characteristic of a traveling wave is its speed, *v*. Look at the figure above and imagine the visible point on the rope moving from its crest position, down to its trough position, and then back up to the crest position. How long did this take? The period, *T*. Behind the screen, the wave moved a distance of one wavelength. *T* is the time required for one wave to travel by a point, and λ is the distance traveled by one wave. Therefore, the equation *distance = rate × time* becomes

$$\lambda = vT$$

$$\lambda \cdot \frac{1}{T} = v$$

$$\lambda f = v$$

The simple equation $v = \lambda f$ shows how the wave speed, wavelength, and frequency are interconnected. *It's the most basic equation in wave theory— know it for the test.*

1. A traveling wave on a rope has a frequency of 2.5 Hz. If the speed of the wave is 1.5 m/s, what are its period and wavelength?

Here's How to Crack It

The period is the reciprocal of the frequency.

$$T = \frac{1}{f} = \frac{1}{2.5 \text{ Hz}} = 0.4 \text{ s}$$

The wavelength can be found from the equation $\lambda f = v$.

$$\lambda = \frac{v}{f} = \frac{1.5 \text{ m/s}}{2.5 \text{ Hz}} = 0.6 \text{ m}$$

2. The period of a traveling wave is 0.5 s, its amplitude is 10 cm, and its wavelength is 0.4 m. What are its frequency and wave speed?

Here's How to Crack It

The frequency is the reciprocal of the period: $f = 1/T = 1/(0.5 \text{ s}) = 2$ Hz. The wave speed can be found from the equation $v = \lambda f$:

$$v = \lambda f = (0.4 \text{ m})(2 \text{ Hz}) = 0.8 \text{ m/s}$$

(Notice that the frequency, period, wavelength, and wave speed have nothing to do with the amplitude.)

Don't be fooled by this formula. The speed of a wave does not depend on the frequency or wavelength. It depends on properties of the **medium**.

> Wave Rule #1: All waves of the same type in the same medium have the same speed.

If you move a rope up and down at a certain frequency and then suddenly increase that frequency, the speed remains unchanged. The wavelength, therefore, decreases. This makes sense since you are creating more pulses per second, each pulse won't have as much time to move down the rope before the next pulse is created. The pulses are closer together, meaning the wavelength has decreased.

Wave Speed on a Stretched String

We can also derive an equation for the speed of a transverse wave on a stretched string or rope. Let the mass of the string be m and its length be L; then its *linear mass density* (μ) is m/L. If the tension in the string is F_T, then the speed of a traveling transverse wave on this string is given by

$$v = \sqrt{\frac{F_T}{\mu}}$$

Notice that v depends only on the physical characteristics of the string—its tension and linear density. So, because $v = \lambda f$ for a given stretched string, varying f will create different waves that have different wavelengths, but v will not vary.

Questions 3-4

A horizontal rope with linear mass density $\mu = 0.5$ kg/m has a tension of 50 N. The non-attached end is oscillated vertically with a frequency of 2 Hz.

3. What are the speed and wavelength of the resulting wave?

4. How would you answer these questions if f were increased to 5 Hz?

Here's How to Crack It

3. Wave speed is established by the physical characteristics of the rope.

$$v = \sqrt{\frac{F_T}{\mu}} = \sqrt{\frac{50 \text{ N}}{0.5 \text{ kg/m}}} = 10 \text{ m/s}$$

With v, we can find the wavelength: $\lambda = v/f = (10 \text{ m/s})/(2 \text{ Hz}) = 5$ m.

4. If f were increased to 5 Hz, then v would not change, but λ would; the new wavelength would be

$$\lambda' = v / f' = (10) \text{ m/s}/ (5 \text{ Hz}) = 2m$$

Wave Rule #2: When a wave passes into a new medium, its frequency stays the same.

This can be understood if we represent a wave as a series of **wavefronts**—lines that represent, say, the crests.

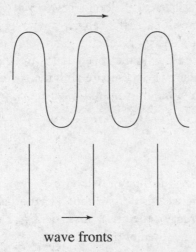

wave fronts

If a wave moves into a new medium, its speed will most likely change. However, the number of wave fronts that approach the boundary per second must be equal to the number of wavefronts that leave the boundary (that is, rate in equals rate out). The number of wave fronts per second is the frequency.

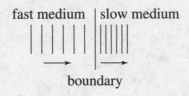

fast medium | slow medium

boundary

While the number of wavefronts leaving the first medium per second equals the number entering the second medium per second, their spacing (wavelength) changes.

———————————○———————————

5. Two ropes of unequal linear densities are connected, and a wave is created in the rope on the left, which propagates to the right, toward the interface with the heavier rope.

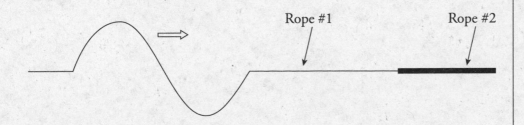

Rope #1   Rope #2

When a wave strikes the boundary to a new medium (in this case, the heavier rope), some of the wave's energy is reflected and some is transmitted. How do the speed and wavelength of the incident wave compare with the speed and wavelength of the transmitted wave?

Here's How to Crack It

Since the wave enters a new medium, it will have a new wave speed. Because rope #2 has a greater linear mass density than rope #1, and because v is inversely proportional to the square root of the linear mass density, the speed of the wave in rope #2 will be less than the speed of the wave in rope #1. Since $v = \lambda f$, and f does not change the fact that v changes means that λ must change too. In particular, since v decreases upon entering rope #2, so will λ.

SUPERPOSITION OF WAVES

When two or more waves meet, the displacement at any point of the medium is equal to the sum of the displacements due to the individual waves. This is **superposition**. The figure shows two wave pulses traveling toward each other along a stretched string. Notice that when they meet and overlap (**interfere**), the displacement of the string is equal to the sum of the individual displacements, but after they pass, the wave pulses continue, unchanged.

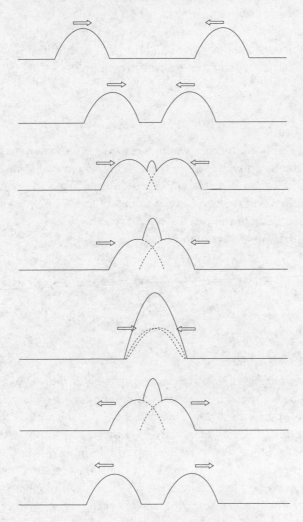

If the two waves have displacements of the same sign when they overlap, the combined wave will have a displacement of greater magnitude than either individual wave; this is called **constructive interference**. Similarly, if the waves have opposite displacements when they meet, the combined waveform will have a displacement of smaller magnitude than either individual wave; this is called **destructive interference**. If the waves travel in the same direction, the amplitude of the combined wave depends on the relative phase of the two waves. If the waves are exactly **in phase**—that is, if crest meets crest and trough meets trough—then the waves will constructively interfere completely, and the amplitude of the combined wave will be the sum of the individual amplitudes. However, if the waves are exactly **out of phase**—that is, if crest meets trough and trough meets crest—then they will destructively interfere completely, and the amplitude of the combined wave will be the difference between the individual amplitudes. In general, the waves will be somewhere in between exactly in phase and exactly out of phase.

---

6. Two waves, one with an amplitude of 8 cm and the other with an amplitude of 3 cm, travel in the same direction on a single string and overlap. What are the maximum and minimum amplitudes of the string while these waves overlap?

Here's How to Crack It
The maximum amplitude occurs when the waves are exactly in phase; the amplitude of the combined waveform will be 8 cm + 3 cm = 11 cm. The minimum amplitude occurs when the waves are exactly out of phase; the amplitude of the combined waveform will then be 8 cm − 3 cm = 5 cm. Without more information about the relative phase of the two waves, all we can say is that the amplitude will be at least 5 cm and no greater than 11 cm.

STANDING WAVES

When our prototype traveling wave on a string strikes the wall, the wave will reflect and travel back toward us. The string now supports two traveling waves; the wave we generated at our end, which travels toward the wall, and the reflected wave. What we actually see on the string is the superposition of these two oppositely directed traveling waves, which have the same frequency, amplitude, and wavelength. If the length of the string is just right, the resulting pattern will oscillate vertically and remain fixed. The crests and troughs no longer travel down the length of the string. This is a **standing wave**, another type of wave that is important for you to know about for this test.

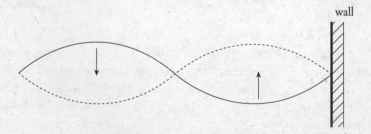

The right end of the string is fixed to the wall, and the left end is oscillated through a negligibly small amplitude so that we can consider both ends to be fixed (no vertical oscillation). The interference of the two traveling waves results in complete destructive interference at some points (marked N in the figure below), and complete constructive interference at other points (marked A in the figure). Other points have amplitudes between these extremes. Notice another difference between a traveling wave and a standing wave: While every point on the string had the same amplitude as the traveling wave went by, each point on a string supporting a standing wave has an individual amplitude. The points marked N are called **nodes**, and those marked A are called **antinodes**.

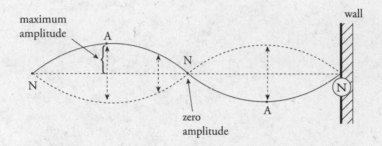

Nodes and antinodes always alternate, they're equally spaced, and the distance between two successive nodes (or antinodes) is equal to $\frac{1}{2}\lambda$. This information can be used to determine how standing waves can be generated. The following figures show the three simplest standing waves that our string can support. The first standing wave has one antinode, the second has two, and the third has three. The length of the string in all three diagrams is L.

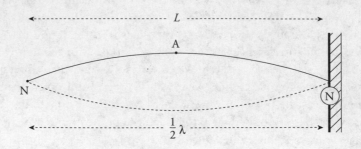

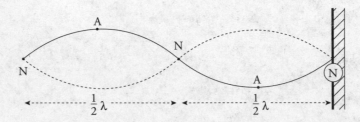

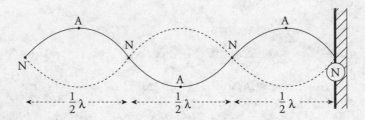

For the first standing wave, notice that L is equal to $1(\frac{1}{2}\lambda)$. For the second standing wave, L is equal to $2(\frac{1}{2}\lambda)$, and for the third, $L = 3(\frac{1}{2}\lambda)$. A pattern is established: A standing wave can only form when the length of the string is a multiple of $\frac{1}{2}\lambda$.

$$L = n(\frac{1}{2}\lambda)$$

Solving this for the wavelength, we get

$$\lambda_n = \frac{2L}{n}$$

These are called the **harmonic** (or **resonant**) **wavelengths**, and the integer n is known as the **harmonic number**.

Since we typically have control over the frequency of the waves we create, it's more helpful to figure out the *frequencies* that generate a standing wave. Because $\lambda f = v$, and because v is fixed by the physical characteristics of the string, the special λ's found above correspond to equally special frequencies. From $f_n = v/\lambda_n$, we get

$$f_n = \frac{nv}{2L}$$

These are the **harmonic** (or **resonant**) **frequencies**. A standing wave will form on a string if we create a traveling wave whose frequency is the same as a resonant frequency. The first standing wave, the one for which the harmonic number, n, is 1, is called the **fundamental standing wave**. From the equation for the harmonic frequencies, we see that the nth harmonic frequency is simply n times the fundamental frequency.

$$f_n = nf_1$$

Likewise, the nth harmonic wavelength is equal to λ_1 divided by n. Therefore, if we know the fundamental frequency (or wavelength), we can determine all the other resonant frequencies and wavelengths.

7. A string of length 12 m that's fixed at both ends supports a standing wave with a total of 5 nodes. What are the harmonic number and wavelength of this standing wave?

Here's How to Crack It
First, draw a picture.

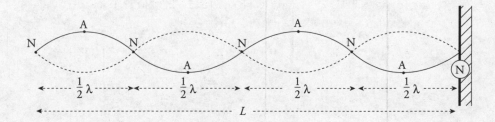

This shows that the length of the string is equal to $4(\frac{1}{2}\lambda)$, so

$$L = 4(\frac{1}{2}\lambda) \quad \Rightarrow \quad \lambda = \frac{2L}{4}.$$

This is the fourth-harmonic standing wave, with wavelength λ_4 (because the expression above matches $\lambda_n = 2L/n$ for $n = 4$). Since $L = 12$ m, the wavelength is

$$\lambda_4 = \frac{2(12 \text{ m})}{4} = 6 \text{ m}.$$

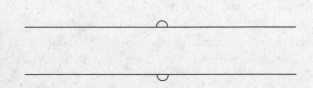

Questions 8-9

A piano tuner causes a piano string to vibrate. He then loosens the string a little, decreasing its tension, without changing the length of the string.

8. What happens to the fundamental frequency?

9. What happens to the fundamental wavelength?

Here's How to Crack It

8. The fundamental frequency for a standing wave is given by the equation $f_1 = \dfrac{v}{2L}$ where v is the speed of a wave on the string and L is the length. The length L doesn't change here, so f_1 depends only on how v changes. We know that the speed of a wave along a string decreases as the tension decreases (look back at the equation preceding example); that is, v will decrease. Therefore, f_1 will decrease, too.

9. The fundamental wavelength is given by $\lambda_1 = 2L$. Since L doesn't change, neither will λ_1.

SOUND WAVES

Sound waves are produced by the vibration of an object, such as your vocal cords, a plucked string, or a jackhammer. The vibrations cause pressure variations in the conducting medium (which can be gas, liquid, or solid), and if the frequency is between 20 Hz and 20,000 Hz, the vibrations may be detected by human ears. The variations in the conducting medium can be positions at which the molecules of the medium are bunched together (where the pressure is above normal), which are called **compressions**, and positions where the pressure is below normal, called **rarefactions**. In the figure below, a vibrating diaphragm sets up a sound wave in an air-filled tube. Each dot represents a great number of air molecules.

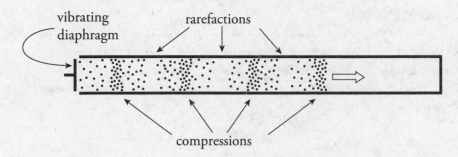

A pipe organ exploits the very phenomenon pictured and described above, to generate different notes.

An important difference between sound waves and the waves we've been studying on stretched strings is that the molecules of the medium transmitting a sound wave move *parallel* to the direction of wave propagation, rather than perpendicular to it. For this reason, sound waves are said to be **longitudinal**. Despite this difference, all of the basic characteristics of a wave—amplitude, wavelength, period, frequency—apply to sound waves as they did for waves on a string. Furthermore, the all-important equation $\lambda f = v$ also holds true. However, because it's very difficult to draw a picture of a longitudinal wave, instead graph the pressure as a function of position.

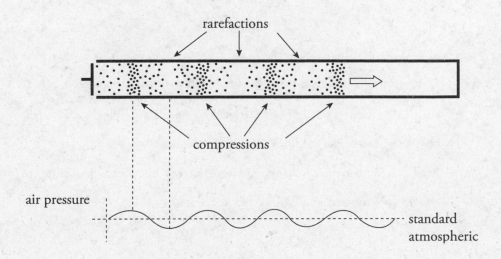

The speed of a sound wave depends on the medium through which it travels. In particular, it depends on the density (ρ) and on the **bulk modulus** (B), a measure of the medium's response to compression. A medium that is easily compressible, like a gas, has a low bulk modulus; liquids and solids, which are much less easily compressed, have significantly greater bulk modulus values. For this reason, sound generally travels faster through solids than through liquids and faster through liquids than through gases. The equation that gives a sound wave's speed in terms of ρ and B is

$$v = \sqrt{\frac{B}{\rho}}$$

The speed of sound through air can also be written in terms of air's mean pressure, which depends on its temperature. At room temperature (approximately 20 °C) and normal atmospheric pressure, sound travels at 343 m/s. This value increases as air warms or pressure increases.

Questions 10-11

A sound wave with a frequency of 343 Hz travels through the air.

10. What is its wavelength?

11. If its frequency increased to 686 Hz, what is its wave speed and the wavelength?

Here's How to Crack It

10. Using v = 343 m/s for the speed of sound through air, we find that

$$\lambda = \frac{v}{f} = \frac{343 \text{ m/s}}{343 \text{ Hz}} = 1 \text{ m}$$

11. Unless the ambient pressure or the temperature of the air changed, the speed of sound would not change. Wave speed depends on the characteristics of the medium, not on the frequency, so v would still be 343 m/s. However, a change in frequency would cause a change in wavelength. Since f increased by a factor of 2, λ would decrease by a factor of 2, to $\frac{1}{2}$ (1 m) = 0.5 m.

---

12. A sound wave traveling through water has a frequency of 500 Hz and a wavelength of 3 m. How fast does sound travel through water?

Here's How to Crack It

$$v = \lambda f = (3 \text{ m})(500 \text{ Hz}) = 1,500 \text{ m/s.}$$

Intensity and Decibel Level

How loud we perceive a sound depends on both frequency and amplitude. Given a fixed frequency, we can say that loudness is measured by **intensity**.

Intensity: $I = \dfrac{P}{A}$

Where P is the power produced by the source and A is the area over which the power is spread. Consider a point source emitting a sound wave in all directions.

At a distance r, the $A = 4\pi r^2$ (the surface area of the sphere). Therefore, $I\alpha\dfrac{1}{r^2}$ If a listener doubles the distance to the source, the sound will be heard one-fourth as loud. An alternate way of measuring loudness is with the **decibel level** (sometimes called *relative intensity*).

Decibel Level: $\beta = 10\log(\dfrac{I}{I_0})$

I_0 is the threshold of hearing and is equal to 10^{-12} watts. Note that, while β is measured in decibels (dB), it is dimensionless.

A useful fact to remember is that if a sound increases by 10dB, the intensity increases by a factor of 10.

───────────○───────────

13. How many times more intense is an 82 dB sound than a 52 dB sound?

Here's How to Crack It
82 dB is 30 dB louder than 52 dB. Each change of 10 dB increases the intensity by a factor of 10. 30 dB is 3•10 so the intensity would be 10 x 10 x 10= 1,000 times more intense.

───────────○───────────

Beats

If two sound waves whose frequencies are close but not identical interfere, the resulting sound modulates in amplitude, becoming loud, then soft, then loud, then soft. This is due to the fact that as the individual waves travel, they are in phase, then out of phase, then in phase again, and so on. Therefore, by superposition, the waves interfere constructively, then destructively, then constructively. When the waves interfere constructively, the amplitude increases, and the sound is loud; when the waves interfere destructively, the amplitude decreases, and the sound is soft. Each time the waves interfere constructively, producing an increase in sound level, we say that a **beat** has occurred. The number of beats per second, known as the beat frequency, is equal to the difference between the frequencies of the two combining sound waves.

$$f_{\text{beat}} = |f_1 - f_2|$$

If frequencies f_1 and f_2 match, then the combined waveform doesn't waver in amplitude, and no beats are heard. For example, pianos can be tuned using the phenomenon of beats. A key is struck, and the corresponding tuning fork is struck; if the piano string is in tune, there should be no beats as the two sounds interfere. If beats are heard, then the piano tuner tightens or loosens the string and repeats until no beats are heard.

Questions 14-15

A piano tuner uses a tuning fork to adjust the key that plays the A note above middle C (whose frequency should be 440 Hz). The tuning fork emits a perfect 440 Hz tone. When the tuning fork and the piano key are struck, beats of frequency 3 Hz are heard.

14. What is the frequency of the piano key?

15. If it's known that the piano key's frequency is too high, should the piano tuner tighten or loosen the wire inside the piano to tune it?

Here's How to Crack It

14. Since f_{beat} = 3 Hz, the tuning fork and the piano string are off by 3 Hz. Since the fork emits a tone of 440 Hz, the piano string must emit a tone of either 437 Hz or 443 Hz. Without more information, we can't decide which one is correct. On the test, only one answer is correct per question; pick the one that you see in the answers.

15. If we know that the frequency of the tone emitted by the out-of-tune string is too high (that is, it's 443 Hz), we need to find a way to lower the frequency. Remember that the resonant frequencies for a stretched string fixed at both ends are given by the equation $f_n = nv/2L$, and that $v = \sqrt{F_T/\mu}$. Since f is too high, v must be too high. To lower v, we must reduce F_T. The piano tuner should loosen the string and listen for beats again, adjusting the string until the beats disappear.

RESONANCE FOR SOUND WAVES

Just as standing waves can be set up on a vibrating string, standing *sound* waves can be established within an enclosure. In the figure below, a vibrating source at one end of an air-filled tube produces sound waves that travel the length of the tube.

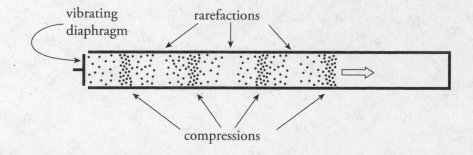

These waves reflect off the far end, and the superposition of the forward and reflected waves can produce a standing wave pattern if the length of the tube and the frequency of the waves are related in a certain way.

Notice that air molecules at the far end of the tube can't oscillate horizontally because they're up against a wall. So the far end of the tube is a displacement node. But the other end of the tube (where the vibrating source is located) is a displacement antinode. A standing wave with one antinode (A) and one node position (N) can be shown as follows:

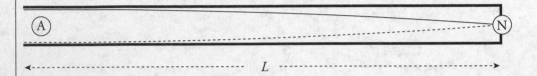

Although sound waves in air are longitudinal, here we'll show the wave as transverse so that it's easier to determine the wavelength. Since the distance between an antinode and an adjacent node is always $\frac{1}{4}$ of the wavelength, the length of the tube, L, in the figure above is $\frac{1}{4}$ the wavelength. This is the longest standing wavelength that can fit in the tube, so it corresponds to the lowest standing wave frequency, the fundamental

$$L = \frac{\lambda_1}{4} \quad \Rightarrow \quad \lambda_1 = 4L \quad \Rightarrow \quad f_1 = \frac{v}{\lambda_1} = \frac{v}{4L}.$$

The next higher-frequency standing wave that can be supported in this tube must have two antinodes and two nodes.

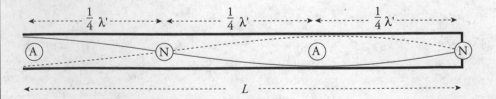

In this case, the length of the tube is equal to $3(\frac{1}{4}\lambda')$, so

$$L = \frac{3\lambda'}{4} \quad \Rightarrow \quad \lambda' = \frac{4L}{3} \quad \Rightarrow \quad f' = \frac{v}{\lambda'} = \frac{3v}{4L}$$

Here's the pattern: Standing sound waves can be established in a tube that's closed at one end if the tube's length is equal to an *odd* multiple of $\frac{1}{4}\lambda$. The resonant wavelengths and frequencies are given by the equations

$$\left.\begin{array}{l} \lambda_n = \dfrac{4L}{n} \\[2em] f_n = n\dfrac{v}{4L} \end{array}\right\} \text{ for any } odd \text{ integer } n$$

If the far end of the tube is not sealed, standing waves can still be established in the tube, because sound waves can be reflected from the open air. A closed end is a displacement node, but an open end is a displacement antinode. In this case, then, the standing waves will have two displacement antinodes (at the ends of the tube), and the resonant wavelengths and frequencies will be given by

$$\left.\begin{array}{l} \lambda_n = \dfrac{2L}{n} \\[2em] f_n = n\dfrac{v}{2L} \end{array}\right\} \text{ for any integer } n$$

Notice that, while an open-ended tube can support any harmonic, a closed-end tube can only support *odd* harmonics.

Question 16-18

A closed-end tube resonates at a fundamental frequency of 343 Hz. The air in the tube is at a temperature of 20°C, and it conducts sound at a speed of 343 m/s.

16. What is the length of the tube?

17. What is the next higher harmonic frequency?

18. Answer the questions posed in questions 15 and 16 assuming that the tube was open at its far end.

16. For a closed-end tube, the harmonic frequencies obey the equation $f_n = \dfrac{nv}{4L}$. The fundamental corresponds to $n = 1$, so

$$f_1 = \frac{v}{4L} \Rightarrow L = \frac{v}{4f_1} = \frac{343 \text{ m/s}}{4(343 \text{ Hz})} = 0.25 \text{ m} = 25 \text{ cm}.$$

17. Since a closed-end tube can support only *odd* harmonics, the next higher harmonic frequency (the first **overtone**) is the *third* harmonic, f_3, which is $3f_1 = 3(343 \text{ Hz}) = 1{,}029 \text{ Hz}$.

18. For an opened-end tube, the harmonic frequencies obey the equation $f_n = nv/(2L)$. The fundamental corresponds to $n = 1$, so

$$f_1 = \frac{v}{2L} \Rightarrow L' = \frac{v}{2f_1} = \frac{343 \text{ m/s}}{2(343 \text{ Hz})} = 0.50 \text{ m} = 50 \text{ cm}.$$

Since an opened-end tube can support any harmonic, the first overtone would be the second harmonic, $f_2 = 2f_1 = 2(343 \text{ Hz}) = 686 \text{ Hz}$.

THE DOPPLER EFFECT

When a source of sound waves and a detector are not in relative motion, the frequency that the source emits matches the frequency that the detector receives.

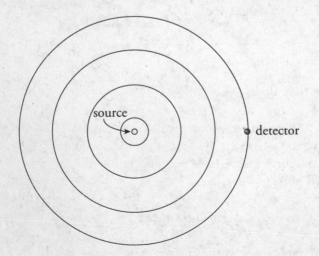

However, if there *is* relative motion between the source and the detector, then the waves that the detector receives are different in frequency. For example, if the detector moves toward the source, then the detector intercepts the waves at a rate higher than the one at which they were emitted; the detector hears a higher frequency than the source emitted. In the same way, if the source moves toward the detector, the wavefronts pile up, and this results in the detector receiving waves with shorter wavelengths and higher frequencies.

Note that when the detector moves and not the source, there is no change in wavelength. Instead, there is a change to the speed with which the detector receives wavefronts.

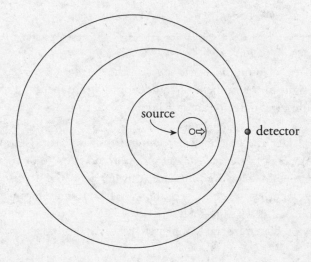

Conversely, if the detector is moving away from the source or if the source is moving away from the detector

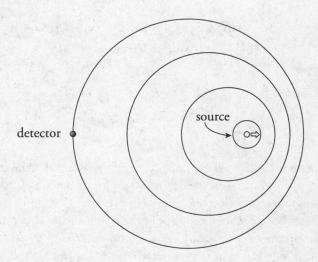

then the detected waves have a lower frequency than they had when they were emitted by the source. The shift in frequency that occurs when the source and detector are in relative motion is known as the **Doppler effect**. In general, relative motion *toward* each other results in a frequency shift upward, and relative motion *away* from each other results in a frequency shift downward.

Let f_S be the frequency of waves that the source emits and f_D the frequency that the detector hears. To determine f_D from f_S, use the following equation:

$$f_D = \frac{v \pm v_D}{v \pm v_S} \cdot f_S$$

where v is the speed of sound, v_D is the speed of the detector, and v_S is the speed of the source. The signs in the numerator and denominator depend on the directions in which the source and detector are moving.

For example, consider the case of a detector moving toward a stationary source. Since the source doesn't move, $v_S = 0$, and there's no decision to be made about the sign in the denominator. However, because v_D is not zero (the detector is moving), we need to decide whether to use the + or the − in the numerator. Since the detector moves *toward* the source, we expect a frequency shift upward. Therefore, to give the higher frequency predicted by the Doppler effect, the + sign must be used.

$$f_D = \frac{v + v_D}{v} \cdot f_S$$

If the detector had been moving *away* from the source, we would have used the − sign in the numerator, to get the lower frequency.

$$f_D = \frac{v - v_D}{v} \cdot f_S$$

If both the source and the detector are moving, simply make each decision (+ or − in the numerator for v_D and + or − in the denominator for v_S) separately. For example, consider a car following a police car whose siren emits a sound of constant frequency. In this case, both the source (the police car) and the detector (the driver of the pursuing car) are moving. Because the detector is moving toward the source, we should use the + sign on v_D in the numerator for an upward contribution to f_D.

Since the source is moving away from the detector, we should use the + sign on v_S in the denominator for a downward contribution to f_D. Therefore, we get

$$f_D = \frac{v + v_D}{v + v_S} \cdot f_S.$$

We can learn something else from this. What if the car were moving at the same speed as the police car? Then, although both are moving relative to the road, *they are not moving relative to each other*. If there is no relative motion between the source and the detector, then there should be no Doppler shift, since $v_D = v_S$ implies that $f_D = f_S$.

Questions 19-20

A source of 4 kHz sound waves travels at $\dfrac{1}{9}$ the speed of sound toward a detector that's moving at $\dfrac{1}{9}$ the speed of sound, toward the source.

19. What is the frequency of the waves as they're received by the detector?

Here's How to Crack It

19. Because the detector moves toward the source, we use the + sign in the numerator of the Doppler effect formula, and since the source moves toward the detector, we use the − sign in the denominator. This gives us

$$f_D = \frac{v + v_D}{v - v_S} \cdot f_S = \frac{v + \frac{1}{9}v}{v - \frac{1}{9}v} \cdot f_S = \frac{5}{4}f_S = \frac{5}{4}(4 \text{ kHz}) = 5 \text{ kHz}$$

---

20. A train sounds its whistle as it travels at a constant speed by a train station. Describe the pitch of the train's whistle as heard by someone standing on the station platform.

Here's How to Crack It

Because the "pitch" of a sound is its frequency, we want to describe the frequency of the train whistle as heard by someone on the platform. As the train *approaches* the platform, the frequency detected will be *higher* than the frequency emitted by the train; then, as the train *recedes* from the platform, the frequency detected will be *lower* than the frequency emitted by the train. So, a person standing on the platform hears a higher pitch as the train approaches and a lower pitch as it travels away.

THE DOPPLER EFFECT FOR LIGHT

Light, or electromagnetic waves, also experience the Doppler effect. As with sound, motion *toward* corresponds to a frequency shift upward and motion *away* corresponds to a frequency shift downward. Because of special relativity (discussed in Chapter 17), the wavelength will change regardless of who moves.

21. Light from a distant galaxy is received on Earth with a wavelength of 650 nm. It's known that the wavelength of this light upon emission was 625 nm. Is the galaxy moving toward us or away from us?

Here's How to Crack It

The fact that the light has a longer wavelength upon detection than it had at emission tells us that the source is receding. Astronomers would say that the light has been **red-shifted**—that is, the wavelength was shifted upward, toward the red end of the visible spectrum.

Chapter 15 Review Questions

Answers are on page 415.

1. What is the wavelength of a 5 Hz wave that travels with a speed of 10 m/s?

   (A) 0.25 m
   (B) 0.5 m
   (C) 1 m
   (D) 2 m
   (E) 50 m

2. A rope of length 5 m is stretched to a tension of 80 N. If its mass is 1 kg, at what speed would a 10 Hz transverse wave travel down the string?

   (A) 2 m/s
   (B) 5 m/s
   (C) 20 m/s
   (D) 50 m/s
   (E) 200 m/s

3. A transverse wave on a long horizontal rope with a wavelength of 8 m travels at 2 m/s. At $t = 0$, a particular point on the rope has a vertical displacement of $+A$, where A is the amplitude of the wave. At what time will the vertical displacement of this same point on the rope be $-A$?

   (A) $t = \dfrac{1}{8}$ s

   (B) $t = \dfrac{1}{4}$ s

   (C) $t = \dfrac{1}{2}$ s

   (D) $t = 2$ s

   (E) $t = 4$ s

4. What is the wavelength of a wave with period 2s and speed 2 cm/s?

   (A) 0.25 cm
   (B) 0.5 cm
   (C) 1 cm
   (D) 2 cm
   (E) 4 cm

5. A string, fixed at both ends, supports a standing wave with a total of 4 nodes. If the length of the string is 6 m, what is the wavelength of the wave?

   (A) 0.67 m
   (B) 1.2 m
   (C) 1.5 m
   (D) 3 m
   (E) 4 m

6. A string, fixed at both ends, has a length of 6 m and supports a standing wave with a total of 4 nodes. If a transverse wave can travel at 40 m/s down the rope, what is the frequency of this standing wave?

   (A) 6.7 Hz
   (B) 10.0 Hz
   (C) 13.3 Hz
   (D) 20.0 Hz
   (E) 26.7 Hz

7. A sound wave travels through a metal rod with wavelength λ and frequency f. Which of the following best describes the wave when it passes into the surrounding air?

	Wavelength	Frequency
(A)	Less than λ	Equal to f
(B)	Less than λ	Less than f
(C)	Greater than λ	Equal to f
(D)	Greater than λ	Less than f
(E)	Greater than λ	Greater than f

8. In the figure below, two speakers, S_1 and S_2, emit sound waves of wavelength 2 m, in phase with each other.

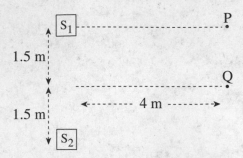

Let A_P be the amplitude of the resulting wave at point P, and A_Q the amplitude of the resultant wave at point Q. How does A_P compare to A_Q?

(A) $A_P < A_Q$
(B) $A_P = A_Q$
(C) $A_P > A_Q$
(D) $A_P < 0, A_Q > 0$
(E) A_P and A_Q vary with time, so no comparison can be made.

9. An observer is 2 m from a source of sound waves. By how much will the sound level decrease if the observer moves to a distance of 20 m ?

(A) 1 dB
(B) 2 dB
(C) 10 dB
(D) 18 dB
(E) 20 dB

10. An organ pipe that's closed at one end has a length of 17 cm. If the speed of sound through the air inside is 340 m/s, what is the pipe's fundamental frequency?

(A) 250 Hz
(B) 500 Hz
(C) 1,000 Hz
(D) 1,500 Hz
(E) 2,000 Hz

11. A bat emits a 40 kHz "chirp" with a wavelength of 8.75 mm toward a tree and receives an echo 0.4 s later. How far is the bat from the tree?

(A) 35 m
(B) 70 m
(C) 105 m
(D) 140 m
(E) 175 m

12. A car is traveling at 20 m/s away from a stationary observer. If the car's horn emits a frequency of 600 Hz, what frequency will the observer hear? (Use $v = 340$ m/s for the speed of sound.)

(A) (34/36)(600 Hz)
(B) (34/32)(600 Hz)
(C) (36/34)(600 Hz)
(D) (32/34)(600 Hz)
(E) (32/36)(600 Hz)

Keywords

mechanical wave
traveling wave
crests
troughs
wavelength
amplitude
propagates
transverse
period
frequency
wavefronts
superposition
interfere
constructive interference
destructive interference
in phase
out of phase
standing wave
nodes
antinodes
harmonic (resonant) wavelengths
harmonic number
harmonic (resonant) frequencies
fundamental standing wave
compressions
rarefactions
longitudinal
bulk modulus
beat
overtone
Doppler effect
red-shifted
intensity
decibel level

Summary

o For traveling waves, in which the peaks and valleys visibly move along the length of a rope, the displacement y of each point depends also on x and t.

o In the point of view in which x varies, and t does not, we "freeze time" and see the-points at which the wave crosses the horizontal, the maximum vertical displacement above the horizontal (crests), and the maximum vertical displacement below the horizontal (the troughs).

o In the point of view in which t varies, and x does not, you designate one position x along the rope to watch as time varies. The point on the rope will oscillate vertically and the wave propagates, or travels, horizontally.

o The five most important characteristics of a traveling wave are its wavelength, amplitude, period, frequency, and speed.

o The equation to determine wave speed on a stretched string is $v = \sqrt{\dfrac{F_T}{\mu}}$.

o Superposition of waves is the concept that when two or more waves meet, the displacement at any point of the medium is equal to the sum of the displacements due to the individual waves. When waves meet and overlap (interfere) the displacement of the string is equal to the sum of the individual displacements.

o Constructive interference creates a combined wave of greater magnitude than either individual wave. Destructive interference results in a combined waveform that has a displacement of a smaller magnitude that either individual wave.

o Standing waves are seen when two oppositely traveling waves that have the same frequency, amplitude, and wavelength oscillate vertically and remain fixed. The crests and troughs do not appear to travel down the length of the string.

o   Sound waves are produced by the vibration of an object. The vibrations cause pressure variations in the conducting medium: Compressions are where the molecules are bunched together (the pressure is above normal). Rarefactions are the positions where the pressure is below normal.

o   Sound waves differ from waves on strings in that the molecules of a medium transmitting a sound wave move parallel to the direction of wave propagation rather than perpendicular to it.

o   Intensity and decibel level measure the loudness of a sound. Decibel level is measured on a logarithmic scale.

o   Resonance for sound waves follows a pattern of nodes and anti-nodes. While an open-ended tube can support any harmonic—any integer times $\frac{1}{4}\lambda$, a closed-end tube can only support odd harmonics—an odd multiple of $\frac{1}{4}\lambda$.

o   The Doppler effect occurs when there is relative motion between the source of the sound waves and the detector. When the detector moves toward the source (or vice-versa), she intercepts the waves at a rate higher than the one at which they were emitted and hears a higher frequency than the source emitted. If the detector is moving away from the source or if the source is moving away from the detector, the detected waves have a lower frequency than originally emitted by the source.

o   Light, or electromagnetic waves, also experiences the Doppler effect. Motion toward the source corresponds to a frequency shift upward (and a wavelength shift downward). Motion away from the source corresponds to a frequency shift downward (and a wavelength shift upward).

Chapter 16
Optics

Optics is the study of light and its interaction with devices such as mirrors, lenses, and prisms. Light (or visible light) makes up only a small part of the entire spectrum of electromagnetic waves, which ranges from radio waves to gamma rays. The waves we studied in the preceding chapter needed a material medium to travel through, but electromagnetic waves can propagate through empty space. Electromagnetic waves consist of time-varying electric and magnetic fields that oscillate perpendicular to each other and to the direction of propagation of the wave.

THE ELECTROMAGNETIC SPECTRUM

Through a vacuum, all electromagnetic waves travel at a fixed speed

$$c = 3.00 \times 10^8 \text{ m/s}$$

regardless of their frequency.

Electromagnetic waves can be categorized by their frequency (or wavelength); the full range of waves is called the **electromagnetic** (or **EM**) **spectrum**. Types of waves include **radiowaves**, **microwaves**, **infrared**, **visible light**, **ultraviolet**, **X-rays**, and **γ-rays** (**gamma rays**), and although they've been placed in the spectrum below, there's no universal agreement on all the boundaries, so many of these bands overlap. You should be familiar with the names of the major categories and, in particular, memorize the order of the colors within the visible spectrum (which, as you can see, accounts for only a tiny sliver of the full EM spectrum). In order of increasing wave frequency, the colors are red, orange, yellow, green, blue, and violet, which is commonly remembered as ROYGBV ("roy-gee-biv"). The wavelengths of the colors in the visible spectrum are usually expressed in nanometers. For example, electromagnetic waves whose wavelengths are between 577 nm and 597 nm are seen as yellow light.

Electromagnetic Spectrum

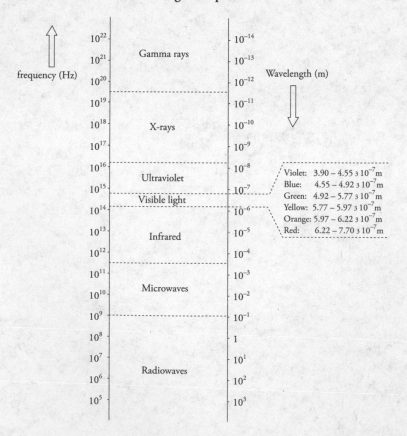

1. What's the approximate frequency range for orange light?

Here's How to Crack It

According to the spectrum, light is orange if its wavelength is between about 6×10^{-7} m and 6.25×10^{-7} m. Using the equation $\lambda f = c$, we find that the upper end of this wavelength range corresponds to a frequency of

$$f_1 = \frac{c}{\lambda_1} = \frac{3.00 \times 10^8 \text{ m/s}}{6.25 \times 10^{-7} \text{ m}} = 4.8 \times 10^{14} \text{ Hz}$$

while the lower end corresponds to

$$f_2 = \frac{c}{\lambda_2} = \frac{3.00 \times 10^8 \text{ m/s}}{6 \times 10^{-7} \text{ m}} = 5 \times 10^{14} \text{ Hz}$$

So the frequency range for orange light is

$$4.8 \times 10^{14} \text{ Hz} \leq f_{\text{orange}} \leq 5 \times 10^{14} \text{ Hz}$$

2. How would you classify electromagnetic radiation that has a wavelength of 1 cm ?

Here's How to Crack It

According to the electromagnetic spectrum presented on the previous page, electromagnetic waves with $\lambda = 10^{-2}$ m are microwaves.

INTERFERENCE AND DIFFRACTION

As we learned in the preceding chapter, waves experience interference when they meet, and whether they interfere constructively or destructively depends on their relative phase. If they meet *in phase* (crest meets crest), they combine constructively, but if they meet *out of phase* (crest meets trough), they combine destructively. The key to the interference patterns we'll study in the next section rests on these points. In particular, if waves that have the same wavelength meet, then the difference in the distances they've traveled determine whether they are in phase. Assuming that the waves are **coherent** (which means that their phase difference remains constant over time and does not vary), if the difference in their path lengths, $\Delta \ell$, is a whole number of wavelengths—0, $\pm\lambda$, $\pm 2\lambda$, etc.—they'll arrive in phase at the meeting point. However, if this difference is a whole number plus one-half a wavelength— $\pm\frac{1}{2}\lambda$, $\pm(1 + \frac{1}{2})\lambda$, $\pm(2 + \frac{1}{2})\lambda$, etc.—then they'll arrive exactly out of phase. That is

$$\left.\begin{array}{ll}\text{constructive interference:} & \Delta\ell = m\lambda \\[2mm] \text{destructive interference:} & \Delta\ell = (m+\frac{1}{2})\lambda\end{array}\right\} \text{where } m \text{ is an integer}$$

Young's Double-Slit Interference Experiment

The following figure shows light incident (shining) on a barrier that contains two narrow slits (perpendicular to the plane of the page), separated by a distance d. On the right is a screen whose distance from the barrier, L, is much greater than d. The question is, What will we see on the screen? You might expect to see just two bright narrow strips of light, directly opposite the slits in the barrier, but this is not what happens.

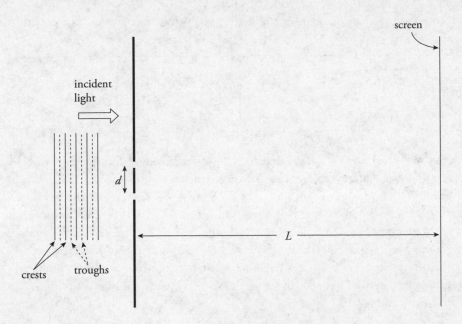

When a wave encounters a slit with a width that's comparable with its wavelength, the wave will fan out after it passes through. This phenomenon is called **diffraction**. In the set-up above, the waves will diffract through the slits and spread out and interfere as they travel toward the screen.

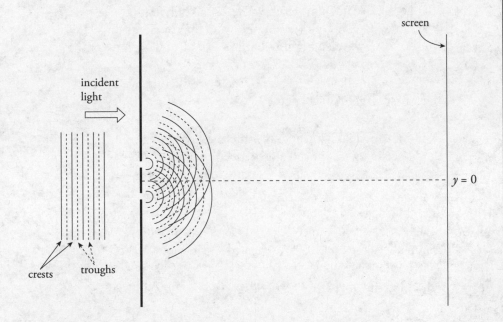

The screen shows the results of this interference: There will be bright bands (**fringes**) centered at those points at which the waves interfere constructively, alternating with dark fringes, where the waves interfere destructively.

To locate the positions of, say, the bright fringes on the screen, we use the equation.

$$y_m = \frac{m\lambda L}{d}$$

Where y measures the vertical displacement along the screen from the center of the screen ($y = 0$, the point directly across from the midpoint of the slits). The bright fringe directly opposite the midpoint of the slits—the **central maximum**—will have the greatest intensity, the bright fringes with $m = \pm 1$ will have a lower intensity, those with $m = \pm 2$ will be fainter still, and so on. If more than two slits are cut in the barrier, the interference pattern becomes sharper, and the distinction between dark and bright fringes becomes more pronounced. Barriers containing thousands of tiny slits per centimeter—called **diffraction gratings**—are used precisely for this purpose.

Questions 3-4

For the experimental set-up we've been studying, assume that $d = 1$ mm, $L = 6.0$ m, and that the light used has a wavelength of 600 nm.

3. How far above the center of the screen will the first bright fringe appear?

4. What would happen to the interference pattern if the slits were moved closer together?

Here's How to Crack It

3.   The central maximum corresponds to $m = 0$ ($y_0 = 0$). The first maximum above the central one is labeled y_1 (since $m = 1$), and the first maximum below the central one is labeled y_{-1} (that is, $m = -1$). The other bright fringes on the screen are labeled accordingly.

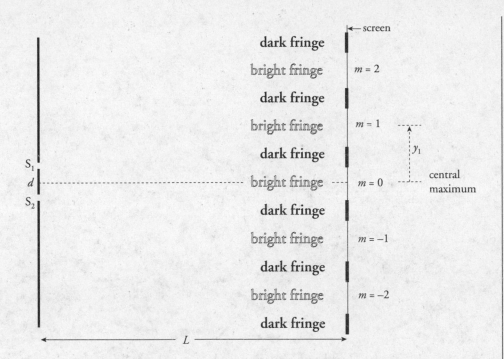

The value of y_1 is

$$y_1 = \frac{1 \cdot \lambda L}{d} = \frac{\left(600 \times 10^{-9}\,\text{m}\right)\left(6.0\,\text{m}\right)}{1 \times 10^{-3}\,\text{m}} = 3.6 \times 10^{-3}\,\text{m} = 3.6\,\text{mm}$$

4. Since $y_m = m\,\lambda\,L/d$, a decrease in d would cause an increase in y_m. In other words, the fringes would become larger and the interference pattern would be more spread out.

Single-Aperture Diffraction

A diffraction pattern will also form on the screen if the barrier contains only one slit. The central maximum will be very pronounced, but lower-intensity maxima will also be seen because of interference from waves arriving from different locations within the slit itself. The width of the central maximum will become wider as the width of the slit is decreased.

REFLECTION AND REFRACTION

Imagine a beam of light directed toward a smooth transparent surface. When it hits this surface, some of its energy will be reflected off the surface and some will be transmitted into the new medium. We can figure out the directions of the reflected and transmitted beams by calculating the angles that the beams make with the normal to the interface. The normal is a line perpendicular to the interface. In the following figure, an incident beam strikes the boundary of another medium; it could be a beam of light in air striking a piece of glass.

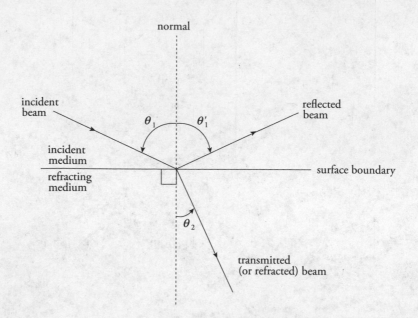

The angle that the **incident beam** makes with the normal is called the **angle of incidence**, or θ_1. The angle that the **reflected beam** makes with the normal is called the **angle of reflection**, θ_1, and the angle that the **transmitted beam** makes with the normal is called the **angle of refraction**, θ_2. The incident, reflected, and transmitted beams of light all lie in the same plane.

The relationship between θ_1 and θ_1' is pretty simple; it is called the **law of reflection**.

$$\theta_1 = \theta_1'$$

To describe how θ_1 and θ_2 are related, we first need to talk about a medium's index of refraction.

When light travels through empty space (vacuum), its speed is $c = 3.00 \times 10^8$ m/s; but when a light travels through a material medium (such as water or glass), it's constantly being absorbed and re-emitted by the atoms of the material and, as a result, its apparent speed, v, is some fraction of c. The reciprocal of this fraction,

$$n = \frac{c}{v}$$

is called the medium's **index of refraction**.

For example, since the speed of light in water is $v = 2.25 \times 10^8$ m/s, the index of refraction of water is

$$n = \frac{3.00 \times 10^8 \text{ m/s}}{2.25 \times 10^8 \text{ m/s}} = 1.33$$

Notice that n has no units; it's also never less than 1.

The equation that relates θ_1 and θ_2 involves the index of refraction of the incident medium (n_1) and the index of refraction of the refracting medium (n_2); it's called **Snell's law** (know this for the test).

$$n_1 \sin \theta_1 = n_2 \sin \theta_2$$

If $n_2 > n_1$ (i.e., when the light slows down in n_2), then Snell's law tells us that $\theta_2 < \theta_1$; that is, the beam will bend (**refract**) *toward* the normal as it enters the medium. On the contrary, if $n_2 < n_1$ (i.e., when the light speeds up in n_2), then $\theta_2 > \theta_1$, and the beam will bend *away* from the normal.

5. A beam of light in air is incident upon a piece of glass, striking the surface at an angle of 60°. If the index of refraction of the glass is 1.5, what are the angles of reflection and refraction?

Here's How to Crack It

If the light beam makes an angle of 60° with the surface, then it makes an angle of 30° with the normal; this is the angle of incidence. By the law of reflection, then, the angle of reflection is also 30°. We use Snell's law to find the angle of refraction. The index of refraction of air is close to 1, so we can say that $n = 1$ for air.

$$n_1 \sin \theta_1 = n_2 \sin \theta_2$$
$$1 \cdot \sin 30° = 1.5 \sin \theta_2$$
$$\sin \theta_2 = 0.33$$
$$\theta_2 = \sin^{-1}(0.33)$$

which is about 19°.

Notice that $\theta_2 < \theta_1$, as we would expect, since the refracting medium (glass) has a greater index than the incident medium (air).

Dispersion of Light

One thing we learned when we studied waves is that wave speed is independent of frequency (Wave Rule #1). For a given medium, different frequencies give rise to different wavelengths because the equation $\lambda f = v$ must always be satisfied and v doesn't vary. But when light travels through a material medium, it displays **dispersion**, which is a variation in wave speed with frequency (or wavelength). So, the definition of the index of refraction, $n = c/v$, should be accompanied by a statement of the frequency of the light used to measure v, since different frequencies have different speeds and different indices. A piece of glass may have the following indices for visible light.

	red	orange	yellow	green	blue	violet
$n =$	1.502	1.506	1.511	1.517	1.523	1.530

Notice that as the wavelength decreases, the refractive index increases. In general, higher frequency waves have higher indices of refraction. Most lists of refractive index values are tabulated using yellow light of wavelength 589 nm (frequency 5.1×10^{14} Hz).

Although the variation in the values of the refractive index across the visible spectrum is pretty small, when white light (which is a combination of all the colors of the visible spectrum) hits a glass prism, the beam is split into its component colors.

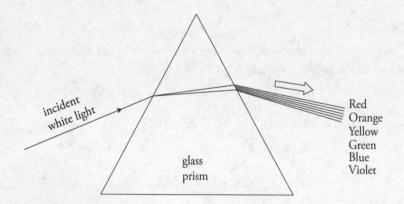

Why? Because each color has its own index. Snell's law tells us that each color will have its own angle of refraction. Therefore, each color emerges from the prism at a slightly different angle, so the light disperses into its component colors.

Total Internal Reflection

When a beam of light strikes the boundary to a medium that has a lower index of refraction, the beam bends away from the normal. As the angle of incidence increases, the angle of refraction becomes larger. At some point, when the angle of incidence reaches a **critical angle**, θ_c, the angle of refraction becomes 90°, which means the refracted beam is directed along the surface.

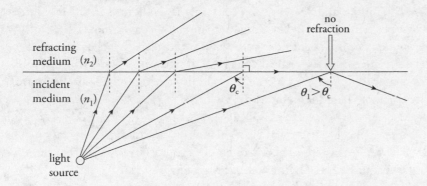

For angles of incidence that are greater than θ_c, there is *no* angle of refraction; the entire beam is reflected back into the original medium. This phenomenon is called **total internal reflection** (sometimes abbreviated **TIR**).

Total internal reflection occurs when

1) $n_1 > n_2$

and

2) $\theta_1 > \theta_c$, where $\theta_c = \sin^{-1}(n_2/n_1)$

Notice that total internal reflection cannot occur if $n_1 < n_2$. If $n_1 > n_2$, then total internal reflection is a possibility; it will occur if the angle of incidence is large enough, that is, if it's greater than the critical angle, θ_c.

Questions 6-7

The critical angle for total internal reflection between air and water is known to be 49°.

6. If a beam of light striking an air/water boundary undergoes total internal reflection, will it stay in the air or in the water?

7. Describe what happens if a beam of light in the air strikes the surface of a calm body of water at an angle of 50° to the normal.

Here's How to Crack It

6. Total internal reflection can occur only if the light is in the medium with the higher index of refraction and strikes a boundary beyond which the index of refraction is lower (and if the angle of incidence is greater than the critical angle). So, if a beam of light striking an air/water boundary experiences total internal reflection, it must have originated (and remain) in the water.

7. The angle of incidence is 50°, which is greater than the critical angle. However, total internal reflection does not occur because the beam is in the air, the medium of lower refractive index. So, the light will experience some reflection (bouncing off the water) and some refraction (bending into the water). The angle of reflection will be the same as the angle of incidence (50°), and the angle of refraction will be smaller than 50° because a beam of light always bends toward the normal when it enters a medium with a greater index of refraction.

MIRRORS

A **mirror** is an optical device that forms an image by reflecting light. We've all looked into a mirror and seen images of nearby objects. Flat mirrors are called **plane mirrors**. Let's begin with a plane mirror; the simplest type of mirror. Then we'll examine curved mirrors; we'll have to use geometrical methods or algebraic equations to analyze the patterns of reflection from these.

Plane Mirrors

The figure below shows an object (denoted by a bold arrow) in front of a flat mirror. Light that's reflected off of the object strikes the mirror and is reflected back to our eyes. The directions of the rays reflected off the mirror determines where we perceive the image to be.

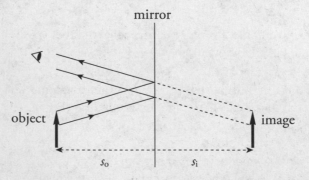

There are four questions we'll answer about the image formed by a mirror.

(1) Where is the image?
(2) Is the image real or is it virtual?
(3) Is the image upright or is it inverted?
(4) What is the height of the image (compared with that of the object)?

When we look at ourselves in a mirror, it seems like our image is *behind* the mirror, and, if we take a step back, our image also takes a step back. The law of reflection can be used to show that the image seems as far behind the mirror as the object is in front of the mirror. This answers question (1).

An image is said to be **real** if light rays actually focus at the image. A real image can be projected onto a screen. For a flat mirror, light rays bounce off the front of the mirror; so, of course, no light focuses behind it. Therefore, the images produced by a flat mirror are not real; they are **virtual**. This answers question (2).

When we look into a flat mirror, our image isn't upside down; flat mirrors produce upright images, and question (3) is answered.

Finally, the image formed by a flat mirror is neither magnified nor diminished (minified) relative to the size of the object. This answers question (4).

Spherical Mirrors

A **spherical mirror** is a mirror that's curved in such a way that its surface forms part of a sphere.

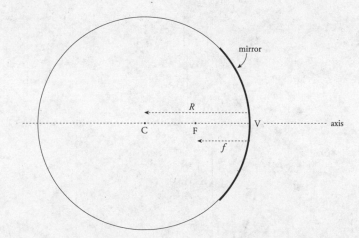

The center of this imaginary sphere is the mirror's **center of curvature**, and the radius of the sphere is called the mirror's **radius of curvature**, R. Halfway between the mirror and the center of curvature, C, is the **focus** (or **focal point**), F. The intersection of the mirror's optic **axis** (its axis of symmetry) with the mirror itself is called the **vertex**, V, and the distance from V to F is called the **focal length**, f, which is equal to one-half of the radius of curvature.

$$f = \frac{R}{2}$$

If the mirror had a parabolic cross-section, then any ray parallel to the axis would be reflected by the mirror through the focal point. Spherical mirrors do this for incident light rays near the axis (**paraxial rays**) because in the region of the mirror that's close to the axis, the shapes of a parabolic mirror and a spherical mirror are nearly identical.

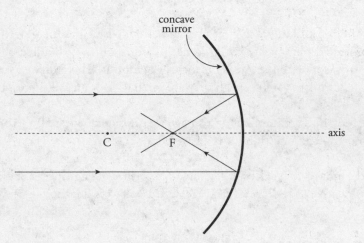

The previous two figures illustrate a **concave mirror**, a mirror whose reflective side is *caved in* toward the center of curvature. The following figure illustrates the **convex mirror**, which has a reflective side that curves away from the center of curvature.

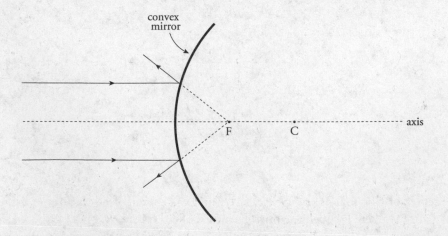

Ray Tracing for Mirrors

One method of answering the four questions we listed earlier involves a geometric approach called **ray tracing**. Representative rays of light are sketched in a diagram that depicts the object and the mirror; the point at which the reflected rays intersect (or appear to intersect) is the location of the image. Some rules governing rays are below.

Concave Mirrors
- An incident ray parallel to the axis is reflected through the focus.
- An incident ray that passes through the focus is reflected parallel to the axis.
- An incident ray that strikes the vertex is reflected at an equal angle to the axis.

Convex Mirrors
- An incident ray parallel to the axis is reflected away from the virtual focus.
- An incident ray directed toward the virtual focus is reflected parallel to the axis.
- An incident ray that strikes the vertex is reflected at an equal angle to the axis.

8. The figure below shows a concave mirror and an object (the bold arrow). Use a ray diagram to locate the image of the object.

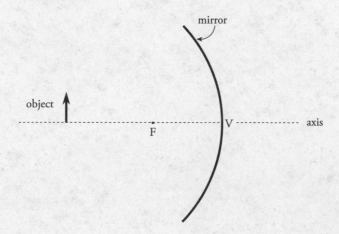

Here's How to Crack It
It only takes two distinct rays to locate the image.

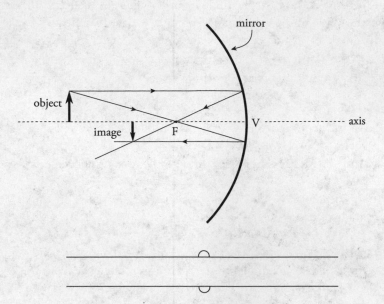

9. The figure below shows a convex mirror and an object (the arrow). Use a ray diagram to locate the image of the object.

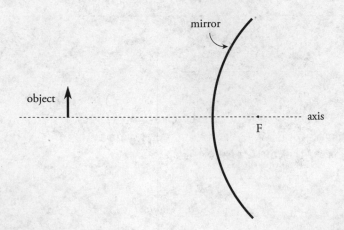

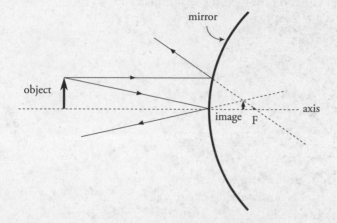

The ray diagrams of the preceding examples can be used to determine the location, orientation, and size of the image. The nature of the image—that is, whether it's real or virtual—can be determined by seeing on which side of the mirror the image is formed. If the image is formed on the same side of the mirror as the object, then the image is real, but if the image is formed on the opposite side of the mirror, it's virtual. Therefore, the image in Question 8 is real, and the image in Question 9 is virtual.

Using Equations to Answer Questions About the Image

The fastest and easiest way to get information about an image is to use two equations and some simple conventions. You should know how to use these two equations for the SAT Physics Subject Test.

> The first equation, called the **mirror equation**, is
>
> $$\frac{1}{s_o} + \frac{1}{s_i} = \frac{1}{f}$$
>
> where s_o is the object's distance from the mirror, s_i is the image's distance from the mirror, and f is the focal length of the mirror.

The value of s_o is *always* positive for a real object, but s_i can be positive or negative. The sign of s_i tells us whether the image is real or virtual: If s_i is positive, the image is real; and if s_i is negative, the image is virtual.

The second equation is called the **magnification equation**

$$m = -\frac{s_i}{s_o}$$

This gives the magnification; the height of the image, h_i, is $|m|$ times the height of the object, h_o. If m is positive, then the image is upright relative to the object; if m is negative, it's inverted. Because s_o is always positive, we can come to two conclusions: If s_i is positive, then m is negative, so real images are always inverted, and, if s_i is negative, then m is positive, so virtual images are always upright.

Finally, to distinguish *mathematically* between concave and convex mirrors, we always write the focal length f as a positive value for concave mirrors and a negative value for convex mirrors. With these two equations and their accompanying conventions, all four questions about an image can be answered. The mirror equation answers questions (1) and (2), and the magnification equation answers (3) and (4).

Image Is Everything
Remember that all real images are inverted and all virtual images are upright.

Mirrors

$$\text{concave} \iff f \text{ positive}$$
$$\text{convex} \iff f \text{ negative}$$

$$\frac{1}{s_o} + \frac{1}{s_i} = \frac{1}{f} \begin{cases} s_o \text{ always positive (real object)} \\ s_i \text{ positive} \implies \text{image is real} \\ s_i \text{ negative} \implies \text{image is virtual} \end{cases}$$

$$m = -\frac{s_i}{s_o} \begin{cases} |m| \times h_o = h_i \\ m \text{ positive} \implies \text{image is upright} \\ m \text{ negative} \implies \text{image is inverted} \end{cases}$$

Question 10-13

An object of height 4 cm is placed 30 cm in front of a concave mirror whose focal length is 10 cm.

10. Where's the image?

11. Is it real or virtual?

12. Is it upright or inverted?

13. What's the height of the image?

Here's How to Crack It

10. With $s_o = 30$ cm and $f = 10$ cm, the mirror equation gives

$$\frac{1}{s_o}+\frac{1}{s_i}=\frac{1}{f} \quad \Rightarrow \quad \frac{1}{30 \text{ cm}}+\frac{1}{s_i}=\frac{1}{10 \text{ cm}} \quad \Rightarrow \quad \frac{1}{s_i}=\frac{1}{15 \text{ cm}} \quad \Rightarrow \quad s_i = 15 \text{ cm}$$

The image is located 15 cm in front of the mirror.

11. Because s_i is positive, the image is real.

12. Real images are inverted.

13. The magnification is

$$m= -\frac{s_i}{s_o}=-\frac{15 \text{ cm}}{10 \text{ cm}}=-\frac{3}{2}$$

(The fact that the magnification is negative confirms that the image is inverted, as we said in Question 12.) The height of the image is

$$h_i = |m| \cdot h_o = \frac{3}{2}(4 \text{ cm})=6 \text{ cm}$$

Question 14-17

An object of height 4 cm is placed 20 cm in front of a
convex mirror whose focal length is –30 cm.

14. Where's the image?

15. Is it real or virtual?

16. Is it upright or inverted?

17. What's the height of the image?

Here's How to Crack It

14.   With $s_o = 20$ cm and $f = -30$ cm, the mirror equation gives us:

$$\frac{1}{s_o}+\frac{1}{s_i}=\frac{1}{f} \;\Rightarrow\; \frac{1}{20\text{ cm}}+\frac{1}{s_i}=\frac{1}{-30\text{ cm}} \;\Rightarrow\; \frac{1}{s_i}=-\frac{1}{12\text{ cm}} \;\Rightarrow\; s_i=-12\text{ cm}$$

So the image is located 12 cm behind the mirror.

15.   Because s_i is negative, the image is virtual.

16.   Virtual images are upright.

17.   The magnification is:

$$m=-\frac{s_i}{s_o}=-\frac{-12\text{ cm}}{20\text{ cm}}=\frac{3}{5}$$

(The fact that the magnification is positive tells us that the image is
upright, as we said in Question 17.) The height of the image is

$$h_i = |m| \times h_o = \tfrac{3}{5}(4\text{ cm}) = 2.4\text{ cm}$$

18. Show how the statements made earlier about plane mirrors can be derived from the mirror and magnification equations.

Here's How to Crack It

A plane mirror can be considered a spherical mirror with an infinite radius of curvature (and an infinite focal length). If $f = \infty$, then $1/f = 0$, and the mirror equation becomes

$$\frac{1}{s_o} + \frac{1}{s_i} = 0 \quad \Rightarrow \quad s_i = -s_o$$

The image is as far behind the mirror as the object is in front. Also, since s_o is always positive, s_i is negative, so the image is virtual. The magnification is

$$m = -\frac{s_i}{s_o} = -\frac{-s_o}{s_o} = 1$$

and the image is upright and has the same height as the object. The mirror and magnification equations confirm our description of images formed by plane mirrors.

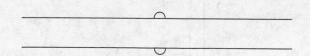

What Produces What?
Only concave mirrors can produce real images (if $s_0 \succ f$). Convex mirrors and plane mirrors can only produce virtual images.

19. Show why convex mirrors can only form virtual images.

Here's How to Crack It

Because f is negative and s_o is positive, the mirror equation

$$\frac{1}{s_o} + \frac{1}{s_i} = \frac{1}{f}$$

immediately tells us that s_i cannot be positive (if it were, the left-hand side would be the sum of two positive numbers, while the right-hand side would be negative). Since s_i must be negative, the image must be virtual.

Question 20-22

An object placed 60 cm in front of a spherical mirror forms a real image at a distance of 30 cm from the mirror.

20. Is the mirror concave or convex?

21. What's the mirror's focal length?

22. Is the image taller or shorter than the object?

Here's How to Crack It

20. The fact that the image is real tells us that the mirror cannot be convex, since convex mirrors form only virtual images. The mirror is concave.

21. With s_o = 60 cm and s_i = 30 cm (s_i is positive since the image is real), the mirror equation tells us that

$$\frac{1}{s_o}+\frac{1}{s_i}=\frac{1}{f} \;\Rightarrow\; \frac{1}{60 \text{ cm}}+\frac{1}{30 \text{ cm}}=\frac{1}{f} \;\Rightarrow\; \frac{1}{f}=\frac{1}{20 \text{ cm}} \;\Rightarrow\; f = 20 \text{ cm}$$

Notice that f is positive; it must be, since the mirror is concave.

22. The magnification is

$$m=-\frac{s_i}{s_o}=-\frac{30 \text{ cm}}{60 \text{ cm}}=-\frac{1}{2}$$

Since the absolute value of m is less than 1, the mirror makes the object look smaller. The image is only half as tall as the object (and is upside down, because m is negative).

23. A concave mirror with a focal length of 25 cm is used to create a real image that has twice the height of the object. How far is the image from the mirror?

Here's How to Crack It

Since h_i (the height of the image) is twice h_o (the height of the object) the value of the magnification is either +2 or −2. To figure out which, we just notice that the image is real; real images are inverted, so the magnification, m, must be negative. Therefore, $m = -2$, so

$$-\frac{s_i}{s_o} = -2 \quad \Rightarrow \quad s_o = \frac{1}{2} s_i$$

Substituting this into the mirror equation gives us

$$\frac{1}{s_o} + \frac{1}{s_i} = \frac{1}{f} \quad \Rightarrow \quad \frac{1}{\frac{1}{2} s_i} + \frac{1}{s_i} = \frac{1}{f} \quad \Rightarrow \quad \frac{3}{s_i} = \frac{1}{f} \quad \Rightarrow \quad s_i = 3f = 3(25 \text{ cm}) = 75 \text{ cm}$$

THIN LENSES

A lens is an optical device that forms an image by *refracting* light. We'll now talk about the equations and conventions that are used to analyze images formed by the two major categories of lenses converging and diverging.

A **converging lens**—like the bi-convex one shown below—converges parallel paraxial rays of light to a focal point on the far side. (This lens is *bi-convex*; both of its faces are convex. Converging lenses all have at least one convex face.) Because light rays actually focus at F, this point is called a **real focus**. Its distance from the lens is the focal length, f.

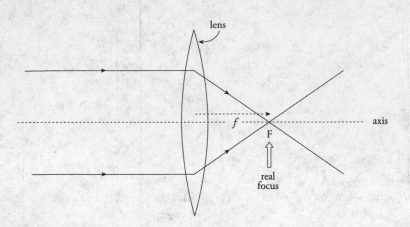

A **diverging lens**—like the *bi-concave* one shown below—causes parallel paraxial rays of light to diverge away from a **virtual focus**, F, on the same side as the incident rays. (Diverging lenses all have at least one concave face.)

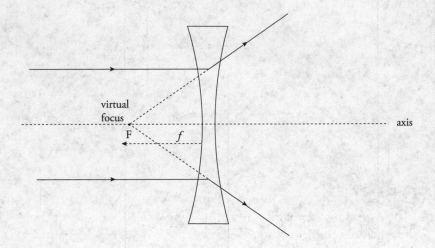

RAY TRACING FOR LENSES

Just as is the case with mirrors, representative rays of light can be sketched in a diagram along with the object and the lens; the point at which the reflected rays intersect (or appear to intersect) is the location of the image. The rules that govern these rays are as follows:

Converging Lenses

- An incident ray parallel to the axis is refracted through the real focus.
- Incident rays pass undeflected through the **optical center**, O (the central point within the lens where the axis intersects the lens).

Diverging Lenses

- An incident ray parallel to the axis is refracted away from the virtual focus.
- Incident rays pass undeflected through the optical center, O.

24. The figure below shows a converging lens and an object (denoted by the bold arrow). Use a ray diagram to locate the image of the object.

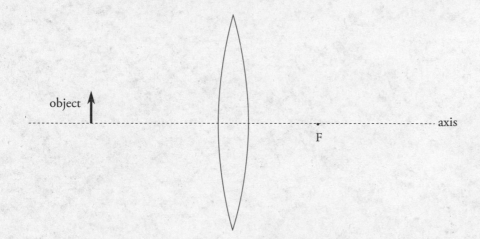

Here's How to Crack It

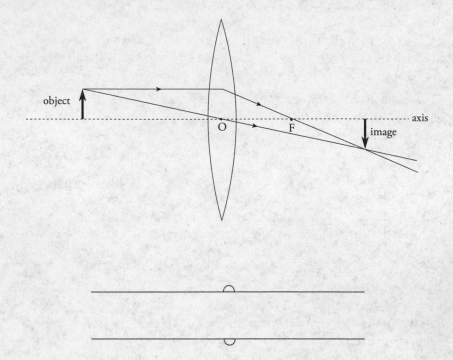

---

25. The figure below shows a diverging lens and an object. Use a ray diagram to locate the image of the object.

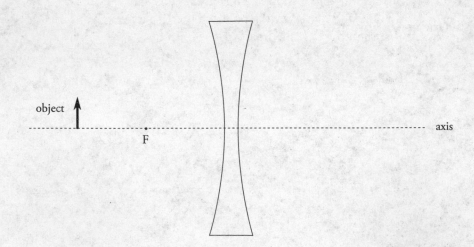

Here's How to Crack It

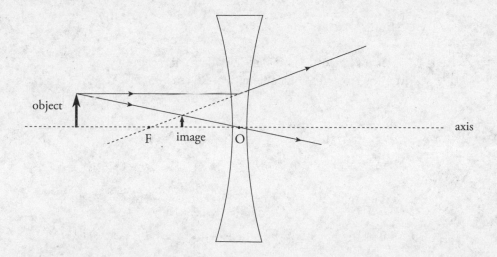

As we mentioned before, the nature of the image—that is, whether it's real or virtual—is determined by the side of the lens upon which the image is formed. If the image is formed on the side of the lens that's opposite the object, then the image is real, and if the image is formed on the same side of the lens as the object, then it's virtual. Therefore, the image in Question 24 is real, while the image in Question 25 is virtual.

Which Side is Real?
For mirrors, the real side (where $s_0 \succ 0$) is the same side as the object. For lenses, the real side is opposite the object.

Using Equations to Answer Questions About the Image

Using the notation we used for mirrors, we can summarize the equations and conventions for analyzing the images formed by lenses. Except for the reversal of the physical locations of real versus virtual images, everything else is the same.

Lenses

$$\text{converging} \quad \Leftrightarrow \quad f \text{ positive}$$
$$\text{diverging} \quad \Leftrightarrow \quad f \text{ negative}$$

$$\frac{1}{s_\text{o}} + \frac{1}{s_\text{i}} = \frac{1}{f} \begin{cases} s_\text{o} \text{ always positive (real object)} \\ s_\text{i} \text{ positive} \quad \Rightarrow \quad \text{image is real} \\ s_\text{i} \text{ negative} \quad \Rightarrow \quad \text{image is virtual} \end{cases}$$

$$m = -\frac{s_\text{i}}{s_\text{o}} \begin{cases} |m| \times h_\text{o} = h_\text{i} \\ m \text{ positive} \quad \Rightarrow \quad \text{image is upright} \\ m \text{ negative} \quad \Rightarrow \quad \text{image is inverted} \end{cases}$$

Question 26-29

An object of height 10 cm is placed 40 cm in front of a converging lens with a focal length of 20 cm.

26. Where's the image?

27. Is it real or virtual?

28. Is it upright or inverted?

29. What's the height of the image?

Here's How to Crack It

26. With s_o = 40 cm and f = 20 cm, the lens equation gives us

$$\frac{1}{s_o} + \frac{1}{s_i} = \frac{1}{f} \Rightarrow \frac{1}{40 \text{ cm}} + \frac{1}{s_i} = \frac{1}{20 \text{ cm}} \Rightarrow s_i = 40 \text{ cm}$$

So the image is located 40 cm from the lens, on the opposite side from the object.

27. Because s_i is positive, the image is real.
28. Real images are inverted.
29. The magnification is

$$m = -\frac{s_i}{s_0} = -\frac{40 \text{ cm}}{40 \text{ cm}} = -1$$

(The fact that the magnification is negative confirms that the image is inverted.) The height of the image is

$$h_i = |m| \bullet h_o = 1(10 \text{ cm}) = 10 \text{ cm}$$

These results are illustrated in Question 24.

Question 30-33

An object of height 9 cm is placed 48 cm in front of a
.diverging lens with a focal length of –24 cm.

30. Where's the image?

31. Is it real or virtual?

32. Is it upright or inverted?

33. What's the height of the image?

What Produces What?
Only converging lenses
can produce real images
(if $s_0 \succ f$). Diverging
lenses can only produce
virtual images.

Here's How to Crack It

30. With s_o = 48 cm and f = –24 cm, the lens equation gives us:

$$\frac{1}{s_o}+\frac{1}{s_1}=\frac{1}{f} \Rightarrow \frac{1}{48\ cm}+\frac{1}{s_i}=\frac{1}{-24\ cm} \Rightarrow s_i=-16\ cm$$

The image is 16 cm from the lens, on the same side as the object.

31. Because s_i is negative, the image is virtual.

32. Virtual images are upright.

33. The magnification is

$$m=-\frac{s_i}{s_o}=-\frac{-16\ cm}{48\ cm}=\frac{1}{3}$$

(The fact that the magnification is positive confirms that the image is upright.) The height of the image is

$$h_i=|m| \bullet \neq h_o=\frac{1}{3}\left(9\ cm\right)=3\ cm$$

These results are illustrated in Question 25.

Chapter 16 Review Questions

Answers are on page 417.

1. What is the wavelength of an X-ray whose frequency is 1.0×10^{18} Hz?

   (A) 3.3×10^{-11} m
   (B) 3.0×10^{-10} m
   (C) 3.3×10^{-9} m
   (D) 3.0×10^{-8} m
   (E) 3.0×10^{26} m

2. In Young's double-slit interference experiment, what is the difference in path length of the light waves from the two slits at the center of the first bright fringe above the central maximum?

   (A) 0

   (B) $\dfrac{1}{4}\lambda$

   (C) $\dfrac{1}{2}\lambda$

   (D) λ

   (E) $\dfrac{3}{2}\lambda$

3. A beam of light in air is incident upon the smooth surface of a piece of flint glass, as shown

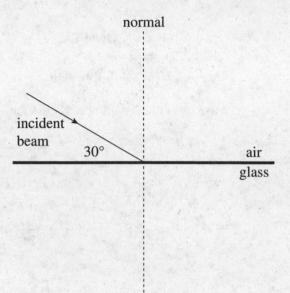

   If the reflected beam and refracted beam are perpendicular to each other, what is the index of refraction of the glass?

   (A) $\dfrac{1}{2}$

   (B) $\dfrac{1}{2}\sqrt{3}$

   (C) $\sqrt{3}$

   (D) 2

   (E) $2\sqrt{3}$

4. When green light (wavelength = 500 nm in air) travels through diamond (refractive index = 2.4), what is its wavelength?

   (A) 208 nm
   (B) 357 nm
   (C) 500 nm
   (D) 700 nm
   (E) 1,200 nm

5. A beam of light traveling in medium 1 strikes the interface to another transparent medium, medium 2. If the speed of light is less in medium 2 than in medium 1, the beam will

   (A) refract toward the normal
   (B) refract away from the normal
   (C) undergo total internal reflection
   (D) have an angle of reflection smaller than the angle of incidence
   (E) have an angle of reflection greater than the angle of incidence

6. If a clear liquid has a refractive index of 1.45 and a transparent solid has an index of 2.90 then, for total internal reflection to occur at the interface between these two media, which of the following must be true?

incident beam originates in	at an angle of incidence greater than
(A) the solid	30°
(B) the liquid	30°
(C) the solid	60°
(D) the liquid	60°

   (E) Total internal reflection cannot occur.

7. An object is placed 60 cm in front of a concave spherical mirror whose focal length is 40 cm. Which of the following best describes the image?

Nature of image	Distance from mirror
(A) Virtual	24 cm
(B) Real	24 cm
(C) Virtual	120 cm
(D) Real	120 cm
(E) Real	240 cm

8. An object is placed 60 cm from a spherical convex mirror. If the mirror forms a virtual image 20 cm from the mirror, what's the magnitude of the mirror's radius of curvature?

   (A) 7.5 cm
   (B) 15 cm
   (C) 30 cm
   (D) 60 cm
   (E) 120 cm

9. The image created by a converging lens is projected onto a screen that's 60 cm from the lens. If the height of the image is $\frac{1}{4}$ the height of the object, what's the focal length of the lens?

   (A) 36 cm
   (B) 45 cm
   (C) 48 cm
   (D) 72 cm
   (E) 80 cm

10. Which of the following is true concerning a biconcave lens?

   (A) Its focal length is positive.
   (B) It cannot form real images.
   (C) It cannot form virtual images.
   (D) It can magnify objects.
   (E) None of the above

Keywords

optics
electromagnetic (EM) spectrum
radiowaves
microwaves
infrared
visible light
ultraviolet
X-rays
γ-rays (gamma rays)
coherent
diffraction
fringes
central maximum
diffraction gratings
incident beam
angle of incidence
reflected beam
angle of reflection
transmitted beam
angle of refraction
law of reflection
index of refraction
Snell's law
refract
dispersion
critical angle
total internal reflection (TIR)
mirror
plane mirrors
real
virtual
spherical mirror
center of curvature
radius of curvature
focus
focal point
axis
vertex
focal length
paraxial rays
concave mirror

convex mirror
ray tracing
mirror equation
magnification
equation
converging lens
real focus
diverging lens
virtual focus
optical center

Summary

For the test, be sure you are familiar with the following concepts from this chapter.

o   Light is a type of electromagnetic wave.

o   The electromagnetic spectrum is a categorization of electromagnetic waves by their frequency or wavelength.

o   Interference can be constructive or destructive.

o   Young's double-slit interference experiment shows the results of interference.

o   Reflection and refraction

o   Dispersion of light

o   Total internal reflection

o   Mirrors

o   Plane mirrors

o   Spherical mirrors

o   Ray tracing for mirrors

o   Use equations to answer questions about the image reflected in a mirror.

o   Thin lenses

o   Ray tracing for lenses

o   Use equations to answer questions about the image viewed through the lens.

Chapter 17
Modern Physics

The subject matter of the previous chapters was developed in the seventeenth, eighteenth, and nineteenth centuries, but as we delve into the physics of the very small, we enter the twentieth century. Let's first look at the structure of the atom, then travel into the nucleus itself. About 10 percent of the questions on the SAT Physics Subject Test will cover the field of modern physics.

THE RUTHERFORD MODEL OF THE ATOM

Around 1900, the atom was just considered a small bunch of positively charged "stuff" embedded with negatively charged electrons. This theoretical structure was known as the **raisin pudding model**; the pudding was the positively charged part of the atom and the raisins were the electrons. However, laboratory experiments in 1909 to 1911 led Ernest Rutherford to propose a radical revision of this model.

Rutherford fired **alpha particles** (α), which were known to be relatively massive and carry an electric charge of $+2e$, at an extremely thin sheet of gold foil. An alpha particle consists of two protons and two neutrons, tightly bound together. If the atom is really just a glob of positive charge dotted with tiny negative electrons, then the heavy alpha particles should sail right through the target atoms, with little deviation.

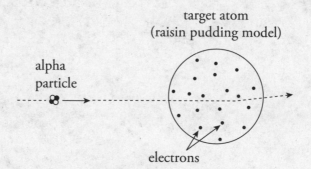

For the most part, this is what the experiments revealed. However, a small percentage of the alpha particles exhibited behavior that was completely unexpected: Some were deflected through very large angles (90° to 180°). This was explained by postulating that the positive charge of the atom was not spread throughout its volume, but was concentrated in a very tiny volume, at the atom's center. Alpha particles that came close to this concentration of positive charge experienced a strong Coulombic repulsive force and were deflected through large angles.

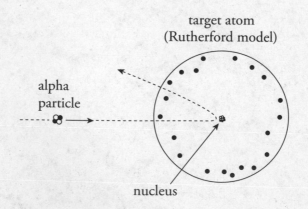

The tiny volume in which the positive charge is concentrated in an atom is known as the **nucleus**, and the nucleus is surrounded by a swarm of negatively charged electrons. This model is known as the **Rutherford nuclear model**.

PHOTONS AND THE PHOTOELECTRIC EFFECT

The particle-like nature of light was revealed and studied through the work of Max Planck in 1900, and later Albert Einstein (who won the 1921 Nobel prize for work in this area). Electromagnetic radiation is emitted and absorbed by matter as though it existed in individual bundles called **quanta**. A quantum of electromagnetic energy is known as a **photon**. Light behaves like a stream of photons, and this is illustrated by the **photoelectric effect**.

When a piece of metal is illuminated by electromagnetic radiation (either visible light, ultraviolet light, or X-rays), the energy absorbed by electrons near the surface of the metal can liberate them from their bound state, and these electrons can fly off. The released electrons are known as **photoelectrons**. In this case, the classical, wave-only theory of light would predict the following three results:

(1)   There would be a significant time delay between the moment of illumination and the ejection of photoelectrons, as the electrons absorbed incident energy until their kinetic energy was sufficient to release them from the atoms' grip.

(2)   Increasing the intensity of the light would cause the electrons to leave the metal surface with greater kinetic energy.

(3)   Photoelectrons would be emitted regardless of the frequency of the incident energy, as long as the intensity was high enough.

Surprisingly, none of these predictions was observed. Photoelectrons were ejected within just a few billionths of a second after illumination, disproving prediction (1). Secondly, increasing the intensity of the light did not cause photoelectrons to leave the metal surface with greater kinetic energy. Although more electrons were ejected as the intensity was increased, there was a maximum photoelectron kinetic energy; prediction (2) was false. And, for each metal, there was a certain **threshold frequency**, f_0: If light of frequency lower than f_0 were used to illuminate the metal surface, *no* photoelectrons were ejected, regardless of how intense the incident radiation was; prediction (3) was also false. Clearly, something was wrong with the wave-only theory of light.

Einstein explained these observations by postulating that the energy of the incident electromagnetic wave was absorbed in individual bundles (photons).

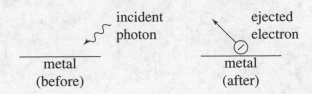

The energy of a photon is proportional to the frequency of the wave,

$$E = hf$$

where h is **Planck's constant** (about $6.63 \times 10{-}34$ J·s).

A certain amount of energy had to be imparted to an electron on the metal surface in order to liberate it; this was known as the metal's **work function**, or ϕ. If an electron absorbed a photon whose energy E was greater than ϕ, it would leave the metal with a maximum kinetic energy equal to $E - \phi$. This process could occur *very* quickly, which accounts for the rapidity with which photoelectrons are produced after illumination.

$$K_{max} = hf - \varnothing$$

Increasing the intensity of the incident energy means bombardment with more photons and results in the ejection of more photoelectrons—but since the energy of each incident photon is fixed by the equation $E = hf$, the value of K_{max} will still be $E - \phi$. This accounts for the observation that disproved prediction (2).

Finally, if the incident energy had a frequency that was less than ϕ/h, the incident photons would each have an energy that was less than ϕ; this would not be enough energy to liberate electrons. Blasting the metal surface with more photons (that is, increasing the intensity of the incident beam) would also do nothing; none of the photons would have enough energy to eject electrons, so whether there were one or one million wouldn't make any difference. This accounts for the observation of a threshold frequency, which we now know is ϕ/h.

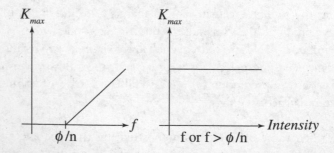

Before we get to some examples, it's worthwhile to introduce a new unit for energy. The SI unit for energy is the joule, but it's too large to be convenient in the domains we're studying now. We'll use a much smaller unit, the **electronvolt** (abbreviated **eV**). The eV is equal to the energy gained (or lost) by an electron accelerated through a potential difference of one volt. Using the equation $\Delta U_{E} = q\Delta V$, we find that

$$1 \text{ eV} = (1 \text{ e})(1 \text{ V}) = (1.6 \times 10^{-19} \text{ C})(1 \text{ V}) = 1.6 \times 10^{-19} \text{ J}$$

In terms of electronvolts, the value of Planck's constant is 4.14×10^{-15} eV•s.

Questions 1-3

The work function for a certain metal is 4.14 eV.

1. What is the threshold frequency required to produce photoelectrons from this metal?

2. To what wavelength does the frequency in Question 1 correspond?

3. Light with frequency 2×10^{15} Hz is directed onto the metal surface. Describe what would happen to the number of photoelectrons and their maximum kinetic energy if the intensity of this light were increased by a factor of 2.

Here's How to Crack It

1. We know from the statement of the question that for a photon to be successful in liberating an electron from the surface of the metal, its energy cannot be less than 4.14 eV. Therefore, the minimum frequency of the incident light—the threshold frequency—must be

$$f_0 = \frac{\phi}{h} = \frac{4.14 \text{ eV}}{4.14 \times 10^{15} \text{ eV} \cdot \text{s}} = 1 \times 10^{15} \text{ Hz}$$

2. From the equation $\lambda f = c$, where c is the speed of light, we find that

$$\lambda = \frac{c}{f} = \frac{3 \times 10^8 \text{ m/s}}{1 \times 10^{15} \text{ Hz}} = 3 \times 10^{-7} \text{ m}$$

3. Since the frequency of this light is higher than the threshold frequency, photoelectrons *will* be produced. If the intensity (brightness) of this light is then increased by a factor of 2, that means the metal surface will be hit with twice as many photons per second, so twice as many photoelectrons will be ejected per second. Thus, making the incident light brighter releases more photoelectrons. However, their maximum

kinetic energy will not change. The only way to increase K_{max} is to increase the *frequency*—not the brightness—of the incident light.

———————————⌒———————————

THE BOHR MODEL OF THE ATOM

In the years immediately following Rutherford's announcement of his nuclear model of the atom, a young physicist, Niels Bohr, added an important piece to the atomic puzzle.

For fifty years it had been known that atoms in a gas discharge tube emitted and absorbed light only at specific wavelengths. The light from a glowing gas, passed through a prism to disperse the beam into its component wavelengths, produced patterns of sharp lines called **atomic spectra**. The visible wavelengths that appeared in the emission spectrum of hydrogen had been summarized by a simple formula. But *why* do atoms emit (or absorb) radiation only at certain discrete wavelengths?

Bohr's model of the atom explains. Using the simplest atom, hydrogen (which has one electron), Bohr postulated that the electron orbits the nucleus only at certain discrete radii. When the electron is in one of these special orbits, it does not lose energy (as the classical theory would predict). However, if the electron absorbs a certain amount of energy, it is **excited** to a higher orbit, one with a greater radius. After spending a short time in this excited state, it returns to a lower orbit, emitting a photon in the process. Since each allowed orbit—or **energy level**—has a specific radius (and corresponding specific energy), the photons emitted in each jump also have specific energies and wavelengths. We say that the electron's energy levels are **quantized**.

The energy levels within the hydrogen atom are given by the formula

$$E_n = \frac{1}{n^2}(-13.6 \text{ eV})$$

and for other one-electron atoms—ionized helium ($Z = 2$), doubly-ionized lithium ($Z = 3$), etc.—the energy levels are

$$E_n = \frac{Z^2}{n^2}(-13.6 \text{ eV})$$

where Z is the number of protons in the atom's nucleus.

When an excited electron drops from energy level $n = j$ to a lower one, $n = i$, the transition causes a photon of energy to be emitted, and the energy of a photon is the difference between the two energy levels:

$$E_{\text{emitted photon}} = \left|\Delta E\right| = E_j - E_i$$

Questions 4-5

Refer to the diagram below.

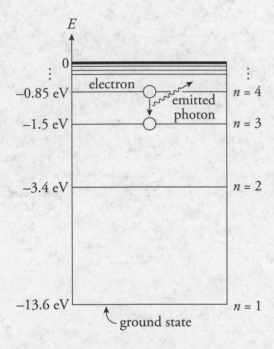

4. How much energy must a ground-state electron in a hydrogen atom absorb to be excited to the $n = 4$ energy level?

5. When the electron is in the $n = 4$ level, what energies are possible for the photon emitted when the electron drops to a lower energy level?

Here's How to Crack It

4.   For an electron to make the transition from E_1 to E_4, it must absorb energy in the amount $E_4 - E_1 = (-0.85 \text{ eV}) - (-13.6 \text{ eV}) = 12.8 \text{ eV}$.

5.   An electron in the $n = 4$ energy level can make several different transitions: It can drop to $n = 3$, $n = 2$, or all the way down to the ground state, $n = 1$.
So, there are three possible values for the energy of the emitted photon, $E_{4 \to 3}$, $E_{4 \to 2}$, or $E_{4 \to 1}$:

$$E_{4 \to 3} = E_4 - E_3 = (-0.85 \text{ eV}) - (-1.5 \text{ eV}) = 0.65 \text{ eV}$$
$$E_{4 \to 2} = E_4 - E_2 = (-0.85 \text{ eV}) - (-3.4 \text{ eV}) = 2.55 \text{ eV}$$
$$E_{4 \to 1} = E_4 - E_1 = (-0.85 \text{ eV}) - (-13.6 \text{ eV}) = 12.8 \text{ eV}$$

WAVE–PARTICLE DUALITY

Light and other electromagnetic waves exhibit wave-like characteristics through interference and diffraction. However, as we saw in the photoelectric effect, light also behaves as if its energy were granular, composed of particles. This is **wave–particle duality**: *Electromagnetic radiation propagates like a wave but exchanges energy like a particle.*

Since an electromagnetic wave can behave like a particle, can a particle of matter behave like a wave? In 1923, the French physicist Louis de Broglie proposed that the answer is *yes*. His conjecture, which has since been supported by experiment, is that a particle of mass m and speed v—and thus with linear momentum $p = mv$—has an associated wavelength, which is called its **de Broglie wavelength**.

$$\lambda = \frac{h}{p}$$

Particles in motion can display wave characteristics, and behave as if they had a wavelength $\lambda = h/p$.

Since the value of h is so small, ordinary macroscopic objects do not display wavelike behavior. For example, a baseball (mass = 0.15 kg) thrown at a speed of 40 m/s has a de Broglie wavelength of

$$\lambda = \frac{h}{p} = \frac{h}{mv} = \frac{6.63 \times 10^{-34} \text{ J} \cdot \text{s}}{(0.15 \text{ kg})(40 \text{ m/s})} = 1.1 \times 10^{-34} \text{ m}$$

This is much too small to measure. However, with subatomic particles, the wave nature is clearly evident.

Questions 6-7

6. Name or describe an experiment that demonstrates that light behaves like a wave.

7. Name or describe an experiment that demonstrates that light behaves like a particle.

Here's How to Crack It

6. Young's double-slit interference experiment shows that light behaves like a wave. Interference is a characteristic of waves, not of particles.

7. The photoelectric effect shows that light behaves like a particle, where the energy of the light is absorbed as photons: individual "particles" of light energy.

NUCLEAR PHYSICS

The nucleus of the atom is composed of particles called **protons** and **neutrons**, which are collectively called **nucleons**. The number of protons in a given nucleus is called the atom's **atomic number**, or Z, and the number of neutrons (the **neutron number**) is denoted N. The total number of nucleons, $Z + N$, is called the **mass number** (or **nucleon number**), and is denoted A. The number of protons in the nucleus of an atom defines the element. For example, the element chlorine (abbreviated Cl) is characterized by the fact that the nucleus of every chlorine atom contains 17 protons, so the atomic number of chlorine is 17; but, different chlorine atoms may contain different numbers of neutrons. In fact, about three-fourths of all naturally occurring chlorine atoms have 18 neutrons in their nuclei (mass number = 35), and most of the remaining one-fourth contain 20 neutrons (mass number = 37). Nuclei that contain the same numbers of protons but different numbers of neutrons are called **isotopes**.

The notation for a **nuclide**—the term for a nucleus with specific numbers of protons and neutrons—is to write Z and A, one above the other, before the chemical symbol of the element.

$$_Z^A X$$

The isotopes of chlorine mentioned earlier would be written as follows:

$$_{17}^{35}Cl \quad \text{and} \quad _{17}^{37}Cl$$

8. How many protons and neutrons are contained in the nuclide $^{63}_{29}\text{Cu}$?

Here's How to Crack It

The subscript (the atomic number, Z) gives the number of protons, which is 29. The superscript (the mass number, A) gives the total number of nucleons. Since $A = 63 = Z + N$, we find that $N = 63 - 29 = 34$.

9. The element neon (abbreviated Ne, atomic number 10) has several isotopes. The most abundant isotope contains 10 neutrons, and two others contain 11 and 12. Write symbols for these three nuclides.

Here's How to Crack It

The mass numbers of these isotopes are $10 + 10 = 20$, $10 + 11 = 21$, and $10 + 12 = 22$. So, we'd write them as follows:

$$^{20}_{10}\text{Ne}, \quad ^{21}_{10}\text{Ne}, \quad \text{and} \quad ^{22}_{10}\text{Ne}$$

Another common notation—which we also use—is to write the mass number after the name of the element. These three isotopes of neon would be written as neon-20, neon-21, and neon-22.

The Nuclear Force

Why wouldn't any nucleus that has more than one proton be unstable? After all, protons are positively charged and would therefore experience a repulsive Coulomb force from each other. Why don't these nuclei explode? And what holds neutrons—which have no electric charge—in the nucleus? These issues are resolved by the presence of another fundamental force, the **strong nuclear force**, which binds together neutrons and protons to form nuclei. Although the strength of the Coulomb force can be expressed by a simple mathematical formula (it's inversely proportional to the square of their separation), the nuclear force is much more complicated; no simple formula can be written for the strength of the nuclear force.

Binding Energy

The masses of the proton and neutron are listed below.

proton: $m_p = 1.6726 \times 10^{-27}$ kg

neutron: $m_n = 1.6749 \times 10^{-27}$ kg

Because these masses are so tiny, a much smaller mass unit is used. With the most abundant isotope of carbon (carbon-12) as a reference, the **atomic mass unit** (abbreviated **amu** or simply **u**) is defined as 1/12 the mass of a ^{12}C atom. The conversion between kg and u is 1 u = 1.6605×10^{-27} kg. In terms of atomic mass units

proton: $m_p = 1.00728$ u

neutron: $m_n = 1.00867$ u

Now consider the **deuteron**, the nucleus of **deuterium**, an isotope of hydrogen that contains 1 proton and 1 neutron. The mass of a deuteron is 2.01356 u, which is a little *less* than the sum of the individual masses of the proton and neutron. The difference between the mass of any bound nucleus and the sum of the masses of its constituent nucleons is called the **mass defect**, Δm. In the case of the deuteron (symbolized **d**), the mass defect is

$$\Delta m = (m_p + m_n) - m_d$$
$$= (1.00728 \text{ u} + 1.00867 \text{ u}) - (2.01356 \text{ u})$$
$$= 0.00239 \text{ u}$$

What happened to this missing mass? It was converted to energy when the deuteron was formed. It also represents the amount of energy needed to break the deuteron into a separate proton and neutron. Since this tells us how strongly the nucleus is bound, it is called the **binding energy** of the nucleus.

The conversion between mass and energy is given by Einstein's **mass–energy equivalence** equation, $E = mc^2$ (where c is the speed of light); the binding energy, E_B, is equal to the mass defect, Δm

$$E_B = (\Delta m)c^2$$

Using $E = mc^2$, the energy equivalent of 1 atomic mass unit is about 931 MeV.

In terms of electronvolts, then, the binding energy of the deuteron is

$$E_B \text{ (deuteron)} = 0.00239 \text{ u} \times \frac{931 \text{ MeV}}{1 \text{ u}} = 2.23 \text{ MeV}$$

Since the deuteron contains 2 nucleons, the **binding energy per nucleon** is

$$\frac{2.23 \text{ MeV}}{2 \text{ nucleons}} = 1.12 \text{ MeV/nucleon.}$$

This is the lowest value of all nuclides. The highest, 8.8 MeV/nucleon, is for an isotope of nickel, ^{62}Ni. Typically, when nuclei smaller than nickel are fused to form a single nucleus, the binding energy per nucleon increases, which tells us that energy is released in the process. On the other hand, when nuclei *larger* than nickel are *split*, binding energy per nucleon again increases, releasing energy.

RADIOACTIVITY

The stability of a nucleus depends on the ability of the nuclear force to balance the repulsive Coulomb forces between the protons. Many nuclides are ultimately unstable and will undergo spontaneous restructuring to become more stable. An unstable nucleus that will spontaneously change into a lower-energy configuration is said to be **radioactive**. Nuclei that are too large (A is too great) or ones in which the neutron-to-proton ratio is unfavorable are radioactive, and there are several different modes of radioactive decay. We'll look at the most important ones: **alpha** decay, **beta** decay (three forms), and **gamma** decay.

Alpha Decay

When a nucleus undergoes alpha decay, it emits an alpha particle, which consists of two protons and two neutrons and is the same as the nucleus of a helium-4 atom. An alpha particle can be represented as

$$\alpha, \ {}^4_2\alpha, \text{ or } {}^4_2\text{He}$$

Very large nuclei can shed nucleons quickly by emitting one or more alpha particles, for example, radon-222 ($^{222}_{86}$Rn) is radioactive and undergoes alpha decay.

$$^{222}_{86}\text{Rn} \rightarrow {}^{218}_{84}\text{Po} + {}^4_2\alpha$$

This reaction illustrates two important features of any nuclear reaction.

> (1)   Mass number is conserved (in this case, 222 = 218 + 4).
>
> (2)   Charge is conserved (in this case, 86 = 84 + 2).

The decaying nuclide is known as the **parent**, and the resulting nuclide is known as the **daughter**. (Here, radon-222 is the parent nuclide and polonium-218 is the daughter.) Alpha decay decreases the mass number by 4 and the atomic number by 2. Therefore, alpha decay looks like the following:

$$_{Z}^{A}X \rightarrow \, _{Z-2}^{A-4}X' + \, _{2}^{4}\alpha$$

Beta Decay

There are three subcategories of **beta** (β) decay, called β^-, β^+, and **electron capture (EC)**.

β^- Decay

When the neutron-to-proton ratio is too large, the nucleus undergoes β^- decay, which is the most common form of beta decay. β^- decay occurs when a neutron transforms into a proton and an electron, and the electron is ejected from the nucleus. The expelled electron is called a **beta particle**. The transformation of a neutron into a proton and an electron (and another particle, the **electron-antineutrino**, $\bar{\nu}_e$) is caused by the action of the **weak nuclear force**, another of nature's fundamental forces. A common example of a nuclide that undergoes β^- decay is carbon-14, which is used to date archaeological artifacts.

$$_{6}^{14}C \rightarrow \, _{7}^{14}N + \, _{-1}^{0}e + \bar{\nu}_e$$

Notice how the ejected electron is written: The superscript is its nucleon number (which is zero), and the subscript is its charge. The reaction is balanced, since 14 = 14 + 0 and 6 = 7 + (−1).

β^+ Decay

When the neutron-to-proton ratio is too small, the nucleus will undergo β^+ decay. In this form of beta decay, a proton is transformed into a neutron and a **positron**, $_{+1}^{0}e$ (the electron's **antiparticle**), plus another particle, the **electron-neutrino**, ν_e, which are then both ejected from the nucleus. An example of a positron emitter is fluorine-17.

$$_{9}^{17}F \rightarrow \, _{8}^{17}O + \, _{+1}^{0}e + \nu_e$$

Electron Capture   Another way in which a nucleus can increase its neutron-to-proton ratio is to capture an orbiting electron and then cause the transformation of a proton into a neutron. Beryllium-7 undergoes this process.

$$^{7}_{4}\text{Be} + ^{0}_{-1}e \rightarrow ^{7}_{3}\text{Li} + \nu_e$$

Gamma Decay

In each of the decay processes defined above, the daughter was a different element from the parent. Radon becomes polonium as a result of α decay, carbon becomes nitrogen as a result of β^- decay, fluorine becomes oxygen from β^+ decay, and beryllium becomes lithium from electron capture. By contrast, gamma decay does not alter the identity of the nucleus; it just allows the nucleus to relax and shed energy. Imagine that potassium-42 undergoes β^- decay to form calcium-42.

$$^{42}_{19}\text{K} \rightarrow ^{42}_{20}\text{Ca}^* + ^{0}_{-1}e + \bar{\nu}_e$$

The asterisk indicates that the daughter calcium nucleus is left in a high-energy, excited state. For this excited nucleus to drop to its ground state, it must emit a photon of energy, a **gamma ray**, symbolized by γ.

$$^{42}_{20}\text{Ca}^* \rightarrow ^{42}_{20}\text{Ca} + \gamma$$

---

10. What's the daughter nucleus in each of the following radioactive decays?

    (a) Strontium-90 ($^{90}_{38}\text{Sr}$); β^- decay

    (b) Argon-37 ($^{37}_{18}\text{Ar}$); electron capture

    (c) Plutonium-239 ($^{239}_{94}\text{Pu}$); alpha decay

    (d) Cobalt-58 ($^{58}_{27}\text{Co}$); β^+ decay

Here's How to Crack It

(a) $^{90}_{38}\text{Sr} \rightarrow ^{90}_{39}\text{Y} + ^{0}_{-1}e + \bar{\nu}_e \quad \Rightarrow \quad$ daughter = yttrium-90

(b) $^{37}_{18}\text{Ar} + ^{0}_{-1}e \rightarrow ^{37}_{17}\text{Cl} + \nu_e \quad \Rightarrow \quad$ daughter = chlorine-37

(c) $^{239}_{94}\text{Pu} \rightarrow ^{235}_{92}\text{U} + ^{4}_{2}\alpha \quad \Rightarrow \quad$ daughter = uranium-235

(d) $^{58}_{27}\text{Co} \rightarrow ^{58}_{26}\text{Fe} + ^{0}_{+1}e^+ + \nu_e \quad \Rightarrow \quad$ daughter = iron-58

Radioactive Decay Rates

Although it's impossible to say precisely when a particular radioactive nuclide will decay, it *is* possible to predict the decay rates of a pure radioactive sample. As a radioactive sample disintegrates, the number of decays per second decreases, but the *fraction* of nuclei that decay per second—the **decay constant**—does not change. The decay constant is determined by the identity of the radioisotope. Boron-9 has a decay constant of 7.5×10^{17} s^{-1} (rapid), while uranium-238 has a decay constant of about 5×10^{-18} s^{-1} (slow).

The **activity** (A) of a radioactive sample is the number of disintegrations it undergoes per second; it decreases with time according to the equation

$$A = A_0 e^{-\lambda t}$$

where A_0 is the activity at time t = 0 and λ is the decay constant (not to be confused with wavelength).

Activity is expressed in disintegrations per second: 1 disintegration per second is one **becquerel** (**Bq**). The greater the value of λ, the faster the sample decays. This equation also describes the number (N) of radioactive nuclei in a given sample, $N = N_0 e^{-\lambda t}$, or the mass (m) of the sample, $m = m_0 e^{-\lambda t}$.

The most common way to indicate the rapidity with which radioactive samples decay is to give their **half-life**. Just as the name suggests, the half-life is the time required for half of a given sample to decay.

Half-life, $T_{1/2}$, is inversely proportional to the decay constant, λ, and in terms of the half-life, the exponential decay of a sample's mass (or activity) can be written as

$$m = m_0 \left(\frac{1}{2}\right)^{t/T_{1/2}}$$

A sample's activity or mass can be graphed as a function of time; the result is the **exponential decay** curve, which you should study carefully.

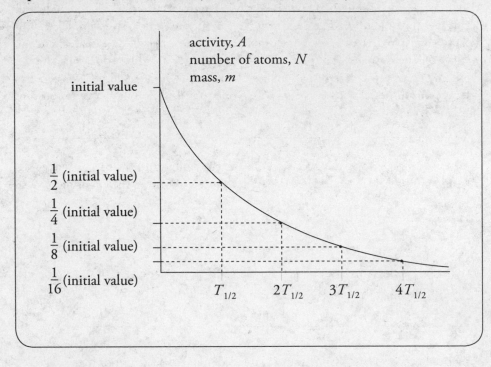

11. The half-life of iodine-131 (a β^- emitter) is 8 days. If a sample of ^{131}I has a mass of 1 gram, what will the mass be 40 days later?

Here's How to Crack It

Every 8 days, the sample's mass decreases by a factor of 2. We can illustrate the decay in the following diagram:

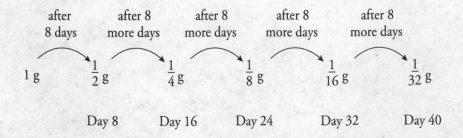

12. Home smoke detectors contain a small radioactive sample of americium-241 ($^{241}_{95}$Am), an alpha-particle emitter that has a half-life of 430 years. What is the daughter nucleus of the decay?

Here's How to Crack It

$$^{241}_{95}\text{Am} \rightarrow {}^{237}_{93}\text{Np} + {}^{4}_{2}\alpha \Rightarrow \quad \text{daughter} = \text{neptunium-237}$$

NUCLEAR REACTIONS

Natural radioactive decay provides one example of a nuclear reaction. Other examples of nuclear reactions include the bombardment of target nuclei with subatomic particles to artificially induce radioactivity (this is **nuclear fission**), and the **nuclear fusion** of small nuclei at extremely high temperatures. In all cases of nuclear reactions that we'll study, nucleon number and charge must be conserved. To balance nuclear reactions, we write $^{1}_{1}\text{p}$ or $^{1}_{1}\text{H}$ for a proton and $^{1}_{0}\text{n}$ for a neutron. Gamma-ray photons can also be produced in nuclear reactions; they have no charge or nucleon number and are represented as $^{0}_{0}\gamma$.

13. A mercury-198 nucleus is bombarded by a neutron, which causes a nuclear reaction.

$$^{1}_{0}\text{n} + {}^{198}_{80}\text{Hg} \rightarrow {}^{197}_{79}\text{Au} + {}^{?}_{?}\text{X}$$

What's the unknown product particle, X?

Here's How to Crack It

In order to balance the superscripts, we must have $1 + 198 = 197 + A$, so $A = 2$, and the subscripts are balanced if $0 + 80 = 79 + Z$, so $Z = 1$.

$$_{0}^{1}\text{n} + {}_{80}^{198}\text{Hg} \rightarrow {}_{79}^{197}\text{Au} + {}_{1}^{2}\text{X}$$

Therefore, X must be a deuteron, $_{1}^{2}\text{H}$ (or just d).

Disintegration Energy

Nuclear reactions not only produce new nuclei and other subatomic particles, but also involve the absorption or emission of energy. Nuclear reactions must conserve total energy, so changes in mass are accompanied by changes in energy according to Einstein's equation $\Delta E = (\Delta m)c^2$.

> A general nuclear reaction is written
>
> $$A + B \rightarrow C + D + Q$$
>
> where Q is the **disintegration energy**.

If Q is positive, the reaction is **exothermic** and the reaction can occur spontaneously; if Q is negative, the reaction is **endothermic** and the reaction cannot occur spontaneously. The energy Q is calculated as follows:

> $$Q = [(m_A + m_B) - (m_C + m_D)]c^2$$

For spontaneous reactions—ones that liberate energy—most of the energy is revealed as kinetic energy of the least massive product nuclei.

SPECIAL RELATIVITY

The SAT Physics Subject Test may ask a question or two on Einstein's theory of special relativity. Since you aren't expected to have an in-depth mastery of this subject, we'll simply state some relevant facts from this theory and present some examples.

Let's begin with the two postulates of special relativity.

> *Postulate 1:*   All the laws of physics are the same in all inertial reference frames.
>
> *Postulate 2:*   The speed of light in vacuum always has the same value ($c = 3 \times 10^8$ m/s), regardless of the motion of the source or the observer.

An **inertial reference frame** is one in which Newton's first law holds. Given one inertial reference frame, any other reference frame that moves with constant velocity relative to the first one will also be inertial. For example, a person standing at a train station considers herself to be in an inertial reference frame. If she places her suitcase on the ground next to her and exerts no forces on it, it stays at rest. Now, if a train moves past the station, traveling on a smooth track in a straight line at constant speed, then a passenger on the train considers himself to be in an inertial reference frame, too. If he places his suitcase on the floor and exerts no forces on it, it stays at rest (relative to him). Now, if the train is speeding by at, say, 40 m/s, then the person standing at the train station would say that the man's suitcase on the train is moving at a speed of 40 m/s, but the man on the train would say that his suitcase is at rest. So, while it's true that these two observers will naturally disagree about the velocity of the suitcase on the train, they won't disagree about physics laws, such as conservation of momentum. This is the essence of Postulate 1. Two people playing a game of billiards on a smoothly moving train (that is, one that travels in a straight line at constant speed) don't have to "adjust" their shots to account for the motion of the train.

Now let's look at Postulate 2 more closely.

1) The Relativity of Velocity

Let's say that the man in the train speeding by the platform at 40 m/s throws a ball down the aisle, parallel to the direction of motion of the train, at a speed of 5 m/s as measured by him. But as measured by the woman standing on the platform, the ball would be moving at a speed of 40 + 5 = 45 m/s. It seems clear that we'd just add the velocities.

This simple addition of velocities does not, however, extend to light or even to objects moving at speeds close to that of light. Imagine a spaceship moving at a speed of $\frac{2}{3}c$ toward a planet. If the spaceship emitted a light pulse toward a planet, the speed of that light pulse, as measured by someone on the planet, would *not* be $\frac{2}{3}c + c = \frac{5}{3}c$; Postulate 2 says that the speed of light would be c, regardless of the motion of the spaceship. Since we haven't been able to travel at speeds even remotely approaching that of light, this result seems very strange.

The correct, *relativistic* formula for the "addition" of velocities—that is, the one that follows from the theory of relativity—looks like this. Imagine that a reference frame, S_{me}, is moving with velocity u past you. Now if an object moves at velocity v (parallel to u), as measured by me in my reference frame, then its speed as measured *by you* would not be $v_{you} = u + v$, but would instead be

$$v_{you} = \frac{u+v}{1+uv/c^2}$$

At normal, everyday speeds, u and v are so small compared with the speed of light that the fraction uv/c^2 is negligibly small, nearly zero. In this case, the denominator in the formula above is nearly 1, and it becomes the formula $v_{you} = u + v$. It's only when u or v is close to the speed of light that the difference becomes measurable.

Let's apply the correct formula to our previous example about the spaceship emitting a pulse of light. With you on the planet and me on the spaceship, $u = \frac{2}{3}c$. Naturally, I measure the speed of the light pulse to be $v = c$, and you would measure its speed to be

$$v_{you} = \frac{u+v}{1+\frac{uv}{c^2}} = \frac{\frac{2}{3}c+c}{1+(\frac{2}{3}c)(c)/c^2} = \frac{\frac{5}{3}c}{1+\frac{2}{3}} = \frac{\frac{5}{3}c}{\frac{5}{3}} = c$$

just as Postulate 2 says you must.

Question 14-15

An enemy spaceship of the Empire is traveling toward the planet Ceti Alpha VI at a speed of $0.4c$. The ship emits a beam of antiprotons at the planet that travel at a speed of $0.5c$ relative to the ship.

14. How fast are the antiprotons traveling relative to the planet?

15. If the Empire ship emits a pulse of red light just before its blast of antiprotons, with what speed does the red light travel, relative to the planet?

Here's How to Crack It

14. With $u = 0.4c$ and $v = 0.5c$, the speed of the antiprotons relative to the planet is

$$v' = \frac{u+v}{1+\dfrac{uv}{c^2}} = \frac{0.4c + 0.5c}{1 + \dfrac{(0.4c)(0.5c)}{c^2}} = \frac{0.9c}{1.2} = 0.75c$$

15. As stated in Postulate 2 of the Theory of Special Relativity, the speed of light through empty space is always measured to be c, regardless of the motion of the source (or observer).

———————————————◯———————————————

2) The Relativity of Time

Let's go back to me on my spaceship, passing by your planet at a speed of $\frac{2}{3}c$. Let's

say, as I'm standing in the ship, I sneeze, and then, 1 second later, I sneeze again.

If you were holding a stopwatch and measured the time between my sneezes, you

would *not* get 1 second. Time is relative. The time as measured by you would not

agree with the time as measured by me.

To see how these time intervals would be related, imagine the following. In my reference frame, let me call the time between my sneezes ΔT_1. If my velocity past you is v, then the time that you'd measure between my sneezes would be

$$\Delta T_2 = \gamma \bullet \Delta T_1$$

where γ is the **relativistic factor**

$$\gamma = \frac{1}{\sqrt{1 - (\frac{v}{c})^2}}$$

Because the denominator of this fraction is never greater than 1, the value of γ

is never less than 1. So unless my spaceship was standing still relative to you, the time that you'd measure between my sneezes would always be *longer* than the time I'd measure. Seems strange? Of course, because, once again, we have no understanding of moving at speeds close to the speed of light, so we don't have any experience for time dilation. In fact, even at $v = \frac{1}{10}c$ (which is about 67 million miles per hour!) the relativistic factor γ is still only 1.005. But highly sensitive atomic clocks have been flown on commercial jet airplanes, and it's been found, upon landing, that they are a little slow relative to their synchronized counterparts that didn't fly. Furthermore, the time difference has been shown to be just what the relativistic formula above predicts.

For all ordinary speeds, where v is very, very small compared to c, the value of γ is negligibly greater than 1, so $\Delta T_2 \approx \Delta T_1$, and we don't notice a difference for ordinary time intervals. But, as v gets closer and closer to c, γ gets bigger and bigger. For example, for passengers on a spaceship moving at, say, $v = 0.99c$ relative to the earth, the value of γ is about 50. So, if someone on the ship says that they've been on the ship for 2 years (as measured by them), we here on Earth would say that the elapsed time is $50 \times 2 = 100$ years.

3) The Relativity of Length

Let's once again go back to me on my spaceship, passing by the earth at a speed of $\frac{2}{3}c$. Let's say I measure the length of my ship to be 100 meters. If you, on earth, were watching my ship fly by, you would *not* measure its length to be 100 m. Length is relative. The length as measured by you would not agree with the length as measured by me.

To see how these lengths would be related, imagine the following. In my reference frame, let me call the length of my spaceship L_1. If my velocity past you is v, then the length that you'd measure for my ship will be

$$L_2 = \frac{L_1}{\gamma}$$

where γ is the relativistic factor. Because γ is greater than 1, the length you'd measure would be *shorter* than what I'd measure. This is known as **length contraction**; lengths that are parallel to the velocity v are shortened by a factor of γ.

Question 16-18

A type of radioactive, subatomic particle, a μ *meson* (also known as a muon, for short) is created by cosmic rays from space entering the earth's atmosphere. Suppose that a muon is traveling downward toward the earth at a speed of 0.99c, relative to the earth.

16. At rest a muon typically lives for about 0.2 microsecond before it decays. How long will the moving muon survive, as measured by observers here on earth?

17. How far does the muon travel, as measured by Earth observers?

18. How far does the muon travel, as measured by the muon itself?

Here's How to Crack It

16. As measured on Earth, the time interval between the moment when the muon is created and the moment it decays is

$$\Delta T_2 = \gamma \cdot \Delta T_1 = \gamma \cdot (0.2 \text{ microsec})$$

In this case, the relativistic factor is

$$\gamma = \frac{1}{\sqrt{1-(v/c)^2}} = \frac{1}{\sqrt{1-(0.99)^2}} \approx \frac{1}{\sqrt{0.02}} = \frac{1}{\sqrt{\frac{1}{50}}} = \sqrt{50} \approx 7$$

So, as measured by observers on Earth, the muon survives for

$$\Delta T_2 = \gamma \cdot \Delta T_1 \approx 7 \cdot (0.2 \text{ microsec}) = 1.4 \text{ microsec}$$

17. Since the speed of the muon is 0.99c, and we measure its lifetime as 1.4 microseconds, the distance it travels, as measured by us, is

$$D = vT = (0.99c)(1.4 \times 10^{-6} \text{ s}) = (0.99)(4.2 \times 10^2 \text{ m}) \approx 420 \text{ m}$$

18. In the reference frame of the muon, it's the earth that's rushing up toward the muon at a speed of $0.99c$. Since, in the muon's frame of reference, it only lives for 0.2 microsecond, the muon measures its distance of travel to be

$$d = vt = (0.99c)(0.2 \times 10^{-6}\,\text{s}) = (0.99)(0.6 \times 10^2\,\text{m}) \approx 60\,\text{m}$$

Notice that since the muon is moving relative to the earth, it measures distances as being shorter than we do. So, from our point of view, the muon lives longer as it travels a proper distance of 420 m. From the muon's point of view, it lives its ordinary, proper lifetime, 0.2 microsecond, but only travels 60 m. These points of view are both correct (remember, distances and time are relative) and they're compatible. In one point of view, the time stretched by a factor of $\gamma = 7$, while in the other point of view it was the distance that shortened by a factor of $\gamma = 7$. (The time interval between two events is said to be *proper* if the two events occur at the same location in the reference frame of the observer. An object's length is said to be *proper* if the object is at rest in the reference frame of the observer.)

Relativistic Energy

You've undoubtedly seen the formula $E = mc^2$, probably the most famous formula in physics. What it says is that mass (m) and energy (E) are *equivalent*, and the formula tells us how much energy is equivalent to a given amount of mass. This energy is called **rest energy** because an object resting, say, on your desk, has energy—in fact, *is* energy—simply by virtue of the fact that it exists and has mass. Because c^2, the square of the speed of light, is such a big number, a small amount of mass is equivalent to a huge amount of energy. When an exothermic nuclear reaction takes place, the total mass of the product nuclei is always less than the total mass of the original nuclei. The "missing mass," Δm, has been converted to energy, ΔE, in accordance with the equation $\Delta E = (\Delta m)c^2$. This is the basis for how the world's nuclear power plants generate energy. The fission of a neutron with a uranium-235 nucleus creates five product particles (a barium-140 nucleus, a krypton-93 nucleus, and 3 neutrons) whose total mass is less than the total mass of the original neutron and uranium-235 nucleus by about 3×10^{-28} kg. Multiplying this Δm by the factor $c^2 = 9 \times 10^{16}$ m²/s², we get $\Delta E = 2.7 \times 10^{-11}$ J.

But what about kinetic energy? Up to now, we've been using the formula KE = $\frac{1}{2}mv^2$ for the kinetic energy of an object of mass m moving with speed v. But if v is close to c (in which case we say that the object is moving at a *relativistic* speed), then this formula won't work. The correct formula is

$$KE = (\gamma - 1)mc^2$$

where γ is the usual relativistic factor. It can be shown that when v is very small compared with c, this formula becomes the familiar KE = $\frac{1}{2}mv^2$.

An object's **total energy**, E_{total}, is now defined as the sum of its rest energy, $E_{rest} = mc^2$, and its kinetic energy.

$$\begin{aligned} E_{total} &= E_{rest} + KE \\ &= mc^2 + (\gamma - 1)mc^2 \\ &= \gamma mc^2 \end{aligned}$$

If we plot the kinetic energy of a particle of mass m as a function of its speed v, we get the following graph:

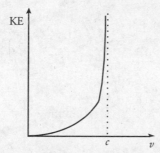

Notice that as v approaches c, the object's kinetic energy approaches infinity. This shows why it's impossible for a material particle to move at the speed of light (or at any speed greater than c). The force accelerating a particle would have to do more and more work to increase the particle's kinetic energy, and it would take an infinite amount of work to push a particle to the speed of light (where its kinetic energy would be infinite). The universe has a speed limit: Light moves at speed c, and everything else moves at a speed less than c.

Chapter 17 Review Questions

Answers are on page 419.

1. What's the energy of a photon whose wavelength is 2.07 nm ?

   (A)   60 eV
   (B)   600 eV
   (C)   960 eV
   (D) 6,000 eV
   (E) 9,600 eV

2. A metal whose work function is 6.0 eV is struck with light of frequency 7.2×10^{15} Hz. What is the maximum kinetic energy of photoelectrons ejected from the metal's surface?

   (A)   7 eV
   (B) 13 eV
   (C) 19 eV
   (D) 24 eV
   (E) No photoelectrons will be produced.

3. An atom with one electron has an ionization energy of 25 eV. How much energy will be released when the electron makes the transition from an excited energy level, where $E = -16$ eV, to the ground state?

   (A)   9 eV
   (B) 11 eV
   (C) 16 eV
   (D) 25 eV
   (E) 41 eV

4. The single electron in an atom has an energy of -40 eV when it's in the ground state, and the first excited state for the electron is at -10 eV. What will happen to this electron if the atom is struck by a stream of photons, each of energy 15 eV ?

   (A) The electron will absorb the energy of one photon and become excited halfway to the first excited state, then quickly return to the ground state, without emitting a photon.
   (B) The electron will absorb the energy of one photon and become excited halfway to the first excited state, then quickly return to the ground state, emitting a 15 eV photon in the process.
   (C) The electron will absorb the energy of one photon and become excited halfway to the first excited state, then quickly absorb the energy of another photon to reach the first excited state.
   (D) The electron will absorb two photons and be excited to the first excited state.
   (E) Nothing will happen.

5. What is the de Broglie wavelength of a proton whose linear momentum has a magnitude of 3.3×10^{-23} kg•m/s ?

   (A) 0.0002 nm
   (B) 0.002 nm
   (C) 0.02 nm
   (D) 0.2 nm
   (E) 2 nm

6. The difference between the mass of an intact phosphorus-31 nucleus and the sum of the masses of its individual protons and neutrons is 0.2825 u. What is the nuclear binding energy per nucleon?

   (A) 4.6 MeV/nucleon
   (B) 6.3 MeV/nucleon
   (C) 8.5 MeV/nucleon
   (D) 12.1 MeV/nucleon
   (E) 17.4 MeV/nucleon

7. Compared to the parent nucleus, the daughter of a β^- decay has

   (A) the same mass number but a greater atomic number
   (B) the same mass number but a smaller atomic number
   (C) a smaller mass number but the same atomic number
   (D) a greater mass number but the same atomic number
   (E) None of the above

8. The reaction $^{218}_{85}\text{At} \rightarrow {}^{214}_{83}\text{Bi}$ is an example of what type of radioactive decay?

   (A) alpha
   (B) β^-
   (C) β^+
   (D) electron capture
   (E) gamma

9. Tungsten-176 has a half-life of 2.5 hours. After how many hours will the disintegration rate of a tungsten-176 sample drop to $\frac{1}{10}$ its initial value?

   (A) 5
   (B) 8.3
   (C) 10
   (D) 12.5
   (E) 25

10. What's the missing particle in the following nuclear reaction?

$$^{2}_{1}\text{H} + {}^{63}_{29}\text{Cu} \rightarrow {}^{64}_{30}\text{Zn} + (?)$$

   (A) Proton
   (B) Neutron
   (C) Electron
   (D) Positron
   (E) Deuteron

11. What's the missing particle in the following nuclear reaction?

$$^{196}_{78}\text{Pt} + {}^{1}_{0}\text{n} \rightarrow {}^{197}_{78}\text{Pt} + (?)$$

   (A) Proton
   (B) Neutron
   (C) Electron
   (D) Positron
   (E) Gamma

12. Two spaceships are traveling directly toward each other, one traveling at a speed of $\frac{c}{6}$ and the other at a speed of $\frac{c}{3}$, as measured by observers on a nearby planet. The faster ship emits a radar pulse directed toward the approaching ship. What is the speed of this radar pulse, as measured by observers on the planet?

   (A) $\frac{c}{2}$
   (B) $\frac{5c}{6}$
   (C) c
   (D) $\frac{7c}{6}$
   (E) $\frac{3c}{2}$

13. An Imperial battle cruiser, sitting in a hanger deck, is measured to have a length of 200 m by a worker on the deck. If the cruiser travels at a speed of $\left(\dfrac{\sqrt{3}}{2}\right) c$ past a planet, what will be the length of the cruiser, as measured by the inhabitants of the planet?

(A) 50 m
(B) 87 m
(C) 100 m
(D) 173 m
(E) 400 m

15. A particle whose rest energy is E is traveling at a speed of $\dfrac{12}{13} c$. What is the particle's kinetic energy?

(A) $\dfrac{7}{169} E$

(B) $\dfrac{5}{13} E$

(C) $\dfrac{3}{5} E$

(D) $\dfrac{8}{5} E$

(E) $\dfrac{13}{5} E$

14. An astronaut lives on a spaceship that is moving at a speed of $\left(\dfrac{4}{5}\right) c$ away from the earth. As measured by a clock on the spaceship, the time interval between her maintenance checks on the ship's main computer is 15 months. In the reference frame of the team here on Earth that monitors the ship's progress, what is the time interval between maintenance checks on the ship's main computer?

(A) 9 months
(B) 12 months
(C) 19 months
(D) 25 months
(E) 30 months

Keywords

raisin pudding model

alpha particles

Rutherford nuclear model

quanta

photon

photoelectric effect

photoelectrons

threshold frequency

Planck's constant

work function

electronvolt (eV)

atomic spectra

excited

energy level

quantized

wave–particle duality

de Broglie wavelength

protons

neutrons

nucleons

atomic number

neutron number

mass number

nucleon number

isotopes

nuclide

strong nuclear force

atomic mass unit (amu)

dueteron

deuterium

mass defect

binding energy

mass–energy equivalence

radioactive

alpha

beta (ß)

gamma

parent

daughter

electron capture (Ec)

beta particle

electron-antineutrino

weak nuclear force

positron

antiparticle

electron-neutrino

gamma ray

decay constant

activity

becquerel (Bq)

half-life

exponential decay

nuclear fission

nuclear fusion

disintegration energy

exothermic

endothermic

inertial reference frame

relativistic factor

length contraction

rest energy

total energy

Summary

For the test, be sure you are familiar with the following concepts from this chapter.

- o   Rutherford model of the atom
- o   Photons and the photoelectric effect
- o   The Bohr model of the atom
- o   Wave–particle duality
- o   Nuclear physics
- o   The nuclear force
- o   Binding energy
- o   Radioactivity
- o   Alpha decay
- o   Beta decay
- o β^- decay
- o β^+ decay
- o   Electron capture
- o   Radioactive decay rates
- o   Nuclear reactions
- o   Disintegration energy
- o   Special relativity
- o   The relativity of velocity
- o   The relativity of time
- o   The relativity of length
- o   Relativistic energy

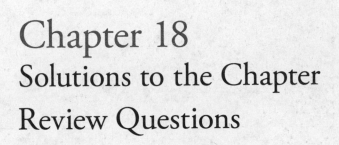

Chapter 18
Solutions to the Chapter
Review Questions

CHAPTER 2 REVIEW QUESTIONS

Question	Answer	Explanation
1	A	Traveling once around a circular path means that the final position coincides with the initial position. Therefore, the displacement is zero. The average speed, which is *total* distance traveled divided by elapsed time, cannot be zero. And since the velocity changed (because its direction changed), there was a nonzero acceleration. Therefore, only statement I is true.
2	C	By definition, $\bar{\mathbf{a}} = \Delta\mathbf{v} / \Delta t$. We determine $\Delta\mathbf{v} = \mathbf{v}_2 - \mathbf{v}_1 = \mathbf{v}_2 + (-\mathbf{v}^1)$ geometrically as follows: Since Δt is a positive scalar, the direction of $\bar{\mathbf{a}}$ is the same as the direction of $\Delta\mathbf{v}$, which is displayed above; choice (C) is best.
3	C	Statement I is false since a projectile experiencing only the constant acceleration due to gravity can travel in a parabolic trajectory. Statement II is true: Zero acceleration means no change in speed (or direction). Statement III is false: An object whose speed remains constant but whose velocity vector is changing direction is accelerating.
4	C	The baseball is still under the influence of Earth's gravity. Its acceleration throughout the *entire* flight is constant, equal to g downward.
5	A	Use Big Five #3 with $v_0 = 0$. $$\Delta s = v_0 t + \frac{1}{2}at^2 = \frac{1}{2}at^2 \;\Rightarrow\; t = \sqrt{\frac{2\Delta s}{a}} = \sqrt{\frac{2(200\text{ m})}{5\text{ m/s}^2}} = 9\text{ s}$$
6	D	Use Big Five #5 with $v_0 = 0$ (calling *down* the positive direction). $$v^2 = v_0^2 + 2a\Delta s = 2a\Delta s \;\Rightarrow\; \Delta s = \frac{v^2}{2a} = \frac{v^2}{2g} = \frac{(30\text{ m/s})^2}{2(10\text{ m/s}^2)} = 45\text{ m}$$
7	C	Apply Big Five #3 to the vertical motion, calling *down* the positive direction. $$\Delta y = v_{0y}t + \frac{1}{2}a_y t^2 = \frac{1}{2}a_y t^2 = \frac{1}{2}gt^2 \;\Rightarrow\; t = \sqrt{\frac{2\Delta y}{g}} = \sqrt{\frac{2(80\text{ m})}{10\text{ m/s}^2}} = 4\text{ s}$$ Notice that the stone's initial horizontal speed ($v_{0x} = 10$ m/s) is irrelevant.

Question	Answer	Explanation
8	B	First we determine the time required for the ball to reach the top of its parabolic trajectory (which is the time required for the vertical velocity to drop to zero). $$v_y \overset{set}{=} 0 \implies v_{0y} - gt = 0 \implies t = \frac{v_{0y}}{g}$$ The total flight time is equal to twice the following value: $$T = 2t = 2\frac{v_{0y}}{g} = 2\frac{v_0 \sin\theta_0}{g} = \frac{2(10 \text{ m/s})\sin 30°}{10 \text{ m/s}^2} = 1 \text{ s}$$
9	C	After 4 seconds, the stone's vertical speed has changed by $\Delta v_y = a_{yt} = (10 \text{ m/s}^2)$ (4 s) = 40 m/s. Since $v_{0y} = 0$, the value of v_y at $t = 4$ is 40 m/s. The horizontal speed does not change. Therefore, when the rock hits the water, its velocity has a horizontal component of 30 m/s and a vertical component of 40 m/s. By the Pythagorean theorem, the magnitude of the total velocity, v, is 50 m/s.
10	E	Since the acceleration of the projectile is always downward (because it's gravitational acceleration), the vertical speed decreases as the projectile rises and increases as the projectile falls. Statements A, B, C, and D are all false.

CHAPTER 3 REVIEW QUESTIONS

Question	Answer	Explanation
1	B	Because the person is not accelerating, the net force he feels must be zero. Therefore, the magnitude of the upward normal force from the floor must balance that of the downward gravitational force. Although these two forces have equal magnitudes, they do not form an action/reaction pair because they both act on the same object (namely, the person). The forces in an action/reaction pair always act on different objects.
2	D	First draw a free-body diagram. "up" is the positive direction The person exerts a downward force on the scale, and the scale pushes up on the person with an equal (but opposite) force, $\mathbf{F_N}$. Thus, the scale reading is F_N, the magnitude of the normal force. Since $F_N - F_w = ma$, we have $$F_N = F_w + ma = (800 \text{ N}) + [800 \text{ N}/(10 \frac{\text{m}}{\text{s}^2})](5 \text{ m/s}^2) = 1200 \text{ N}.$$
3	A	The net force that the object feels on the inclined plane is $mg \sin\theta$, the component of the gravitational force that is parallel to the ramp. Since $\sin\theta = (5 \text{ m})/(20 \text{ m}) = 1/4$, we have $F_{net} = (2 \text{ kg})(10 \text{ N/kg})(\frac{1}{4}) = 5 \text{ N}$.
4	C	The net force on the block is $F - F_f = F - \mu_k F_N = F - \mu_k F_w = (18 \text{ N}) - (0.4)(20 \text{ N}) = 10 \text{ N}$. Since $F_{net} = ma = (\frac{F_w}{g})a$, we find that $10 \text{ N} = [\frac{20 \text{ N}}{10 \text{ m/s}^2}]a$, which gives $a = 5 \text{ m/s}^2$.
5	A	The force pulling the block down the ramp is $mg \sin\theta$, and the maximum force of static friction is $\mu_s F_N = \mu_s mg \cos\theta$. If $mg \sin\theta$ is greater than $\mu_s mg \cos\theta$, then there is a net force down the ramp, and the block will accelerate down. So, the question becomes, "Is $\sin\theta$ greater than $\mu_s \cos\theta$?" Since $\theta = 30°$ and $\mu_s = 0.5$, the answer is *yes*.

Question	Answer	Explanation
6	E	One way to attack this question is to notice that if the two masses happen to be equal, that is, if $M = m$, then the blocks won't accelerate (because their weights balance). The only expression given that becomes zero when $M = m$ is the one given in choice (E). If we draw a free-body diagram, Newton's second law gives us the following two equations: $$F_T - mg = ma \quad (1)$$ $$Mg - F_T = Ma \quad (2)$$ Adding these equations yields $Mg - mg = ma + Ma = (M + m)a$, so $$a = \frac{Mg - mg}{M + m} = \frac{M - m}{M + m}g$$
7	E	If $\mathbf{F}_{net} = 0$, then $\mathbf{a} = 0$. No acceleration means constant speed (possibly, but not necessarily, zero) with no change in direction. Therefore, statements B, C, and D are false, and statement A is not necessarily true.
8	D	The horizontal motion across the frictionless tables is unaffected by (vertical) gravitational acceleration. It would take as much force to accelerate the block across the table on earth as it would on the moon. (If friction *were* taken into account, then the smaller weight of the block on the moon would imply a smaller normal force by the table and hence a smaller frictional force. Less force would be needed on the moon in this case.)
9	D	The maximum force that static friction can exert on the crate is $\mu_s F_N = \mu_s F_w = \mu_s mg = (0.4)(100 \text{ kg})(10 \text{ N/kg}) = 400$ N. Since the force applied to the crate is only 344 N, static friction is able to apply that same magnitude of force on the crate, keeping it stationary. [Choice (B) is incorrect because the static friction force is *not* the reaction force to $\mathbf{F}$; both $\mathbf{F}$ and $\mathbf{F}_{f(static)}$ act on the same object (the crate) and therefore cannot form an action/reaction pair.]

Question	Answer	Explanation
10	A	With crate #2 on top of crate #1, the force pushing downward on the floor is greater, so the normal force exerted by the floor on crate #1 is greater, which increases the friction force. Statements B, C, D, and E are all false.
11	E	Neither the velocity nor the acceleration is constant because the direction of each of these vectors is always changing as the object moves along its circular path. And the net force on the object is not zero because a centripetal force must be acting to provide the necessary centripetal acceleration to maintain the object's circular motion.

CHAPTER 4 REVIEW QUESTIONS

Question	Answer	Explanation
1	A	Since the force **F** is perpendicular to the displacement, the work it does is zero.
2	B	By the work–energy theorem $$W = \Delta K = \frac{1}{2}m(v^2 - v_0^2) = \frac{1}{2}(4 \text{ kg})[(6 \text{ m/s})^2 - (3 \text{ m/s})^2] = 54 \text{ J}$$
3	B	Since the box (mass m) falls through a vertical distance of h, its gravitational potential energy decreases by mgh. The length of the ramp is irrelevant here.
4	C	Since the centripetal force always points along a radius toward the center of the circle, and the velocity of the object is always tangent to the circle (and thus perpendicular to the radius), the work done by the centripetal force is zero. Alternatively, since the object's speed remains constant, the work–energy theorem tells us that no work is being performed.
5	A	The gravitational force points downward while the book's displacement is upward. Therefore, the work done by gravity is $-mgh = -(2 \text{ kg})(10 \text{ N/kg})(1.5 \text{ m}) = -30$ J.
6	D	First, the kinetic energy the block gains is the same as the potential energy it loses, which is mgh. Since this is equal to $\frac{1}{2}mv^2$, we find that $v = \sqrt{2gh}$. Plugging in $g = 10 \text{ m/s}^2$ and $h = 4$ m, we get $v = \sqrt{80} \approx 9$ m/s.
7	C	Apply conservation of mechanical energy (including the negative work done by $\mathbf{F}_f$, the force of sliding friction). $$K_i + U_i + W_{\text{frict}} = K_f + U_f$$ $$0 + mgh - F_f L = \frac{1}{2}mv^2 + 0$$ $$v = \sqrt{\frac{2}{m}(mgh - F_f L)}$$ $$= \sqrt{\frac{2}{3}(3 \cdot 10 \cdot 4 - 16 \cdot 6)}$$ $$= \sqrt{16}$$ $$= 4 \text{ m/s}$$ Note: $W_{total} = \Delta K$ could also be used.

Question	Answer	Explanation
8	E	Apply conservation of mechanical energy (including the negative work done by $\mathbf{F}_r$, the force of air resistance). $$K_i + U_i + W_r = K_f + U_f$$ $$0 + mgh - F_r h = \frac{1}{2}mv^2 + 0$$ $$v = \sqrt{\frac{2h(mg - F_r)}{m}}$$ $$= \sqrt{\frac{2(40\text{ m})[(4\text{ kg})(10\text{ N/kg}) - 20\text{ N}]}{4\text{ kg}}}$$ $$= \sqrt{\frac{2(40\text{ m})[20\text{ N}]}{4\text{ kg}}}$$ $$= \sqrt{2(10)(20)\frac{\text{m}^2}{\text{s}^2}}$$ $$= 20\text{ m/s}$$ Again, $W_{total} = \Delta K$ could also be used.
9	E	Because the rock has lost half of its gravitational potential energy, its kinetic energy at the halfway point is half of its kinetic energy at impact. Since K is proportional to v^2, if $K_{\text{at halfway point}}$ is equal to $\frac{1}{2}K_{\text{at impact}}$, then the rock's speed at the halfway point is $\sqrt{\frac{1}{2}} = \frac{1}{\sqrt{2}}$ its speed at impact.
10	D	Using the equation $P = Fv$, we find that $P = (200\text{ N})(2\text{ m/s}) = 400\text{ W}$.

CHAPTER 5 REVIEW QUESTIONS

Question	Answer	Explanation
1	C	The magnitude of the object's linear momentum is $p = mv$. If $p = 6$ kg · m/s and $m = 2$ kg, then $v = 3$ m/s. Therefore, the object's kinetic energy is $K = \frac{1}{2}mv^2 = \frac{1}{2}(2\text{ kg})(3\text{ m/s})^2 = 9$ J.
2	C	The impulse delivered to the ball, $J = F\Delta t$, equals its change in momentum. Since the ball started from rest, we have $$F\Delta t = mv \;\Rightarrow\; \Delta t = \frac{mv}{F} = \frac{(0.5\text{ kg})(4\text{ m/s})}{20\text{ N}} = 0.1\text{ s}$$
3	E	The impulse delivered to the ball, $J = \bar{F}\Delta t$, equals its change in momentum. Thus, $$\bar{F}\Delta t = \Delta p = p_f - p_i = m(v_f - v_i) \;\Rightarrow\; \bar{F} = \frac{m(v_f - v_i)}{\Delta t} = \frac{(2\text{ kg})(8\text{ m/s} - 4\text{ m/s})}{0.5\text{ s}} = 16\text{ N}$$
4	D	The impulse delivered to the ball is equal to its change in momentum. The momentum of the ball was $m\mathbf{v}$ before hitting the wall and $m(-\mathbf{v})$ after. Therefore, the change in momentum is $m(-\mathbf{v}) - m\mathbf{v} = -2m\mathbf{v}$, so the magnitude of the momentum change (and the impulse) is $2mv$.
5	B	By definition of *perfectly inelastic*, the objects move off together with one common velocity, $\mathbf{v}'$, after the collision. By conservation of linear momentum, $$m_1\mathbf{v}_1 + m_2\mathbf{v}_2 = (m_1 + m_2)\mathbf{v}'$$ $$\mathbf{v}' = \frac{m_1 v_1 + m_2 v_2}{m_1 + m_2}$$ $$= \frac{(3\text{ kg})(2\text{ m/s}) + (5\text{ kg})(-2\text{ m/s})}{3\text{ kg} + 5\text{ kg}}$$ $$= -0.5\text{ m/s}$$

Question	Answer	Explanation
6	D	First, apply conservation of linear momentum to calculate the speed of the combined object after the (perfectly inelastic) collision. $$m_1 v_1 + m_2 v_2 = (m_1 + m_2) v'$$ $$v' = \frac{m_1 v_1 + m_2 v_2}{m_1 + m_2}$$ $$= \frac{m_1 v_1 + (2m_1)(0)}{m_1 + 2m_1}$$ $$= \frac{1}{3} v_1$$ Therefore, the ratio of the kinetic energy after the collision to the kinetic energy before the collision is $$\frac{K'}{K} = \frac{\frac{1}{2} m' v'^2}{\frac{1}{2} m_1 v_1^2} = \frac{\frac{1}{2}(m_1 + 2m_1)(\frac{1}{3} v_1)^2}{\frac{1}{2} m_1 v_1^2} = \frac{1}{3}$$
7	C	Total linear momentum is conserved in a collision during which the net external force is zero. If kinetic energy is lost, then by definition, the collision is not elastic.

Question	Answer	Explanation
8	B	First replace each rod by concentrating its mass at its center of mass position.

The center of mass of the two m's is at their midpoint, at a distance of $\frac{1}{2}L$ below the center of mass of the rod of mass $2m$.

Now, applying the equation for locating the center of mass (letting $y = 0$ denote the position of the center of mass of the top horizontal rod), we find

$$y_{cm} = \frac{(2m)(0) + (2m)(\frac{1}{2}L)}{2m + 2m} = \frac{1}{4}L$$ |
| 9 | D | The linear momentum of the bullet must have the same magnitude as the linear momentum of the block in order for their combined momentum after impact to be zero. The block has momentum MV to the left, so the bullet must have momentum MV to the right. Since the bullet's mass is m, its speed must be $v = \frac{MV}{m}$. |
| 10 | C | In a perfectly inelastic collision, kinetic energy is never conserved; some of the initial kinetic energy is always lost to heat and some is converted to potential energy in the deformed shapes of the objects as they lock together. |

CHAPTER 6 REVIEW QUESTIONS

Question	Answer	Explanation
1	C	By combining the equation for centripetal acceleration, $a_c = v^2/r$, with $v = r\omega$, we find $$a_c = \frac{v^2}{r} = \frac{(r\omega)^2}{r} = \omega^2 r \implies \omega = \sqrt{\frac{a_c}{r}} = \sqrt{\frac{9 \text{ m/s}^2}{0.25 \text{ m}}} = 6 \text{ s}^{-1}$$
2	C	Use Big Five #3 for rotational motion. $$\Delta\theta = \omega_0 t + \frac{1}{2}\alpha t^2 = \frac{1}{2}\alpha t^2 \implies \alpha = \frac{2\Delta\theta}{t^2} = \frac{2(60 \text{ rad})}{(10 \text{ s})^2} = 1.2 \text{ rad/s}^2$$
3	D	The torque is $\tau = rF = (0.20 \text{ m})(20 \text{ N}) = 4 \text{ N} \cdot \text{m}$.
4	D	From the diagram we calculate that $$\tau = rF\sin\theta = Lmg\sin\theta$$ $$= (0.80 \text{ m})(0.50 \text{ kg})(10 \text{ N/kg})(\sin 30°)$$ $$= 2.0 \text{ N} \cdot \text{m}$$

Question	Answer	Explanation
5	B	The stick will remain at rest in the horizontal position if the torques about the suspension point are balanced.

$$\tau_{CCW} = \tau_{CW}$$
$$r_1 F_1 = r_2 F_2$$
$$r_1 m_1 g = r_2 m_2 g$$
$$m_2 = \frac{r_1 m_1}{r_2} = \frac{(50 \text{ cm})(3 \text{ kg})}{30 \text{ cm}} = 5 \text{ kg}$$

Note that the center of mass formula could also be used to find m_2, though it would require algebra. Typically, the center of mass forma is useful for determining where the balance point is. If the balance point is known, then torque is usually easier.

CHAPTER 7 REVIEW QUESTIONS

Question	Answer	Explanation
1	A	Gravitational force obeys an inverse-square law: $F_{grav} \propto \dfrac{1}{r^2}$. Therefore, if r increases by a factor of 2, then F_{grav} decreases by a factor of $2^2 = 4$.
2	E	Mass is an intrinsic property of an object and does not change with location. This eliminates choices A and C. If an object's height above the surface of the earth is equal to $2R_E$, then its distance from the center of the earth is $3R_E$. Thus, the object's distance from the earth's center increases by a factor of 3, so its weight decreases by a factor of $3^2 = 9$.
3	C	The gravitational force that the moon exerts on the planet is equal in magnitude to the gravitational force that the planet exerts on the moon (Newton's third law).
4	D	The gravitational acceleration at the surface of a planet of mass M and radius R is given by the equation $g = GM/R^2$. Therefore $$g_{Pluto} = G\frac{M_{Pluto}}{R_{Pluto}^2} = G\frac{\frac{1}{500}M_{Earth}}{\left(\frac{1}{15}R_{Earth}\right)^2} = \frac{15^2}{500} \cdot G\frac{M_{Earth}}{R_{Earth}^2} = \frac{225}{500}(10 \text{ m/s}^2) = 4.5 \text{ m/s}^2$$
5	B	The gravitational pull by the earth provides the centripetal force on the satellite, so $\dfrac{GMm}{R^2} = \dfrac{mv^2}{R}$. This gives $\dfrac{1}{2}mv^2 = \dfrac{GMm}{2R}$, so the kinetic energy K of the satellite is inversely proportional to R. Therefore, if R increases by a factor of 2, then K decreases by a factor of 2.
6	E	The gravitational pull by Jupiter provides the centripetal force on its moon. $$G\frac{Mm}{R^2} = \frac{mv^2}{R}$$ $$G\frac{M}{R} = v^2$$ $$= \left(\frac{2\pi R}{T}\right)^2$$ $$= \frac{4\pi^2 R^2}{T^2}$$ $$M = \frac{4\pi^2 R^3}{GT^2}$$

Question	Answer	Explanation
7	B	Kepler's Third Law says that $T^2 \propto R^3$ for a planet with a circular orbit of radius R. Since $T \propto R^{\frac{3}{2}}$, if R increases by a factor of 9, then T increases by a factor of $9^{\frac{3}{2}} = \left(3^2\right)^{\frac{3}{2}} = 3^3 = 27$.
8	D	Apply conservation of mechanical energy. $$K_0 + U_0 = K_f + U_f$$ $$0 - G\frac{Mm}{3R} = \frac{1}{2}mv_f^2 - G\frac{Mm}{R}$$ $$\frac{1}{2}mv_f^2 = G\frac{2Mm}{3R}$$ $$v_f = \sqrt{\frac{\frac{4}{3}GM}{R}}$$
9	A	Since the centripetal force on each satellite is equal to the gravitational force it feels due to the earth, the question is equivalent to, "How does F_A, the gravitational force on satellite A, compare to F_B, the gravitational force on satellite B?" Because both satellites have the same mass, Newton's law of gravitation tells us that the gravitational force is inversely proportional to r^2. Since satellite B is 3 times farther from the center of the earth than satellite A, the gravitational force that satellite B feels is $\frac{1}{3}^2 = \frac{1}{9}$ the gravitational force felt by satellite A. (Be careful if you tried to apply the formula $F_c = \frac{mv^2}{r}$ for centripetal force and concluded that the answer was B. This is wrong because even though both satellites orbit at a constant speed, they don't orbit at the *same* speed, so the formula for centripetal force cannot be used directly.)

CHAPTER 8 REVIEW QUESTIONS

Question	Answer	Explanation
1	D	The acceleration of a simple harmonic oscillator is not constant, since the restoring force—and, consequently, the acceleration—depends on position. Therefore, statement I is false. However, both statements II and III are fundamental, defining characteristics of simple harmonic motion.
2	C	The acceleration of the block has its maximum magnitude at the points where its displacement from equilibrium has the maximum magnitude (since $a = \dfrac{F}{m} = \dfrac{kx}{m}$). At the endpoints of the oscillation region, the potential energy is maximized and the kinetic energy (and hence the speed) is zero.
3	E	By conservation of mechanical energy, $K + U_S$ is a constant for the motion of the block. At the endpoints of the oscillation region, the block's displacement, x, is equal to $\pm A$. Since $K = 0$ here, all the energy is in the form of potential energy of the spring, $\frac{1}{2} kA^2$. Because $\frac{1}{2} kA^2$ gives the total energy at these positions, it also gives the total energy at any other position. Using the equation $U_S(x) = \frac{1}{2} kx^2$, we find that, at $x = \frac{1}{2} A$ $$K + U_S = \frac{1}{2} kA^2$$ $$K + \tfrac{1}{2} k (\tfrac{1}{2} A)^2 = \frac{1}{2} kA^2$$ $$K = \frac{3}{8} kA^2$$ Therefore, $$K/E = \frac{\frac{3}{8} kA^2}{\frac{1}{2} kA^2} = \frac{3}{4}$$
4	C	As we derived in Question 2, the maximum speed of the block is given by the equation $v_{max} = A\sqrt{\dfrac{k}{m}}$. Therefore, v_{max} is inversely proportional to $\sqrt{m}$. If m is increased by a factor of 2, then v_{max} will decrease by a factor of $\sqrt{2}$.
5	D	The period of a spring–block simple harmonic oscillator is independent of the value of g. (Recall that $T = 2\pi\sqrt{\dfrac{m}{k}}$.) Therefore, the period will remain the same.

Question	Answer	Explanation
6	D	The frequency of a spring–block simple harmonic oscillator is given by the equation $f = (\frac{1}{2}\pi)\sqrt{\frac{k}{m}}$. Squaring both sides of this equation, we get $f^2 = \left(\frac{k}{4\pi^2}\right)\left(\frac{1}{m}\right)$. Therefore, if f^2 is plotted versus $(1/m)$, then the graph will be a straight line with slope $\left(\frac{k}{4\pi^2}\right)$. (Note: The slope of the line whose equation is $y = ax$ is a.)
7	A	The only equation that gives $x = 6$ when $t = 0$ is the one in choice A.
8	B	The period of the spring-block simple harmonic oscillator is given by the equation $T = 2\pi\sqrt{\frac{m}{k}}$. So, to make T as small as possible, we want m to be as small as possible and k to be as large as possible. Since m_2 is the smaller mass and k_1 is the larger spring constant, this combination will give the oscillator the shortest period.
9	C	For small angular displacements, the period of a simple pendulum is essentially independent of amplitude.
10	B	First draw a free-body diagram. The net force toward the center of the bob's circular path is $F_T - mg\cos\theta_{max}$. This must provide the centripetal force, $\frac{mv^2}{L}$. But since the speed of the bob at this moment is zero ($v = 0$), we get $F_T = mg\cos\theta_{max}$. (The acceleration is purely tangential here, equal to $\frac{(mg\sin\theta_{max})}{m} = g\sin\theta_{max}$.)

CHAPTER 9 REVIEW QUESTIONS

Question	Answer	Explanation
1	C	Use the equation $Q = mc\,\Delta T$. $$Q = (0.04\text{ kg})(0.50\text{ kJ/kg}\cdot{}^\circ\text{C})(50{}^\circ\text{C} - 20{}^\circ\text{C}) = 0.6\text{ kJ} = 600\text{ J}$$
2	D	Phase changes obey the equation $Q = mL$, where m is the mass of the sample and L is the latent heat of transformation. In this case, we find that $$m = \frac{Q}{L} = \frac{2000\text{ J}}{200\text{ kJ/kg}} = \frac{2000\text{ J}}{200\times 10^3\text{ J/kg}} = \frac{1}{100}\text{ kg}$$
3	A	First, let's figure out how much heat is required to bring the water to its boiling point. $$Q = mc\Delta T = (0.1\text{ kg})(4.186\text{ kJ/kg}\cdot{}^\circ\text{C})(100{}^\circ\text{C} - 20{}^\circ\text{C}) = 33\text{ kJ}$$ Once the water reaches 100°C, any additional heat will be absorbed and begin the transformation to steam. To completely vaporize the sample requires $$Q = mL = (0.1\text{ kg})(2260\text{ kJ/kg}) = 226\text{ kJ}$$ Since the 20°C water absorbed only 100 kJ of heat, enough heat was provided to bring the water to boiling, but not enough to completely vaporize it (at which point, the absorption of more heat would begin to increase the temperature of the steam). Thus, the water will reach and remain at 100°C.
4	D	The equation for volume expansion is $\Delta V = \beta V_i \Delta T$, so $$\Delta V = \beta V_i \Delta T = \frac{4.0\times 10^{-5}}{{}^\circ\text{C}}(2.0\text{ m}^3)(35{}^\circ\text{ C} - 5{}^\circ\text{ C}) = 0.0024\text{ m}^3 \times \left(\frac{10^2\text{ cm}}{1\text{ m}}\right)^3 = 2{,}400\text{ cm}^3$$
5	B	Because the gas is confined, n remains constant, and because we're told the volume is fixed, V remains constant as well. Since R is a universal constant, the ideal gas law, $PV = nRT$, tells us that P and T are proportional. Therefore, if T increases by a factor of 2, then so does P.

Question	Answer	Explanation
6	E	Neither choice A nor B can be correct. Using $PV = nRT$, both containers have the same V, n is the same, P is the same, and R is a universal constant. Therefore, T must be the same for both samples. Choice C is also wrong, since R is a universal constant. The kinetic theory of gases predicts that the rms speed of the gas molecules in a sample of molar mass M and temperature T is $$v_{rms} = \sqrt{\frac{3RT}{M}}$$ Hydrogen has a smaller molar mass than does helium, so v_{rms} for hydrogen must be greater than v_{rms} for helium (because both samples are at the same T).
7	A	By convention, work done *on* the gas sample is designated as negative, so in the first law of thermodynamics, $\Delta U = Q - W$, we must write $W = -320$ J. Therefore, $Q = \Delta U + W = 560$ J $+ (-320$ J$) = +240$ J. Positive Q denotes heat *in*.
8	C	No work is done during the step from state b to state c because the volume doesn't change. Therefore, the work done from a to c is equal to the work done from a to b. Since the pressure remains constant (this step is isobaric), we find that $W = P \Delta V = (3.0 \times 10^5 \text{ Pa})[(25 - 10) \times 10^{-3} \text{ m}^3] = 4,500$ J.
9	B	Since the engine takes in 400 J of energy and produces only 400 J – 300 J = 100 J of useful work, its efficiency is $\frac{(100 \text{ J})}{(400 \text{ J})} = \frac{1}{4}$.
10	D	Statement A is the first law of thermodynamics. Statements C and E are true, but they are not equivalent to the second law of thermodynamics. Choice B is false, but if it read, "The efficiency of a heat engine can never be equal to 100 percent," then it would be equivalent to the Second Law. Choice D is one of the several equivalent forms of the second law of thermodynamics.

CHAPTER 10 REVIEW QUESTIONS

Question	Answer	Explanation
1	D	Electrostatic force obeys an inverse-square law: $F_E \propto \dfrac{1}{r^2}$. Therefore, if r increases by a factor of 3, then F_E decreases by a factor of $3^2 = 9$.
2	C	The strength of the electric force is given by $\dfrac{kq^2}{r^2}$, and the strength of the gravitational force is $\dfrac{Gm^2}{r^2}$. Since both of these quantities have r^2 in the denominator, we simply need to compare the numerical values of kq^2 and Gm^2. There's no contest since $$kq^2 = \left(\dfrac{9 \times 10^9 \ N \cdot m^2}{C^2}\right)(1 \ C)^2 = 9 \times 10^9 \ \text{N·m}^2$$ and $$Gm^2 = \left(\dfrac{6.7 \times 10^{-11} \ N \cdot m^2}{\text{kg}^2}\right)(1 \ \text{kg})^2 = 6.7 \times 10^{-11} \ \text{N·m}$$ we see that $kq^2 > Gm^2$, so F_E is much stronger than F_G.
3	C	If the net electric force on the center charge is zero, the electrical repulsion by the $+2q$ charge must balance the electrical repulsion by the $+3q$ charge $$k\dfrac{(2q)(q)}{x^2} = k\dfrac{(3q)(q)}{y^2} \ \Rightarrow \ \dfrac{2}{x^2} = \dfrac{3}{y^2} \ \Rightarrow \ \dfrac{y^2}{x^2} = \dfrac{3}{2} \ \Rightarrow \ \dfrac{y}{x} = \sqrt{\dfrac{3}{2}}$$
4	E	Since P is equidistant from the two charges, and the magnitudes of the charges are identical, the strength of the electric field at P due to $+Q$ is the same as the strength of the electric field at P due to $-Q$. The electric field vector at P due to $+Q$ points away from $+Q$, and the electric field vector at P due to $-Q$ points toward $-Q$. Since these vectors point in the same direction, the net electric field at P is (E to the right) + (E to the right) = ($2E$ to the right).

Question	Answer	Explanation
5	D	The acceleration of the small sphere is $$a = \frac{F_E}{m} = k\frac{Qq}{mr^2}$$ As r increases (that is, as the small sphere is pushed away), a decreases. However, since a is always positive, the small sphere's speed, v, is always increasing.
6	B	Since F_E (on q) = qE, it must be true that F_E (on $-2q$) = $-2qE = -2F_E$.
7	D	All excess electric charge on a conductor resides on the outer surface.
8	D	By definition, electric field vectors point *away from* a *positive* source charge and *toward* a *negative* source charge. Furthermore, since an electron (which is negatively charged) would be repelled from a negative source charge, the resulting electric force on an electron would point away from a negative source charge, in the opposite direction from the electric field vector.
9	A	The individual electric field vectors at P due to the two source charges have the same magnitude and point in opposite directions. Therefore, the net electric field at point P will be zero.
10	A	The individual electric field vectors at the center of the square due to the two negative source charges cancel each other out. So we simply need to make sure that the individual electric field vector at the center of the square due to the bottom-right source charge cancels the individual electric field vector at the center of the square due to the upper-left source charge. Since the upper-left source charge is $+Q$, the bottom-right source charge must be $+Q$ also.

CHAPTER 11 REVIEW QUESTIONS

Question	Answer	Explanation
1	E	A counterexample for statement I is provided by two equal positive charges; at the point midway between the charges, the electric field is zero, but the potential is not. A counter-example for statement II is provided by an electric dipole (a pair of equal but opposite charges); at the point midway between the charges, the electric potential is zero, but the electric field is not. As for statement III, consider a single positive point charge $+Q$. Then at a distance r from this source charge, the electric field strength is $E = \dfrac{kq}{r^2}$ and the potential is $V = \dfrac{kQ}{r}$. Thus, $V = rE$, so V is not inversely proportional to E.
2	C	By definition, $U_E = -W_E$, so if W_E is negative, then ΔU_E is positive. This implies that the potential energy, U_E, increases.
3	B	The work required to assemble the configuration is equal to the potential energy of the system. $$W = U_E = k\sum_{i<j}\frac{q_i q_j}{r_{ij}}$$ $$= k\left(\frac{q_1 q_2}{r_{12}} + \frac{q_1 q_3}{r_{13}} + \frac{q_1 q_4}{r_{14}} + \frac{q_2 q_3}{r_{23}} + \frac{q_2 q_4}{r_{24}} + \frac{q_3 q_4}{r_{34}}\right)$$ $$= k\left(\frac{q^2}{s} + \frac{q^2}{s\sqrt{2}} + \frac{q^2}{s} + \frac{q^2}{s} + \frac{q^2}{s\sqrt{2}} + \frac{q^2}{s}\right)$$ $$= k\frac{q^2}{s}(4+\sqrt{2})$$
4	B	Use the definition $\Delta V = -\dfrac{W_E}{q}$. If an electric field accelerates a negative charge doing positive work on it, then $W_E > 0$. If $q < 0$, then $-\dfrac{W_E}{q}$ is positive. Therefore, ΔV is positive, which implies that V increases.

Question	Answer	Explanation
5	E	By definition $$V_{A \to B} = \frac{\Delta U_E}{q}, \text{ so } V_B - V_A = \frac{\Delta U_E}{q}$$
6	C	Because **E** is uniform, the potential varies linearly with distance from either plate ($\Delta V = Ed$). Since points 2 and 4 are at the same distance from the plates, they lie on the same equipotential. (The equipotentials in this case are planes parallel to the capacitor plates.)
7	D	As we move from point A to point B, the potential decreases by 10 V, so $\Delta V = -10$ V. Now, since $\Delta U = q\Delta V$, we have $\Delta U = (-2 \text{ C})(-10 \text{ V}) = +20$ J.
8	A	Since Q cannot change and C is increased (because of the dielectric), $\Delta V = Q/C$ must decrease. Also, since $U_E = \dfrac{Q^2}{(2C)}$, an increase in C with no change in Q implies a decrease in U_E.
9	B	By definition, $W_E = -q\Delta V$, which gives $$W_E = -q(V_B - V_A) = -(-0.05 \text{ C})(100 \text{ V} - 200 \text{ V}) = -5 \text{ J}$$ Notice that neither the length of the segment AB nor that of the curved path from A to B is relevant.

CHAPTER 12 REVIEW QUESTIONS

Question	Answer	Explanation
1	A	Let ρ_S denote the resistivity of silver and let A_S denote the cross-sectional area of the silver wire. Then $$R_B = \frac{\rho_B L}{A_B} = \frac{(5\rho_S)L}{4^2 A_S} = \frac{5}{16}\frac{\rho_S L}{A_S} = \frac{5}{16}R_S$$
2	D	The equation $I = \dfrac{V}{R}$ implies that increasing V by a factor of 2 will cause I to increase by a factor of 2.
3	C	Use the equation $P = \dfrac{V^2}{R}$. $$P = \frac{V^2}{R} \quad \Rightarrow \quad R = \frac{V^2}{P} = \frac{(120 \text{ V})^2}{60 \text{ W}} = 240 \ \Omega$$
4	B	The current through the circuit is $$I = \frac{\mathcal{E}}{r+R} = \frac{40 \text{ V}}{(5 \ \Omega) + (15 \ \Omega)} = 2 \text{ A}$$ Therefore, the voltage drop across R is $V = IR = (2 \text{ A})(15 \ \Omega) = 30 \text{ V}$.
5	E	The 12 Ω and 4 Ω resistors are in parallel and are equivalent to a single 3 Ω resistor, because $\dfrac{1}{(12 \ \Omega)} + \dfrac{1}{(4 \ \Omega)} = \dfrac{1}{(3 \ \Omega)}$. This 3 Ω resistor is in series with the top 3 Ω resistor, giving an equivalent resistance in the top branch of 3 Ω + 3 Ω = 6 Ω. Finally, this 6 Ω resistor is in parallel with the bottom 3 Ω resistor, giving an overall equivalent resistance of 2 Ω, because $\dfrac{1}{(6 \ \Omega)} + \dfrac{1}{(3 \ \Omega)} = \dfrac{1}{(2 \ \Omega)}$.
6	D	If each of the identical bulbs has resistance R, then the current through each bulb is $\mathcal{E}/R$. This is unchanged if the middle branch is taken out of the parallel circuit. (What *will* change is the total amount of current provided by the battery.)

Question	Answer	Explanation
7	B	The three parallel resistors are equivalent to a single 2 Ω resistor, because $\frac{1}{(8\ \Omega)} + \frac{1}{(4\ \Omega)} + \frac{1}{(8\ \Omega)} = \frac{1}{(2\ \Omega)}$. This 2 Ω resistance is in series with the given 2 Ω resistor, so their equivalent resistance is $2\ \Omega + 2\ \Omega = 4\ \Omega$. Therefore, three times as much current will flow through this equivalent 4 Ω resistance in the top branch as through the parallel 12 Ω resistor in the bottom branch, which implies that the current through the bottom branch is 3 A, and the current through the top branch is 9 A. The voltage drop across the 12 Ω resistor is therefore $V = IR = (3\ \text{A})(12\ \Omega) = 36\ \text{V}$.
8	E	Since points a and b are grounded, they're at the same potential (call it zero). Traveling from b to a across the battery, the potential increases by 24 V, so it must decrease by 24 V across the 8 Ω resistor as we reach point a. Thus, $I = V/R = \dfrac{(24\ \text{V})}{(8\ \Omega)} = 3\ \text{A}$
9	D	The equation $P = I^2R$ gives $$P = (0.5\ \text{A})^2(100\ \Omega) = 25\ \text{W} = 25\ \text{J/s}$$ Therefore, in 20 s, the energy dissipated as heat is $$E = Pt = (25\ \text{J/s})(20\ \text{s}) = 500\ \text{J}$$
10	B	Resistors in series always share the same current, so we can eliminate choices D and E. Now, using Ohm's law, $V = IR$, we see that if I is constant, then V is proportional to R. Since $R_A = 4R_B$, we know that $V_A = 4V_B$.

CHAPTER 13 REVIEW QUESTIONS

Question	Answer	Explanation
1	D	Statement I is false: The magnetic field lines due to a current-carrying wire encircle the wire in closed loops. Statement II is also false: Since the magnetic force is always perpendicular to the charged particle's velocity vector, it can do work on the charged particle; therefore, it cannot change the particle's kinetic energy. Statement III, however, is true: If the charged particle's velocity is parallel (or antiparallel) to the magnetic field lines, then the particle will feel no magnetic force.
2	C	The magnitude of the magnetic force is $F_B = qvB$, so the acceleration of the particle has magnitude $$a = \frac{F_B}{m} = \frac{qvB}{m} = \frac{(4.0 \times 10^{-9} \text{ C})(3 \times 10^4 \text{ m/s})(0.1 \text{ T})}{2 \times 10^{-4} \text{ kg}} = 0.06 \text{ m/s}^2.$$
3	D	By the right-hand rule, the direction of $\mathbf{F}_B$ is out of the plane of the page (since the particle carries a negative charge).
4	D	Since $\mathbf{F}_B$ is always perpendicular to $\mathbf{v}$, $\mathbf{v}$ cannot be upward or downward in the plane of the page; this eliminates choices (B) and (C). The velocity vector also cannot be to the right choice (A), since then $\mathbf{v}$ would be antiparallel to $\mathbf{B}$, and $\mathbf{F}_B$ would be zero. Using the right-hand rule, $\mathbf{v}$ must be out of the plane of the page.
5	A	The magnetic force provides the centripetal force on the charged particle. Therefore, $$qvB = \frac{mv^2}{r} \quad \Rightarrow \quad qB = \frac{mv}{r} \quad \Rightarrow \quad mv = qBr \quad \Rightarrow \quad p = qBr$$
6	A	The strength of the magnetic field at a distance r from a long, straight wire carrying a current I is proportional to I/r; that is, B is inversely proportional to r. So, at $\frac{1}{2}$ the distance from the wire, the magnetic field will be twice as strong.
7	E	The magnetic force provides the centripetal force on the charged particle. It follows that $$qvB = \frac{mv^2}{r} \quad \Rightarrow \quad qB = \frac{mv}{r} \quad \Rightarrow \quad r = \frac{mv}{qB}$$ Increasing m or v, or decreasing q or B, would make r larger, not smaller. Therefore, the answer must be (E).

Question	Answer	Explanation
8	D	The magnetic field **B** cannot be in the plane of the page (because both **v** and $\mathbf{F_B}$ are), so we can eliminate choices (A), (B), and (C). If **B** pointed into the plane of the page, it's easy to see that the right-hand rule tells us that $\mathbf{F_B}$ would point upward in the plane of the page. Therefore, **B** must point out of the plane of the page.
9	E	Since **v** is perpendicular to **B**, the strength of the magnetic force, $\mathbf{F_B}$, is just qvB, where q is the magnitude of the charge. In this case, then, we find that $$\mathbf{F_B} = (0.04 \text{ C})(2 \times 10^4 \text{ m/s})(0.5 \text{ T}) = 400 \text{ N}$$
10	C	The period T is the time it takes the charge to complete one revolution: $T = \dfrac{2\pi r}{v}$. Since the magnetic force is providing the centripetal force, $qVB = \dfrac{mv^2}{r}$ or $r = \dfrac{mv}{qB}$. Therefore, $T = \dfrac{2\pi m}{qB}$. Since T is independent of v, it will remain unchanged.

CHAPTER 14 REVIEW QUESTIONS

Question	Answer	Explanation
1	E	Since **v** is upward and **B** is out of the page, the direction of $\mathbf{F}_B$ on the free electrons will be to the left, leaving an excess of positive charge at the right. Therefore, the potential at point b will be higher than at point a, by $\varepsilon = vBL$ (motional emf).
2	C	If the plane of a loop enclosing an area A is perpendicular to a uniform magnetic field of strength B, then the magnetic flux through the loop, Φ_B, is simply equal to the product BA. Since both these loops have the same area, the magnetic fluxes through them will be the same, regardless of their shape.
3	C	To the right of the long straight wire, the magnetic field points into the plane of the page, and it is stronger at x_1 than at x_2. This means that the "into-the-page magnetic flux" through the loop increases as the loop is moved from x_1 to x_2. Since the flux is into the page and increasing, Lenz's law says that the current induced in the loop will be counterclockwise to produce its own *out*-of-the-page magnetic flux.
4	E	Since the current in the straight wire is steady, there is no change in the magnetic field, no change in magnetic flux, and, therefore, no induced emf or current.
5	C	By definition, magnetic field lines emerge from the north pole and enter at the south pole. Therefore, as the north pole is moved upward through the loop, the upward magnetic flux increases. To oppose an increasing upward flux, the direction of the induced current will be clockwise (as seen from above) to generate some downward magnetic flux. Now, as the south pole moves away from the center of the loop, there is a decreasing upward magnetic flux, so the direction of the induced current will be counterclockwise.

CHAPTER 15 REVIEW QUESTIONS

Question	Answer	Explanation
1	D	From the equation $\lambda f = v$, we find that $$\lambda = \frac{v}{f} = \frac{10 \text{ m/s}}{5 \text{ Hz}} = 2 \text{ m}$$
2	C	The speed of a transverse traveling wave on a stretched rope is given by the equation $v = \sqrt{F_T / \mu}$. Therefore $$v = \sqrt{\frac{F_T}{m/L}} = \sqrt{\frac{80 \text{ N}}{(1 \text{ kg})/(5 \text{ m})}} = \sqrt{400 \text{ m}^2/\text{s}^2} = 20 \text{ m/s}$$
3	D	The time interval from a point moving from its maximum displacement above $y = 0$ (equilibrium) to its maximum displacement below equilibrium is equal to one-half the period of the wave. In this case $$T = \frac{1}{f} = \frac{\lambda}{v} = \frac{8 \text{ m}}{2 \text{ m/s}} = 4 \text{ s}$$ so the desired time is $\frac{1}{2}$ (4 s) = 2 s.
4	E	From the equations $\lambda f = v$ and $f = 1/T$, we get $\lambda = vT = 2(\text{cm/s})(2 \text{ s}) = 4 \text{ cm}$.
5	E	The distance between successive nodes is always equal to $\frac{1}{2}\lambda$. If a standing wave on a string fixed at both ends has a total of 4 nodes, the string must have a length L equal to $3(\frac{1}{2}\lambda)$. If $L = 6$ m, then λ must equal 4 m.
6	B	We found in the previous question that $\lambda = 4$ m. Since $v = 40$ m/s, the frequency of this standing wave must be $$f = \frac{v}{\lambda} = \frac{40 \text{ m/s}}{4 \text{ m}} = 10 \text{ Hz}$$
7	A	In general, sound travels faster through solids than through gases. Therefore, when the wave enters the air from the metal rod, its speed will decrease. The frequency, however, will not change. Since $v = \lambda f$ must always be satisfied, a decrease in v implies a decrease in λ.

Question	Answer	Explanation
8	A	The distance from S_2 to P is 5 m (it's the hypotenuse of a 3-4-5 triangle), and the distance from S_1 to P is 4 m. The difference between the path lengths to point P is 1 m, which is half the wavelength. Therefore, the sound waves are always exactly out of phase when they reach point P from the two speakers, causing destructive interference there. By contrast, since point Q is equidistant from the two speakers, the sound waves will always arrive in phase at Q, interfering constructively. Since there's destructive interference at P and constructive interference at Q, the amplitude at P will be less than at Q.
9	E	The intensity (power per unit area) is proportional to $1/r^2$, where r is the distance between the source and the detector. If r increases by a factor of 10, the intensity decreases by a factor of 100. Because the decibel scale is logarithmic, if the intensity decreases by a factor of $100 = 10^2$, the decibel level decreases by $10 \log (10^2) = 20$ dB.
10	B	An air column (such as an organ pipe) with one closed end resonates at frequencies given by the equation $f_n = \dfrac{nv}{(4L)}$ for odd integers n. The fundamental frequency corresponds, by definition, to $n = 1$. Therefore $$f_1 = \frac{v}{4L} = \frac{340 \text{ m/s}}{4(0.17 \text{ m})} = 500 \text{ Hz}$$
11	B	The speed of the chirp is $$v = \lambda f = (8.75 \times 10^{-3} \text{ m})(40 \times 10^3 \text{ Hz}) = 350 \text{ m/s}$$ If the distance from the bat to the tree is d, then the wave travels a total distance of $d + d = 2d$ (round-trip distance). If T is the time for this round-trip, then $$2d = vT \implies d = \frac{vT}{2} = \frac{(350 \text{ m/s})(0.4 \text{ s})}{2} = 70 \text{ m}$$
12	A	Since the car is traveling away from the stationary detector, the observed frequency will be lower than the source frequency. This eliminates choices (B) and (C). Using the Doppler effect equation, we find that $$f_D = \frac{v}{v + v_S} \cdot f_S = \frac{340 \text{ m/s}}{(340 + 20) \text{ m/s}} \cdot (600 \text{ Hz}) = \frac{34}{36}(600 \text{ Hz})$$

CHAPTER 16 REVIEW QUESTIONS

Question	Answer	Explanation
1	B	From the equation $\lambda f = c$, we find that $$\lambda = \frac{c}{f} = \frac{3.0 \times 10^8 \text{ m/s}}{1.0 \times 10^{18} \text{ Hz}} = 3.0 \times 10^{-10} \text{ m}$$
2	D	Since the fringe is bright, the waves must interfere constructively. This implies that the difference in path lengths must be a whole number times the wavelength, eliminating choices (B), (C), and (E). The central maximum is equidistant from the two slits, so $\Delta \ell = 0$ there. At the first bright fringe above the central maximum, we have $\Delta \ell = \lambda$.
3	C	First, eliminate choices (A) and (B): The index of refraction is never smaller than 1. Refer to the following diagram: Since the reflected and refracted beams are perpendicular to each other, we have $\theta_2 = 30°$. Snell's law then becomes $$n_1 \sin\theta_1 = n_2 \sin\theta_2$$ $$1 \times \sin 60° = n_2 \sin 30°$$ $$\frac{1}{2}\sqrt{3} = n_2 \cdot \frac{1}{2}$$ $$\sqrt{3} = n_2$$
4	A	The frequency is unchanged, but because the speed of light in diamond is less than in air, the wavelength of the light in diamond is shorter than its wavelength in air. $$\lambda_{\text{in diamond}} = \frac{1}{f}v_{\text{in diamond}} = \frac{1}{f}\frac{c}{n_{\text{diamond}}} = \frac{1}{n_{\text{diamond}}}\lambda_{\text{in air}} = \frac{500 \text{ nm}}{2.4} = 208 \text{ nm}$$

Question	Answer	Explanation
5	A	If the speed of light is less in medium 2 than in medium 1, then medium 2 must have the higher index of refraction; that is, $n_2 > n_1$. Snell's law then implies that $\theta_2 < \theta_1$: The beam will refract toward the normal upon transmission into medium 2.
6	A	The critical angle for total internal reflection is computed as follows: $$\sin\theta_c = \frac{n_2}{n_1} = \frac{1.45}{2.90} = \frac{1}{2} \quad \Rightarrow \quad \theta_c = 30°$$ Total internal reflection can happen only if the incident beam originates in the medium with the higher index of refraction and strikes the interface of the other medium at an angle of incidence greater than the critical angle.
7	D	If $s_o = 60$ cm and $f = 40$ cm, the mirror equation tells us that $$\frac{1}{s_o} + \frac{1}{s_i} = \frac{1}{f} \quad \Rightarrow \quad \frac{1}{60\text{ cm}} + \frac{1}{s_i} = \frac{1}{40\text{ cm}} \quad \Rightarrow \quad \frac{1}{s_i} = \frac{1}{120\text{ cm}} \quad \Rightarrow \quad s_i = 120\text{ cm}$$ and, since s_i is positive, the image is real.
8	D	Because the image is virtual, we must write the image distance, s_i, as a negative quantity: $s_i = -20$ cm. Now, with $s_o = 60$ cm, the mirror equation gives $$\frac{1}{s_o} + \frac{1}{s_i} = \frac{1}{f} \quad \Rightarrow \quad \frac{1}{60\text{ cm}} + \frac{1}{-20\text{ cm}} = \frac{1}{f} \quad \Rightarrow \quad \frac{1}{f} = \frac{1}{-30\text{ cm}} \quad \Rightarrow \quad f = -30\text{ cm}$$ The focal length is half the radius of curvature, so $$f = \frac{R}{2} \quad \Rightarrow \quad R = 2f = 2(-30\text{ cm}) = -60\text{ cm} \quad \Rightarrow \quad |R| = 60\text{ cm}$$
9	C	Since the image is projected onto a screen, it must be real, and therefore inverted. The magnification must be negative, so $$m = -\frac{1}{4} \quad \Rightarrow \quad -\frac{s_i}{s_o} = -\frac{1}{4} \quad \Rightarrow \quad s_o = 4s_i$$ Because $s_i = 60$ cm, the object distance, s_o, must be 240 cm. Therefore $$\frac{1}{s_o} + \frac{1}{s_i} = \frac{1}{f} \quad \Rightarrow \quad \frac{1}{240\text{ cm}} + \frac{1}{60\text{ cm}} = \frac{1}{f} \quad \Rightarrow \quad \frac{1}{f} = \frac{1}{48\text{ cm}} \quad \Rightarrow \quad f = 48\text{ cm}$$
10	B	A bi-concave lens is a diverging lens. Diverging lenses (like convex mirrors) have negative focal lengths and therefore cannot form real images. (Notice that statement (D) is false; diverging lenses and convex mirrors always form diminished, virtual images, as you can verify using the mirror and magnification equations.)

CHAPTER 17 REVIEW QUESTIONS

Question	Answer	Explanation
1	B	Combining the equation $E = hf$ with $f = c/\lambda$ gives us $$E = \frac{hc}{\lambda} = \frac{(4.14 \times 10^{-15} \text{ eV} \cdot \text{s})(3.00 \times 10^{8} \text{ m/s})}{2.07 \times 10^{-9} \text{ m}} = 600 \text{ eV}$$
2	D	The energy of the incident photons is $$E = hf = (4.14 \times 10^{-15} \text{ eV} \cdot \text{s})(7.2 \times 10^{15} \text{ Hz}) = 30 \text{ eV}$$ Since $E > \phi$, photoelectrons will be produced, with maximum kinetic energy $$K_{max} = E - \phi = 30 \text{ eV} - 6 \text{ eV} = 24 \text{ eV}$$
3	A	If the atom's ionization energy is 25 eV, then the electron's ground-state energy must be –25 eV. Making a transition from the –16 eV energy level to the ground state will cause the emission of a photon of energy. $$\Delta E = (-16 \text{ eV}) - (-25 \text{eV}) = 9 \text{ eV}$$
4	E	The gap between the ground-state and the first excited state is $$-10 \text{ eV} - (-40 \text{ eV}) = 30 \text{ eV}$$ Therefore, the electron must absorb the energy of a 30 eV photon (at least) to move even to the first excited state. Since the incident photons have only 15 eV of energy, the electron will be unaffected.
5	C	The de Broglie wavelength of a particle whose momentum is p is $\lambda = h/p$. For this proton, we find that $$\lambda = \frac{h}{p} = \frac{6.63 \times 10^{-34} \text{ J} \cdot \text{s}}{3.3 \times 10^{-23} \text{ kg} \cdot \text{m/s}} = 2.0 \times 10^{-11} \text{ m} = 0.02 \text{ nm}$$
6	C	Converting the given mass defect into energy gives the binding energy $$E_{B} = (0.2825 \text{ u}) \times \frac{931 \text{ MeV}}{1 \text{ u}} = 263 \text{ MeV}$$ Since the nucleus contains 31 nucleons, the binding energy per nucleon is $$\frac{263 \text{ MeV}}{31 \text{ nucleons}} = 8.5 \text{ MeV/nucleon}$$ Note: Choices (D) and (E) are impossible. The maximum binding energy of any stable nucleus is about 8.8 MeV/nucleon, and choices (A) and (B) are too low for a nucleus containing 31 nucleons. Only small nuclei ($A < 12$) have binding energy per nucleon values less than 7.5 MeV/nucleon.

Question	Answer	Explanation
7	A	In β^- decay, a neutron is transformed into a proton and an electron. Therefore, the total nucleon number (mass number) doesn't change, but the number of protons (the atomic number) increases by one.
8	A	Since the mass number decreased by 4 and the atomic number decreased by 2, this is an alpha decay.
9	B	After 3 half-lives, the activity will drop to $(1/2)^3 = 1/8$ its initial value, and after 4 half-lives, it will drop to $(1/2)^4 = 1/16$ its initial value. Since $1/10$ is between $1/8$ and $1/16$, the time interval in this case is between 3 and 4 half-lives, that is, between $3(2.5 \text{ h}) = 7.5 \text{ h}$ and $4(2.5 \text{ h}) = 10 \text{ h}$. Only choice (B) is in this range.
10	B	In order to balance the mass number (the superscripts), we must have $2 + 63 = 64 + A$, so $A = 1$. In order to balance the charge (the subscripts), we need $1 + 29 = 30 + Z$, so $Z = 0$. A particle with a mass number of 1 and no charge is a neutron, $_0^1 \text{n}$.
11	E	To balance the mass number (the superscripts), we must have $196 + 1 = 197 + A$, so $A = 0$. To balance the charge (the subscripts), we need $78 + 0 = 78 + Z$, so $Z = 0$. The only particle listed that has zero mass number and zero charge is a gamma-ray photon, $_0^0 \gamma$.
12	C	Radar waves are electromagnetic waves, and the speed of all electromagnetic waves through empty space is measured by all observers to always be c (Postulate 2 of the theory of special relativity).
13	C	If $v = (\frac{\sqrt{3}}{2})c$, then the relativistic factor is $$\gamma = \frac{1}{\sqrt{1-(\frac{\sqrt{3}}{2})^2}} = \frac{1}{\sqrt{1-\frac{3}{4}}} = \frac{1}{\sqrt{\frac{1}{4}}} = \frac{1}{\frac{1}{2}} = 2$$ So, as measured by the inhabitants of the planet, the length of the cruiser as it passes by will be $$l = \frac{L}{\gamma} = \frac{200 \text{ m}}{2} = 100 \text{ m}$$

Question	Answer	Explanation
14	D	If $v = \dfrac{4}{5}c$, then the relativistic factor is $$\gamma = \frac{1}{\sqrt{1-(\frac{4}{5})^2}} = \frac{1}{\sqrt{1-\frac{16}{25}}} = \frac{1}{\sqrt{\frac{9}{25}}} = \frac{1}{\frac{3}{5}} = \frac{5}{3}$$ So, as measured by the team on the earth, the time interval between maintenance checks of the computer will be $$\Delta T_2 = \gamma \cdot \Delta T_1 = \frac{5}{3} \cdot (15\,\text{months}) = 25\,\text{months}$$
15	D	Because v is close to c, the particle is relativistic, so it would be incorrect to use the formula $\text{KE} = \dfrac{1}{2}mv^2$. Instead, we must use the formula $\text{KE} = (\gamma - 1)mc^2$. Since $v = \dfrac{12}{13}c$, the relativistic factor is $$\gamma = \frac{1}{\sqrt{1-(\frac{12}{13})^2}} = \frac{1}{\sqrt{1-\frac{144}{169}}} = \frac{1}{\sqrt{\frac{25}{169}}} = \frac{1}{\frac{5}{13}} = \frac{13}{5}$$ So, the kinetic energy of this particle is $$\text{KE} = (\gamma - 1)mc^2 = (\frac{13}{5}-1)mc^2 = \frac{8}{5}mc^2 = \frac{8}{5}E$$

Chapter 19
The Princeton Review
Practice SAT Physics
Subject Test 1

SAT PHYSICS SUBJECT TEST 1

TEST 1

Your responses to the Physics Subject Test questions should be filled in on Test 1 of your answer sheet (at the back of the book).

PHYSICS SUBJECT TEST 1

75 Questions • Time limit = 1 hour • You may NOT use a calculator.

Part A

Directions: Each set of lettered choices below refers to the numbered questions immediately following it. Select the one letter choice that best answers each question or best fits each statement, and then fill in the corresponding oval on the answer sheet. *A choice may be used once, more than once, or not at all in each set.*

Questions 1-4

   (A) Displacement
   (B) Velocity
   (C) Acceleration
   (D) Linear momentum
   (E) Kinetic energy

1. Which one is NOT a vector?

2. If an object's mass and the net force it feels are both known, then Newton's second law could be used to directly calculate which quantity?

3. Which quantity can be expressed in the same units as impulse?

4. If an object's speed is changing, which of the quantities could remain constant?

Questions 5-8

For an object traveling in a straight line, its velocity (*v*, in m/s) as a function of time (*t*, in s) is given by the following graph.

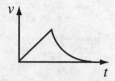

Questions 5-8 relate to the following graphs.

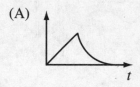
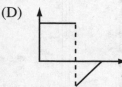

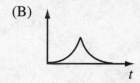
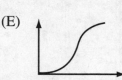

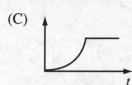

5. Which graph best depicts the object's momentum?

6. Which graph best illustrates the object's acceleration?

7. Which graph best depicts the object's kinetic energy?

8. Which graph best illustrates the object's distance from its starting point?

Questions 9-10

    (A) Newton's law of universal gravitation
    (B) Red shift of light from other galaxies
    (C) The fact that every element of atomic number greater than 83 is radioactive
    (D) The zeroth law of thermodynamics
    (E) Mass–energy equivalence

9. Which provides the basis for the observation that the universe is expanding?

10. Which principle could be used to help calculate the amount of radiation emitted by a star?

Questions 11-12

    (A) Reflection
    (B) Refraction
    (C) Polarization
    (D) Diffraction
    (E) Interference

11. Which is due to the change in wave speed when a wave strikes the boundary to another medium?

12. Which phenomenon is NOT experienced by sound waves?

GO ON TO THE NEXT PAGE

Part B

Directions: Each of the questions or incomplete statements below is followed by five suggested answers or completions. Select the one that is best in each case and then fill in the corresponding oval on the answer sheet.

13. An astronaut standing on the surface of the moon (mass = M, radius = R) holds a feather (mass = m) in one hand and a hammer (mass = $100m$) in the other hand, both at the same height above the surface. If he releases them simultaneously, what is the acceleration of the hammer?

    (A) $\dfrac{mv^2}{r}$

    (B) $\dfrac{GM}{R^2}$

    (C) $\dfrac{GMm}{R^2}$

    (D) $100\dfrac{GM}{R^2}$

    (E) $100\dfrac{GMm}{R^2}$

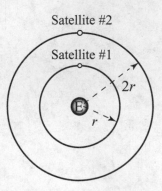

14. Two satellites orbit the earth. Their orbits are circular, and each satellite travels at a constant speed. If the mass of Satellite #2 is twice the mass of Satellite #1, which satellite's speed is greater?

    (A) Satellite #1, by a factor of $\sqrt{2}$
    (B) Satellite #1, by a factor of 2
    (C) Satellite #2, by a factor of $\sqrt{2}$
    (D) Satellite #2, by a factor of 2
    (E) Neither; the satellites' speeds are the same.

Questions 15-17 refer to the collision of two blocks on a frictionless table. Before the collision, the block of mass m is at rest.

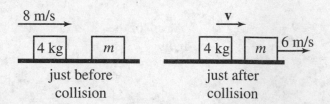

15. What is the total momentum of the blocks just AFTER the collision?

    (A) 12 kg-m/s
    (B) 16 kg-m/s
    (C) 18 kg-m/s
    (D) 24 kg-m/s
    (E) 32 kg-m/s

16. If the collision were elastic, what is the total kinetic energy of the blocks just AFTER the collision?

    (A) 16 J
    (B) 32 J
    (C) 64 J
    (D) 128 J
    (E) 256 J

17. If the blocks had instead stuck together after the collision, with what speed would they move if $m = 12$ kg ?

    (A) 2.0 m/s
    (B) 2.7 m/s
    (C) 3.2 m/s
    (D) 4.0 m/s
    (E) 4.6 m/s

GO ON TO THE NEXT PAGE

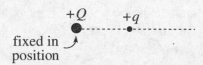

fixed in
position

18. The figure above shows two positively charged
particles. The +Q charge is fixed in position, and
the +q charge is brought close to +Q and released
from rest. Which of the following graphs best
depicts the acceleration (a) of the +q charge as a
function of its distance (r) from +Q ?

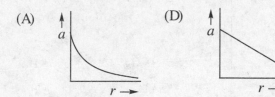

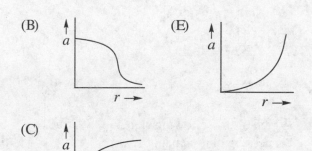

19. Two particles have unequal charges; one is
+q and the other is –2q. The strength of the
electrostatic force between these two stationary
particles is equal to F. What happens to F if the
distance between the particles is halved?

(A) It decreases by a factor of 4.
(B) It decreases by a factor of 2.
(C) It remains the same.
(D) It increases by a factor of 2.
(E) It increases by a factor of 4.

20. A simple harmonic oscillator has a frequency of
2.5 Hz and an amplitude of 0.05 m. What is the
period of the oscillations?

(A)   0.4 sec
(B)   0.2 sec
(C)   8 sec
(D)   20 sec
(E)   50 sec

21. A light wave, traveling at 3×10^8 m/s has a
frequency of 6×10^{15} Hz. What is its wavelength?

(A) 5×10^{-8} m
(B) 2×10^{-7} m
(C) 5×10^{-7} m
(D) 5×10^{-6} m
(E) 2×10^7 m

22. A beam of monochromatic light entering a glass
window pane from the air will experience a
change in

(A) frequency and wavelength
(B) frequency and speed
(C) speed and wavelength
(D) speed only
(E) wavelength only

GO ON TO THE NEXT PAGE

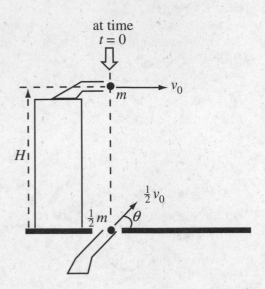

at time
$t = 0$

Questions 23-25

Two cannons shoot cannonballs simultaneously. The cannon embedded in the ground shoots a cannonball whose mass is half that of the cannonball shot by the elevated cannon. Also, the initial speed of the cannonball projected from ground level is half the initial speed of the cannonball shot horizontally from the elevated position. Air resistance is negligible and can be ignored. Each cannonball is in motion for more than 2 seconds before striking the level ground.

23. Let a_1 denote the acceleration of the cannonball of mass m one second after launch, and let a_2 denote the acceleration of the cannonball of mass $m/2$ one second after launch. Which of the following statements is true?

    (A) $a_1 = 4a_2$
    (B) $a_1 = 2a_2$
    (C) $a_1 = a_2$
    (D) $a_2 = 2a_1$
    (E) $a_2 = 4a_1$

24. If the cannonball projected from ground level is in flight for a total time of T, what horizontal distance does it travel?

    (A) $\frac{1}{2}v_0 T$

    (B) $v_0 T$

    (C) $\frac{1}{2}v_0 T \sin\theta_0$

    (D) $\frac{1}{2}v_0 T \cos\theta_0$

    (E) $\quad v_0 T \cos\theta_0$

25. For the cannonball of mass m, which of the following quantities decreases as the cannonball falls to the ground?

    (A) Kinetic energy
    (B) Potential energy
    (C) Momentum
    (D) Speed
    (E) Mass

26. Which of the following statements is true concerning phase changes?

    (A) When a liquid freezes, it releases thermal energy into its immediate environment.
    (B) When a solid melts, it releases thermal energy into its immediate environment.
    (C) For most substances, the latent heat of fusion is greater than the latent heat of vaporization.
    (D) As a solid melts, its temperature increases.
    (E) As a liquid freezes, its temperature decreases.

GO ON TO THE NEXT PAGE

27. Four point charges are labeled Charge 1, Charge 2, Charge 3, and Charge 4. It is known that Charge 1 attracts Charge 2, Charge 2 repels Charge 3, and Charge 3 attracts Charge 4. Which of the following must be true?

(A) Charge 1 attracts Charge 4.
(B) Charge 2 attracts Charge 3.
(C) Charge 1 repels Charge 3.
(D) Charge 2 repels Charge 4.
(E) Charge 1 repels Charge 4.

Questions 28-30

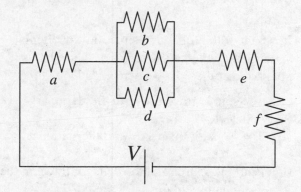

All six resistors in the circuit have the same resistance, R, and the battery is a source of constant voltage, V.

28. How does the current through Resistor a compare with the current through Resistor b ?

(A) The current through Resistor a is 9 times the current through Resistor b.
(B) The current through Resistor a is 3 times the current through Resistor b.
(C) The current through Resistor a is the same as the current through Resistor b.
(D) The current through Resistor b is 3 times the current through Resistor a.
(E) The current through Resistor b is 9 times the current through Resistor a.

29. If the total resistance in the circuit is $\dfrac{10R}{3}$, the amount of current that passes through resistor a is what constant times $\dfrac{V}{R}$?

(A) $\dfrac{1}{20}$

(B) $\dfrac{1}{10}$

(C) $\dfrac{3}{10}$

(D) $\dfrac{10}{9}$

(E) $\dfrac{10}{3}$

30. If the power dissipated by resistor e is P, how much power is dissipated by resistor f ?

(A) $\dfrac{P}{6}$

(B) $\dfrac{P}{3}$

(C) $\dfrac{P}{2}$

(D) P

(E) $2P$

31. An object of mass 5 kg is acted upon by exactly four forces, each of magnitude 10 N. Which of the following could NOT be the resulting acceleration of the object?

(A) 0 m/s^2
(B) 2 m/s^2
(C) 4 m/s^2
(D) 8 m/s^2
(E) 10 m/s^2

GO ON TO THE NEXT PAGE

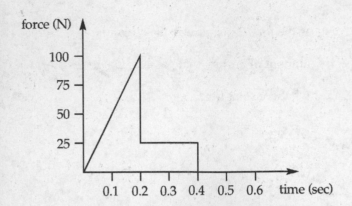

32. The total force acting on an object as a function of time is given in the graph above. What is the magnitude of the change in momentum of the object between $t = 0$ and $t = 0.4$ sec?

    (A) 2 kg-m/sec
    (B) 5 kg-m/sec
    (C) 10 kg-m/sec
    (D) 12 kg-m/sec
    (E) 15 kg-m/sec

33. An object is placed 20 cm from a diverging lens. If the distance between the lens and the image is 8 cm, what is the magnification?

    (A) $\dfrac{1}{15}$

    (B) $\dfrac{2}{5}$

    (C) $\dfrac{1}{2}$

    (D) 2

    (E) $\dfrac{5}{2}$

34. A rope stretched between two fixed points can support transverse standing waves. What is the ratio of the sixth harmonic frequency to the third harmonic frequency?

    (A) $\dfrac{1}{2}$

    (B) $\dfrac{1}{\sqrt{2}}$

    (C) 2

    (D) $2\sqrt{2}$

    (E) 4

35. In which of the following situations involving a source of sound and a detector of the sound is it possible that there is NO perceived Doppler shift?

    (A) The source travels toward the stationary detector.
    (B) The detector travels toward the stationary source.
    (C) Both the source and the detector travel in the same direction.
    (D) Both the source and detector travel in opposite directions, with the source and detector moving away from each other.
    (E) Both the source and detector travel in opposite directions, with the source and detector moving toward each other.

GO ON TO THE NEXT PAGE

36. Sound waves travel at 350 m/s through warm air and at 3,500 m/s through brass. What happens to the wavelength of a 700 Hz acoustic wave as it enters brass from warm air?

    (A) It decreases by a factor of 20.
    (B) It decreases by a factor of 10.
    (C) It increases by a factor of 10.
    (D) It increases by a factor of 20.
    (E) The wavelength remains unchanged when a wave passes into a new medium.

37. Which of the following types of electromagnetic radiation has the longest wavelength?

    (A) Gamma rays
    (B) Ultraviolet
    (C) Blue light
    (D) X-rays
    (E) Orange light

38. The circular metal plate has a concentric circular hole. If the plate is heated uniformly, so that the outer circumference of the plate increases by 4 percent, then the circumference of the hole will

    (A) decrease by 16 percent
    (B) decrease by 8 percent
    (C) decrease by 4 percent
    (D) increase by 4 percent
    (E) increase by 8 percent

39. A box of mass 40 kg is pushed in a straight line across a horizontal floor by an 80 N force. If the force of kinetic friction acting on the box has a magnitude of 60 N, what is the acceleration of the box?

    (A) 0.25 m/s^2
    (B) 0.5 m/s^2
    (C) 1.0 m/s^2
    (D) 2.0 m/s^2
    (E) 3.5 m/s^2

	mass (in kg)	speed (in m/s)
Trial 1:	0.5	4
Trial 2:	1	3
Trial 3:	2	2
Trial 4:	3	1

40. The table records the mass and speed of an object traveling at constant velocity on a frictionless track, as performed by a student conducting a physics lab exercise. In her analysis, the student had to state the trial in which the object had the greatest momentum and the trial in which it had the greatest kinetic energy. Which of the following gives the correct answer?

	Greatest Momentum	Greatest Kinetic Energy
(A)	Trial 1	Trial 3
(B)	Trial 2	Trial 2
(C)	Trial 3	Trial 2
(D)	Trial 3	Trial 3
(E)	Trial 4	Trial 4

GO ON TO THE NEXT PAGE

41. What did Rutherford's experiments on alpha particle scattering indicate about the structure of the atom?

    (A) Atoms are roughly spherical with a radius of about 10^{-10} m.
    (B) The electrons occupy quantized energy levels, absorbing or emitting energy only when they make a quantum jump between these levels.
    (C) The density of positive charge within an atom is not uniform throughout the atom's volume.
    (D) Allowed electron orbits must have a circumference equal to a whole number times the electron's de Broglie wavelength.
    (E) Alpha particles are positively charged.

42. What happens to the pressure, P, of an ideal gas if the temperature is increased by a factor of 2 and the volume is increased by a factor of 8 ?

    (A) P decreases by a factor of 16.
    (B) P decreases by a factor of 4.
    (C) P decreases by a factor of 2.
    (D) P increases by a factor of 4.
    (E) P increases by a factor of 16.

43. How much current does a 60-watt lightbulb draw if it operates at a voltage of 120 volts?

    (A) 0.25 amp
    (B) 0.5 amp
    (C) 2 amps
    (D) 4 amps
    (E) 30 amps

$$^2_1H + {}^2_1H \rightarrow {}^3_2He + X$$

44. Identify the particle X resulting from the nuclear reaction shown above.

    (A) Positron
    (B) Electron
    (C) Proton
    (D) Neutron
    (E) Alpha particle

45. If a 50 g block of solid marble (specific heat = 0.9 kJ/kg·°C), originally at 20°C, absorbs 100 J of heat, which one of the following best approximates the temperature increase of the marble block?

    (A) 1°C
    (B) 2°C
    (C) 4°C
    (D) 10°C
    (E) 20°C

46. A sample of an ideal gas is heated, doubling its absolute temperature. Which of the following statements best describes the result of heating the gas?

    (A) The root-mean-square speed of the gas molecules doubles.
    (B) The average kinetic energy of the gas molecules increases by a factor of $\sqrt{2}$.
    (C) The average kinetic energy of the gas molecules increases by a factor of 4.
    (D) The speeds of the gas molecules cover a wide range, but the root-mean-square speed increases by a factor of $\sqrt{2}$.
    (E) The speeds of the gas molecules cover a wide range, but the root-mean-square speed increases by a factor of 2.

GO ON TO THE NEXT PAGE

47. A block of ice, initially at –20°C, is heated at a steady rate until the temperature of the sample reaches 120°C. Which of the following graphs best illustrates the temperature of the sample as a function of time?

(A)
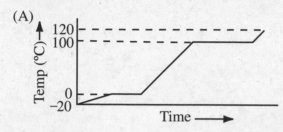

(B)
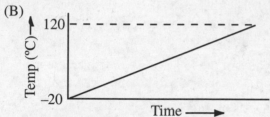

(C)
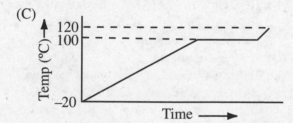

(D)
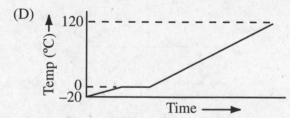

(E)
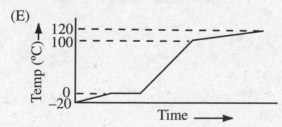

48. Which of the following changes to a double-slit interference experiment with light would increase the widths of the fringes in the diffraction pattern that appears on the screen?

(A) Use light of a shorter wavelength
(B) Move the screen closer to the slits
(C) Move the slits closer together
(D) Use light with a lower wave speed
(E) Increase the intensity of the light

49. In an experiment designed to study the photoelectric effect, it is observed that low-intensity visible light of wavelength 550 nm produced no photoelectrons. Which of the following best describes what would occur if the intensity of this light were increased dramatically?

(A) Almost immediately, photoelectrons would be produced with a kinetic energy equal to the energy of the incident photons.
(B) Almost immediately, photoelectrons would be produced with a kinetic energy equal to the energy of the incident photons minus the work function of the metal.
(C) After several seconds, necessary for the electrons to absorb sufficient energy from the incident energy, photoelectrons would be produced with a kinetic energy equal to the energy of the incident photons.
(D) After several seconds, necessary for the electrons to absorb sufficient energy from the incident energy, photoelectrons would be produced with a kinetic energy equal to the energy of the incident photons minus the work function of the metal.
(E) Nothing would happen.

GO ON TO THE NEXT PAGE

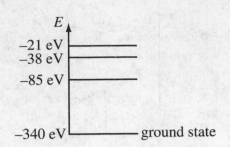

50. The diagram (not drawn to scale) gives the first few electron energy levels within a single-electron atom. Which of the following gives the energy of a photon that could NOT be emitted by this atom during an electron transition?

    (A)　17 eV
    (B)　42 eV
    (C)　64 eV
    (D) 255 eV
    (E) 302 eV

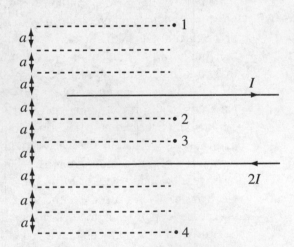

51. The figure above shows a pair of long, straight current-carrying wires and four marked points. At which of these points is the net magnetic field zero?

    (A) Point 1 only
    (B) Points 1 and 2 only
    (C) Point 2 only
    (D) Points 3 and 4 only
    (E) Point 3 only

52. A nonconducting sphere is given a nonzero net electric charge, $+Q$, and then brought close to a neutral conducting sphere of the same radius. Which of the following will be true?

    (A) An electric field will be induced within the conducting sphere.
    (B) The conducting sphere will develop a net electric charge of $-Q$.
    (C) The spheres will experience an electrostatic attraction.
    (D) The spheres will experience an electrostatic repulsion.
    (E) The spheres will experience no electrostatic interaction.

53. Which of the following would increase the capacitance of a parallel-plate capacitor?

    (A) Using smaller plates
    (B) Replacing the dielectric material between the plates with one that has a smaller dielectric constant
    (C) Decreasing the voltage between the plates
    (D) Increasing the voltage between the plates
    (E) Moving the plates closer together

    A ————

    B ——————

    C �-----

    D ——————

54. The four wires are each made of aluminum. Which wire will have the greatest resistance?

    (A) Wire A
    (B) Wire B
    (C) Wire C
    (D) Wire D
    (E) All the wires have the same resistance because they're all composed of the same material.

GO ON TO THE NEXT PAGE

Questions 55-57

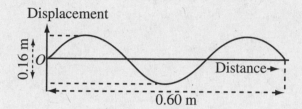

55. What is the amplitude of the wave?

    (A) 0.08 m
    (B) 0.16 m
    (C) 0.32 m
    (D) 0.48 m
    (E) 0.60 m

56. What is the wavelength of the wave?

    (A) 0.08 m
    (B) 0.16 m
    (C) 0.20 m
    (D) 0.40 m
    (E) 0.60 m

57. The drawing shows the displacement of a traveling wave at time $t = 0$. If the wave speed is 0.5 m/sec, and the wavelength is λ m, what is the period of the wave (in seconds)?

    (A) $\dfrac{1}{4\lambda}$

    (B) $\dfrac{1}{2\lambda}$

    (C) $\dfrac{1}{\lambda}$

    (D) 2λ

    (E) 4λ

58. Lead-199 has a half-life of 1.5 hours. If a researcher begins with 2 grams of lead-199, how much will remain after 6 hours?

    (A) 0.125 grams
    (B) 0.25 grams
    (C) 0.375 grams
    (D) 0.5 grams
    (E) 0.625 grams

GO ON TO THE NEXT PAGE

59. The square shown is the same size in each of the following diagrams. In which diagram is the electrical potential energy of the pair of charges the greatest?

(A)

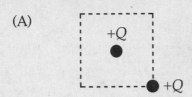

(B)

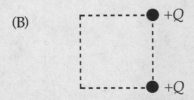

(C)

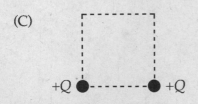

(D)

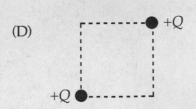

(E)

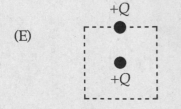

60. Four point charges, two positive and two negative, are fixed in position at the corners of a square, as shown below.

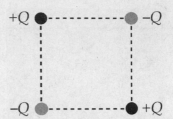

Which one of the following arrows best illustrates the total electrostatic force on the charge in the lower right-hand corner of the square?

(A) ↖

(B) ←

(C) ↘

(D) →

(E) The electric force on this charge is 0.

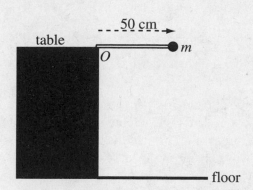

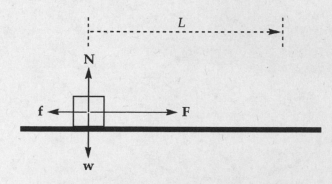

61. One end of a rigid, massless rod of length 50 cm is attached to the edge of the table at point O; at the other end of the rod is a ball of clay of mass $m = 0.2$ kg. The rod extends horizontally from the end of the table. What is the torque of the gravitational force on the clay ball relative to point O ?

    (A)   0.01 N-m
    (B)   0.1 N-m
    (C)   1 N-m
    (D)   10 N-m
    (E)   100 N-m

62. Two rocks are dropped simultaneously from the top of a tall building. Rock 1 has mass M_1, and rock 2 has mass M_2. If air resistance is negligible, what is the ratio of rock 1's momentum to rock 2's momentum just before they hit the ground?

    (A) $\dfrac{\sqrt{M_1}}{M_2}$

    (B) $\dfrac{M_1}{M_2}$

    (C) $\left(\dfrac{M_1}{M_2}\right)^2$

    (D) 1

    (E) None of the above

63. The four forces act on the block as it moves the distance L. What is the total work performed on the block by these forces?

    (A) $(F + f)L$
    (B) $(F - f)L$
    (C) $(N - w)L$
    (D) $(N + w)L$
    (E) $(F - N + f - w)L$

GO ON TO THE NEXT PAGE

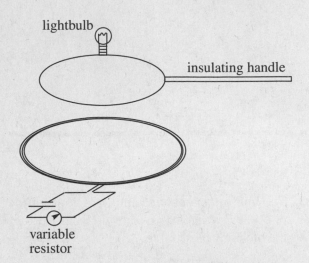

lightbulb

insulating handle

variable resistor

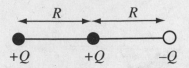

R R

$+Q$ $+Q$ $-Q$

64. A loop of metal wire containing a tiny lightbulb is attached to an insulating handle and placed over a coil of wire in which a current can be established by a source of emf and controlled by a variable resistor. The plane of the top loop is parallel to the plane of the bottom coil. Which of the following could NOT cause the bulb to light?

(A) Rotating the handle 90° while keeping the plane of the top loop parallel to the plane of the bottom coil
(B) Raising the handle up and away from the coil
(C) Lowering the handle down toward the coil
(D) Decreasing the resistance of the coil
(E) Increasing the resistance of the coil

65. During each cycle, a heat engine with an efficiency of 25% takes in 800 J of energy. How much waste heat is expelled during each cycle?

(A) 100 J
(B) 200 J
(C) 300 J
(D) 400 J
(E) 600 J

66. Three point charges are arranged along a straight line. If k denotes Coulomb's constant, what is the strength of the electrostatic force felt by the positive charge at the left end of the line?

(A) $\dfrac{kQ^2}{2R^2}$

(B) $\dfrac{kQ^2}{R^2}$

(C) $\dfrac{3kQ^2}{4R^2}$

(D) $\dfrac{5kQ^2}{4R^2}$

(E) $\dfrac{3kQ^2}{2R^2}$

67. Consider two adjacent transparent media. The speed of light in Medium 1 is v_1, and the speed of light in Medium 2 is v_2. If $v_1 < v_2$, then total internal reflection will occur at the interface between these media if a beam of light is

(A) incident in Medium 1 and strikes the interface at an angle of incidence greater than $\sin^{-1}(v_1/v_2)$.
(B) incident in Medium 1 and strikes the interface at an angle of incidence greater than $\sin^{-1}(v_2/v_1)$.
(C) incident in Medium 2 and strikes the interface at an angle of incidence greater than $\sin^{-1}(v_1/v_2)$.
(D) incident in Medium 2 and strikes the interface at an angle of incidence greater than $\sin^{-1}(v_2/v_1)$.
(E) Total internal reflection is impossible in the situation described.

GO ON TO THE NEXT PAGE

Questions 68-69

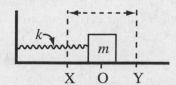

A block is attached to the end of a linear spring, the other end of which is anchored to a wall. The block is oscillating between extreme positions X and Y on a frictionless table, and when the block is at Point O, the spring is at its natural length. The value of the spring's force constant, k, is known, but the mass of the block, m, is unknown.

68. Knowing which one of the following would permit you to calculate the value of m ?

    (A) The acceleration of the block at Point O
    (B) The acceleration of the block at Point Y
    (C) The speed of the block as it passes through O
    (D) The distance between X and Y
    (E) The time required for the block to travel from X to Y

69. If $\omega = \sqrt{\dfrac{k}{m}}$, and the distance between O and Y is d, what is the speed of the block at point O ?

    (A) $\dfrac{d\omega}{2}$

    (B) $d\omega$

    (C) $2d\omega$

    (D) $d^2\omega$

    (E) $d\omega^2$

70. A particle travels in a circular path of radius 0.2 m with a constant kinetic energy of 4 J. What is the net force on this particle?

    (A) 4 N
    (B) 16 N
    (C) 20 N
    (D) 40 N
    (E) Cannot be determined from the information given

Questions 71-72

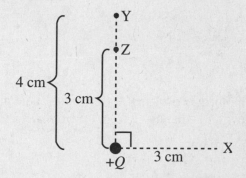

71. How much work is done by the electric field created by the stationary charge $+Q = +2.0$ C to move a charge of $+1.0 \times 10^{-9}$ C from position X to position Z ? (Note: The value of Coulomb's constant, k, is 9×10^9 N-m²/C².)

    (A)   0 J
    (B)   150 J
    (C)   300 J
    (D)   560 J
    (E) 1,000 J

GO ON TO THE NEXT PAGE

72. If E_Y is the electric field strength at position Y and E_Z is the electric field strength at position Z, what is the value of $\dfrac{E_Z}{E_Y}$?

    (A) $\dfrac{\sqrt{3}}{4}$

    (B) $\dfrac{\sqrt{4}}{3}$

    (C) $\dfrac{4}{3}$

    (D) $\dfrac{9}{16}$

    (E) $\dfrac{16}{9}$

73. An object is placed 100 cm from a plane mirror. How far is the image from the object?

    (A) 50 cm
    (B) 100 cm
    (C) 200 cm
    (D) 300 cm
    (E) 400 cm

74. Why do baseball catchers wear mitts rather than just using their bare hands to catch pitched baseballs?

    (A) The impulse delivered to the catcher's hand is reduced due to the presence of the mitt.
    (B) The force on the catcher's hand is reduced because of the increased area provided by the mitt.
    (C) The baseball's change in momentum is reduced due to the presence of the mitt.
    (D) The force on the catcher's hand is reduced because the mitt increases the time of impact.
    (E) The force on the catcher's hand is reduced because the mitt decreases the time of impact.

75. A spaceship is moving directly toward a planet at a speed of $\dfrac{c}{2}$. When the spaceship is 4.5×10^8 m from the planet (as measured by someone on the spaceship), a pulse of light is emitted by someone on the planet. As measured by someone on the spaceship, how long does it take the light pulse to travel from the planet to the ship?

    (A) 0.5 sec
    (B) 1.0 sec
    (C) 1.5 sec
    (D) 2.0 sec
    (E) 2.5 sec

STOP

IF YOU FINISH BEFORE TIME IS CALLED, YOU MAY CHECK YOUR WORK ON THIS TEST ONLY.

DO NOT TURN TO ANY OTHER TEST IN THIS BOOK.

ANSWERS TO THE PRINCETON REVIEW
PRACTICE SAT PHYSICS SUBJECT TEST 1

Question Number	Correct Answer	Right	Wrong	Question Number	Correct Answer	Right	Wrong	Question Number	Correct Answer	Right	Wrong
1.	E	___	___	26.	A	___	___	51.	A	___	___
2.	C	___	___	27.	E	___	___	52.	C	___	___
3.	D	___	___	28.	B	___	___	53.	E	___	___
4.	C	___	___	29.	C	___	___	54.	B	___	___
5.	A	___	___	30.	D	___	___	55.	A	___	___
6.	D	___	___	31.	E	___	___	56.	D	___	___
7.	B	___	___	32.	E	___	___	57.	D	___	___
8.	E	___	___	33.	B	___	___	58.	A	___	___
9.	B	___	___	34.	C	___	___	59.	E	___	___
10.	E	___	___	35.	C	___	___	60.	A	___	___
11.	B	___	___	36.	C	___	___	61.	C	___	___
12.	C	___	___	37.	E	___	___	62.	B	___	___
13.	B	___	___	38.	D	___	___	63.	B	___	___
14.	A	___	___	39.	B	___	___	64.	A	___	___
15.	E	___	___	40.	C	___	___	65.	E	___	___
16.	D	___	___	41.	C	___	___	66.	C	___	___
17.	A	___	___	42.	B	___	___	67.	A	___	___
18.	A	___	___	43.	B	___	___	68.	E	___	___
19.	E	___	___	44.	D	___	___	69.	B	___	___
20.	A	___	___	45.	B	___	___	70.	D	___	___
21.	A	___	___	46.	D	___	___	71.	A	___	___
22.	C	___	___	47.	A	___	___	72.	E	___	___
23.	C	___	___	48.	C	___	___	73.	C	___	___
24.	D	___	___	49.	E	___	___	74.	D	___	___
25.	B	___	___	50.	B	___	___	75.	C	___	___

Chapter 20
Answers and Explanations
to Practice SAT Physics
Subject Test 1

Answers and Explanations

Question	Answer	Explanation
1	E	Kinetic energy is a scalar, equal to one-half an object's mass times the square of its speed. Like potential energy and work, kinetic energy does not have a direction associated with it.
2	C	Newton's second law is $F_{net} = ma$, so if we know F_{net} and m, we can calculate the acceleration, a.
3	D	Impulse is equal to force multiplied by time, so its units are N-s. Because 1 N = 1 kg-m/s², we see that 1 N-s = 1 kg-m/s, which we immediately notice is the same as the units of mass (kg) times those of velocity (m/s), and mv is linear momentum choice (D). You may also have remembered the impulse–momentum theorem, which says that the impulse delivered to an object is equal to the resulting change in its linear momentum. Since impulse gives the change in linear momentum, it must be true that impulse can be expressed in the same units as linear momentum.
4	C	If an object's speed is changing, it must be moving, so its displacement is changing. Since velocity, $\mathbf{v}$, is speed plus direction, a change in speed automatically means a change in velocity. Now, since the velocity is changing, the linear momentum, $\mathbf{p}$, must be changing also, since $\mathbf{p} = m\mathbf{v}$. Finally, because kinetic energy is equal to $\frac{m}{2}$ times the square of the speed, a changing speed implies a changing kinetic energy. The answer must be (C). An object undergoing a change in speed may certainly be subject to a constant acceleration (gravitational acceleration, for example).
5	A	Momentum is mass times velocity. Since the mass of the object is just a positive constant, the graph of momentum should have the same shape as the graph of the velocity.
6	D	If the velocity vs. time graph has a corner, then the acceleration vs. time graph will be discontinuous (have a jump). As shown in the diagram, the first part of the velocity vs. time graph is a straight line with a positive slope. Thus, the corresponding acceleration graph should be a horizontal line above the axis. Next on the velocity vs. time graph there is a curvy part, decreasing but concave up (like the left half of a cup). The slope of that is negative to begin with and then becomes less negative as we approach the center of the cup. Thus a straight line on the acceleration vs. time graph–negative but getting less negative.

Question	Answer	Explanation
7	B	Kinetic energy is proportional to v^2. Since the first part of the v versus t graph is a straight line, it must have the form $v = at$ for some constant, a. Squaring this gives us something proportional to t^2, the graph of which is parabolic. This eliminates choices (A) and (D). Next, since v drops to 0 in the original graph, the kinetic energy must also drop to 0, so now choice (E) is eliminated. Finally, we can eliminate the graph in (C), because if it were correct, it would mean that the object had a constant kinetic energy for the latter part of its motion (since the graph is flat); but the original graph shows us that v is never constant.
8	E	Since the given graph of v versus t is always above the t axis, that means v is never negative. From this we can conclude that the object never changes direction (because the velocity would change from positive to negative if this were true). If the object is always traveling in the same direction, its distance from the starting point must always increase. This behavior is only illustrated by the graph in (E).
9	B	The red shift of light refers to the increase in the wavelength (or, equivalently, the decrease in the frequency) of light from a distant source when it's measured here. This change in wavelength (and frequency) is the Doppler effect and implies that the source and detector are moving away from each other. This provides evidence for the expansion of the Universe.
10	E	Stars are huge nuclear-fusion reactors. When nuclei fuse, the mass of the product nucleus is less than the combined masses of the original nuclei. The "missing" mass has become energy, which is radiated away. Einstein's famous mass-energy equivalence equation, $E = mc^2$, can be used to calculate the amount of energy resulting from a fusion reaction.
11	B	Refraction, the change in the direction of a wave when it enters a new medium, is caused by the change in the speed of the wave as it travels within the new medium.
12	C	Only a transverse wave, defined to be a wave in which the oscillation is perpendicular to the direction of wave propagation, can be polarized. Since sound waves are longitudinal, they cannot be polarized.
13	B	The gravitational force on an object of mass m can be expressed either by mg or by $\frac{GMm}{r^2}$. Setting mg equal to $\frac{GMm}{r^2}$, we get $g = \frac{GM}{R^2}$, which is the object's (free-fall) acceleration. Notice that the mass of the object cancels out, so whether we're asked for the acceleration of the feather or the hammer, the answer would be the same. (By the way, the experiment described in this question was actually performed by Apollo 15 astronaut David Scott on July 30, 1971. Both the feather and the hammer hit the lunar surface at the same time, verifying the fact—first stated by Galileo—that under conditions of no air resistance, all objects fall with the same acceleration, regardless of their mass.)

Question	Answer	Explanation
14	A	Let m be the mass of a satellite orbiting the earth in a circular orbit of radius r at a constant speed of v. Since the centripetal force is provided by the gravitational force due to the earth (mass M), we can write $\frac{mv^2}{r} = \frac{GMm}{r^2}$. Solving for v gives us $v = \sqrt{\frac{GM}{r}}$. This result tells us that the mass of the satellite is irrelevant; only the mass of the earth, M, remains in the formula. Since v is inversely proportional to the square root of r, the satellite that's *closer* will have the greater speed. In this case, since Satellite #1 has the smaller orbit radius, it has the greater speed, and, since the radius of its orbit is $\frac{1}{2}$ the radius of Satellite #2's orbit, its orbit speed is greater by a factor of $\sqrt{2}$.
15	E	Using the equation $p = mv$, we can figure out that before the collision, the momentum of the left-hand block was (4 kg)(8 m/s) = 32 kg-m/s, and that of the right-hand block was zero (since it was at rest), so the total momentum before the collision was 32 kg-m/s. Since total momentum is conserved in the collision, the total momentum *after* the collision must also be 32 kg-m/s.
16	D	Using the equation $K = mv^2/2$, we can figure out that before the collision, the kinetic energy of the left-hand block was (4 kg)(8 m/s)^2/2 = 128 J and that of the right-hand block was zero (since it was at rest), giving a total kinetic energy before the collision of 128 J. Since kinetic energy is conserved in an *elastic* collision, the total kinetic energy *after* the collision must also be 128 J.
17	A	If the blocks stick together after the collision—a perfectly inelastic collision—then conservation of momentum gives us 32 kg-m/s = (4 + m)v, where v denotes the common speed of the blocks after the collision. If m = 12 kg, then v = 32/(4 + 12) = 32/16 = 2 m/s.
18	A	If the mass of the $+q$ charge is m, then its acceleration is $$a = \frac{F_E}{m} = \frac{kQq}{m}\frac{1}{r^2}$$ The graph in (A) best depicts an inverse-square relationship between a and r.
19	E	Since Coulomb's law is an inverse-square law (that is, F is inversely proportional to r^2), if r decreases by a factor of 2, then F increases by a factor of $2^2 = 4$.
20	A	The period is the reciprocal of the frequency: $T = 1/f = 1/(2.5 \text{ Hz}) = 0.4$ sec.
21	A	We use the equation that relates wavelength, frequency, and wave speed $$\lambda f = c \implies \lambda = \frac{c}{f} = \frac{3\times10^8 \text{ m/s}}{6\times10^{15} \text{ Hz}} = 0.5\times10^{-7} \text{ m} = 5\times10^{-8} \text{ m}$$

Question	Answer	Explanation
22	C	When a wave enters a new medium, its frequency does not change, but its wave speed does. Since $\lambda f = v$, the change in wave speed implies a change in wavelength also.
23	C	While the cannonballs are in flight, the only force they feel is the gravitational force, so the acceleration of each cannonball is equal to g.
24	D	For an ideal projectile, the horizontal velocity while in flight is constant and equal to the initial horizontal velocity. In this case, the initial horizontal speed of the cannonball shot from ground level is $(\frac{1}{2}v_0)\cos\theta_0$. Now, multiplying this rate by the time of flight, T, gives the total horizontal distance covered.
25	B	As the cannonball falls, it accelerates downward and its speed increases; this eliminates choices (A), (C), and (D). The mass of the cannonball does not change, eliminating choice (E). The answer is (B). As the cannonball falls, its height decreases, so its gravitational potential energy decreases.
26	A	Statement (B) is false, because a solid must *absorb* thermal energy in order to melt. Statement (C) is false since it generally requires much more energy to break the intermolecular bonds of a liquid to change its state to vapor than to loosen the intermolecular bonds of a solid to change its state to liquid. And statements (D) and (E) are false: While a substance undergoes a phase change, its temperature remains constant. The answer must be (A).

27	E	We know that like charges repel and opposite charges attract. So, we can put Charges 1, 2, 3, and 4 into two "camps." Because Charge 1 attracts Charge 2, these charges must be in opposite camps
		
		               1 2
		
		Next, since Charge 2 repels charge 3, Charge 3 is in the same camp as Charge 2
		
		               1 2
		                                    3
		
		And, finally, since Charge 3 attracts Charge 4, these charges are in opposite camps, giving us
		
		               1 2
		               4 3
		
		We now see that only statement (E) can be correct.

28	B	The current entering the parallel combination containing Resistors b, c, and d will split evenly among the resistors since all their resistances are the same. Because there are 3 resistors in the parallel combination, each resistor in this combination will get 1/3 of the current. Another way of saying that the current through Resistor b is 1/3 the current through Resistor a is to say that the current through Resistor a is 3 times the current through Resistor b.

Question	Answer	Explanation
29	C	Using Ohm's law in the form $I = V/R$, we find that the current through resistor a is $I = V/(10R/3) = (3/10)(V/R)$.
30	D	The power dissipated by a resistor carrying current is given by $P = IV$ or by $P = I^2R$. Since resistors e and f carry the same current I (because they're in series) and have the same resistance R, they dissipate the same power.
31	E	The maximum net force on the object occurs when all four forces act in the same direction, giving $F_{net} = 4F = 4(10\ N) = 40\ N$, and a resulting acceleration of $a = F_{net}/m = (40\ N)/(5\ kg) = 8\ m/s^2$. These four forces could not give the object an acceleration greater than this.
32	E	The impulse-momentum theorem says that the change in momentum is equal to the impulse, which is the area under the force versus time graph. The region under the graph from $t = 0$ to $t = 0.4$ sec is composed of a right triangle (from $t = 0$ to $t = 0.2$ sec) plus a rectangle (from $t = 0.2$ sec to $t = 0.4$ sec), so the total area under the graph from $t = 0$ to $t = 0.4$ sec is $(1/2)(0.2)(100) + (0.4 - 0.2)(25) = 10 + 5 = 15$ kg-m/sec.
33	B	Apart from sign, the magnification factor, m, is equal to i/o, where i is the image distance from the lens and o is the object distance. In this case then, we have $m = i/o = (8\ cm)/(20\ cm) = 2/5$.
34	C	The nth harmonic frequency is equal to n times the fundamental frequency, f_1. Therefore $$\frac{f_6}{f_3} = \frac{6f_1}{3f_1} = 2$$
35	C	If both the source and detector travel in the same direction and at the same speed, there will be no relative motion and hence no Doppler shift.
36	C	The frequency does not change, so the wavelength must change (because the wave speed changes). $$\lambda_{in\ brass} = \frac{v_{in\ brass}}{f} = \frac{10v_{in\ air}}{f} = 10\lambda_{in\ air}$$
37	E	Gamma rays and X-rays are very high-energy, short-wavelength radiations. Ultraviolet light has a higher energy and shorter wavelength than visible light. Within the visible spectrum, the colors are—in order of increasing frequency—ROYGBV, so orange light ("O") has a lower frequency—and thus a longer wavelength—than blue light ("B").

Question	Answer	Explanation
38	D	All linear dimensions within the plate—including the radius and circumference of the hole—will increase by the same amount during thermal expansion. (To see that the hole does indeed get bigger, imagine that it was filled with a flat circular plug of metal. This plug would get bigger as the entire plate expanded, so if the plug were removed, it would leave behind a bigger hole.)
39	B	The net force acting on the block is 80 N – 60 N = 20 N. Dividing the net force by the object's mass gives the acceleration (Newton's second law), so we find that $a = F_{net}/m = (20\ N)/(40\ kg) = 0.5\ m/s^2$.
40	C	Since momentum, p, is equal to mv, we just multiply the two entries (m and v) in each row of the table and see which one is the greatest. This occurs in Trial 3, where $p = (2\ kg)(2\ m/s) = 4$ kg-m/s. So, the answer must be either choice C or choice D. To decide which, we only need to find the kinetic energy of the object in Trial 2 and Trial 3 and choose the one that's greater. Since $\frac{1}{2}mv^2 = \frac{1}{2}(1\ kg)(3\ m/s)^2 = \frac{9}{2}$ J in Trial 2, but only $\frac{1}{2}(2\ kg)(2\ m/s)^2 = 4$ J in Trial 3, we see that the object's kinetic energy is greater in Trial 2, so the answer is (C).
41	C	Statements (A) and (E) were known before Rutherford conducted this series of experiments, and statements (B) and (D) concerning the electrons were proposed later by Bohr. What Rutherford discovered with these experiments was that an atom's positive charge was not uniformly distributed throughout the entire atom but was instead concentrated into a very small volume at the atom's center (the nucleus).
42	B	Use the ideal gas law. $$P' = \frac{nRT'}{V'} = \frac{nR(2T)}{8V} = \frac{1}{4}\frac{nRT}{V} = \frac{1}{4}P$$
43	B	We use the equation for the power dissipated by a resistor, $P = IV$. $$I = \frac{P}{V} = \frac{60\ W}{120\ V} = 0.5\ A$$
44	D	To balance the superscripts, we write 2 + 2 = 3 + A, and get A = 1. Now, to balance the subscripts, we write 1 + 1 = 2 + Z, so Z = 0. Therefore, the particle X has a mass number of 1 and a charge of 0; it's a neutron.
45	B	We use the equation $q = mc\Delta T$ to find ΔT. $$\Delta T = \frac{q}{mc} = \frac{0.1\ kJ}{(0.05\ kg)(0.9\ kJ/kg \cdot °C)} = \frac{2}{0.9}°C \approx 2°C$$

Question	Answer	Explanation
46	D	From the kinetic theory of gases, we know that the average kinetic energy of the molecules of an ideal gas is directly proportional to the absolute temperature. This eliminates choices (B) and (C). Furthermore, the fact that $\mathrm{KE}_{avg} \propto T$ implies that the root-mean-square speed of the gas molecules, v_{ms}, is proportional to the square root of the absolute temperature. This eliminates choices (A) and (E).
47	A	Ice melts at 0°C and boils at 100°C. During these phase transitions, the temperature remains constant. Therefore, the graph of the sample's temperature must be momentarily flat at both 0°C and at 100°C.
48	C	Relative to the central maximum, the locations of the bright fringes on the screen are given by the expression $mL(\lambda/d)$, where λ is the wavelength of the light used, L is the distance to the screen, d is the separation of the slits, and m is an integer. The width of a fringe is, therefore $(m + 1)L(\lambda/d) - mL(\lambda/d) = \lambda L/d$. One way to increase $\lambda L/d$ is to decrease d.
49	E	If the photons of the incident light have insufficient energy to liberate electrons from the metal's surface, then simply increasing the number of these weak photons (that is, increasing the intensity of the light) will do nothing. To produce photoelectrons, each photon of the incident light must have an energy at least as great as the work function of the metal.
50	B	The energies emitted during electron transitions are equal to the differences between the allowed energy levels. Choice (A), 17 eV, is equal to the energy emitted by the photon when an electron drops from the –21 eV level to the –38 eV level. Choice (C), 64 eV, is equal to the energy emitted by the photon when an electron drops from the –21 eV level to the –85 eV level. Choice (D), 255 eV, is equal to the energy emitted by the photon when an electron drops from the –85 eV level to the –340 eV level. And choice (E), 302 eV, is equal to the energy emitted by the photon when an electron drops from the –38 eV level to the –340 eV level. However, no electron transition in this atom could give rise to a 42 eV photon.

Question	Answer	Explanation
51	A	Call the top wire (the one carrying a current I to the right) Wire 1, and call the bottom wire (carrying a current $2I$ to the left) Wire 2. In the region between the wires, the individual magnetic field vectors due to the wires are both directed into the plane of the page (use the right-hand rule with your right hand wrapped around the wire and your right thumb pointing in the direction of the current), so they could not cancel in this region. Therefore, the total magnetic field could not be zero at either Point 2 or Point 3. This eliminates choices (B), (C), (D), and (E), so the answer must be (A). (Because the magnetic field created by a current-carrying wire is proportional to the current and inversely proportional to the distance from the wire, the fact that Point 1 is in a region where the individual magnetic field vectors created by the wires point in opposite directions and that Point 1 is twice as far from Wire 2 as from Wire 1 imply that the total magnetic field there will be zero.)
52	C	The proximity of the charged sphere will induce negative charge to move to the side of the uncharged sphere closer to the charged sphere. Since the induced negative charge is closer than the induced positive charge to the charged sphere, there will be a net electrostatic attraction between the spheres.
53	E	The capacitance of a parallel-plate capacitor is $C = K\varepsilon_0 A/d$, where K is the dielectric constant, A is the area of each plate, and d is their separation distance. Decreasing d will cause C to increase.
54	B	The resistance of a wire made of a material with resistivity ρ and with length L and cross-sectional area A is given by the equation $R = \rho L/A$. Since Wire B has the greatest length and smallest cross-sectional area, it has the greatest resistance.
55	A	The amplitude of a wave is the maximum displacement from equilibrium (the position of zero displacement). Since the distance between the maximum positive displacement and the maximum negative displacement is 0.16 m, the amplitude is half this: 0.08 m.

Question	Answer	Explanation
56	D	Each "hump" along the wave represents half a cycle, or half a wavelength. The drawing given with the question shows three such consecutive humps having a total length of 0.6 m, so each one has a length of 0.2 m. Since this is half a wavelength, the full wavelength must be 0.4 m.
57	D	The period, T, is the reciprocal of the frequency, and the frequency, f, always satisfies the equation $\lambda f = v$. So, we find that $$T = \frac{1}{f} = \frac{\lambda}{v} = \frac{\lambda m}{\frac{1}{2} \text{ m/sec}} = (2\lambda) \text{ sec.}$$
58	A	Because each half-life is 1.5 hours, a time interval of 6 hours is equal to 4 half-lives. After each half-life elapses, the mass of the sample is cut in half, so after 4 half-lives, the mass of the sample decreases from 2 grams to 1 gram to 0.5 grams to 0.25 grams and, finally, to 0.125 grams.
59	E	The electrical potential energy of a pair of charges is given by kq_1q_2/r, where r is the distance between the charges. Therefore, the electrical potential energy of the pair of charges $+Q$ and $+Q$ will be greatest when the distance between them is the *smallest*. Of the five diagrams given, the charges are closest together in diagram (E).
60	A	By the principle of superposition, the total electric force on the charge in the lower right-hand corner is simply the sum of the individual electric forces produced by each of the charges in the other three corners. The first diagram below shows the directions of the individual electric forces that each of the other three charges exerts separately on the lower right-hand charge. The second and third diagrams then show how these three vectors add together to give the net electric force. Note that F_2 and F_3 are each larger than F_1 since $F_E = \dfrac{k\lvert q_1 q_2 \rvert}{r^2}$. Therefore, $\mathbf{F}_2 + \mathbf{F}_3$ is also larger than $\mathbf{F}_1$.
61	C	The torque is equal to rF, where $F = mg$. In this case, then, we find that torque $= rmg = (0.5 \text{ m})(0.2 \text{ kg})(10 \text{ N/kg}) = 1$ N-m.

Question	Answer	Explanation
62	B	Because the rocks are dropped from rest simultaneously and air resistance is negligible, both rocks will accelerate at the same rate and have the same speed, v, at impact. So, the ratio of Rock 1's momentum to Rock 2's momentum will be $(M_1 v)/(M_2 v) = M_1/M_2$.
63	B	Because the forces **N** and **w** are vertical while the displacement of the block is horizontal, the work done by each of these forces is zero, so they contribute nothing to the total work performed. This eliminates choices (C), (D), and (E). Since the force **f** is opposite to the direction of the displacement, the work it does is *negative*; in fact, it's $-fL$. The work done by the force **F** is FL, so the total work performed on the block is $-fL + FL = (F - f)L$.
64	A	Choices (B), (C), (D), and (E) all change the magnetic flux through the loop containing the light bulb, thus inducing an emf and a current. However, just swinging the handle over as described in choice A changes neither the area presented to the magnetic field lines from the bottom coil nor the density of the field lines at the position of the loop. No change in magnetic flux means no induced emf and no induced current.
65	E	If the efficiency of the engine is 25%, then the energy that is output for useful work is 25% of the input energy, which is $(25\%)(800\ \text{J}) = 200\ \text{J}$. The remaining $800\ \text{J} - 200\ \text{J} = 600\ \text{J}$ is expelled as waste heat.
66	C	Label the charges 1, 2, and 3, in order from left to right. We're asked to find the force on Charge 1 due to the other two charges. The electrostatic force on Charge 1 due to Charge 2 is a repulsive force, of magnitude $\dfrac{kQ^2}{R^2}$, and the electrostatic force on Charge 1 due to Charge 3 is a weaker, attractive force, of magnitude $\dfrac{kQ^2}{(2R)^2} = \dfrac{kQ^2}{4R^2}$. Since these individual forces act in opposite directions, the magnitude of the net force is found by *subtracting* the magnitudes of the individual forces. So, the total electric force on Charge 1 has magnitude $$F_{net} = F_{2\text{-on-}1} - F_{3\text{-on-}1} = \frac{kQ^2}{R^2} - \frac{kQ^2}{4R^2} = \frac{3kQ^2}{4R^2}$$
67	A	In order for total internal reflection to occur, the beam must be incident in the medium with the higher index of refraction and strike the interface at an angle of incidence greater than the critical angle. Since $v_1 < v_2$, the refractive index of Medium 1, $n_1 = c/v_1$, must be *greater* than the index of Medium 2 ($n_2 = c/v_2$), and the critical angle is $\theta_{crit} = \sin^{-1}(n_2/n_1) = \sin^{-1}(v_1/v_2)$.

Question	Answer	Explanation
68	E	The frequency of the oscillations, f, can be found from the equation $f = \frac{1}{2\pi}\sqrt{k/m}$. Since k is known, all we need is f in order to calculate m. If we know the quantity given in choice (E), we can double it to get the period, then take its reciprocal to obtain f.
69	B	When the block is at Point Y, all its energy is due to the potential energy of the stretched spring, which is $\frac{1}{2}kd^2$. At the moment the block passes through the equilibrium position, O, this energy has been converted entirely to kinetic. By setting $\frac{1}{2}mv^2$ equal to $\frac{1}{2}kd^2$, we find that $$\frac{1}{2}mv^2 = \frac{1}{2}kd^2 \implies v = d\sqrt{k/m} = d\omega.$$
70	D	Because the particle travels in a circular path with constant kinetic energy (which implies constant speed), the net force on the particle is the centripetal force. $$F = \frac{mv^2}{r} = \frac{2\left(\frac{1}{2}mv^2\right)}{r} = \frac{2K}{r} = \frac{2(4\text{ J})}{0.2\text{ m}} = 40\text{ N}$$
71	A	The change in the electrical potential energy as a charge q moves from position X to position Z is equal to q times the difference in potential between the points: $\Delta PE = qV = q\Delta\phi = q(\phi_Z - \phi_X)$. Because positions X and Z are equidistant from the source charge ($+Q$), the potentials at these locations are the same. Since $\Delta\phi = 0$, there is no change in potential energy, so the work done by the electric field is also zero.
72	E	The electric field strength is given by $E = \frac{kQ}{r^2}$. Therefore $$\frac{E_Z}{E_Y} = \frac{kQ/r_Z^2}{kQ/r_Y^2} = \frac{r_Y^2}{r_Z^2} = \frac{(4\text{ cm})^2}{(3\text{ cm})^2} = \frac{16}{9}$$
73	C	The distance from the mirror to the image is equal to the distance from the mirror to the object. Therefore, the distance from the object to the image is 100 cm + 100 cm = 200 cm.

Question	Answer	Explanation
74	D	The impulse delivered to the ball is equal to the ball's change in momentum, and the presence of the mitt does not change this, eliminating choices (A) and (C). The extra area may decrease the *pressure* on the catcher's hand, but not the force (eliminating choice (B). The padding of the mitt causes the time during which the ball comes to a stop to increase (just as an air bag increases the time it takes for an automobile passenger involved in an accident to come to a stop), which *decreases* the magnitude of the ball's acceleration (since $a = \Delta v / \Delta t$). A decrease in the magnitude of the acceleration means a decrease in the magnitude of the force (since $a = F/m$).
75	C	The second postulate of Einstein's theory of special relativity states that the speed of light is a universal constant ($c = 3 \times 10^8$ m/s), regardless of the motion of the source or the detector. So despite the fact that the spaceship is approaching the planet at a speed of $c/2$, occupants of the ship will still measure the speed of light to be c. The time it takes the light pulse to travel a distance of 4.5×10^8 m is $$t = \frac{d}{c} = \frac{4.5 \times 10^8 \text{ m}}{3.0 \times 10^8 \text{ m/s}} = 1.5 \text{ s}$$

The Princeton Review Practice SAT Physics Subject Tests Scoring Grid

Recall from the Introduction that your raw score is equal to the number of questions you answered correctly minus $\frac{1}{4}$ of the number of questions you answered incorrectly,

$$(\text{number of correct answers}) - \frac{1}{4}(\text{number of wrong answers})$$

then rounded to the nearest whole number. Questions that you leave blank do not count toward your raw score.

Raw Score	Approximate Scaled Score
≥ 60	800
56–59	780–790
50–55	750–770
45–49	720–740
40–44	690–710
36–39	660–680
30–35	630–650
25–29	600–620
20–24	570–590
16–19	540–560
11–15	510–530
7–10	480–500
2–6	450–470
–4–1	410–440
≤ -5	≤ 400

Chapter 21
The Princeton Review
Practice SAT Physics
Subject Test 2

SAT PHYSICS SUBJECT TEST 2

TEST 2

Your responses to the Physics Subject Test questions should be filled in on Test 2 of your answer sheet (at the back of the book).

PHYSICS SUBJECT TEST 2

75 Questions • Time limit = 1 hour • You may NOT use a calculator.

Part A

Directions: Each set of lettered choices below refers to the numbered questions immediately following it. Select the one letter choice that best answers each question or best fits each statement, and then fill in the corresponding oval on the answer sheet. *A choice may be used once, more than once, or not at all in each set.*

Questions 1-5

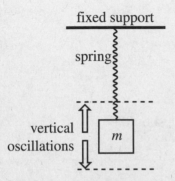

A block of mass *m* undergoing simple harmonicmotion. Frictional forces are negligible and can be ignored. Questions 1-5 relate to the following quantities:

(A) Amplitude
(B) Frequency
(C) Period
(D) Position of block
(E) Total mechanical energy of the block

1. Once the motion is underway, which quantity does NOT remain constant?

2. Which quantity is inversely proportional to the square root of the block's mass?

3. Which quantity would always be greater if the block oscillated with a smaller force constant?

4. The maximum speed of the block is proportional to what quantity?

5. The graph of which quantity (versus time) would look like a sine wave?

Questions 6-9

(A) Alpha decay
(B) β^- decay
(C) β^+ decay
(D) Electron capture
(E) Gamma decay

6. Which type of decay would cause the number of neutrons in the nucleus to decrease by 1 ?

7. In which type of decay is the identity of the nucleus unchanged?

8. Which type of decay ejects the heaviest particle?

9. Which type of decay would cause the atomic number of the nucleus to increase?

GO ON TO THE NEXT PAGE

Questions 10-12

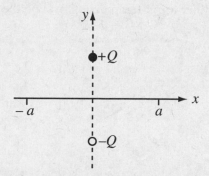

An electric dipole, a pair of equal but opposite charges. Two isolated point charges are fixed in the positions shown on the *y* axis; the positive charge is located at the point $(0, b)$ and the negative charge is located at the point $(0, -b)$. Questions 10-12 relate to the graphs labeled (A) through (E) that appear below.

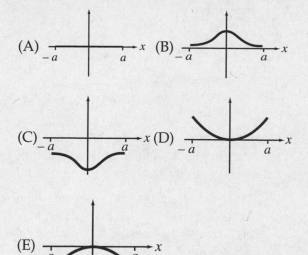

10. Which graph best depicts the electric field magnitude along the *x* axis, from $x = -a$ to $x = a$?

11. Which graph best illustrates the electric potential along the *x* axis, from $x = -a$ to $x = a$?

12. If a negative charge, $-q$, were moved along the *x* axis from $x = -a$ to $x = a$, which graph best depicts the magnitude of the electric force it would feel during this motion?

GO ON TO THE NEXT PAGE

Directions: Each of the questions or incomplete statements below is followed by five suggested answers or completions. Select the one that is best in each case and then fill in the corresponding oval on the answer sheet.

13. Two people, one of mass 100 kg and the other of mass 50 kg, stand facing each other on an ice-covered (essentially frictionless) pond. If the heavier person pushes on the lighter one with a force F, then

    (A) the force felt by the heavier person is $-\frac{1}{2}F$

    (B) the force felt by the heavier person is $-2F$

    (C) the magnitude of the acceleration of the lighter person will be $\frac{1}{2}$ of the magnitude of the acceleration of the heavier person

    (D) the magnitude of the acceleration of the lighter person will be twice the magnitude of the acceleration of the heavier person

    (E) None of the above

14. Each of the following particles is projected with the same speed into a uniform magnetic field **B** such that the particle's initial velocity is perpendicular to **B**. Which one would move in a circular path with the largest radius?

    (A) Proton
    (B) Beta particle
    (C) Alpha particle
    (D) Electron
    (E) Positron

15. Which of the following best describes the magnetic field lines created by a long, straight, current-carrying wire?

    (A) Rays that emanate from the wire
    (B) Circles centered on the wire
    (C) Lines parallel to the wire
    (D) Lines perpendicular to the wire
    (E) Noncircular ellipses centered on the wire

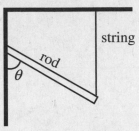

16. If the rod is uniform and has mass m, what is the tension in the supporting string?

    (A) $\dfrac{(mg \sin \theta)}{2}$

    (B) $\dfrac{mg \sin}{2}$

    (C) $\dfrac{(mg \cos \theta)}{2}$

    (D) $\dfrac{mg}{2}$

    (E) mg

17. A lightweight toy car crashes head-on into a heavier toy truck. Which of the following statements is true as a result of the collision?

    I. The car will experience a greater impulse than the truck.
    II. The car will experience a greater change in momentum than the truck.
    III. The magnitude of the acceleration experienced by the car will be greater than that experienced by the truck.

    (A) I and II only
    (B) II only
    (C) III only
    (D) II and III only
    (E) I, II, and III

GO ON TO THE NEXT PAGE

Questions 18-19

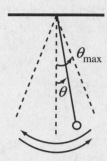

A simple pendulum, composed of a bob of mass m connected to the end of a massless rod, executes simple harmonic motion as it swings through small angles of oscillation. The largest angle the pendulum makes with the vertical is denoted by θ_{max}. Frictional effects are negligible and can be ignored, and the pendulum is near the surface of the earth, where $g = 9.8$ m/s^2.

18. Which one of the following statements is true?

    (A) At $\theta = 0$, the tangential acceleration is 0.
    (B) At $\theta = \theta_{max}$, the tangential acceleration is 0.
    (C) At $\theta = 0$, the speed is 0.
    (D) At $\theta = 0$, the restoring force is maximized.
    (E) At $\theta = \theta_{max}$, the speed is maximized.

19. Knowing which one of the following would enable you to calculate the length of the pendulum?

    (A) The mass of the bob
    (B) The period of the oscillations
    (C) The tangential acceleration at $\theta = 0$
    (D) The maximum speed of the bob
    (E) The acceleration at $\theta = \theta_{max}$

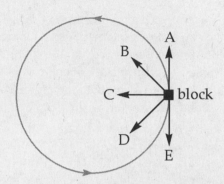

20. A block is moving counter-clockwise in a circular path on a flat table. If the speed of the block is increasing at the moment it is at the position shown, which one of the five arrows best illustrates the direction of the acceleration on the block?

    (A) A
    (B) B
    (C) C
    (D) D
    (E) E

21. If a particle of charge –0.2 mC were placed at a certain location within an electric field, the magnitude of the electric force it would feel is 1 N. What is the magnitude of the electric field at this location? (1 mC = 10^{-3} C)

    (A)   2,000 N/C
    (B)   5,000 N/C
    (C)   20,000 N/C
    (D)   50,000 N/C
    (E) 500,000 N/C

GO ON TO THE NEXT PAGE

22. Traveling at an initial speed of 1.5×10^6 m/s, a proton enters a region of constant magnetic field, B, of magnitude 1.0 tesla. If the proton's initial velocity vector makes an angle of 30° with the direction of B, compute the proton's speed 4 seconds after entering the magnetic field.

    (A) 5.0×10^5 m/s
    (B) 7.5×10^5 m/s
    (C) 1.5×10^6 m/s
    (D) 3.0×10^6 m/s
    (E) 6.0×10^6 m/s

23. An object of mass 2 kg increases in speed from 2 m/s to 4 m/s in 3 s. What was the total work performed on the object during this time interval?

    (A) 4 J
    (B) 6 J
    (C) 12 J
    (D) 24 J
    (E) 36 J

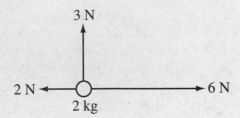

24. The figure above shows the forces acting on an object of mass 2 kg. What is the object's acceleration?

    (A) 2 m/s²
    (B) 2.5 m/s²
    (C) 3 m/s²
    (D) 3.5 m/s²
    (E) 4 m/s²

25. Two traveling waves of equal frequency, one of amplitude 4 cm and the other of amplitude 6 cm, superimpose in a single medium. Which of the following best describes the amplitude, A, of the resultant wave?

    (A) 2 cm $\leq A \leq 10$ cm
    (B) $A = 5$ cm
    (C) $A = 10$ cm
    (D) 10 cm $\leq A \leq 12$ cm
    (E) 12 cm $\leq A \leq 24$ cm

26. A uniform bar is lying on a flat table. Besides the gravitational and normal forces (which cancel), the bar is acted upon by exactly two other forces, F_1 and F_2, which are parallel to the surface of the table. If the net force on the rod is zero, then which one of the following is true?

    (A) The net torque on the bar must also be zero.
    (B) The bar can accelerate translationally if F_1 and F_2 are not applied at the same point.
    (C) The net torque will be zero if F_1 and F_2 are applied at the same point.
    (D) The bar cannot accelerate translationally or rotationally.
    (E) None of the above

GO ON TO THE NEXT PAGE

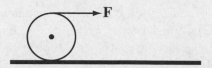

27. A uniform cylinder, initially at rest on a frictionless, horizontal surface, is pulled by a constant force F from time $t = 0$ to time $t = T$. From time $t = T$ on, this force is removed. Which of the following graphs best illustrates the speed, v, of the cylinder's center of mass from $t = 0$ to $t = 2T$?

(A)

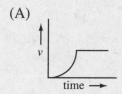

(B)

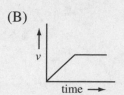

(C)

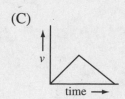

(D)

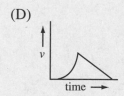

(E)

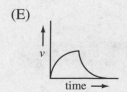

Questions 28-30

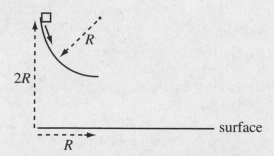

A small box slides down a frictionless track in the shape of a quarter-circle of radius R. The box starts from rest at the top of the track, a height equal to $2R$ above a horizontal surface. At the moment the box leaves the bottom of the track, a ball of the same mass as the box is dropped from the same height at the bottom of the track.

28. How fast is the box moving when it reaches the end of the track?

(A) $v = \sqrt{gR}$
(B) $v = \sqrt{2gR}$
(C) $v = \sqrt{\pi gR}$
(D) $v = \sqrt{2\pi gR}$
(E) $v = \pi\sqrt{2gR}$

29. Which of the following quantities must decrease as the box slides down the track?

(A) The normal force on the box
(B) The net force on the box
(C) The kinetic energy of the box
(D) The potential energy of the box
(E) The total mechanical energy (kinetic + potential) of the box

GO ON TO THE NEXT PAGE

30. Once the box leaves the bottom of the slide, which of the following statements best describes the motions of the box and the ball?

    (A) The ball hits the floor at the same time as the box.
    (B) The ball hits the floor before the box does.
    (C) The ball hits the floor after the box does.
    (D) The acceleration of the box is greater than the acceleration of the ball.
    (E) The acceleration of the ball is greater than the acceleration of the box.

31. An ellipsoid-shaped conductor is negatively charged. Which one of the following diagrams best illustrates the charge distribution and electric field lines?

    (A)

    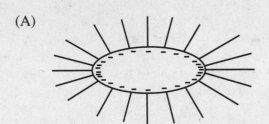

    (B)

    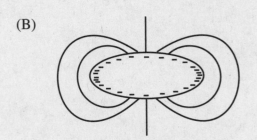

    (C)

    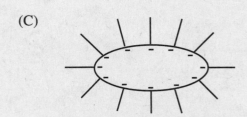

    (D)

    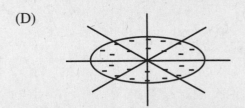

    (E)

    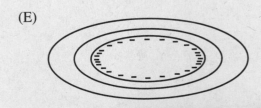

GO ON TO THE NEXT PAGE

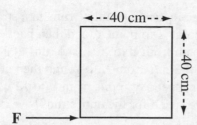

32. The figure above shows a square metal plate of side length 40 cm and uniform density, lying flat on a table. A force F of magnitude 10 N is applied at one of the corners, parallel to one of the sides, as shown. What's the torque produced by F relative to the center of the square?

    (A) 0 N-m
    (B) 1.0 N-m
    (C) 1.4 N-m
    (D) 2.0 N-m
    (E) 4.0 N-m

33. A mover, exerting a steady force of 200 N, pushes a box of mass 50 kg across a flat wooden floor. If the velocity of the box does not change while he pushes, what is the coefficient of kinetic friction between the box and the floor?

    (A) 0.2
    (B) 0.4
    (C) 0.5
    (D) 0.6
    (E) 0.8

34. What principle is the basis for the transmission of light through glass (fiber optic) cables, allowing the signal to be sent even if the cable is bent?

    (A) Photoelectric effect
    (B) Uncertainty principle
    (C) Light diffraction
    (D) Light polarization
    (E) Total internal reflection

35. A student is monitoring the pressure and absolute temperature in a container of fixed volume filled with an ideal gas as the gas is heated. Which of the following graphs best illustrates the relationship between the pressure (P) and absolute temperature (T) of the gas, assuming that none of the gas escapes from the container?

(A)

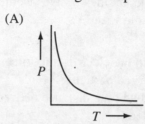

(B)

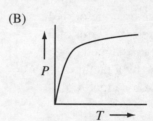

(C)

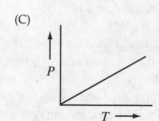

(D)

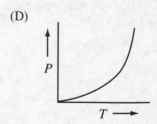

(E)

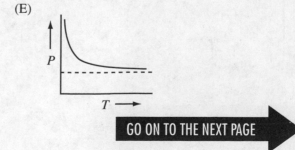

GO ON TO THE NEXT PAGE

36. Of the following types of waves, which type travels at the greatest speed through vacuum?

    (A) Radio waves
    (B) Microwaves
    (C) Ultraviolet light
    (D) X-rays
    (E) None of the above; all these waves would travel at the same speed.

37. What would happen to the electrostatic force between a pair of charged particles if both charges were doubled and the distance between them were also doubled?

    (A) It would decrease by a factor of 4.
    (B) It would decrease by a factor of 2.
    (C) It would remain unchanged.
    (D) It would increase by a factor of 2.
    (E) It would increase by a factor of 4.

38. As a bat flies at a constant speed of $0.04V$ toward a large tree trunk (where V denotes the speed of sound), the bat emits an ultrasonic pulse. The pulse is reflected off the tree and returns to the bat, which can detect and analyze the returning signal. If the returning signal has a frequency of 61 kHz, at approximately what frequency did the bat emit the original ultrasonic pulse?

    (A) 56 kHz
    (B) 62 kHz
    (C) 68 kHz
    (D) 74 kHz
    (E) 78 kHz

39. During practice, an athlete runs in a straight line from point X to point Y, and then back along the same path from Y to X. If she runs at a constant speed of 3 m/s from X to Y, and then at a constant speed of 6 m/s from Y to X, what is her average speed for the entire run?

    (A) 3.5 m/s
    (B) 4 m/s
    (C) 4.5 m/s
    (D) 5 m/s
    (E) 5.5 m/s

40. A sky diver jumps from an airplane. After "free falling" for a while, she opens her parachute and her descent speed begins to decrease. While her descent speed decreases, let F denote the magnitude of the gravitational force on the sky diver and let D denote the magnitude of the upward force of air resistance (drag). Which of the following is then true?

    (A) $F > D$
    (B) $F < D$
    (C) $F + D <$ weight of the sky diver
    (D) $F - D >$ weight of the sky diver
    (E) $F - D > 0$

GO ON TO THE NEXT PAGE

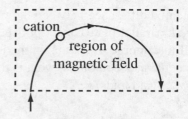

41. The figure above shows a cation (a positive ion—that is, an atom that has lost one or more electrons) entering a mass spectrometer, which contains a region with a uniform magnetic field, **B**. Once in the magnetic field, the cation moves in a semicircular path in the direction indicated. What is the direction of **B** ?

    (A) Upward in the plane of the page
    (B) To the left in the plane of the page
    (C) To the right in the plane of the page
    (D) Out of the plane of the page
    (E) Into the plane of the page

42. A traveling wave has a frequency of 6.0 Hz, an amplitude of 0.2 m, and a wavelength of 0.5 m. What is its wave speed?

    (A) 0.1 m/s
    (B) 0.6 m/s
    (C) 1.2 m/s
    (D) 2.4 m/s
    (E) 3.0 m/s

Questions 43-45

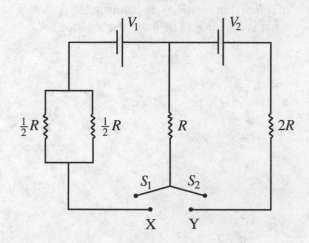

The circuit shown contains two switches: S_1, which can connect to point X, and S_2, which can connect to point Y.

43. If switch S_1 is left in the position shown in the figure but switch S_2 is connected to point Y, what is the current through the resistor R ?

    (A) $\dfrac{V_2}{3R}$

    (B) $\dfrac{V_2}{R}$

    (C) $\dfrac{3V_2}{2R}$

    (D) $\dfrac{V_1 + V_2}{3R}$

    (E) $\dfrac{V_1 - V_2}{R}$

GO ON TO THE NEXT PAGE

44. If switch S_2 is left in the position shown in the diagram, but switch S_1 is connected to point X, what is the current through the resistor R ?

(A) $\dfrac{V_1}{4R}$

(B) $\dfrac{V_1}{2R}$

(C) $\dfrac{4V_1}{5R}$

(D) $\dfrac{5V_1}{4R}$

(E) $\dfrac{(V_1 + V_2)}{2R}$

45. If both switches are left in the positions shown in the diagram, what is the current through the resistor R ?

(A) 0

(B) $\dfrac{2(V_1 + V_2)}{11R}$

(C) $\dfrac{4(V_1 + V_2)}{13R}$

(D) $\dfrac{2(V_1 + V_2)}{5R}$

(E) $\dfrac{6(V_1 + V_2)}{7R}$

46. What does the second law of thermodynamics say should happen to an isolated, ordered system?

(A) Heat will flow into the system.
(B) Heat will flow out of the system.
(C) Work will be done by the system.
(D) Work will be done on the system.
(E) The entropy within the system will increase.

47. The potential difference between the plates of a charged, parallel-plate capacitor is equal to X volts. If the amount of charge on the POSITIVE plate is equal to Y coulombs, what is the capacitance (in farads)?

(A) $\dfrac{X}{2Y}$

(B) $\dfrac{Y}{2X}$

(C) $\dfrac{Y}{X}$

(D) $\dfrac{2Y}{X}$

(E) $\dfrac{2X}{Y}$

48. A car, starting from rest, accelerates uniformly at 4 m/s^2 along a straight track. How far will it travel in 6 s ?

(A) 24 m
(B) 48 m
(C) 64 m
(D) 72 m
(E) 144 m

49. An object is executing uniform circular motion. Which of the following quantities remain(s) constant during the object's motion?

(A) Velocity and acceleration
(B) Speed and velocity
(C) Speed and acceleration
(D) Acceleration only
(E) Speed only

GO ON TO THE NEXT PAGE

Questions 50-53

In the diagram accompanying each question, representative light rays from an illuminated object (labeled "O" in the diagrams) interact with an optical device (or devices): a mirror, a lens, or a combination of both. In each case, identify the optical device(s)—from among the choices below—that is/are most likely in the dotted box.

(A) Plane mirror
(B) Converging lens
(C) Diverging lens
(D) Plane mirror and a converging lens
(E) Plane mirror and a diverging lens

50.

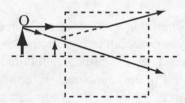

51.

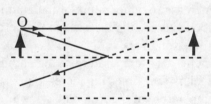

52.

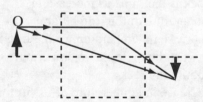

53.

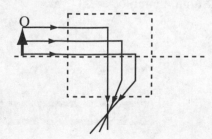

54. A superconductor is

(A) a device used to study the collisions of subatomic particles that have been accelerated to near light speeds
(B) a hollow, doughnut-shaped device containing a strong magnetic field for confinement of very high temperature plasmas
(C) an element used to generate high-energy coherent laser light
(D) an element whose supercooled vapor fills a cloud chamber to detect the tracks of charged particles when they initiate condensation of the vapor
(E) an element or alloy whose electrical resistivity vanishes when cooled to extremely low temperatures

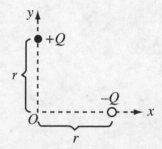

55. Two equal but opposite point charges are fixed in position on the x and y axes, as shown in the figure above. Which of the following arrows best illustrates the direction of the resulting electric field at the origin, O ?

(A) ↗
(B) ↘
(C) ↙
(D) ↘
(E) ←

GO ON TO THE NEXT PAGE

56. The planet Jupiter is 5 times farther from the sun than the earth, and the mass of Jupiter is 300 times the mass of the earth. If F_J is the strength of the gravitational force exerted by the sun on Jupiter, and F_E is the strength of the gravitational force exerted by the sun on the earth, what's the value of the ratio $\dfrac{F_J}{F_E}$?

   (A) $\dfrac{1}{60}$

   (B) $\dfrac{1}{12}$

   (C) 8

   (D) 12

   (E) 60

57. Consider a double-slit interference experiment using yellow light of wavelength λ, with the slits labeled S_1 and S_2. If P is the center of a dark fringe on the screen on which the resulting diffraction pattern is projected, which of the following equations relating S_1P and S_2P, the distances from slits S_1 and S_2, respectively, to the point P could be true?

   (A) $S_1P - S_2P = \dfrac{1}{2}\lambda$

   (B) $S_1P - S_2P = \lambda$

   (C) $S_1P - S_2P = 2\lambda$

   (D) $S_1P - S_2P = 3\lambda$

   (E) $S_1P = S_2P$

58. A pair of tuning forks produce sound waves that travel through the air. The frequency of the sound waves produced by the first tuning fork is 440 Hz, and the frequency of the sound waves produced by the second tuning fork is 880 Hz. If v_1 denotes the speed of the sound waves produced by the first tuning fork and v_2 denotes the speed of the sound waves produced by the second turning fork, then

   (A) $v_1 = 2v_2$
   (B) $v_1 = 4v_2$
   (C) $v_1 = v_2$
   (D) $v_2 = 2v_1$
   (E) $v_2 = 4v_1$

59. A block of aluminum and a block of iron each absorb the same amount of heat, and both blocks remain solid. The mass of the aluminum block is twice the mass of the iron block. If the specific heat of aluminum is twice the specific heat of iron, then

   (A) the increase in temperature of the aluminum block is twice the increase in temperature of the iron block
   (B) the increase in temperature of the aluminum block is four times the increase in temperature of the iron block
   (C) the increase in temperature of the aluminum block is the same as increase in temperature of the iron block
   (D) the increase in temperature of the iron block is twice the increase in temperature of the aluminum block
   (E) the increase in temperature of the iron block is four times the increase in temperature of the aluminum block

GO ON TO THE NEXT PAGE

60. If a container contains a mixture of two ideal gases (of different molecular masses) at thermal equilibrium, which of the following is true?

    (A) The average kinetic energy of the molecules of the lighter gas is less than the average kinetic energy of the molecules of the heavier gas.
    (B) The average kinetic energy of the molecules of the lighter gas is greater than the average kinetic energy of the molecules of the heavier gas.
    (C) The average speed of the molecules of the lighter gas is less than the average speed of the molecules of the heavier gas.
    (D) The average speed of the molecules of the lighter gas is equal to the average speed of the molecules of the heavier gas.
    (E) The average speed of the molecules of the lighter gas is greater than the average speed of the molecules of the heavier gas.

61. A vertically polarized plane wave (an AM radio wave) is emitted by a radio antenna and travels across flat ground. Which of the following could describe the direction of the magnetic field component of the wave?

    (A) Parallel to the ground and perpendicular to the direction of propagation
    (B) Perpendicular to the ground and to the direction of propagation
    (C) Parallel to the ground and to the direction of propagation
    (D) Perpendicular to the ground and parallel to the direction of propagation
    (E) Parallel to the electric field component of the wave

62. Which of the following best describes the relationship between the frequency and amplitude of a sound wave?

    (A) Frequency is proportional to amplitude.
    (B) Frequency is proportional to the square of the amplitude.
    (C) Frequency is inversely proportional to amplitude.
    (D) Frequency is inversely proportional to the square of the amplitude.
    (E) Frequency and amplitude are independent.

63. An atom whose nucleus contains 17 protons and 20 neutrons is a chlorine atom. Which of the following describes the composition of the nucleus of an isotope of chlorine?

    (A) 20 protons, 17 neutrons
    (B) 19 protons, 18 neutrons
    (C) 18 protons, 18 neutrons
    (D) 17 protons, 19 neutrons
    (E) 16 protons, 20 neutrons

64. When a projectile moving in a parabolic path reaches its highest point above the ground,

    (A) its velocity is instantaneously zero
    (B) its acceleration is instantaneously zero
    (C) its weight balances the force of air resistance
    (D) the net force it feels is instantaneously zero
    (E) None of the above

GO ON TO THE NEXT PAGE

Questions 65-66

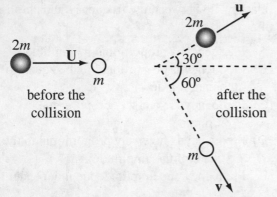

before the collision

after the collision

An object of mass 2*m* moving with velocity **U** strikes an object of mass *m* initially at rest. After the collision, the objects move away with velocities **u** and **v**, as shown.

65. Which one of the following equations correctly relates *u* and *v* ?

 (A) $2u \cos 30° = v \cos 60°$
 (B) $u \cos 30° = 2v \cos 60°$
 (C) $2u \sin 30° = v \sin 60°$
 (D) $u \sin 30° = 2v \sin 60°$
 (E) $u \sin 30° = v \cos 60°$

66. If the collision is elastic, then

 (A) $U^2 = u^2 - \frac{1}{2}v^2$

 (B) $U^2 = u^2 + \frac{1}{2}v^2$

 (C) $U = u - \frac{1}{2}v$

 (D) $U = u + \frac{1}{2}v$

 (E) $(U - u)^2 = \frac{1}{2}v^2$

67. The acceleration due to gravity on the moon is 1/6 of its value on Earth. If an object weighs 20 N on the moon, what is its mass on Earth?

 (A) 2 kg
 (B) 7.2 kg
 (C) 12 kg
 (D) 60 kg
 (E) 72 kg

68. The electric field strength at a point some distance away from a source charge does NOT depend on

 (A) the magnitude of the source charge.
 (B) the sign of the source charge.
 (C) the distance from the source charge.
 (D) the nature of the medium surrounding the source charge.
 (E) None of the above

GO ON TO THE NEXT PAGE

69. Which of the following equations best states the relationship between a material's coefficient of volume expansion due to heating, β, and its coefficient of linear expansion, α ?

    (A) $\beta = \alpha$
    (B) $\beta = 3\alpha$
    (C) $\beta = \alpha + \alpha^2$
    (D) $\beta = \alpha^3$
    (E) $\beta = 3\alpha^3$

70. The ends of a long, taut tightrope are attached to two platforms. A tightrope artist walks along the tightrope and, upon reaching the middle, stops. Someone standing on one of the platforms grabs the rope near one end and sends a transverse wave pulse down the rope. When the pulse reaches the tightrope walker, he briefly rises upward, and the wave passes. This illustrates the fact that the wave transports

    (A) momentum
    (B) mass
    (C) weight
    (D) wavelength
    (E) density

Questions 71-72

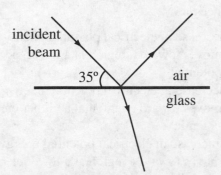

Note: The figure is not drawn to scale.

The figure above shows a beam of light striking the surface of a piece of glass from the air.

71. If the reflected beam and refracted beam are perpendicular to each other, what is the index of refraction of the glass?

    (A) sin 55°
    (B) 1/sin 55°
    (C) 1/sin 35°
    (D) sin 55°/sin 35°
    (E) sin 35°/sin 55°

72. Let *n* denote the index of refraction of the glass. If the incident light has a frequency of *f* when traveling through the air, what is the wavelength of the light when it travels through the glass?

    (A) *fc*/*n*
    (B) *n*/*fc*
    (C) *c*/*f*
    (D) *nc*/*f*
    (E) *c*/*nf*

GO ON TO THE NEXT PAGE

73. An electron that accelerates from a point near a collection of negative source charges toward a point near a collection of positive source charges experiences

   (A) a decrease in electrical potential energy as it moves toward a region at a lower electric potential
   (B) a decrease in electrical potential energy as it moves toward a region at a higher electric potential
   (C) an increase in electrical potential energy as it moves toward a region at a lower electric potential
   (D) an increase in electrical potential energy as it moves toward a region at a higher electric potential
   (E) no change in electrical potential energy

74. As the air around the base of a candle flame is heated, it rises and is replaced by cooler air. This illustrates what type of heat transfer?

   (A) Conduction
   (B) Convection
   (C) Radiation
   (D) Diffraction
   (E) Latent heat

75. Five identical spaceships take off from Planet X, and each passes by Planet Y at a constant speed on its way to Planet Z. A science station on Planet Y observes them passing by. The spaceship traveling at which of the following speeds would be observed to have the greatest length?

   (A) 6×10^7 m/s
   (B) 9×10^7 m/s
   (C) 1×10^8 m/s
   (D) 1.5×10^8 m/s
   (E) 2×10^8 m/s

STOP

IF YOU FINISH BEFORE TIME IS CALLED, YOU MAY CHECK YOUR WORK ON THIS TEST ONLY.

ANSWERS TO THE PRINCETON REVIEW
PRACTICE SAT PHYSICS SUBJECT TEST 2

Question Number	Correct Answer	Right	Wrong	Question Number	Correct Answer	Right	Wrong	Question Number	Correct Answer	Right	Wrong
1.	D	___	___	26.	C	___	___	51.	A	___	___
2.	B	___	___	27.	B	___	___	52.	B	___	___
3.	C	___	___	28.	B	___	___	53.	D	___	___
4.	A	___	___	29.	D	___	___	54.	E	___	___
5.	D	___	___	30.	A	___	___	55.	D	___	___
6.	B	___	___	31.	A	___	___	56.	D	___	___
7.	E	___	___	32.	D	___	___	57.	A	___	___
8.	A	___	___	33.	B	___	___	58.	C	___	___
9.	B	___	___	34.	E	___	___	59.	E	___	___
10.	B	___	___	35.	C	___	___	60.	E	___	___
11.	A	___	___	36.	E	___	___	61.	A	___	___
12.	B	___	___	37.	C	___	___	62.	E	___	___
13.	D	___	___	38.	A	___	___	63.	D	___	___
14.	C	___	___	39.	B	___	___	64.	E	___	___
15.	B	___	___	40.	B	___	___	65.	C	___	___
16.	D	___	___	41.	D	___	___	66.	B	___	___
17.	C	___	___	42.	E	___	___	67.	C	___	___
18.	A	___	___	43.	A	___	___	68.	B	___	___
19.	B	___	___	44.	C	___	___	69.	B	___	___
20.	B	___	___	45.	A	___	___	70.	A	___	___
21.	B	___	___	46.	E	___	___	71.	D	___	___
22.	C	___	___	47.	C	___	___	72.	E	___	___
23.	C	___	___	48.	D	___	___	73.	B	___	___
24.	B	___	___	49.	E	___	___	74.	B	___	___
25.	A	___	___	50.	C			75.	A	___	___

Chapter 22
Answers and Explanations to Practice SAT Physics Subject Test 2

Answers and Explanations

Question	Answer	Explanation
1	D	As the block moves up and down, its position changes.
2	B	According to the equation for the frequency of a spring–block simple harmonic oscillator, $f = \dfrac{1}{2\pi}\sqrt{k/m}$, we see that the frequency is inversely proportional to the square root of m, the mass of the block.
3	C	According to the equation for the period of a spring–block simple harmonic oscillator, $T = 2\pi\sqrt{m/k}$, we see that the period is inversely proportional to the square root of k, the force constant of the spring. So, if k is smaller, T will be greater.
4	A	If A is the amplitude of the oscillations, then the maximum potential energy of the spring is $\dfrac{1}{2}kA^2$. When the block passes through the equilibrium position, all this energy is completely converted to kinetic energy, at which point the block has its maximum speed. Setting $\dfrac{1}{2}mv_{max}^2$ equal to $\dfrac{1}{2}kA^2$, we find that $v_{max} = A\sqrt{k/m}$, so v_{max} is proportional to A.
5	D	If A is the amplitude of the oscillations, then the position of the block varies sinusoidally between $y = -A$ and $y = +A$. The equation for the position (as a function of time, t) will have the form $y = A\sin(\omega t + \phi)$, where $\omega = 2\pi f$.
6	B	When a nucleus undergoes β^- decay, a neutron is converted into a proton and an electron, and the electron is ejected. Because of this, the number of neutrons in the nucleus is decreased by 1.
7	E	A nucleus in an excited energy state can "relax" to a lower energy state by releasing energy. If the photon(s) emitted in this process are in the gamma-ray portion of the electromagnetic spectrum, we refer to this "decay" as gamma decay. The numbers of protons and neutrons remain unchanged.
8	A	When a nucleus undergoes alpha decay, it ejects an alpha particle, which is a helium-4 nucleus, composed of 2 protons and 2 neutrons. This is by far the heaviest decay particle that is ejected from a radioactive nucleus.
9	B	When a nucleus undergoes β^- decay, a neutron is converted into a proton and an electron, and the electron is ejected. Because of this, the number of protons in the nucleus—the atomic number—is increased by 1.
10	B	The electric field strength is strongest at $x = 0$. It increases from $x = -a$ to $x = 0$, then decreases from $x = 0$ to $x = a$. Therefore, only graphs (B) and (E) are possible. However, since the electric field strength at $x = 0$ is not zero, the answer cannot be (E).
11	A	Every point on the x axis is equidistant from the source charges. For any given point, P, on the x axis, let R denote its distance from the $+Q$ charge and from the $-Q$ charge. Then the potential at P is $k(+Q)/R + k(-Q)/R = 0$. Therefore, the potential is zero everywhere along the x-axis, so graph A is the answer.

Question	Answer	Explanation
12	B	If a charge $-q$ is at a location where the electric field is **E**, then the electric force on the charge is $\mathbf{F} = (-q)\mathbf{E}$, and the magnitude of this force is qE. Since the magnitude of the electric force, F, is proportional to the electric field strength, the graph of F should have the same shape as the graph of E.
13	D	By Newton's third law, the force on the heavier person is equal but opposite to the force on the lighter person, eliminating choices (A) and (B). Since the lighter person has $\frac{1}{2}$ the mass of the heavier person and acceleration is inversely proportional to mass, the magnitude of the lighter person's acceleration will be twice that of the heavier person.
14	C	When the particle enters the magnetic field, the magnetic force provides the centripetal force to cause the particle to execute uniform circular motion. $$\lvert q \rvert vB = \frac{mv^2}{r} \quad \Rightarrow \quad r = \frac{mv}{\lvert q \rvert B}$$ Since v and B are the same for all the particles, the largest r is found by maximizing the ratio $m/\lvert q \rvert$. The value of $m/\lvert q \rvert$ for an alpha particle is about twice that for a proton and thousands of times greater than that of an electron or positron.
15	B	The magnetic field lines created by a long, straight, current-carrying wire are circles centered on the wire.
16	D	With respect to the point at which the rod is attached to the vertical wall, the tension in the string exerts a counterclockwise (CCW) torque, and the gravitational force—which acts at the rod's center of mass—exerts a clockwise (CW) torque. If the rod is in equilibrium, these torques must balance. Letting L denote the length of the rod, this gives us $$\tau_{\text{CCW}} = \tau_{\text{CW}}$$ $$F_{\text{T}} L \sin\theta = (\tfrac{1}{2}L)(mg)\sin\theta$$ $$F_{\text{T}} = \tfrac{1}{2}mg$$
17	C	By Newton's third law, both vehicles experience the same magnitude of force and, therefore, the same impulse; so Statement I is false. Invoking Newton's second law, in the form *impulse = change in momentum*, we see that Statement II is therefore also false. However, since the car has a smaller mass than the truck, its acceleration will be greater in magnitude than that of the truck, so Statement III is true.
18	A	At the instant a simple harmonic oscillator passes through equilibrium, the restoring force is zero. Since the restoring force on the bob is zero at equilibrium, the tangential acceleration of the bob is also zero at this point.

Question	Answer	Explanation
19	B	Using the equation for the period of a simple pendulum (oscillating with a small amplitude so we can approximate the motion as simple harmonic), $T = 2\pi\sqrt{L/g}$, we see that we can solve for L if we know T (since g is known).
20	B	Because the block moves in a circular path, it must experience a centripetal acceleration (that is, an acceleration directed toward the center of the circle). Now, since the speed of the block is changing, it must also be experiencing a tangential acceleration; in particular, because the block's speed is *increasing*, this tangential acceleration must be in the *same* direction as the block's velocity. Therefore, the total acceleration of the block is the sum of the centripetal acceleration $\mathbf{a}_c$ and the tangential acceleration $\mathbf{a}_t$. The figure below shows that this sum points upward and to the left, so arrow B is best.
21	B	From the equation $F = qE$, where q is the magnitude of the charge in the electric field, we find that $$E = \frac{F}{q} = \frac{1\,\text{N}}{0.2 \times 10^{-3}\,\text{C}} = 5 \times 10^{3}\ \text{N/C}$$
22	C	Since the magnetic force is always perpendicular to the object's velocity, it does zero work on any charged particle. Zero work means zero change in kinetic energy (a direct consequence of the work–energy theorem), so the speed remains the same. Remember: The magnetic force can only change the direction of a charged particle's velocity, not its speed.
23	C	Use the work–energy theorem. $$W = \Delta\text{KE} = \frac{1}{2}m(v_f^2 - v_i^2) = \frac{1}{2}(2\ \text{kg})[(4\ \text{m/s})^2 - (2\ \text{m/s})^2] = 12\ \text{J}$$

Question	Answer	Explanation
24	B	First, if we add the 2 N force to the left and the 6 N force to the right, we get a 4 N force to the right. Then, adding this to the 3 N force gives us a net force whose magnitude is 5 N (this follows from the famous 3-4-5 right triangle). Since $a = F_{net}/m$, we get $a = (5\ \text{N})/(2\ \text{kg}) = 2.5\ \text{m/s}^2$.
25	A	If these waves interfere completely destructively, the amplitude of the resultant wave will be 6 cm − 4 cm = 2 cm. If they interfere completely constructively, then the amplitude of the resultant wave will be 6 cm + 4 cm = 10 cm. In general, then, the amplitude of the resultant wave will be no less than 2 cm and no greater than 10 cm.

Question	Answer	Explanation
26	C	Since $\mathbf{F}_{net} = \mathbf{F}_1 + \mathbf{F}_2 = \mathbf{0}$, the bar cannot accelerate translationally, so (B) is false. The net torque does *not* need to be zero, as the following diagram shows (eliminating choices A and D). 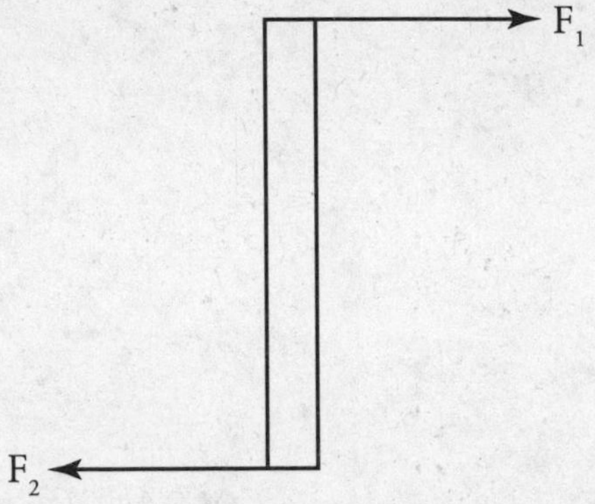 However, since $\mathbf{F}_2 = -\mathbf{F}_1$, choice (C) is true; one possible illustration of this is given below. 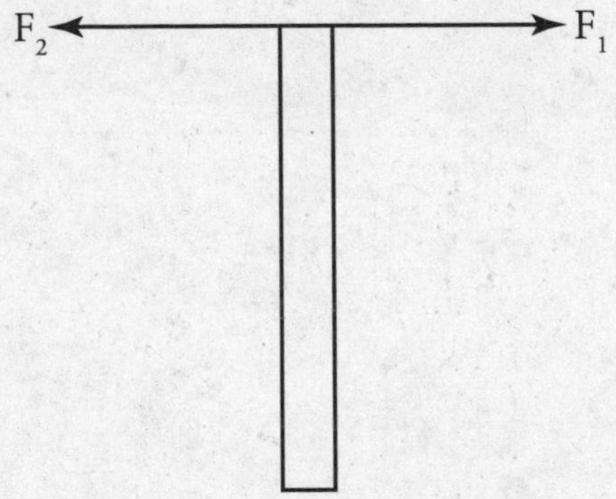
27	B	The cylinder slides across the surface with acceleration $a = F/m$ until time $t = T$, when a drops to zero (because F becomes zero). Therefore, from time $t = 0$ to $t = T$, the velocity is steadily increasing (because the acceleration is a positive constant), but, at $t = T$, the velocity remains constant. This is illustrated in graph (B).
28	B	We'll use conservation of mechanical energy. Let the flat surface be our $PE_{grav} = 0$ level. Then $$K_0 + U_0 = K_f + U_f$$ $$0 + mg(2R) = \frac{1}{2}mv^2 + mgR$$ $$\frac{1}{2}mv^2 = mgR$$ $$v = \sqrt{2gR}$$

Question	Answer	Explanation
29	D	As the box slides down the track, it loses height, so it loses gravitational potential energy. The quantities in choices (A), (B), and (C) *increase* as the box slides down the track, and the quantity in choice (E) remains constant.
30	A	Since both the box and the ball have zero vertical velocity at the moment when they're released, they'll both take the same amount of time to fall to the surface. The box's horizontal velocity at the moment it leaves the track is irrelevant to this question.
31	A	Electric field lines are always perpendicular to the surface of a conductor, eliminating choices (B) and (E). Excess charge on a conductor always resides on the surface (eliminating choice (D)), and there is a greater density of charge at points where the radius of curvature is smaller, which eliminates choice (C).
32	D	Since the line of action of the force coincides with one of the sides of the square, the lever arm of the force, ℓ (the distance from the center of the square to the bottom side), is simply equal to $\frac{1}{2}s$, half the length of each side of the square. This gives us $$\tau = \ell F = \tfrac{1}{2}(0.40 \text{ m})(10 \text{ N}) = 2.0 \text{ N-m}$$
33	B	Since the velocity does not change, the acceleration of the box is zero, so the net force the box feels must also be zero. Since the mover pushes on the box with a force of 200 N, the force of kinetic friction must also be 200 N (in the opposite direction) to give a net force of zero. Because the strength of the force of kinetic friction, F_{friction}, is equal to μF_N, where $F_N = mg$ (since the floor is flat), we find that $$\mu = \frac{F_{\text{friction}}}{F_N} = \frac{F_{\text{friction}}}{mg} = \frac{200 \text{ N}}{(50 \text{ kg})(10 \text{ m/s}^2)} = 0.4$$
34	E	Fiber optic cables transmit light using total internal reflection. Choices (A), (B), (C), and (D) do not apply here.
35	C	The ideal gas law says that $PV = nRT$. Since V, n, and R are constants here, P is proportional to T. The graph of a proportion is a straight line through the origin.
36	E	All electromagnetic waves—regardless of frequency—travel at speed c (the speed of light) through vacuum.
37	C	Applying Coulomb's law, we see that the electric force will not change. $$F' = k\frac{Q'q'}{r'^2} = k\frac{(2Q)(2q)}{(2r)^2} = k\frac{4Qq}{4r^2} = k\frac{Qq}{r^2} = F$$

Question	Answer	Explanation
38	A	Because the bat flies *toward* the tree, the frequency of the waves as they hit the tree is *higher* than the frequency with which they were emitted by the bat. Then as these waves reflect off the tree, they are detected by the bat, which is still flying toward the tree, so the frequency gets shifted higher again. Therefore, if the returning signal is detected by the bat as having a frequency of 61 kHz, the original pulse must have been emitted at a frequency lower than 61 kHz. Only choice (A) is lower than 61 kHz.
39	B	Perhaps the easiest way answer this question is to choose a numerical value for the distance between X and Y. Let's choose 180 m. Then the time it takes the athlete to run from X to Y is 60 seconds, and the time it takes to run from Y back to X is 30 seconds. Her average speed for the entire run is the *total* distance traveled, 180 m + 180 m = 360 m, divided by the *total* time, 60 s + 30 s = 90 s. This gives an average speed for the entire trip of (360 m)/(90 s) = 4 m/s. (Note: You would get the same answer, 4 m/s, no matter what positive value you chose for the distance between X and Y.)
40	B	Choices (A) and (E) are identical, so both may be eliminated. Since F is equal to the weight of the sky diver, choices (C) and (D) don't make sense. If the sky diver's downward velocity is decreasing, she must be experiencing an upward acceleration. Therefore, the net force on the sky diver must be upward. Since D is an upward force and F is a downward force, D must be greater than F to give a net force, $D - F$, that's upward.
41	D	At the top of the semicircle, the cation's velocity, **v**, is to the right, and the net force it feels, **F**, must be downward in the plane of the page (that is, toward the center of the circle since it's undergoing uniform circular motion).

center of path

For a positive charge moving to the right to feel a downward magnetic force in the plane of the page, the magnetic field must point *out* of the plane of the page (according to the right-hand rule). |

Question	Answer	Explanation
42	E	Use the equation that relates wavelength, frequency, and wave speed. $$v = \lambda f = (0.5\,\text{m})(6.0\,\text{Hz}) = 3.0\text{ m/s}$$
43	A	With switch S_2 connected to Point Y and switch S_1 left open, only the right-hand half of the pictured circuit is a closed circuit (the battery V_1 and the parallel combination of resistors are effectively removed from the circuit in this situation). The total resistance is $R + 2R = 3R$, so the current in the circuit is $I = V_2/3R$.
44	C	With switch S_1 connected to Point X and switch S_2 left open, only the left-hand half of the pictured circuit is a closed circuit (the battery V_2 and resistor of resistance $2R$ are effectively removed from the circuit in this situation). The parallel combination of resistors is equivalent to a single resistance of $R/4$, since $$\frac{1}{R_\text{P}} = \frac{1}{\frac{1}{2}R} + \frac{1}{\frac{1}{2}R} = \frac{2}{\frac{1}{2}R} = \frac{4}{R} \quad \Rightarrow \quad R_\text{P} = \frac{R}{4}$$ So, because the total resistance is $R + R/4 = \dfrac{5R}{4}$, the current through resistor R is $$I = \frac{V_1}{(5R/4)} = \frac{4V_1}{5R}$$
45	A	If *both* switches S_1 and S_2 are open, the middle, vertical branch of the pictured circuit is effectively removed. There'll be current around the perimeter of the circuit, but none down the middle branch.
46	E	By definition of an *isolated* system, statements (A), (B), (C), and (D) are all false. The second law of thermodynamics tells us that in this situation, an ordered system will become more disordered, moving toward a state of maximum entropy.
47	C	Don't let the emphasis of the word "positive" in the question throw you. In the equation $Q = CV$, Q is the magnitude of charge on either the positive or the negative plate of the capacitor. So, in this case, $Y = CX$, which gives us $C = Y/X$.
48	D	Using Big Five #3 (with $v_0 = 0$), we get $\Delta s = \dfrac{1}{2}at^2 = \dfrac{1}{2}(4\text{ m/s}^2)(6\text{ s})^2 = 72\text{ m}$.
49	E	The velocity of an object undergoing uniform circular motion is always changing (because the direction is always changing), so choices (A) and (B) are eliminated. Furthermore, since the acceleration is centripetal, it must always point toward the center of the circle; so, as the object moves around the circle, the acceleration vector is also constantly changing direction. Since the acceleration changes, the answer must be (E). Notice that for an object in uniform circular motion, both the velocity and the acceleration are changing because the *directions* of these vectors are always changing, even though their magnitudes stay the same.

Question	Answer	Explanation
50	C	The ray diagram is consistent with a diverging lens as the optical device, forming an upright, virtual image on the same side of the lens as the object.
51	A	This ray diagram is consistent with a plane mirror as the optical device, forming an upright, virtual image on the opposite side of the mirror.
52	B	The ray diagram is consistent with a converging lens as the optical device, forming an inverted, real image on the opposite side of the lens from the object.
53	D	Since the rays first reflect then are converged as they exit the box, this ray diagram is consistent with having a plane mirror and then a converging lens within the dotted box.
54	E	Choice (E) is the definition of a superconductor. (Choice (A) describes a particle accelerator/collider, and choice (B) describes a device known as a tokamak.)
55	D	The electric field vector at the origin is the sum of the individual electric field vectors due to the two source charges. The diagrams below show that the net electric field vector at the origin points down and to the right.
56	D	Let M be the mass of the sun, M_J the mass of Jupiter, and M_E the mass of Earth. In addition, let R_J denote the distance from the sun to Jupiter and R_E the distance from the sun to the earth. We're told that $M_J = 300M_E$ and $R_J = 5R_E$, so using Newton's law of gravitation, we find that $$F_{on\,J} = G\frac{MM_J}{R_J^2} = G\frac{M(300M_E)}{(5R_E)^2} = \frac{300}{25} \bullet G\frac{MM_E}{R_E^2} = 12F_{on\,E} \;\Rightarrow\; \frac{F_{on\,J}}{F_{on\,E}} = 12$$

Question	Answer	Explanation
57	A	Since P is the center of a dark fringe, it is a location of completely destructive interference. In order for this to occur, the waves must be exactly out of phase when they reach P. This will happen if the difference between their path lengths from the slits is an odd number of half wavelengths. Only the equation in choice (A) satisfies this requirement.
58	C	The speed of a wave is determined by the properties of the medium, not by the frequency. (An exception to this general rule includes light through a transparent material medium such as glass—the speed depends slightly on the frequency, and this accounts for the phenomenon of dispersion, which can be seen in the familiar spreading of white light into its component colors when it passes through a prism.) Since wave speed is independent of frequency in the situation described here, the answer is (C).
59	E	We use the equation $q = mc\Delta T$. Since both the aluminum block and the iron block absorb the same amount of heat, we have $m_{Al}c_{Al}\Delta T_{Al} = m_{Fe}c_{Fe}\Delta T_{Fe}$, where "Al" denotes aluminum and "Fe" denotes iron. Now, because $m_{Al} = 2m_{Fe}$ and $c_{Al} = 2c_{Fe}$, we have $$(2m_{Fe})(2c_{Fe})\Delta T_{Al} = m_{Fe}c_{Fe}\Delta T_{Fe} \quad \Rightarrow \quad 4\Delta T_{Al} = \Delta T_{Fe}$$
60	E	Since the gases are in thermal equilibrium in the same container, they're at the same temperature, and because the average kinetic energy of the molecules is proportional to the temperature, the fact that their temperatures are the same implies that the average kinetic energy of their molecules is the same also. This eliminates choices (A) and (B). Now, in order for the lighter molecules to have the same average kinetic energy as the heavier ones, the lighter molecules must be moving faster on average, so statement (E) is correct.
61	A	By definition, if the wave is vertically polarized, the electric field component, **E**, of the wave always oscillates vertically. That is, **E** is perpendicular to the ground. Since the direction of propagation, **S**, is parallel to the ground, and the vectors **E**, **B**, and **S** are always mutually perpendicular, **B** must be parallel to the ground and perpendicular to **S**.

Question	Answer	Explanation
62	E	The frequency determines the pitch of a sound, and the amplitude determines the intensity (or loudness). Pitch and loudness are independent. (A sound can be soft and low pitched, soft and high pitched, loud and low pitched, or loud and high pitched; there's no connection.)
63	D	Isotopes of an element contain the same number of protons but different numbers of neutrons. So any isotope of chlorine *must* contain 17 protons.
64	E	When a projectile moving in a parabolic path reaches the top of its path, its *vertical* velocity is instantaneously zero. Choice (A) is a trap; it is wrong because the projectile has a (constant) *horizontal* velocity during its entire flight. Choices (B) and (D) are equivalent, so both can be eliminated. Choice (C) can also be eliminated; the weight of the projectile points downward, and when the projectile is at the top of its path and has a purely horizontal velocity, the force of air resistance is also horizontal. There is no reason why the vertical force must have the same magnitude as the horizontal force. The answer must be (E).
65	C	Momentum is conserved in the collision. Before the collision, the vertical component of the momentum was zero (since there was only one moving object and it was moving horizontally only). Therefore, the total vertical momentum *after* the collision must be zero also. The vertical component of the momentum of the $2m$ mass after the collision is $(2m)(u \sin 30°)$, and the vertical component of the momentum of the other mass after the collision is $(m)(-v \sin 60°)$. Since the total vertical momentum after the collision is zero, we find that $$(2m)(u \sin 30°) + (m)(-v \sin 60°) = 0$$ $$(2m)(u \sin 30°) = mv \sin 60°$$ $$2u \sin 30° = v \sin 60°$$
66	B	If the collision is elastic, then kinetic energy is conserved. Therefore $$\frac{1}{2}(2m)U^2 + 0 = \frac{1}{2}(2m)u^2 + \frac{1}{2}mv^2 \quad \Rightarrow \quad U^2 = u^2 + \frac{1}{2}v^2$$
67	C	Since we know $g = 10 \text{ m/s}^2$ on the earth, the value of g on the moon must be $\frac{1}{6}(10) = \frac{5}{3} \text{ m/s}^2$. So, if an object weighs 20 N on the moon, its mass must be $$m = \frac{w_{\text{on moon}}}{g_{\text{on moon}}} = \frac{20 \text{ N}}{\frac{5}{3} \text{ m/s}^2} = 12 \text{ kg}$$ Since mass does not vary with location, if the mass is 12 kg on the moon, it's 12 kg here on Earth (and everywhere else).

Question	Answer	Explanation
68	B	The strength of the electric field at a point that is a distance r from a point charge of magnitude Q is given by the expression $\frac{kQ}{r^2}$. If the source charge is surrounded by an insulating medium other than vacuum, then the value of k we use in this expression is actually $\frac{k_0}{K}$, where k_0 is Coulomb's constant ($\frac{9 \times 10^9 \text{ N-m}^2/\text{C}^2}{\text{C}^2}$) and K is the dielectric constant of the medium. The sign of the source charge will affect the *direction* of the electric field vector at a point but not the *strength* of the field.
69	B	Since the coefficient of thermal expansion has units of deg^{-1} whether it's for linear, area, or volume expansion, we can eliminate choices (C), (D), and (E), because the units of β would be wrong if any of these equations were true. Now, all you need to remember is that the coefficient of volume expansion is different from the coefficient of linear expansion to eliminate (A) and choose (B). [In case you want to see how (B) is derived, notice that since each linear dimension, L, of a solid increases by $\alpha L \Delta T$, the new volume of a heated solid, V', is $V(1 + \alpha \Delta T)^3 =$ $V(1 + 3\alpha\Delta T + 3\alpha^2\Delta T + \alpha^3\Delta T)$. Since α is so small, the terms involving α^2 and α^3 are *really* small and can be ignored. Therefore $\beta \approx 3\alpha$.]
70	A	While the tightrope artist is just standing there in the middle of the rope, he has no momentum. But, as the wave passes, he moves upward, meaning he now has vertical momentum. Therefore, the wave pulse transmitted vertical momentum (and energy).
71	D	The diagram below (which *is* drawn to scale) shows that the angle of incidence, θ_1, is 55° and the angle of refraction, θ_2, is 35°.

Now by using Snell's law, we find that

$$n_1 \sin\theta_1 = n_2 \sin\theta_2$$
$$(1)\sin 55^\circ = n_2 \sin 35^\circ$$
$$\frac{\sin 55^\circ}{\sin 35^\circ} = n_2$$

Question	Answer	Explanation
72	E	Don't let the underlined phrase in the question throw you. When a wave enters a new medium, its frequency does not change. So if the frequency of the light was f in the air, it's still f in the glass. Using the equation that relates wavelength, frequency, and wave speed, along with the equation $v = c/n$ (which follows immediately from the definition of index of refraction), we find that $$\lambda_{\text{in glass}} = \frac{v_{\text{in glass}}}{f} = \frac{c/n}{f} = \frac{c}{nf}$$
73	B	Since the electron is naturally being accelerated toward a region containing positive source charges, its potential energy decreases. (It's like a ball dropping to the ground; it is accelerated downward by the gravitational field, and it loses gravitational potential energy.) Therefore, the answer is either (A) or (B). Now since the potential due to a positive charge is higher than the potential due to a negative charge (because positive numbers are greater than negative numbers), the electron is accelerating toward a region of higher electric potential choice (B).
74	B	The transfer of heat due to a moving fluid (such as air) is known as convection. (Choices (D) and (E), by the way, are not modes of heat transfer and can therefore be eliminated immediately.)
75	A	The faster a spaceship passes by the station, the shorter its length is observed to be. This is because as v increases, the relativistic factor γ increases, so the amount of length contraction increases. Therefore, the *smaller* the v, the smaller the value of γ, and the *longer* the ship will be observed to be. Of the choices given, the speed in choice (A) is the smallest. (Note that the spaceship traveling at the speed given in choice (E) will be observed to be the shortest as it passes by the station.)

The Princeton Review Practice SAT Physics Subject Tests Scoring Grid

Recall from the Introduction that your Raw Score is equal to the number of questions you answered correctly minus $\frac{1}{4}$ of the number of questions you answered incorrectly

$$(\text{number of correct answers}) - \frac{1}{4}(\text{number of wrong answers})$$

then rounded to the nearest whole number. Questions that you leave blank do not count toward your raw score.

Raw Score	Approximate Scaled Score
≥ 60	800
56–59	780–790
50–55	750–770
45–49	720–740
40–44	690–710
36–39	660–680
30–35	630–650
25–29	600–620
20–24	570–590
16–19	540–560
11–15	510–530
7–10	480–500
2–6	450–470
–4–14	10–440
≤ -5	≤ 400

About the Authors

Steve Leduc has been teaching at the university level since the age of 19. He earned his Sc.B. in theoretical mathematics from MIT at 20 and his M.A. in mathematics from UCSD at 22. After his graduate studies, Steve cofounded Hyperlearning, Inc., an educational services company that provided supplemental courses in undergraduate math and science for students from the University of California, where he lectured in seventeen different courses in mathematics and physics. He has published four math books, *Differential Equations* in 1995, *Linear Algebra* in 1996, The Princeton Review's *Cracking the GRE Math Subject Test* in 2000, and *Cracking the Virginia SOL Algebra II* in 2001, as well as a physics book, The Princeton Review's *Cracking the AP Physics B & C Exams* in 1999. Through Hyperlearning, Steve has directed the creation and administration of the most successful preparation course for the medical school entrance exam (the MCAT) in California, where he has taught mathematics and physics to thousands of undergraduates. Hyperlearning merged with The Princeton Review in 1996. He currently owns two-to-the-eleventh-power CDs and has seen *Monty Python and The Holy Grail, Star Trek II: The Wrath of Khan,* and *Blade Runner* about two-to-the-eleventh-power times.

—*Paul Kanarek*

NOTES

NOTES

NOTES

NOTES

NOTES

NOTES

NOTES

NOTES

NOTES

NOTES

NOTES

NOTES

NOTES

NOTES

AP Exams

**Cracking the AP Biology Exam,
2009 Edition**
978-0-375-42884-5 • $18.00/C$21.00

**Cracking the AP Calculus AB & BC Exams,
2009 Edition**
978-0-375-42885-2 • $19.00/C$22.00

**Cracking the AP Chemistry Exam,
2009 Edition**
978-0-375-42886-9 • $18.00/C$22.00

**Cracking the AP Computer Science A & AB,
2006–2007**
978-0-375-76528-5 • $19.00/C$27.00

**Cracking the AP Economics Macro & Micro
Exams, 2009 Edition**
978-0-375-42887-6 • $18.00/C$21.00

**Cracking the AP English Language &
Composition Exam, 2009 Edition**
978-0-375-42888-3 • $18.00/C$21.00

**Cracking the AP English Literature &
Composition Exam, 2009 Edition**
978-0-375-42889-0 • $18.00/C$21.00

**Cracking the AP Environmental
Science Exam, 2009 Edition**
978-0-375-42890-6 • $18.00/C$21.00

**Cracking the AP European History Exam,
2009 Edition**
978-0-375-42891-3 • $18.00/C$21.00

**Cracking the AP Physics B Exam,
2009 Edition**
978-0-375-42892-0 • $18.00/C$21.00

**Cracking the AP Physics C Exam,
2009 Edition**
978-0-375-42893-7 • $18.00/C$21.00

**Cracking the AP Psychology Exam,
2009 Edition**
978-0-375-42894-4 • $18.00/C$21.00

**Cracking the AP Spanish Exam,
with Audio CD, 2009 Edition**
978-0-375-76530-8 • $24.95/$27.95

**Cracking the AP Statistics Exam,
2009 Edition**
978-0-375-42848-7 • $19.00/C$22.00

**Cracking the AP U.S. Government
and Politics Exam, 2009 Edition**
978-0-375-42896-8 • $18.00/C$21.00

**Cracking the AP U.S. History Exam,
2009 Edition**
978-0-375-42897-5 • $18.00/C$21.00

**Cracking the AP World History Exam,
2009 Edition**
978-0-375-42898-2 • $18.00/C$21.00

SAT Subject Tests

**Cracking the SAT Biology E/M Subject Test,
2009–2010 Edition**
978-0-375-42905-7 • $19.00/C$22.00

**Cracking the SAT Chemistry Subject Test,
2009–2010 Edition**
978-0-375-42906-4 • $19.00/C$22.00

**Cracking the SAT French Subject Test,
2009–2010 Edition**
978-0-375-42907-1 • $19.00/C$22.00

**Cracking the SAT U.S. & World History
Subject Tests, 2009–2010 Edition**
978-0-375-42908-8 • $19.00/C$22.00

**Cracking the SAT Literature Subject Test,
2009–2010 Edition**
978-0-375-42909-5 • $19.00/C$22.00

**Cracking the SAT Math 1 & 2 Subject Tests,
2009–2010 Edition**
978-0-375-42910-1 • $19.00/C$22.00

**Cracking the SAT Physics Subject Test,
2009–2010 Edition**
978-0-375-42911-8 • $19.00/C$22.00

**Cracking the SAT Spanish Subject Test,
2009–2010 Edition**
978-0-375-42912-5 • $19.00/C$22.00